D1500298

AMERICAN EDUCATION

Its Men,

Ideas,

and

Institutions

Advisory Editor

Lawrence A. Cremin
Frederick A. P. Barnard Professor of Education
Teachers College, Columbia University

A MERICAN EDUCATION: *Its Men, Ideas, and Institutions*
presents selected works of thought and scholarship that have
long been out of print or otherwise unavailable. Inevitably, such
works will include particular ideas and doctrines that have been
outmoded or superseded by more recent research. Nevertheless,
all retain their place in the literature, having influenced educational thought and practice in their own time and having provided
the basis for subsequent scholarship.

THEN & NOW IN EDUCATION

1845:1923

A MESSAGE OF ENCOURAGEMENT
FROM THE PAST TO THE PRESENT

By OTIS W. CALDWELL

AND STUART A. COURTIS

ARNO PRESS & THE NEW YORK TIMES

*New York * 1971*

Reprint Edition 1971 by Arno Press Inc.

Reprinted from a copy in
  The Newark Public Library

American Education:
  Its Men, Ideas, and Institutions - Series II
ISBN for complete set: 0-405-03600-0
See last pages of this volume for titles.

Manufactured in the United States of America

Library of Congress Cataloging in publication Data

Caldwell, Otis William, 1869-1947.
    Then & now in education, 1845:1923.
    (American education: its men, ideas, and
institutions. Series II)
    1. Education--Massachusetts--Boston.
2. Educational tests and measurements--Boston.
I. Courtis, Stuart Appleton, 1874-   joint author.
II. Title. III. Series.
LA306.B7C35 1971   371'.009744'61   77-165711
ISBN 0-405-03700-7

THEN & NOW IN
EDUCATION
1845:1923

Drawn by Robert W. Weir.

For George P. Morris, Esq.

Washington's Head Quaters, Newburg, N. Y.

This was the Frontispiece and the only illustration in a school textbook (Cobb's *North American Reader*) in common use seventy-five years ago.

THEN & NOW IN EDUCATION
1845 : 1923

A MESSAGE OF ENCOURAGEMENT
FROM THE PAST TO THE PRESENT

By OTIS W. CALDWELL
*Director of the Lincoln School
and Professor of Education, Teachers College
Columbia University*

AND STUART A. COURTIS
*Director of Instruction,
Teacher Training, and Research
and Dean, Detroit Teachers College*

Yonkers-on-Hudson, New York
WORLD BOOK COMPANY
1925

WORLD BOOK COMPANY

THE HOUSE OF APPLIED KNOWLEDGE

Established 1905 by Caspar W. Hodgson

YONKERS-ON-HUDSON, NEW YORK

2126 PRAIRIE AVENUE, CHICAGO

Much talk has been made in comparing schools today with those of "the fathers." Surveys have shown many ways in which schools may be improved. Often the work of particular schools or individual teachers has been shown to be ineffective. In an age of scientific study of how the human race educates its young, it is not uncommon for the public and the "rank and file" of teachers to possess the uneasy feeling that something is badly wrong. This volume is by men who believe profoundly in the scientific study of education. They also believe that education was never so effective as today; that our practices have improved; but most of all that our ideals have far outrun our practices, thus showing the way to further progress. The volume presents genuine foundations for much encouragement to all classes of citizens, since all in one way or another are interested in modern education

CCTNE-2

Copyright 1923 by World Book Company
Copyright in Great Britain
All rights reserved

PRINTED IN U.S.A.

AUTHORS' PREFACE

Oh wad some power the giftie gie us
To see oursel's as ithers see us!
It wad frae monie a blunder free us
And foolish notion.

BURNS

THE poet's fervent wish awakens few responses in the heart of the average American school teacher. During the past decade the teacher has been given repeated opportunity to see herself through the eyes of survey experts and specialists of many types, but the vision has been conducive neither to peace of mind nor to professional happiness.

Survey after survey has revealed unsuspected inadequacy or inefficiency in American education. Both teachers and teaching accordingly have been exposed to severe public censure. Superintendents and teachers have been dismissed, school systems and methods reorganized, and the advent of a new era properly heralded in the public press. But in these survey reports one can search almost in vain for adequate recognition of the value of the services rendered by teachers, of their desire and their efforts to do their best, and of records of the progress in educational matters which has actually taken place.

One might erroneously conclude that the primary purpose of surveys is to reveal our defects. Intelligent criticism is essential to growth, it is true, but even more essential is a consciousness of the successful mastery of past difficulties, the glow of pleasure and content which comes from merited approval of faithful service rendered, the conviction of power to deal adequately with future difficulties as they arise. Without these elements of encouragement, criticism alone is depressing, disheartening, destructive. With them it becomes a challenge to effort, a stimulus to courage and hope, a revealer of opportunities for further service.

v

This book is written to bring a long-delayed message of encouragement to all who have participated in accomplishing the educational progress of the last fifty years. In 1845 a survey was made of the Boston schools — a survey so objective in its nature, so modern in its methods, that suggestive comparisons are possible between then and now on the basis of valid scientific evidence. Dull and phlegmatic indeed must the person be who can read the story presented in the following pages and not be thrilled by the progress made in seventy-five years and by what that progress means to the age-long, world-wide struggle for the betterment of human living.

This book presents an opportunity to look at school conditions in Boston in 1845 through the eyes of the educational authorities of that day, and thus indirectly to see ourselves as Horace Mann would see us, were he to return to American schools after an absence of seventy-five years.

Acknowledgment is gratefully made for assistance of various types: to Dr. Paul Monroe of Teachers College, Columbia University, for suggestive encouragement and scholarly guidance in planning the investigation; to Dr. Edward H. Reisner of Teachers College, Columbia University, for critical reading of the manuscript; to the Research Committee of the American Association for the Advancement of Science for a grant of funds used in partial payment for reprinting test materials; and to the many superintendents and teachers throughout the country who have assisted in collecting the data presented in this volume. Most of all should appreciation be expressed to the unnumbered teachers who, by their devoted and unselfish services, have brought about the improved conditions revealed by the comparison between Then and Now.

THE AUTHORS

CONTENTS

ILLUSTRATIONS FROM PHOTOGRAPHS

GRAPHS

TABLES

THEN AND NOW IN EDUCATION

CHAPTER ONE

HISTORIC THUNDERBOLTS

HORACE MANN was appointed Secretary of the State Board of Education in Massachusetts in 1837. The office was a new one, and its creation was opposed by many of the sturdy individualists of that period as another evidence of a growing tendency toward a centralization that seemed to them an ominous departure from the ideal of individual liberty which the republic was established to perpetuate. Perhaps none were more jealous of their individual prerogatives, none more outspoken in their views, none more violent in their opposition, than the little band of some thirty schoolmen who served as masters of the Boston Public Schools.

In those days there was no centralized municipal school organization. School affairs were managed by a " School Committee," a relic of the days of the old town meeting which in some places has persisted, in name at least, down to the present day. Each school was a separate organization, each master an independent personage of considerable importance politically within his own district, and truly " master " in his own school. As a class the Boston schoolmasters were conservative, bound by convention, jealous of encroachment on what they considered their rights and privileges, and in the main opposed to all change and progress.

The newly appointed Secretary was a gentleman of warm heart and keen vision, as well as a man of unusual ability. Education to him was a type of calling as fine and as sacred as the ministry itself. His proverbial love of children manifested itself in a passionate zeal to improve instruction; to try to make the schools contribute to the development of character. Neither expediency, tradition, nor convention was considered by him when the betterment of child training

1

was at stake. Up and down the state he went, attacking boldly evils as he found them and preaching his message of reform.

Horace Mann, in the discharge of his secretarial duties, issued public documents and gave addresses throughout the state, presenting a program of general educational improvement and reform. He made no direct attack on the Boston schoolmasters. It was inevitable, however, that his vigorous advocacy of a progressive program should arouse these conservative schoolmen. His arguments were accepted as criticisms, and the Boston schoolmasters were not slow to reply. Thirty-one of them banded together in defense of their practices, and in a public statement attacked the position of the Secretary of the State Board of Education. They ridiculed his program and belittled his knowledge and purposes.

If Horace Mann did not precipitate the controversy with the Boston schoolmasters, at least he welcomed their opposition as an opportunity to direct the attention of the wealthiest and most ambitious city in the state to conditions much in need of change. He made a vigorous public reply. Rejoinder followed reply, and the famous controversy between Horace Mann and the Boston schoolmasters was on.

We must know something of the school organization of that day in order to appreciate the situation. The relation of the Boston School Committee of that period to the masters of the various schools is difficult for a modern schoolman to understand. The school committee was not responsible for the administration of the schools. There was no supervision, and no school system, as we now know these terms. The school committee built the necessary buildings, prescribed certain rules and regulations, and hired masters to carry them out. Once a year a formal inspection by the school committee took place. The children were examined orally, and a report was made as to the condition of school work. In the early days, when the total number of pupils was small, this inspection was probably thorough and reasonably adequate, but by 1845 the annual inspection had become little more than a traditional formality and the school committee's report had become an official convention. For instance, the statement of the committee appointed to inspect the Boston Latin School reads as follows:

REPORT

OF THE

SUB-COMMITTEE OF THE LATIN SCHOOL

Made August 5, 1845

To the School Committee of Boston:
The Sub-Committee of the Latin School, respectfully report that they examined said School on the 24th ultimo, and found it in its usual good condition.

The whole number of pupils was 139
      Average attendance in July 126

EDWARD WIGGLESWORTH,
WILLIAM HAGUE,
THEOPHILUS PARSONS,
J. I. T. COOLIDGE.

Boston, August 5, 1845.

The report of the English High School was nearly as conventional:

REPORT

OF THE

SUB-COMMITTEE OF THE ENGLISH HIGH SCHOOL

Made August 5, 1845

The Sub-Committee of the English High School respectfully report,
That they visited the School on four different days in the month of July, for the purpose of making the Quarterly and Annual Examinations. They examined the School in its several departments,

and were impressed with the thoroughness and accuracy manifested by the scholars generally in their various studies. In Algebra and Geometry, especially, there was great proficiency, and the only thing in which there appeared any deficiency was the pronunciation of the French language, entire accuracy of which can of course be obtained only from a French teacher. The result of the examination has satisfied the Committee that the School maintains the high character which it has long held; and although they are far from intimating that there is no further room for improvement, they are fully of the opinion that this Board and the Public have no reason to be dissatisfied with its present condition.

All of which is respectfully submitted.

ALEXANDER YOUNG,
AURELIUS D. PARKER,
WINSLOW LEWIS,
SAMUEL G. HOWE,
EZRA PALMER, JR.

Boston, August 4, 1845.

The controversy of the Boston schoolmasters, whatever its merits and whatever else it accomplished, aroused public consciousness to a state of extreme sensitiveness with respect to public education. In 1845 the citizens of Boston, like all true Americans, were proud of their schools and considered them the best in the world. Horace Mann, in commenting on the report, is responsible for the following statements:

If there is anything in the institution of the city, or in the character of its inhabitants, to which we have always referred with a feeling of exultation, it is the heartiness and the bounteousness with which our noble system of Free Schools has been sustained by the popular voice. In no city in the world, has there been one half so much pecuniary liberality for the maintenance of Common Schools, as in the city of Boston. In no city of the world, have the generous appropriations made in behalf of the schools, been seconded and advocated by the citizens with so great a degree of unanimity. In no city in the world, have the wealthy made so little clamor or opposition, in regard to that great fundamental principle of Republicanism, — that the property of the country must secure the education of the country. It is an extraordinary fact, that, for the last six or eight years the annual appropriations of money for the support of Public Schools, in the city of Boston, with its eighty thousand, its one hundred thousand, or its one hundred and twenty thousand inhabitants, has constantly kept in advance of the appropriations made by the Parliament of Great Britain, in behalf of Popular Education, for all England, with its sixteen, seventeen, and now, as it is supposed, its eighteen millions of people. When the Parliament granted £20,000 for all England, Boston granted more than $100,000. When the Parliament rose to £30,000, Boston had risen to more than $150,000; and now, when the Parliament, in spite of the opposition of lords and bishops, has strained itself up to £40,000, the appropriations of the city of Boston are more than $212,000. This money is not raised to be squandered on place-holders, but by a glorious alchemy, to be transmuted into intelligence, good feeling, and good habits.

It was disturbing to the people of Boston to have their costly schools attacked by a public official and compared unfavorably with schools in Germany and other foreign countries. When the time came for the annual inspection of the common schools, as the grade schools were called, they determined that the occasion called for something more thoroughgoing than the conventional inspection. No direct reference was made in the Survey Report itself to the controversy which had been carried on during the three years previous, yet it is easy to read between the lines. The following brief but pointed Authorization of the Committee is of interest:

CITY OF BOSTON

In School Committee, May 6, 1845.

Ordered That Messrs. Parsons, Howe and Neale be a Committee to make the annual examination of the several Grammar Schools, and report at the quarterly meeting in August.

S. F. McCLEARY, Secretary.

Excerpts from the authorized report[1] which follow show the ways in which the committee worked.

To THE SCHOOL COMMITTEE OF THE CITY OF BOSTON
Gentlemen :

Your Sub-Committee, appointed for the purpose of making the Annual Examinations in the Grammar Department of all the Schools, have attended to their duty, and submit the following :

It has long been the custom to appoint an Annual Committee to visit and examine the Writing Department in all these Boston Schools, and another to visit and examine the Grammar Department, and for each to make a separate report. It was, however, found to be impossible to do anything like justice on the examination, for Committeemen could not be found who could give the time necessary to examine over 7,000 children. A few years ago it was ordered, that the Annual Committee might limit their examination to the first class in each School; and it was under this order that your Committee was appointed. But although we were to examine only the first class in nineteen schools, still the task was a very difficult one, for we were expected to judge of the real and comparative merits of the whole School; because long custom, — the common law of the Committee, — required us to attend to many points of inquiry not especially named in the order.

The School Committee has no way of obtaining a condensed and comparative view of the condition of all the Schools, except through the Reports of its Annual Committee ; and it does not obtain these until more than half the year for which it is chosen has expired. It was in view of the great importance of the subject, that your Committee, anxious to do all that could possibly be done towards a thorough and satisfactory examination of the Schools, resolved to adopt, in addition to the usual mode of oral examination, the plan of submitting to the scholars a series of printed questions on all the subjects studied in the schools.

The committee proceeded with its plan with commendable care and thoroughness. Written examinations were given,

[1] Throughout the pages which follow the authors have pieced together excerpts from the report to make the type of connected account required for the purposes of this volume. Since the complete report is given in the Appendix, it is not thought necessary to indicate in detail the pages from which particular excerpts are taken.

and scored under uniform conditions, and the tabulated results published in detail, question by question and school by school. Illustrations of type answers were also given and in the comments upon the results and in the recommendations made, many additional details are supplied. Taken as a whole, therefore, and in connection with other available reports and documents, the report of what is probably the first survey of an American system gives a fairly complete and detailed picture of the school life and achievement of Boston children of 14 years of age.

The inefficiency revealed by the survey was as great a surprise and disappointment to the school committee as many of our modern survey reports have proved to be to those who have made them. Nevertheless, with absolute honesty and frankness they published every figure.

The interest of Horace Mann in the report can well be imagined. In a personal letter to a friend he wrote:

What a pile of thunderbolts! Jupiter never had more lying by his side when he ordered a lot to punish the wicked. If the masters see fit to assail me again, I think I can answer them in such a way as to make it redound to the glory of God.[1]

Officially, however, he contented himself with publishing the report in full in *The Common School Journal,* of which he was the editor, and with commenting with fine professional skill upon both the method and the conclusions of the Boston School Committee.

Horace Mann recognized at once the significance of the scientific method applied to education and hailed the report as the dawn of a new era. *The Common School Journal* of 1845 supplies us with Horace Mann's own appraisal of the functions and value of careful measurement applied to educational problems, as well as his views in regard to the particular educational problems raised by the survey.

[1] *Horace Mann,* by Hinsdale.

The survey held the attention of the public for a few short weeks and of schoolmen for a few months longer. The recommendations of the report, at first violently attacked as unwarranted and revolutionary, were gradually put into effect. Very few schoolmen proved to have the intelligence of Horace Mann, and the era foreseen by him did not begin to materialize until more than fifty years later.

In time, however, the inevitable occurred. Dr. Rice, in 1898, once again proved the value of the comparative examination. Professor Thorndike, following along the same path, developed a scientific scale for measuring an educational product. This time the world was ready, and soon a host of workers were busy developing other tests and scales. Now the scientific study of educational problems has become general in American schools.

In the meantime the 1845 survey reports and the old school journals were turning yellow and disintegrating upon library shelves. Again the inevitable occurred. A man who believed in measurement in education, in attempting to trace the history of examinations and tests used in American schools found the 1845 report. The content of this report proved of such unusual value, that it seemed desirable to make it available to all who are interested in discerning the trends of progress in American education. In its original form the report was prepared to meet a distinct local need. It has been necessary to reorganize, reproduce, and supplement the text of the report.

Almost as soon as the report was discovered, the suggestion came, " Reprint the tests; give them in detail in our schools and compare the achievement of the present with the past." Careful study from this point of view, however, showed that simple repetition of the tests would not suffice. So great has been the change from then to now, that questions adjusted to the content of the courses of that day are in general not applicable to those of the present. Nevertheless, the work of the examiners of 1845 was skillfully done and certain of the questions, particularly in geography and history, were found suitable for any age. Accordingly a careful selection was made, tests printed, the coöperation of schoolmen secured, and the revised tests were given from Maine to California. The results of this comparison are included with the other material in this volume.

The finding of the report stimulated many other investigations besides the repetition of the tests. Indeed, the test results constitute but a minor part of the book. Copies of the textbooks used at the time were brought to light from dusty shelves. Details of organization and administration, copies of rules and regulations of the Boston School Board, were discovered in reports. Comments were taken from the public press of the day. Such material affords an opportunity to reconstruct the past and to compare school conditions in 1845 with those of the present. Accordingly, most of what follows necessarily deals with the presentation of a reconstructed picture of the past; but there will also be presented in one chapter (Chapter VIII) a generalized picture of a modern city school unit in order that the progress from then to now may be appreciated, and such a discussion should reveal how great has been the progress of the last seventy-five years.

CHAPTER TWO

THE BOSTON PUBLIC SCHOOLS IN THE DAYS OF HORACE MANN

THE survey committee did not realize that they were writing for posterity. They wasted no words on descriptions of existing conditions known to all in that day. Nevertheless, here and there, in the report of the committee, in the tests given, in Horace Mann's comments, or in other documents and newspaper comment published at or near the same time, it is possible to glean one fragment of information after another, and to piece together an interesting picture of what the Boston schools were like in 1845. That picture is presented in this chapter.

Horace Mann writes: [1]

We commence in the present number of the *Journal* the publication of copious extracts from the late Reports of the Annual Examining Committees of the Boston Grammar and Writing Schools. To prevent misapprehension, it should be premised, that there are five grades of Public Schools in the City of Boston — namely, the Latin, the English High, the Grammar and Writing, the Intermediate, and the Primary. The reports from which we are about to quote, relate to the Grammar and Writing Schools only.

From one of the questions in the arithmetic tests we learn that in 1845, "the City of Boston has 120,000 inhabitants, half males, and its property liable to taxation is one hundred millions." Reference has already been made to the fact that the total money raised for school purposes was $212,000. Horace Mann is the authority also for the further information that "By far the largest item in the expenditure (for education) is for the Grammar and Writing Schools. The salaries of all the teachers of the Primary Schools, where there are about 8,000 children, are less, in the aggregate,

---

[1] *The Common School Journal*, Vol. VII, No. 19, October 1, 1845.

than $30,000, while the salaries of the teachers in the Grammar and Writing Schools, where there are but about the same number of children, amount to more than $77,000." In Boston masters were paid $125 a month for 12 months ($1,500 per year), a salary which was good when considered in the light of prices and values of that time. Throughout the state, however, the average paid male teachers was $32.11 per month. Women teachers were paid still less. Even in Boston the salary of women teachers at that time was about $20 per month.

From the survey tables and from comments on the various schools and masters we learn that in 1845 there were nineteen public grammar schools in the city of Boston.[1] Five of those were for boys only, five for girls only, eight received both boys and girls, and one was set apart for colored children. In the main, the buildings were square two-story affairs, one room on each floor, each room holding 200 or more children. The largest membership given for any school is 549 for the Hancock School. One school, the Franklin, is recorded as having five recitation rooms, but for the most part a schoolroom was a single large room with a platform across one end and with seats for from 200 to 300 children.[2] The seats were plain, solid, securely fastened to the floor, and arranged in orderly rows with narrow aisles between.

The organization of the Boston schools was peculiar. There were really two complete schools or school organizations within each school building, one being known as a Grammar School, the other as a Writing School. Each school had its master, neither of which was responsible to the other in the management and instruction of his school. As both the survey committee and Horace Mann violently attacked this system and others defended it, considerable information is here given as to its mode of operation.

[1] See page 219.   [2] See diagram, page 140.

For instance, the following statements are taken from the survey report:

Another defect in our schools, which operates upon them injuriously, is that which gives to each school two heads. There are in each, one called a grammar master, who teaches grammar and certain other branches, and one called a writing master, who teaches writing and also some other branches. These two are both masters, and equal masters, with equal pay, no difference in rank or authority, neither having exclusive control or responsibility. . . . We do not deny that there must have been powerful motives, or interests, or influences of some kind, which could have caused the adoption and continuance of so strange an arrangement. . . . Indeed, the only argument of any weight in its favor is this — the departments of writing and arithmetic being very important require we should secure the most competent instructors and we can do this only by giving to such instructors the same pay, and the same rank, and the same power, that we give to the Grammar masters. Now to say nothing of the notorious fact, that inferior men are very often chosen to this office, the argument itself is very feeble. . . .

It is a fact of some significance in this connection that the masters, as the schools are now organized, do not really have much to do with either the instruction or the discipline of the lower classes, and in most cases positively nothing to do with their moral training. Our schools are not only double-headed, but they are triple-headed, if not quadruple-headed. Each of the masters is nominally the responsible head of his own department; but he confines his attention almost entirely to the upper classes, and leaves his usher and his assistants to manage the lower as they can.

In some schools the masters, in reply to the printed questions of the committee, say they have but sixty under their personal care; and it is a fact beyond question, that some of them do nothing and know nothing, about the instruction of the lower classes.

We have alluded, elsewhere, to some of the evils of this management, of which the only ostensible benefit is, that it affords comfortable places and salaries for persons otherwise, perhaps, out of employment.

A paragraph from Horace Mann's comments contributes a little further information:

In one department, there is a Grammar Master (so called) who has sole charge of orthography, reading, grammar, geography, and history, to which if he pleases, he may add natural philosophy and astronomy; and, in the other department, there is a Writing Master (so called) who has charge of arithmetic and handwriting, with perhaps a little of algebra, geometry, and bookkeeping. The children pass from one master to the other each half day.

One or two other sentences in the report throw additional light on the situation. The statement is explicitly made that " in sixteen schools there are thirty-two masters and sixteen ushers, each master having equal jurisdiction; one (type) being master of one half (a school) all the morning, the other of the other half; and then exchanging in the afternoon." Apparently the ushers and women teachers were constant morning and afternoon; it was only the masters who changed.

The length of the daily session was apparently six clock hours, but varied somewhat at different times in the year. From the first Monday in May to the first Monday in October, school began at eight o'clock and closed at five. For the balance of the year the hours are given as 9 : 00 to 12, 2 : 00 to 5 : 00. Ordinarily there was a fifteen-minute recess each half day, but from the first Monday in November until the first of March the afternoon recess was omitted and the schools closed at four.

Schools were in session all the year round, but apparently there were many and frequent vacations, of varying length. Every Wednesday and Saturday afternoon throughout the year and all fast days were holidays. National holidays, like Christmas, Thanksgiving, Fourth of July, Election Day, etc., were also observed, and there were many short special vacations. Specifically mentioned as vacations are the week beginning on the first Monday in June and the remainder of the week after the exhibit in August and the two succeeding weeks.

No complete statement of these regulations was found anywhere, but by searching through the reports of the Boston School Committee for this period, one after another was brought to light. Whether or not all these regulations were operative in 1845 is not made clear in the available reports.

A study of the rules of the school committee and the indirect references in the survey reports show that children could not be admitted from the primary to the grammar and writing schools until they had attained to their seventh birthday: were acquainted with the common stops — as punctuation marks were called — and abbreviations, had been exercised in the spelling book, were able to name the chapters, recite verses, and read fluently in the New Testament. Boys were required to leave school at the end of the term next after their fourteenth birthday, girls after their sixteenth birthday. Schools were ungraded in these days. That is, there was no regular grouping of children into definite classes of approximately equal ability, as at the present time. The whole body of children did not recite at once, however. There was a division of younger from older children, and there were four recitation groups, corresponding in a general way to present-day grades. For instance, children in the "first classes" in the various schools were those about to graduate and on the average were 14 years, 2 months old, resembling our present eighth grade in age. Grading was an individual and flexible matter. For instance, a child on entering school was put with children of about his own age. If, however, he proved more competent than this group, he might at any time be called upon to recite with a higher class. No pupil could give exclusive attention to one department, grammar or writing, without special permission. In general, about one teacher was provided for each sixty children.

In the report mention is made of medal scholars. These were supposed to be pupils of exceptional ability to whom

Modern schools provide facilities for pupils' meetings, parents' and community meetings, and amateur theatricals, as well as for swimming and many other activities not included in the school program of a generation ago.

prize medals were awarded each year. The money for these medals came partly from a fund provided by Benjamin Franklin. As the schools grew, additions to the medal funds were made from time to time from city funds. In 1845 the whole system of prizes was being vigorously discussed, and a few years later it was abolished. At the time of the report, however, medal scholars are to be understood as individuals of exceptional ability.

The subjects taught and the standard texts were as follows:

GRAMMAR SCHOOL

SUBJECT	AUTHOR OF TEXT	SCHOOLS STUDYING SUBJECT [2]
Spelling	Kelley	19
Reading	Cobb	19
Grammar	Whately	19
Geography		19
History	Worcester	17
Natural Philosophy [1] .	Smellie	13
Astronomy [1]		4

WRITING SCHOOL

SUBJECT	AUTHOR OF TEXT	SCHOOLS STUDYING SUBJECT [2]
Arithmetic	Emerson	19
Handwriting	Root System [1]	19
Algebra [1]		12
Geometry [1]		2
Bookkeeping [1] . . .		11

[1] Elective.

[2] No school had studied Rhetoric, fifteen declined to be questioned on Astronomy, six on Natural Philosophy, and two upon History. All the schools were examined in Geography, English, Grammar, and Definitions (taken from reading books).

The distribution of time to the various subjects is not given, except for the writing schools. The statement of the survey committee is:

From thirty minutes to one hour each day (four days a week) is devoted to writing by all the pupils of each class. In most of the schools, one hour is spent in this way, and this without regard to sex, age, or acquirements.

The girl at seven and seventeen gives the same time to these studies (writing and arithmetic). From one half to an hour in each day is devoted to writing, so that two hours to two hours and a half are set apart for arithmetic during the seven or nine years the pupils may remain in school. The rules give the masters no discretion in this matter, and the child who studies nothing but arithmetic, and who, in fact, can learn nothing except that during the recitation, is compelled to spend two or two and a half hours per day in this way. The committee do not doubt that the older pupils may spend this time in the study of arithmetic profitably, but they believe that with the younger it is not only partially lost, but tends to weary and disgust them.

The textbooks of 1845 must be seen to be appreciated. Mature, formal, dry, barren, designedly intricate and perplexing, are descriptive statements which roughly characterize all of them. Yet they formed the chief instruments of instruction, as the following quotations from the survey reports will show:

Most of the questions [in the survey tests] might be answered by children who are familiar with the text books used in our schools, all of them by children to whom these text books had been fully and familiarly explained by good teachers. (Survey Committee.)

In what condition are these children (failures in definition test) to read the Bible, or to hear a sermon? In what condition are they to read an essay, or a speech, or any instructive subject? The great end of education is to fit them to become men. Where is the evidence that the minds of these children have been trained to precision and exactness of thought? (Horace Mann.)

All pupils of average ability who have been properly taught should have a command, not merely of the particular fact, or the general statement of a truth or principle, but also of its connection, relations, and applications. Text books contain a much greater proportion of isolated facts and of abstract principles, than of relations and applications. This is the circumstance which gives pertinency and significance to their distinctive appellation, — text books. They are books containing texts. These texts the teacher is to expound. Each one of them should be the foundation of a discourse, or a series of discourses. This is teaching. Hearing recitations from a book is not teaching. It is the exposition of the principle contained in the books; showing its connection with life, with action, with duty; making it the nucleus around which to gather all related facts and all collateral principles; — it is this and this only, which can appropriately be called teaching. All short of this is mere journey-work, rude mechanical labor and drudgery. (Horace Mann.)

The conclusion to be drawn from these and many similar statements is that in 1845 education on the intellectual side was conceived as a process by which the children acquired knowledge and skill as a result of the instruction and exposition by their teachers of the texts in the textbooks. The children's business was to learn and to recite; that of the teachers to expound and to appraise; and the function of the training given was supposed to be preparation for living. There were usually one small blackboard to a school, a few small globes, no maps, no supplementary reading, and no legitimate child activity, much routine memorization, endless drill and recitation, and constant repression of childish desire for exercise and play.

In one respect the Boston schools of 1845 differed markedly from those of the present day. The religious and moral elements were much in evidence. There was daily reading of the Scriptures. The Lord's Prayer and the Ten Commandments were required to be read and repeated at least once a week. Masters and teachers were expected as part of their duties to develop the character and moral natures of their young charges. High ideals for teachers and teaching are ex-

pressed in the survey reports and in Horace Mann's comment
on them. Witness the following:

Far be it from me to consider intellectual activity and intellectual
acquirements as alone worthy of consideration. Let us look, also,
to the cultivation of the religious sense, the supremacy of conscience, the duty of self-culture, the love of knowledge, the respect
for order, — let the presence or absence and measure of these be
taken into account, before we say which school is first or which is
last. (Survey Report.)

Nor must we forget, that if our schools are to be places where
human beings shall be taught and trained, there must be discipline,
restraint, and positive authority. He who hopes for an escape from
this necessity, knows nothing of human nature. He has not
learned the most universal law of human life, who does not know
that every man from his cradle to his grave, errs and sins, and suffers the punishments by which Providence would restrain, instruct,
and reform him. It is thus man learns, and so must the child learn
to become a man.

Who is entitled to more respect, to a more affectionate regard
by the whole community, than the faithful and useful schoolmaster?
When Providence in its mercy gives us children, we receive from
its hands these germs of human life and with them the solemn duty
of watching over them, of training them in their growth, and so
preparing them in the morning of their lives for the hours of noonday toil, that the various uses and employments of life may be discharged by the men and women who are to follow us in such wise
as to promote their own good and the good of mankind. We feel
the burden of this task, and we call upon the schoolmaster to aid
us. We tell him to stand in the place of the parent; we put in
his hands a large part of our authority; we lay on his shoulders
a heavy portion of our own responsibility. Whoso enters our schoolrooms, and is able to see there only feebleness and imperfection,
and the day of small things, forgets, or is incapable of knowing that,
in the immature and slight seeming Present before him there lies
an indefinite Future. There are the men and women of a time that
is near at hand; there is the nation of the coming age. Within
those walls are a large part, — no man can say how large, — of
the influences that are to set their seal upon that nation, to form
its character and determine its destiny. There is the beginning of
Education. And the end of it is not when as men and women they

take their places in society, but afar off, in the distance of Eternity these never ending influences go on; and every step of their eternal progress is colored and qualified by this beginning.

On the other hand, for the benefit of those who, deceived by these and many other pious and idealistic phrases, imagine that daily living in 1845 was on a higher plane than in the twentieth century, there is much indirect evidence that both in the school and out of it, human nature was often quite as mean and selfish as it is today. For instance, pages of the report are devoted to an arraignment of corporal punishment in the school, although in 1844 the Board had passed a rule requiring a full report of each case. In one of the open letters written at this time reference is made to the fact that for a representative school the Boston Survey Committee found the floggings to average 65 per day for four hundred children, or one every six minutes throughout the six-hour session, — a reasonably busy day for teachers whose time seems to have been pretty full otherwise. Nor were these floggings simple affairs. But perhaps it is best to let the committee speak for itself.

We are forced to believe that there has been gross abuse of the power of corporal punishment. Undoubtedly there are some persons who look upon the rod as if it had a magic power, as if chaos must come again if it were abandoned and forgotten. They quote the saying of Solomon as if it contained all his wisdom and regard the rod as if it must be the chief instrument of education. We hope the regulations of the committee and the power of public opinion will break the force of the blows and save the little victims from outrage.

We have referred principally to the habitual use of corporal punishment in our boys' schools, for we are ready to say of him, who in this age and city avows that he cannot teach our girls without resort to blows, that he cannot so use the respect, the docility and the affectionate temper, which characterize the many, as to subdue the perversity of the few, he is not yet fit for the high vocation of teacher.

It will be found upon examination that in most of the cases where severe injury has followed corporal punishment in our schools, the offence was very trifling and no great severity intended when the master began to strike.   Moreover, it is beyond all question that in the majority of cases of corporal punishment and other kinds of punishment in our schools, it is inflicted for violations of arbitrary rules of discipline, — for whispering, for disorderly conduct, arising perhaps from mere physical uneasiness, and it is equally certain that the fault in most cases is as much that of the school as of the scholar.

The report also throws indirect light on the spirit and attitudes which prevail among the masters.   Many precautions were taken by the survey committee to avoid cheating on the part of both pupils and masters, and the statement, "We were pained, however, to find that though many of the masters coöperated with us some did not," is significant, as is also this comment:

Those masters, or others, who may attempt to undervalue the accuracy or importance of the returns for the sake of saving the character of particular schools will sink all the schools low indeed. For if, with the aid of previous knowledge of the questions, the answers are so very unsatisfactory, what must they have been if no one had meddled with a trial which was designed as a fair one?

Other quotations are equally significant.

The masters evidently are very desirous of obeying implicitly and in some cases blindly every wish of the General Committee, but they seem to fear a secret power which may govern them and the committee, too.

Most of the masters declined answering the question, "Can you suggest any improvement in the text books studied in our schools?" Those who did answer, touched it as one would handle the edge of a very sharp instrument; the only full, free, and valuable communication was given by an energetic and able master, after assurance that no public use would be made of it.   Such a state of things ought not to be.   It is discreditable to this committee and injurious to the masters and to their schools to have them placed in such relations that they dare not express their honest opinion of any text book used in any department of instruction, let who will own the copyright.

Horace Mann throws further light on the situation by pleading for open advertisement of the teaching position to be filled. He urged that public examination of candidates be held. He says:

Who does not know that the lucrative and honorable station of a mastership in the Boston schools, has been sought for, in some instances, by persons who relied more on the partiality of friends, or the efficacy of the selfish motives they could arouse in some member of the committee, than on their own personal merits or fitness for the office; and who would as soon have put their hands into Nebuchadnezzar's furnace as to have entered an arena where their merits were to be weighed with those of others, in an even balance.

Suppose a member of the school committee, — and we take the supposition from fact and not from the imagination, — should make overtures to a teacher in another town, to apply for a mastership in one of the Boston schools, and should engage to second the application; but before the conversation should close, suppose this same school committeeman should propose to the teacher, that, before leaving the town where he was then employed, he should cause the aforesaid committee man's books to be introduced into the schools of that town; — does not every one see that the person thus dishonorably approached, must either comply with the suggestion made to him; or, if he should become a candidate for the place, without such compliance, that he must encounter the opposition of the suborner, whose selfish purposes he had disappointed?

The inference to be made from the committee's report is that influence and graft were at least as much if not more to be reckoned with "in the good old days of 1845" as in the present. Even the School Committee itself was not ideal.

The first of the causes which operate unfavorably upon our schools may be found in the constitution of the School Committee. Numerous, chosen without concert, in many different parts of the city, offering to those of its members who cannot turn it to their pecuniary benefit, no motive but the mere love of usefulness to induce them to remain long in office, it is necessarily an uncertain, fluctuating and inexperienced body. The duties which its members ought to discharge, are burdensome, and would require great labor, and occupy a large portion of our time. The duties which we do perform, though quite as much as can be expected or ought to be asked of men who give to these duties only their leisure, and give it without compensation, are but a small part of these which lie upon us.

Nor is it possible for us to perform even these as they should be performed. The schools are divided among Sub-Committees. Each Sub-Committee consisting of three members, the whole number for the nineteen Grammar Schools, is fifty-seven. And as only twenty-four members serve on the Sub-Committees, it is obvious that each member must serve on two schools and nine must serve on three. The Sub-Committees are required to visit each school at least once a quarter. Now, not to dwell at present upon the necessary insufficiency of so brief an examination, we would ask attention to one inevitable result from this practice. In fact, no one man, and no Sub-Committee, is ever required or expected to know the actual condition of all the Grammar Schools in Boston. It is, we repeat, impossible that the present School Committee should perform this work of supervision. But while it constitutes, as in fact it does, the Board of Education for the City, and is therefore supposed to do this work, it protects and perpetuates defects, by preventing that personal examination by parents, which might, in some degree at least, be given, if it were supposed to be needed; — thus verifying the saying of Jeremy Bentham, in his argument in favor of individual responsibility, that "a Board is but too apt to become a screen."

Such were the Boston schools in 1845. In their conception of education, narrow; in buildings and equipment, meager and barren; in methods of control, primitive. They were without organization and supervision, there was little grading, the classes were large, the membership shifting, the attendance variable. The head master was often primarily an efficient flogger of children, a ward heeler subject to the influence, control, and graft of the influential ward politician, working through a large school committee !

Not all the Boston masters were of this type, of course; yet it must be remembered that thirty-one out of thirty-two were sufficiently like-minded to sign a public statement attacking Horace Mann, well known for his proved ability and zeal for the public good in other fields, whose only fault was that he dared publicly to plead for the improvement of the public schools.

It is a rather shocking picture of school conditions but seventy-five years ago. And yet, in the words of the survey committee, we must remember

That many of our schools are far better than they once were, we well know and gladly acknowledge. But the knowledge that there are such improvements has only made us look to the possibility of further progress and resolve to do all in our power to leave for our children schools as much better than the present, as the present are better than those of olden times.

CHAPTER THREE

The First American Survey

TO the courageous and resourceful committees appointed to examine the Grammar and Writing Schools in 1845 much honor is due. We cannot now tell in whose fertile brain originated the Boston plan to secure positive, objective information about the products of classroom instruction, nor whose brave and determined persistency carried the plan through to completion. We do know that the committee on writing schools made a less thorough report, and prepared the less satisfactory tests, so that it is probable the moving spirit is to be sought among the members of the Grammar School Committee. It is even possible, though not proved, that the idea of tests and detailed tabulations was inspired by Horace Mann himself. In his comments on the mode of examination used by the committees, he says:

> We call it novel, because, although such a plan of examination is common in Europe, and has been partially adopted in some places in this country, yet we have seen nothing on this side of the Atlantic so thorough and complete and embracing in one view so large a number of schools and scholars, as the Boston Committees' Report.

Be that as it may, we can all subscribe to his further statement that

> Not the City of Boston alone, but the whole state and the cause of education generally, are under a vast debt of obligation to the committee who assumed and who have carried through the labors of this novel mode of examination.

Accordingly, the names of these pioneer American surveyors are listed here, that we may pay at least the only tribute in our power, respectful memory.

SURVEY COMMITTEES

Grammar Schools	*Writing Schools*
Theophilus Parsons	William Brigham
S. G. Howe	J. I. T. Coolidge
Rollin H. Neale	Hiram A. Graves

The reasons for the use of printed tests are clearly given by the committee:

It is our wish to have as fair an examination as possible; to give the same advantages to all; to prevent leading questions; to carry away, not loose notes, or vague remembrances of the examination, but positive information, in black and white; to ascertain with certainty what the scholars did not know, as well as what they did know; to test their readiness at expressing their ideas upon paper; to have positive and undeniable evidence of their ability or inability to construct sentences grammatically, to punctuate them, and to spell the words. One of the papers prepared was a list of words to be defined, all of them taken from the reading book and used in the class; another was a set of questions upon Geography; another upon Grammar; one upon Civil History; one upon Natural Philosophy; one upon Astronomy; one upon Whately's Rhetoric, and one upon Smellie's Philosophy.

Writing specimens were also collected and a test given in arithmetic.

Copies of the test papers will be found in the Appendix, but some analysis of them is necessary. The committees' own statements are as follows:

In Geography, there were 31 questions, some very simple, some rather difficult, but not one which well taught children of fourteen years of age should not answer.

In History, a list containing 30 questions was submitted and certainly there is hardly a question which a child of thirteen who had studied history should not answer.

In Definitions, there were 28 words selected from the reading book, which the classes have probably read through during the year, and some probably more than once. Some of the words are the very titles and headings of reading lessons; some of them occur

The older type of clothes-room provided a place where pupils piled their coats, hats, overshoes, etc., in uncleanly, unhealthful, and troublesome fashion. Modern schools provide individual lockers in corridors or in special locker rooms.

several times in the book. It is true that some of the words are not in common use, and are what are called "hard words," but these are the very words which should be explained in our upper classes; — as for the easy words, they learn them in conversation. We admit that Thanatopsis (like some other words selected) is a rare and difficult one, and it would not have been chosen, were it not the heading of one of the lessons in the Reader, and the name prefixed to one of the most beautiful gems in the whole collection of American poetry.

In Natural Philosophy, we gave printed papers containing 20 very simple questions and required answers to as many of them as could be written in an hour.

In Astronomy, 21 questions were put varying from those of the simplest nature, such as, what is the radius of a circle, up to questions about tides, change of seasons, etc.

The whole number of questions in Grammar was 14; — some being merely requisitions to write a simple sentence containing an active transitive verb and an objective case, and others being sentences which contain false syntax to be corrected.

In forming an estimate of the relative rank of the several schools in Writing, the Committee confined themselves wholly to the specimens offered by the first class.

The written examination in Arithmetic was adopted in all the schools except the Smith. It was limited to the first division of the first class, which varied in numbers from four to twenty-six. The committee prepared ten questions for solution on a variety of subjects, and caused them to be printed on a single sheet, leaving between each a sufficient blank space to enable the pupil to record the process of solution. It was not expected any considerable number could work out all the sums in so short a time (1 hour and 10 minutes) but it was thought expedient to propose such questions that even those who had made the greatest advancement might find employment during the allotted period. It was intended to have these questions embrace such a variety of subjects as to require a pretty thorough knowledge of the whole science of arithmetic to give the right answers to all of them.

The committee men showed great skill and wisdom in preparing the tests. Not only did they begin with easy, conventional classroom questions, and gradually increase the difficulty of the questions, but they included questions which required the application of knowledge to new situations, — reasoning or thought questions, as they are often called. For instance, the question, " In what year was the embargo laid by President Jefferson and when was non-intercourse substituted for it? " is a pure memory question, a question of fact. But the question, " Explain what is meant by an embargo," calls for understanding and clear expression. Analysis of the tests from this point of view reveals the following facts:

ANALYSIS OF TESTS

SUBJECT	TOTAL QUESTIONS	TYPES OF QUESTIONS		
		Memory or Skill	Intermediate	Thought
1. History	30	13	8	9
2. Geography . .	31	8	13	10
3. Grammar . . .	14	11	3	9
4. Philosophy . .	20	8	5	7
5. Astronomy . .	24	10	6	8
6. Arithmetic . .	10	4	0	6
Total . . .	129	54	35	40
Per cent . .	100	42	27	31

Questions which can be answered by direct statements of fact (presumably given in the textbook) have been classified as memory questions; those evidently given to test the children's powers to apply what they have learned to new situations are called thought questions; those involving summarization or generalization of facts have been called intermediate. It is, of course, impossible at this time to classify the questions as the examiners classified them, but the analysis serves to show what was clearly the intention of the examiners, to arrange comprehensive tests.

The grammar questions are difficult to classify. Parse, punctuate, define, state rules, are all questions involving chiefly memory skill. There are no thought questions of the kind given in the other tests.

The arithmetic examination was probably a very poor test. There were four examples involving computations, and six problems. Only one of these problems was within the children's ability. For two problems, not a single one of the 308 children who attempted them obtained a correct answer, and for three others the number of correct answers were 1, 2, and 3, respectively. Such results make it probable that the examiners were not familiar with the work of the schools and that they greatly overestimated the attainments of the children.

Of the words to be defined the committee says:

There are two or three of these words, as Thanatopsis, Zoonamia, etc., which, being in the reading lessons, the scholars would meet with, and not being in the dictionary, they would not be likely to understand unless the masters taught them their meaning. They are, therefore, a better test than words which may be found in the dictionary, of the endeavors of the masters to secure on the part of the children, an understanding of what they read. It is so obvious, as hardly to need the authority of the best instructors and of all good writers on education, that the habit of reading without understanding and without knowing whether one understands or not, is easily formed and confirmed, and is most injurious; while the pupil who never passes a word without knowing whether he understands it, and inquiring into the meaning if he does not, has acquired a habit of mind which will be almost sufficient, of itself, to insure constant improvement.

The tests were given by the examiners themselves under uniform conditions. The Grammar School Committee's statement of its procedure, in giving the examination, is most interesting.

Our plan of proceeding was as follows: In order to prevent the children of one school from having an advantage over those of another by ascertaining what the questions were to be, they were privately prepared and printed; then, without any previous notice, each member of the Committee commenced at 8 o'clock in the morning with one school, and spread before the first division of the first class the printed questions in geography. The maps and books were put out of the way; the scholars were placed at a distance from each other, so as to prevent communication by whispers; they were told that they would have one hour to answer the questions, and that they should not lose time in trying to write handsomely, as the chirography would not be taken into account. Then they were set to work. Notwithstanding all that was said about their being taken by surprise, about their being unused to such mode of questioning, about their inability to express what they knew in so short a time, we found that in a few minutes they were all busily at work; all adapted themselves to their new circumstances with that readiness which characterizes our countrymen, without embarrassment, and, generally, they had exhausted their power to answer before the hour expired.

At the end of the hour, the Committee man gathered up his papers, and went as quickly as possible to the next School, remained there an hour, and then proceeded to a third. After the noon intermission, the Committee commenced again and visited three more Schools; thus each Committee man finished the examination in geography of six schools; and the three finished all the Schools in the City. The next day we took the questions on another subject, and thus finished the whole.

We extended our examination into some of the Schools in the neighboring towns and states, and gained much useful information from them. But we include only the Dudley School in Roxbury among our returns. We examined this first, and were certain that neither master nor scholars knew anything beforehand of our questions. Of those examined afterwards, there was some doubt, and we therefore omit them.

With regard to the Schools in the City proper, we believe that upon no one subject except definitions, was a knowledge of the questions obtained by the scholars of any School previously to their being presented by the Committee; and even in regard to definitions, very little advantage was gained by any one School. Fraud ever carries a suspicious front; the natural language of a cheat can be detected even in his mode of writing; and the unfairness in one School was discovered by a glance at the written answers. But in almost every set of answers obtained from the Schools, there is internal evidence of honesty; — honest ignorance, and honest error, as well as honest accuracy.

But we repeat the assertion, that, to the best of our knowledge and belief, the statistical returns which we submit will present the fullest and the fairest means for judging of the real merits and demerits of our Schools, and of their comparative rank, which have ever been embodied so as to be within the reach of any but actual examiners of the Schools. We may say this safely, because it is perhaps the only statistical information which has ever been so embodied.

The whole number of pupils present in the Schools on the days when we examined, was 7,526; the whole number offered for examination, — a number comprising the flower of the Boston Public Schools, — was 530; their average age being about thirteen years, six months.

The children were also examined verbally, although no details are given as to their examination except that it confirmed the results of the written tests.

The Committee on Writing Schools state that they

Commenced their examination early in June and continued the same from time to time, to the middle of July. In arithmetic they examined the pupils by submitting printed questions for their solution and also by propounding questions orally.

The whole number of children belonging to the schools at the time of the examination was 8,343, of whom 308, comprising the best scholars in each school, were examined in this manner.

The committee members evidently scored the papers themselves and painstakingly, question by question. Both the committee and Horace Mann refer repeatedly to the labor involved. Fortunately they did more than merely score the papers; they gave the general rules governing their procedure and also specimen answers and papers.

For instance, the committee says:

The results would have been more surprising had we rigidly adhered to the rules of criticism, and set down every answer as incorrect which was not faultless; but we have put the most lenient construction upon the answers, and whenever it appeared that the scholar had any tolerable idea of the subject, we have recorded his answer as correct. If we had put down as correct only those answers which were perfect in regard to sense, to grammatical constructions, to spelling and to punctuation, the record would have been very short.

These tables have been prepared with very great labor and care. It was necessary, however, to have them printed in haste, and a work which should have occupied several months, has been done in a few weeks. It may be, therefore, that there are some errors in them; but it is believed that they will generally be found in favor of the schools. For instance, in looking for errors in definitions, the rule has been, that when the scholar expressed himself obscurely, but seemed to have an idea of the meaning of the word, he should be considered as having answered correctly. So in geography, history, philosophy, etc., though the answers were ungrammatical, and contained errors in spelling and punctuation, still they have been recorded in the column of correct answers, if the scholar seemed to have a correct idea of the subject.

As to the columns containing the errors in spelling, grammar and punctuation, they probably fall short of the real number, because while none would be found that were not in the scholars' answers, hundreds may have been overlooked in such a mass of papers. The number of errors in punctuation seems so enormous, that the Committee may be suspected of hypercriticism; it may be said that punctuation is a mere matter of taste, and that any man may point out hundreds of errors in the works of the best authors. But in looking over the answers written by our scholars, care has been taken to record only the most palpable errors in punctuation. The list has been swelled mainly by the omission of commas and periods where the sense absolutely required them.

Sometimes errors will be found set down in the columns of errors in punctuation and spelling, against a question which is recorded as not having been answered; and this is the explanation: A boy writes against the question: "I dont know never studeid the subject." Here the question would be recorded as unanswered, and yet one error in spelling and two errors in punctuation would be recorded against him.

Lest the form of the tables should not be understood, we here observe, that the first column on the left hand refers to the number of the question, to prevent repetition in printing, though at the time of writing every scholar had the question plainly printed, before his eyes, and wrote his answers under them. The second column contains the number of answers correct as to sense; the third contains those incorrect as to sense; the fourth, fifth and sixth contain, respectively, the number of errors in grammar, spelling and punctuation; the seventh contains the number of questions not answered, and the eighth the percentage of correct answers relatively to the whole number of answers that should have been given, supposing all the questions to have been answered.

The column representing the percentage of correct answers in each school in each study, is obtained by taking the number of scholars examined, and multiplying it by the whole number of questions; this shows the number of answers which they should have given; then taking the number of correct answers which they did give, and ascertaining the proportion between them.

The relative rank of each school in each study, is obtained by multiplying the percentage of correct answers by the percentage of the scholars examined.

In the Appendix to the original report are given a number of sets of specimen papers " printed carefully from their papers, exactly as they spelled the words and punctuated the sentences and used capital or small letters." These specimen papers comprise:

a. One history paper from each of 15 " medal scholars," one from each school and chosen at random from the list of medal scholars.

b. Same for test on definitions.

c. Exact copies of the answers in natural philosophy written by 5 scholars of the first division, first class, in one of the schools which ranks above mediocrity.

d. Answers of same 5 scholars to questions in English Grammar.

e. Exact answers to questions in geography given by

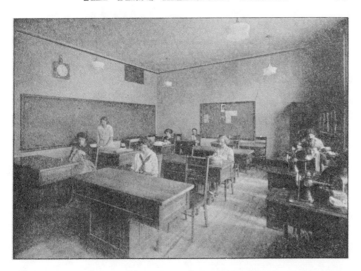

A good schoolroom includes plenty of blackboard and bulletin space, pictures, and movable seatings with individual desks, as shown in the upper picture. Below is shown a science room with desks and seatings suited to experimentation, study, and recitation within one room.

10 scholars, taken in alphabetical order from a girls' school in Boston and a girls' school in Roxbury, the average of their ages being about the same.

The committee also gave three summary tables, one giving the average age of the classes examined in each school, one the comparative rank of each school in the required studies, and one the comparative rank in the allowed studies.

Well might the committee say:

The mode of examination by written questions has been used with great success in many schools and colleges; but we are not aware of any tabularization like this having been attempted.

CHAPTER FOUR

Unanswerable Arguments from the Past

BY no means the least interesting reading in connection with the 1845 report is the portion of the *Common School Journal* in which Horace Mann justifies the use of printed tests by the survey committee. He saw at once the meaning and value of objective measurement, and even now when the conflict for the scientific study of educational processes by means of standard tests has been won, his appraisal of the method of the first American survey is still most enlightening.

Briefly, Horace Mann states that the new method of examination has a "decided superiority over any and all other methods" for the following reasons:

1. It is impartial.
2. It is just to the pupils.
3. It is more thorough than older forms of examination.
4. It prevents the "officious interference" of the teacher.
5. It "determines, beyond appeal or gainsaying, whether the pupils have been faithfully and competently taught."
6. It takes away "all possibility of favoritism."
7. It makes the information obtained available to all.
8. It enables all to appraise the ease or difficulty of the questions.

The arguments must be submitted in some detail. Whenever possible the extended statements are condensed, but they contain so much of general interest, reveal so much of the practices, difficulties, and dangers inherent in the system of inspection of schools by observation and oral examination which was the rule in 1845, that they have a distinct value for all administrative and supervisory officers who to this

Above is a modern school library, with equipment and books suited to all ages of school pupils and contributing to all school studies and activities.   Below is a classroom for little children, with low blackboards, bulletin boards, and table, work bench, and movable tables and chairs.

day still place a large degree of dependence upon the oral methods.

Horace Mann calls the new method impartial,

for it submits the same question not only to all the scholars who are to be examined, in the same school, but to all the schools of the same class or grade. Scholars in the same school, therefore, can be equitably compared with each other; and all the different schools are subjected to a measurement by the same standard. Take the best school committee man who ever exposed the nakedness of ignorance, or detected fraud, or exploded the bubbles of pretension, and let him examine a class orally, and he cannot approach exactness, in judging of the relative merits of the pupils, by any very close approximation. And the reason is apparent. He must propound different questions to different scholars; and it is impossible that these questions should be equal, in point of ease or difficulty. A poor scholar may be asked a very easy question, and answer it. A good scholar may be asked a very difficult one, and miss it. In some cases, a succeeding scholar may profit by the mistakes of a preceding one; so that, if there had been a different arrangement of their seats, the record would have borne a different result of plus and minus. The examiner may prepare himself beforehand as carefully as he pleases, and mark out the precise path he intends to pursue, and yet, in spite of himself, he may be thrown out of his course by unforeseen circumstances. But when the questions are the same, there is exactness of equality. Balances cannot weigh out the work more justly. So far as the examination is concerned, all the scholars are "born free and equal."

Suppose a race were to be run by twenty men, in order to determine their comparative fleetness; but instead of bringing them upon the same course, where they could all stand abreast and start abreast, one of them should be selected to run one mile, and then a second, starting where the first one stopped, should run another mile, and so on until the whole had entered the lists; might it not, and would it not so happen that one would have the luck of running up hill, and another down; that one would run over a good turnpike and another over a "corduroy"? Pupils required to answer dissimilar questions, are like runners obliged to test their speed by running on dissimilar courses.

Again, it is clear that the larger the number of questions put to a scholar, the better is the opportunity to test his merits. If but a single question is put the best scholar in the school may miss it, though he would answer the next twenty without a blunder; or the poorest scholar may succeed in answering one question, though certain to fail in twenty others. Each question is a partial test, and the greater the number of questions, therefore, the nearer does the test approach to completeness. It is very uncertain which face of a die will be turned up at the first throw; but if the dice are thrown all day, there will be a great equality in the number of the different faces turned up.

In fine, the method adopted by the committees was not merely impartial, — for this is only an adjective, — but it was the noun substantive, Impartiality itself.

In discussing justice to pupils, Horace Mann writes:

Suppose, under the form of oral examination, an hour is assigned to a class of thirty pupils, this gives two minutes apiece. But under the late mode of examination, we have the paradox, that an hour for thirty is sixty minutes apiece. Now it often happens that a sterling scholar is modest, diffident, and easily disconcerted under new circumstances. Such a pupil requires time to collect his faculties. Give him this, and he will not disappoint his best friends. Debar him from this, and a forth-putting, self-esteeming competitor may surpass him. In an exercise of two minutes, therefore, the best scholar may fail, because he loses his only opportunity while he is summoning his energies to improve it, but give him an hour, and he will have time to rally and do himself justice. It is one of the principal recommendations of this method, indeed, that it excludes surprise as one of the causes of failure, and takes away the simulation of it as an excuse.

Evidently school committees bent on examining schools had their troubles with teachers in 1845 as in the present day. Horace Mann's comments on this point are exceedingly illuminating.

It sometimes happens that when an examiner has brought a pupil or class to a test-question, — to a point that will reveal their condition as to ignorance or knowledge, — the teacher bolts out with some suggestion or leading question that defeats the whole purpose at a breath. We would look with all possible lenity upon teachers who take such a course; for we perceive the vehemence of the temptation under which they labor. When the pupils of their favorite class, and perhaps in their favorite study, are in danger of being sunk in the abysses of their own ignorance, how natural it is for a kind-hearted and quick-feeling teacher to wish to throw them a rope. But such interference is unjust, not to say ungentlemanly. The case supposed is the very juncture where the teacher should abstain from intermeddling though he should be obliged to thrust his pocket handkerchief into his mouth, or put his head out of the window. Of what use to examine a school, if each boy and girl is to be like Punch and Judy in the puppet-show, and to be told by another the things they are to say? While, then, we respect the feelings which prompt the teacher to interfere with the course of the examination, we consider it a great point gained, to prevent the mischief of their indulgence. Now where a school is examined by written or printed questions, distributed on the instant, by the examining committee, questions of which the teachers themselves are as ignorant as the pupils, — they must, perforce, look on at their leisure. Though they writhe in anxiety, yet their ill-judged kindness can do no harm; their improper suggestions are excluded. They are obliged to reflect that the day of probation has passed; the time for trial and judgment has come.

Compared with the above is his appraisal of the reliability of the method used by the examining committee.

All pupils of average ability, who have been properly taught, should have a command, not merely of the particular fact, or the general statement of a truth or principle, but also of its connections, relations and applications; and every faithful examiner will strive to know whether they possess the latter as well as the former species of information. Now the method of examination lately adopted by the Boston School Committee, settles the question, — what kind or quality of instruction has been given by the masters, as it does — what amount or extent of proficiency has been made by the pupils. A pupil may most faithfully commit the whole of one of our grammars to memory, and yet know nothing more of the science of English Grammar, than a parrot, who has been taught to say "Pretty Poll," knows of the power and copiousness of the

English language; or he may con Geography and Atlas, till he can repeat every line in the one and remember every island speck in the other, and yet have no distinct conception of anything beyond the visible horizon. A child may know, — as any child, unless it be an idiotic one, does, — that water will run down hill, and yet never be led to embrace the truth, that it is mountain ridges and table-lands that give descent and direction to the course of rivers. Nay, because he has faithfully learned the fact that the upper part of the map represents the north, he may conscientiously deny that the waters of Lake Erie run into Lake Ontario, because, as he holds his map before him, it looks as though they must, for that purpose, run up hill. A child may know how to spell from a spelling book, and yet, when put to the twofold operation of writing and spelling, he may bring vowels and consonants into very strange juxtapositions. Or he may be introduced to ten thousand English words, and not know the real meaning and use of more than five hundred of them.

We repeat, then, that this method of examination tests, in a most admirable manner, the competency or sufficiency of the teaching which the pupils have received; for, as a workman is not taught any art or handicraft, until he can execute it, so a child is not taught any principle until he can explain it, or apply it. Where children of ordinary abilities have been continuously and for a long time under instruction, any deficiencies, of the kinds above specified, are not to be laid to their charge, but to that of their instructors. How should pupils know what lies beyond text books, or what is necessary in order to understand the text book, unless they have been taught it?

An unimportant but interesting sidelight is contained in the following:

A most unpleasant, and generally, we doubt not, an unfounded accusation, is sometimes brought against examiners: — namely, that they are guilty of partiality in putting out questions; that they visit the iniquities of fathers upon children, by selecting difficult questions for the child of an adversary or opponent, and reserving the easy ones for the children of friends. Now, in its practical mischiefs, the next worse thing to their committing so unjust an act, is the suspicion that they have committed it. Either the fact or the suspicion greatly impairs the value, if it does not defeat the object of an examination. We have known instances where it would have been far better that there should have been no examination at all, than to have the cry of injustice raised, and the feelings of the district exasperated against committee men. But by putting the same questions to all, not only the odious offence of favoritism, but even an indulgence of the suspicion of it, is excluded.

The following comment is worthy of a permanent place in our educational literature and might apply to modern tests as well as those used by the Boston examiners:

When the oral method is adopted, none but those personally present at the examination can have any accurate or valuable idea of the appearance of the school. By hearing the questions asked and the answers given they may form a notion, more or less correct, of the attainments of the pupils, and the readiness with which they can command them. But all the information which approaches authenticity is confined within the walls of the schoolroom. Whoever is not therein and is not there at the time, too, must rely upon rumor for his opinions. Not so, however, when the examination is by printed questions and written answers. A transcript, a sort of Daguerreotype likeness, as it were, of the state and condition of the pupils' minds, is taken and carried away, for general inspection. Instead of being confined to committees and visitors, it is open to all; instead of perishing with the fleeting breath that gave it life, it remains a permanent record. All who are, or who may afterwards become interested in it, may see it. The school, during successive years too, can be compared with itself, in order to determine whether it is advancing or retrograding; or whether it has improved under one teacher, while it deteriorates under another. It is true that the committees, from year to year, under the old method, may have known their opinion, — they may write it out and publish it, — but the different committees will have different standards of excellence; and thus it is that a school may have a brightening reputation, while in reality it is running down, and a waning one while it is improving. If every man's foot is to be taken as twelve inches long, it becomes an important question by whose foot we shall measure. So of the different standards of judging in the minds of different men. . . .
Where the questions are all printed and preserved, their char-

acter as to ease or difficulty can be seen. Should the question be
too difficult for children of the age and opportunities of those examined, equitable abatement can be made for their failures. If,
on the other hand, the questions are simple, and yet the children
blunder, the censure must fall upon them with proportionate severity. If the scholars fail to answer, with promptitude and correctness, such questions as are found in the books, they must bear
a portion at least of the dishonor; but if they answer from the book
accurately and readily, but fail in those cases which involve relations and application of principles, the dishonor must settle upon
the heads of the teachers. Whether one or the other, whether
more or less of either, cannot be sufficiently known, unless the
character of the questions is known. This important knowledge
can be obtained only when the questions can be inspected;
that is, only when the written method of examination has been
employed.

From the foregoing it will be evident that Horace Mann
was scientifically minded on educational matters long before
his time. The measure of a man is often his open-minded-
ness toward that which is new. It is only the man of exceptional ability who has the power to set aside the instinc-
tive aversion to change which all adults have and to consider
a novel action on its merits. Horace Mann had that power.
His statement, " We venture to predict that the mode of
examination by printed questions and written answers will
constitute a new era in the history of our schools," is proof
of his clear-sighted vision and sound judgment. He would
have welcomed standard tests, and would have been quick
to appreciate the value of the experimental method in education. Perhaps there is no better tribute to his far-seeing
genius than that the new era foreseen by him did not begin
to materialize until two generations later, and even the year
1923 finds many who are blind to the value of objective,
impartial comparison. Be that as it may, the schools of the
future, in attempting to compare themselves with the present, will suffer from no meagerness of data. Today a com-

These are the old and the new rural school buildings.   Until three years
before the date of publication of this book the building shown in the
upper picture was in use.   The children may now be proud of their
school home.

petent superintendent's annual report gives in great detail
a wealth of objective information upon which valid comparisons may be based.   In the future, therefore, it will not be
difficult to establish growth and determine improvement.
But in the past the case was different.

CHAPTER FIVE

School Efficiency in 1845

THE average American teacher will inspect the results of the Boston tests with a most keen interest and a measure of anxiety. What will they show? The teacher's work in 1920, as measured by tests, has been cross-sectioned, dissected, analyzed, and held up to public comment, often to scorn and ridicule. It is true that the results of modern tests have been a surprise to all, even to the teachers themselves. The scores made by children are ridiculously low, the individual variation enormous, the progress from year to year much smaller than expected and supposed to exist. The greatest chagrin from the situation has come from the frequent and uncomplimentary comparisons with the past. Parents have not hesitated to say: "When we went to school, teaching was more effective." "In the good old days of drill and discipline, the children really learned something." "We learned when I was in school." Parents and the public generally have not only said these things, they have believed them, and have blamed teachers and schoolmen generally for "new-fangled methods" although the same have been developed with the intent and for the purpose of making the schools better. Teachers feel and know that the schools are better, that they themselves are entitled to praise, not blame, to reward, not censure. Criticism alone would be welcome. Teachers more than others are interested in improving the schools. Ridicule and condemnation as a reward for effort are not stimulating to further effort, and to compare unfavorably the present which is known with the past which is out of reach and imperfectly known, is to undermine the confidence of the profession in respect to its own ability and progress. For there has been no way to confirm or refute the comparisons as usually made, except a very few relatively meager comparative studies.

The records of the Boston Survey, however, open the door to an inspection of the past, an inspection which in many ways is comparable to the survey inspections of the present. How did the Boston schools of 1845 appear to the surveyors of that day? What was the character of their achievements? We have already seen that school conditions have changed greatly and for the better. What about the products of classroom teaching?

The first American surveyors were men of truth and courage. They believed in calling things by their correct names, and their survey comments should afford gleeful reading to many modern school teachers. What teacher whose work has been " surveyed " will fail to be interested in the following statement of the committee?

The first feeling occasioned by looking over these returns is that of entire incredulity. It is very difficult to believe that, in the Boston Schools, there should be so many children in the first classes unable to answer such questions; that there should be so many who try to answer, and answer imperfectly; that there should be so many absurd answers, so many errors in spelling, in grammar, and in punctuation. If by any accident these documents should be destroyed, we could hardly hope that your faith in our accuracy would induce you to believe the truth if we told you. But the papers are all before you, each signed by the scholar who wrote it.

There is one painful reflection forced upon the mind by the answers generally; and this is that while in some schools the scholars seem to be conscientious, and do not answer questions about which they are ignorant; in others they appear to be perfectly reckless, and put down answers quite at hazard, in the hope of hitting upon something that may pass for an answer. This shows an habitual carelessness in giving answers, or a want of that nicely-trained conscientiousness, which deters from trying to appear what one is not.

There is another sad reflection suggested by these answers. They show beyond all doubt, that a large proportion of the scholars of our first classes, boys and girls of fourteen or fifteen years of age, when called upon to write simple sentences, to express their thoughts on common subjects, without the aid of a dictionary or a master, cannot write, without such errors in grammar, in spelling, and in punctuation, as we should blush to see in a letter from a son or daughter of their age. And most of these children are about finishing their school career; they are going out into life; some to learn trades; some to assist their mothers in the house; the larger part never to receive any supplementary education; and how, we ask, are they, by and by, to write a letter that they would not be ashamed to exhibit?

But there is still a more melancholy consideration, which is, that, if the first class, — if the children who have, during a year, enjoyed that special care and attention which our teachers give to the upper classes, go out imperfectly instructed, what must be the case with the hundreds and thousands of the children of our less favored citizens, whom necessity forces to leave the schools without even reaching the first class? We know that the value of the services of most of our ushers would be underrated by proportioning it to their salaries; and that great injustice would be done to the many excellent instructresses, by supposing their work, as assistants, to be worth to the scholars only one-sixth the work of the masters, — but if there be anything like justice in the low rate at which the City remunerates their services, those who receive their instruction alone must go out from the schools but very poorly taught.

Upon the whole, the Committee have, reluctantly, come to the conclusion that the Grammar Schools of Boston have not the excellence and usefulness that they should possess. Our citizens manifest their strong desire, that their children should have the best possible education, by a very liberal expenditure for this purpose; and it is certain that their children have not this education. We cannot but believe, for we see, that other schools are better than most of ours; and that the majority of our Schools are further below the best that we have, than any thing in the peculiar condition of the scholars, or other similar causes can explain. And your Committee do not think they should discharge their duty, if they did not suggest some, at least, of the causes which seem to them to operate unfavorably upon our Schools.

In *The Common School Journal* for October, 1845, the editor says:

The facts disclosed by the Reports, have spread through the city a general and deep feeling of sorrow and mortification, no one will be so presumptuous as to deny. Sad indeed would it be, if this feeling should die away without producing a reform.

We have no wish to blazon abroad the defects of these schools; but if this occasion should not be made use of, for admonition and warning, the calamity of their present condition would not only be gratuitously suffered, but it might be perpetuated for years to come.

It was surely not to be expected beforehand, that, in other towns, the pupils would be found superior to the pupils in the Boston Schools. Yet such is proved to be the fact; and it has filled the intelligent citizens of Boston, — those who have the interests of the schools most deeply at heart, and who are not blinded or biased by any mercenary or sinister motives, — with amazement and grief. The Report of the Grammar Committee, from which we have quoted so largely, leaves no doubt of the humiliating fact. The committee have not sent out their conjectures, or their opinions merely, — had they done so, it would have been denied and denounced by acclamation, — but they have presented the data from which the fact is deducible with mathematical certainty.

The late examination of the Boston Grammar and Writing Schools, has demonstrated for the thousandth time, — though perhaps more fully than ever before, — that children who have been kept in their copy-books until they can write a fair and legible hand, will, if required to write down sentences of their own construction, produce the most illegible and disgraceful scrawls. We hesitate not to say, that in all the schools of Massachusetts we have ever visited, we have never seen so great a proportion of disreputable specimens of handwriting, and of errors in spelling and punctuation, as in the children's answers, now on file in the office of the city clerk.

No one can look carefully into the details of this examination without discovering an accumulation and redundancy of evidence in support of the declaration made by both of the committees, that the children have been superficially taught. There is a painful superabundance of proof, that the children have experienced but little of the highest, and indeed the only valuable kind of instruction, — an indoctrination into principles.

But the most extraordinary, and we may add, frightful ignorance, was exhibited in regard to definitions. Here, in this most important branch of an intellectual education, ignorance was the rule, and intelligence the exception.

Such a result (arithmetic scores) repels comment. No friendly attempt at palliation can make it any better. No severity of just censure can make it any worse.

Let us look for a few moments a little more in detail to the results which called forth these blasts of criticism and censure. The full tables will be found in the Appendix, but the summaries and illustrations given by the committee themselves may be summarized.

A total of 154 questions were asked in the Grammar Schools. To these there should have been 57,873 answers, if each scholar had been able to answer; but there were only 31,159, of which only 17,216 were correct in sense, leaving unanswered 26,714. The 31,159 answers contained 2,801 errors in grammar, 3,733 errors in spelling, and 35,947 errors in punctuation.

In geography there should have been 15,097 answers, but 5,233 questions were not answered at all, 4,871 were answered incorrectly, and only 5,193 or about one-third of the whole number were answered correctly.

In history, instead of the 13,140 answers which should have been given, there were only 5,933, of which only 3,567 were correct; 2,366 were incorrect.

In definitions, out of 516 children who had the questions before them one hour, not a single one defined correctly every word; only 47 defined half of them, and 39 could not define correctly a single one of the 28 words.

As a general thing, the answers in natural philosophy are better than in the other branches, but even here there is too much teaching by rote, as will be seen by the tables. To the question: "What do you understand by the center of gravity of bodies?" — 195 out of the 279 answered correctly. To the next: "Define momentum," — 133 out of the 279 answered correctly. But to the question: "If a grindstone should suddenly split in pieces while whirling

rapidly around, would the pieces fall directly to the ground or not ?"
— only 63 of the 279 answered correctly; and to the simple question, which involves an important principle, whether a pound of
water occupies more space when liquid or when in the shape of ice?
— 151 out of the 279 answered wrong, and 55 answered not at all.

Out of the whole number of questions in astronomy, 977
were answered correctly, 634 were answered incorrectly, and
1,613 were not answered at all.

The questions in grammar are the best proof that scholars may
parse technically, and point out the relations of words, their mood,
tense, case, person, number and gender; and yet, in the very
sentences which they make use of to express these relations, and in
quoting rules in justification of what they write, be continually
making blunders; and may parse their sentences grammatically,
in the most ungrammatical language. The whole number of answers given was 4,183, and these contained 962 errors in spelling,
2,247 errors in grammar, and 8,980 errors in punctuation.

In writing, the highest mark given was 12. The distribution of ranks assigned the various schools was as follows:

	HIGHEST								LOWEST
Rank	12	11	10	9	8	7	6	5	4
Number of schools receiving rank .	3	1	4	6	1	1	3	1	1

In arithmetic, the possible number of right answers was
3,080, the actual number 1,078.

In considering these results it must be remembered that
not all the pupils in the first division of the first class were
examined; only those whom the masters chose to present for
examination. For instance, out of 1,251 scholars in the first
class in the Writing Schools, only a carefully selected 308
took the arithmetic tests. These selected pupils — "brag
scholars," as Horace Mann says they are sometimes called —
made a score of 35% in accuracy. That is, the total correct
answers were but 35% of the possible number of correct answers.

The results above may be summarized as follows:

PERCENTAGE OF CORRECT ANSWERS [1]

HISTORY	ASTRONOMY	ARITHMETIC	GEOGRAPHY	ALL SUBJECTS
45%	39%	35%	34%	30%

Therefore, the degree of success attained by the teachers in " the good old days " of 1845 was, to say the least, very poor and keenly disappointing to all.

The survey conclusions drawn from the results are equally interesting:

The careful observer will learn, by looking over our tables, the general system of instruction pursued in our schools; namely, that of verbal or book knowledge. Generally speaking, the questions which would be asked by one who teaches from books, as the names of the principal lakes, rivers, etc., are answered correctly, but take such questions as this: — Do the waters of Lake Erie run into Lake Ontario, or those of Ontario into Erie? — and 287 answer correctly, while 130 answer it incorrectly. Now, if we take into consideration what is unquestionably true, that many of those who did not know, answered by guess, and that they were just as likely to guess right as wrong, much the largest proportion (68%) of our best scholars could not tell which way the waters run, in spite of all the fame of Niagara.

The verbal examination in geography confirmed the opinion which would be drawn from the answers to the printed questions. In a few schools, the children seem to have been taught orally, and upon correct principles; but generally they were lost when taken out of the common routine of questions. They could bound states and countries; name capitals, capes, and mountains; enumerate rivers, lakes, and bays; and answer a series of questions put by the master, of half an hour's duration; but questioned as to the drainage of countries, their capacities for commerce, the causes which direct streams and determine the force of water, — their want of comprehension of these and other similar subjects, showed plainly, in almost every school, that they had learned geography as if it were only a catalogue of names of all the divisions of water, from ponds up to oceans; of land, from towns to empires.

[1] The returns from certain of the tests are not given in detail, but the committee gives the summary figures upon which this score is based.

In history, the scholars have, for the most part, learned to recite the words of the text-book, without having had its spirit illustrated, and without having been accustomed to think about the meaning of what they have learned. The answers to the following questions show most undeniably, that in many schools, nothing but the words of the books are learned, and that those are often learned without understanding their meaning. First came the question, — When was the embargo laid by President Jefferson, and when was the non-intercourse act substituted for it? To this many scholars could answer correctly, while they could not answer correctly the question which came soon after, viz.: "What is an embargo?" In one school, the Adams, 15 out of 20 answered correctly as to the date of the embargo, while only one of them could tell what an embargo meant. In another, the Hawes, 13 out of 17 knew about the date of the fact, but only 4 could tell what the fact was, — what the word embargo means — and 6 gave an incorrect definition of it. On the other hand, in the Bowdoin School, only 15 out of 42 knew when the embargo was laid; but 29 out of the 42 defined it correctly. In the Brimmer School, where 6 knew the date of the embargo, 13 could define it correctly.

Now this is a case illustrative of that to which we shall often allude : — the practice of teaching the name of the thing rather than the nature of the thing. It is worth positively nothing to know the date of an embargo, if one does not know what an embargo is. Nay, it may be worse than nothing, because some erroneous idea will be attached to it, as must be the case in the minds of those scholars who defined embargo to be "a duty."

In definitions, some of the answers were so supremely absurd and ridiculous, that one might suspect the boys of attempting to jest with the Committee, were it not that there are marks of honest attempts to trace analogies between words which they did know and words which they did not know. Many of the children were probably set upon the chase after their meanings for the first time, and it was not strange if they should make great mistakes.

In astronomy, the same peculiarities were observed here as in the other studies, — a more familiar acquaintance with the text-books than with the principles involved, — although a remarkable deficiency of knowledge, even upon subjects defined in the books and of essential importance, was observable.

One general inference to be drawn from an examination of these answers is that it is difficult for our scholars to learn to spell correctly, without being more in the habit of writing than they now are. Scores and hundreds of errors, of the most palpable kind, have been committed in their written answers, by children who could spell the very same words correctly, if they were called upon in the usual way, and had the words pronounced aloud to them. The principle is the same as that by which they were trained to read words correctly, which they do not understand. The visible form of the word suggests the idea of the audible sound by which it is to be expressed; in spelling aloud, the audible sound recalls the visible form, or the arrangement of the letters; but if called upon to arrange the letters, or to spell without the aid of the sound, or of the spoken word, that is, if called upon to write, they were very apt to go wrong.

The Boston Schools, we think, would be rated very high in comparison with the best schools in the world, on the subject of technical parsing. It would seem impossible for a scholar to take up a stanza of Childe Harold and parse the words correctly, to perceive, that is, the connection and relations of the words, and yet fail to feel the force of the metaphors, or to understand the sense of the whole stanza. Nevertheless, this is done sometimes. Such is the power of drilling. Such is the effect of close attention to the mere osteology of language; to the tones and articulations, in forgetfulness of the substance that covers, and the spirit that animates them.

Upon the teachers must, in a great degree, depend whether the pupils shall confine their acquisitions to the letter and rules of the text-book, or whether they shall understand the principles of the studies which they pursue.

In this respect there is a most striking difference in our schools. In some the pupils seem to understand what they have studied, and to know how to apply it to the cases which may arise; in others they can repeat rules with great fluency and accuracy, answer printed questions in arithmetic, while the book is before them, and, in fact, recite all their lessons in the book in a manner which would seem to do them great credit. When, however, these landmarks are thrown aside, and they are called to the blackboard and requested to answer questions not found in the book, and for which they have no prescribed rules, they come to a dead stand, and lose the whole skill which before they apparently exhibited.

It seems to the Committee that this latter mode of instruction is quite prevalent in some of the schools; that the pupils learn rules rather than principles, and that the text-books are made quite too much their guide. It is believed that no school can be very successful while this plan is adhered to, that a good and sufficient education will not be acquired by keeping within the pages of text-books, and that no person can be a successful teacher without constant instruction in the principles and applications of the studies pursued.

Horace Mann reaches the same conclusion as the Committee. He says:

Take, for instance, the question in geography, "On what range of mountains is the line of perpetual snow most elevated above the ocean, — on the Rocky Mountains of North America, or on the Cordilleras of Mexico?" — and it appears that only 91 pupils answered the question correctly; while 154 answered it wrong, and 242 did not answer it at all, being either ignorant of the meaning of the terms used, or unable to form any conclusions respecting the fact. Now this precise question may never have been put to the classes before, and we should not feel disposed to blame a teacher, even if it could be proved that he had propounded this particular question to his scholars. But, that children who have professedly studied geography for years, and who have recited in anything but the most parrot-like manner, should not have discovered the principles which would lead them inevitably to the correct decision of such a question, is wholly inconceivable. That less than one in five, — less than 20%, — of the flower of the Boston Grammar Schools, should have been ignorant of the true answer to such a question, and ignorant also of the principles which would conduct them to it, almost transcends credibility. It proves conclusively that the great majority of the children must have committed to memory the names of the zones, without any adequate conception of the different temperatures belonging to each; that all their recitations about the sun's altitude and declination, must have been unconnected with any idea of the calorific effects of his more or less vertical rays, and that the varieties of climate and of vegetation, of cold and of heat, had never been considered in connection with their natural causes.

Take another fact stated in the Committee's Report, which, if it were not authenticated by the testimony of men whose honesty and intelligence are above suspicion, and if an inspection of the answers on file did not corroborate every word of the statement, we should be inclined to pronounce a libellous misrepresentation of the Boston Schools.   The committees after asking the two questions, "What is the general course of the rivers in North and South Carolina?" and "What is the general course of the rivers in Kentucky and Tennessee?" inquire, in the next question, "What is the cause of the rivers of these four contiguous States running in opposite directions?"   And what is the result of the answers given by the first division of the first class of the Boston Grammar Schools, to a question which seems almost too simple to be put to any child over ten years of age?   It is this: 130 answered correctly; 61 answered incorrectly, and 308, — more than three-fifths of the whole number, — could not answer the question at all.   One child said the rivers ran in those opposite directions, "because it was the will of God," — a remarkably easy method of answering questions in physical geography, natural philosophy, astronomy, chemistry, or anything else; and one which would save philosophers an immense amount of labor.

We will give but one more illustration on the subject in geography.   The pupils were directed to "draw an outline map of Italy." It is obvious that no other country in the world could have been selected, so easily depicted, as Italy, upon slate, paper, or blackboard.   We should have said beforehand, that every child in all our schools above the Primary, must have heard that Italy is shaped like a boot and spur; and also that the mind of every child must have been so agreeably and vividly impressed with the similitude that no amount of lifeless teaching would ever efface the image. Is not map-drawing taught in the Boston Grammar Schools? Does any professional teacher, at the present day, pretend to teach geography without drawing maps himself, and insisting that all his pupils shall do so?   Does not every competent teacher know that there can be no adequate security that a child understands physical and political geography, unless he can produce, from his own mind, and through his own fingers, the outlines of countries and boundaries of nations?   When we see a pupil draw the map of a country, sketch its mountains, trace its rivers, dot down its cities, etc., from memory, we know that he has an image of them in his mind; but this knowledge we can never fully possess until we find

Children work better when free to adjust themselves to their physical surroundings.

that he is able to do so.   Hence the Committee required one outline map to be drawn, and selected the easiest case possible from
among all the countries in the world.   The results we give in the
Committee's own words:

"Each scholar was required to sketch on his paper an outline of
Italy, and many attempted it, but of the whole number (500) only
seventeen made a drawing which could have been recognized as a
representation of Italy by one who did not know what the scholar
was trying to do.   In the Dudley School (Roxbury) more than 50
percent of the scholars drew such an outline as could be recognized."

More than 50 percent in a Roxbury School, against less than 4 percent in the Boston Schools!   We have seen the original drawings
themselves made by the Boston children; and surely nothing even
of a barbarian rudeness can surpass them.   Any boot made after
the similitude of any of these outlines of Italy, must be designed
for a club or a cloven foot, and the spur would be as appropriate
on one side as on the other.   In one instance, the toe of the boot
points towards the east, as though it menaced an assault upon
Greece or Asia Minor.   In another case, the scholar has made a
pair of shanks and feet, with the toes pointing inward, like the limbs
of those unfortunate cripples, who, when they walk, lift one foot
over the other!

We feel bound to say, that to suffer children to read without
understanding what they read, is one of the most flagrant cases
of incompetent teaching.   The proper pronunciation of words,
according to the standard of the best speakers, is a desirable accomplishment.   Distinct enunciation, the length of sounds, the
pitch and power of the voice, should be attended to by all teachers;
but the signification of the words, — the meaning of the author, —
is primary, is principal, is indispensable.   Whatever else is omitted,
this must be attended to.   There can be no compromise here.
However outlandish or brogue-like the voice; however slovenly
or slipshod the enunciation; the sense of the author must be sought
out and brought out, and made the sure possession of each pupil.
The elocutionary part of reading is but its body, the intellectual
part is the soul, and the former without the latter is only a dead
mass of matter.   It would be painful to find that a teacher had
abandoned his children and had spent his time in fitting up a hundred of Maelzel's automata, which could be made to utter words
by the turning of a crank; but it would not be half so deplorable

as to find living minds, with faculties all hungering and thirsting
for information, with powers capacious of old thoughts, and capable of originating new ones — to find such minds turned into
automata, and made to utter pages of words, month after month,
and year after year, with no proper conception of their beauty,
their wisdom, or their truth. It is not enough, that children
should understand four words out of five, or nine words out of ten,
or ninety-nine words out of a hundred; for, if they do not understand the fifth, the tenth, the hundredth word, they may lose all
the soul of whatever they read. No one thing at the present day,
draws so broad a line of demarcation between the competent and
the incompetent teacher, as the intelligence or the ignorance of
their pupils in regard to what they read.

But we need not enlarge here. Whoever has read the pages of
this Journal, from its commencement, knows with what earnestness,
with what unwearable importunity, we have dwelt upon this point.
Committees and teachers, through the country, have seconded our
endeavors, until such a change has been effected that we believe
there is hardly a school in any of the country towns of the State,
where, if the same proportion of the advanced classes should be
taken, they would not appear better, if subjected to a similar examination, than the Boston Schools have done. Soon after the
report of the committee was made, a few of the definitions given
by the children were published in some of the city papers; and,
of course, they were read, more or less, in different parts of the
State. So extraordinary were they, so improbably ridiculous and
absurd, that we know they were regarded by many persons as a
fiction, a *jeu d'esprit*, got up by some wag to caricature the Boston
Schools. The only proof of their genuineness consisted in the fact,
that they were worse than any mortal could have invented. Sheridan, in the character of Mrs. Malaprop, fell infinitely short of them.
Here follow a few of these wonderful definitions :

Monotony, — Change of names, Thick-headed, — A plant, — Is a word
which means a variety, Music, — Time, — A Study, — Scene, — Silent, —
Musing, — Discord, — A song sung by one person, — Alone, from the Latin
word, Monoo, alone, — the bones of human animals, — Sameless, — Motion, — Monitory, — Cold, Ceremonious, — Indifference, — Motion, —
Smoothness, Sootments, — A moaning noise, — Dolorousness, — Moaning
noise, — Pleasant, — Silence, — Many, — etc., etc.

Connoisseur, — Lover, — People who write funeral services, — A Juryman, — a rich merchant, — a person who composes requiems, — A stranger

from places unknown, — A Poet, — A requiem for the dead, — A picture, — Soldiers, — A Wealthy gentlemen, — One who has everything that he wants that money can produce, — It is the name of some foreign person, — Some great personage, — A great personage, — A great person, — A person of importance, — A look out, — Governor, — One that is dead, — A person who corrects letters, — A name by which Frenchmen are called, — A piece of money, — A journey, — One who spies, — A gentleman, — A kind of brigands, — Is a name applied to some nation, — Friend, — A soldier, — Ambassador, &c. &c.

Infatuated, — Filled with air, — charmed, — Bound up, — Bound up, — Charmed, — Charmed, — Charmed, — Charmed, — Charmed, — Renewed force, — Renewed force, — To have your attention taken up by anything means that you are infatuated with the idea, — Delighted, — Being very much pleased with anything, — Drunk, — Induced, — Filled with, — Pleased, — Delighted with, — Exhausted, — Enraged, — Not fatuated, — Not fatuated, — Taken up with, — Not fatuated, — To deprive, — Taken up with, — Absorption, — Triannical, &c. &c.

Misnomer, — Truth, — A reality, — Wonder, — Wonderful thing, — A hoax, — A name, — A True thing, — A name, — A name, — A name, — A person who makes an arrow, — A person who makes an arrow, — A name, — A name, — A name, — A name, — A name, — A story not authenticated, or a story the truth of which is doubtful, — A story the truth of which is doubtful, — A fabulous thing, — Means a soldier or people, — Was an ancient writer, — The real thing, — Humbug, — Humbug, — A mistake, — Humbug, — Cheat, — Cheat, — Having no name, — A true story, — Something great, — Something that never existed, — A thing that never was, — Bad, — A dream name, — False, — A strange thing, — Wrong story, — A fable, — A lie, — Belonging to several places, or claimed by several places, — A falsehood, — Accident, — Something bad for which we are corrected, — No name, — Fiction, — Fictitious, — A wrong action, — A wise man, — A namesake, — Namesake, — A false indictment, — A namesake, — A false indictment, — Not true, — Namesake, — True thing, — &c. &c.

Face to face with these revelations, what recommendations for improvements did the Committee have to make? There is not space to repeat in full detail all the suggestions and the supporting arguments, but from the point of view of subsequent progress it is interesting to appraise the judgment and foresight of the Committee. Accordingly the attempt has been made to list recommendations made by each Committee and by Horace Mann and, as a symptom of the importance

attached to the recommendations by the Committee themselves, to count the number of pages devoted to the discussions.

RECOMMENDATIONS BY GRAMMAR SCHOOL COMMITTEE

NATURE OF RECOMMENDATION	PAGES DEVOTED TO DISCUSSION	ACHIEVED BY 1920
1. * Change Method of Instruction	9½	Yes
2. Provide more maps, globes, in schools .	1½	Yes
* Establish Superintendent of Schools . .	6	Yes
3. * Simplify School Organization to provide for single principal	10½	Yes
4. * Decrease use of corporal punishment .	9	Yes
5. Improve the quality of teachers and relation between teachers and scholars .	3	Yes

RECOMMENDATIONS BY WRITING SCHOOL COMMITTEE

NATURE OF RECOMMENDATION	PAGES DEVOTED TO DISCUSSION	ACHIEVED BY 1920
1. * Change Method of Instruction	1	Yes
2. Improvement in School Buildings . . .	½	Yes
3. * Simplify School Organization to provide single principal	2½	Yes
4. * Abolish prize and medals	1	Yes
5. Improve attendance	½	Yes

RECOMMENDATIONS BY HORACE MANN

NATURE OF RECOMMENDATION	PAGES DEVOTED TO DISCUSSION	ACHIEVED BY 1920
1. * Simplify School Organization to provide a single principal	6½	Yes
2. * Abolish prizes and medals	½	Yes
3. * Change Method of Instruction	12	Yes
4. * Decrease corporal punishment	4	Yes
5. Selection of teachers on merit basis by public competitive examination . .	3½	Partially

* Common to two or more groups.

The Boston Schools of 1845, therefore, must be judged to have been exceedingly inefficient, although then, as now, the causes were many, not few.   That the Committee was wise in its recommendations is shown by the fact that every reform urged by them has ultimately been achieved.   Succeeding chapters will present the evidence which makes plain the extent of the progress which has taken place.

CHAPTER SIX

ADJUSTING OLD EXAMINATIONS TO MODERN USES

THE determination to repeat the Boston Tests led to an analysis of the 1845 test material from the point of view of its suitability to present-day conditions. This analysis was in itself instructive. Some of the questions were found to be just such questions as any teacher might ask today. Others, while not based directly upon subject matter taught in the classroom, could be answered by any one who had really learned to think correctly. Still others proved totally foreign to the range of knowledge and beyond the intelligence of eighth-grade children.

Accordingly, selection was made of thirty questions, five in each of six subjects, which seemed to have possibilities for twentieth-century children. The reasons for the selection of these questions has so much bearing on the interpretation of the results that each question and the answer accepted as correct will be discussed in some detail.

HISTORY

Question 1. *What is history?*

The 1845 children answered in terms of the textbook definition. Much less attention is now paid to learning definitions by heart than formerly. The questions give an opportunity to see how far the change in emphasis in history teaching has operated to prevent modern children from being able to formulate a definition on demand.

Any statement expressing the idea that history is a narrative of past events was accepted as correct. That is, the story, record, account, or any equivalent expression.

Question 2. *About what year did the first colonists come to New England and what were the supposed motives for leaving the mother country?*

64

There are really two questions here, and both may be classified as vital information. Every American citizen should know approximately the year when colonization in New England began and have some conception of the beginnings of American ideals. Consequently both a date and a reason were required for a score of " correct." If either were missing and the other correct, one-half credit was given.

For the date, answer 1620, 1607, any year from 1600 to 1635, or an expression indicating the early part of the seventeenth century was accepted as correct. Acceptable reasons were, to escape religious persecutions, to enjoy civil and religious liberty, to get liberty, or equivalent statements.

Question 3. *When did the war of the American Revolution commence and who were the allies of the Americans?*

Here again two answers were required, a date and an ally. Both are essential elements of knowledge.

For the year, 1775 or 1776 was accepted as correct. For an ally, the French.

Question 4. *About what year was the embargo laid by President Jefferson and when was non-intercourse substituted for it?*

This question is of relatively little value in itself. However, it is one of several pairs of questions which become significant when taken together. For instance, comparison of the percentage of correct answers with the percentage of correct answers to the fifth question, *What is an embargo?*, shows at once whether children are being taught merely to remember dates or to understand the event for which the date stands.

There are really two questions here also, but both in 1845 and in 1919 most children gave a single response. Therefore, full credit was allowed for either answer or both.

The answers accepted as correct were 1807, 1809, any year from 1804 to 1812.

Any definition of embargo which expressed the idea that

an embargo is a restraint of trade was accepted as correct; that is, a stopping of trade, prohibition to sail, etc.

Very few of the remaining questions of the 1845 test proved suitable for 1919. Many of the questions (Numbers 1, 2, 3, 29, 30) appear to call for the answers given in the textbook used. Questions 5 to 19 dealt with general ancient and medieval history, which today are not ordinarily studied below high school level. The questions used (Numbers 1, 19, 20, 24, 26) were, in the judgment of the authors, those most likely to yield results of value for purposes of comparison.

GEOGRAPHY

In the field of geography, there was a wider range of choice. Thirteen of the questions were definite memory questions beginning " Name the." The one chosen for the 1919 test, *Name the principal rivers in North America*, seemed to offer a chance for a fair comparison of the efficiency of this type of instruction at the two periods.

A study of the published answers to this question and consultation with a number of geography teachers led to the following formulation, which is much more comprehensive than expected by those who gave the 1845 tests:

The list below contains most of the principal rivers that will be named. The names of other rivers will appear, however, and they should be counted, if they are names of American rivers and if, in the opinion of the teacher, they are of importance, either locally or because they have been taught. Such additional rivers should be recorded on this sheet.

1. Arkansas	9. Hudson	17. Ohio	24. St. Lawrence
2. Alleghany	10. Kennebec	18. Penobscot	25. Savannah
3. Alabama	11. Kentucky	19. Potomac	26. San Joaquin
4. Columbia	12. Mackenzie	20. La Platte	27. Saskatchewan
5. Colorado	13. Merrimac	21. Red	28. Sacramento
6. Connecticut	14. Mississippi	22. Red River	29. Susquehanna
7. Cumberland	15. Missouri	of the North	30. Tennessee
8. Delaware	16. Nelson	23. Rio Grande	31. Yellowstone

In the answers on the test papers, count the number of rivers which are found in the list above, and record this number in column A in place of the C and X answers. Write O for no correct response.[1]

Many of the questions formed a series of related inquiries, the first revealing the extent to which the children possessed the essential information, the second or third whether the children were able to apply this knowledge. Such a series is formed by the three questions: What is the general course of the rivers in North and South Carolina? What is the general course of the rivers in Kentucky and Tennessee? What is the cause of the rivers in these four contiguous states running in opposite directions? As a representative of this type, the question, *Do the waters of Lake Erie run into Lake Ontario, or the waters of Ontario into Erie?* was chosen.

Any statement indicating the direction from Erie into Ontario was correct. Many children answered that the waters of Lake Erie run into the Welland Canal, and while this probably represents what they had been taught, it was nevertheless counted wrong as not answering the question.

Three other questions involving general comprehension of relationship rather than specific information were taken. The first deals with the relative accessibility in the interior parts to ships and commerce of Europe and Africa, the second with the relative length of the route from England to India by the Cape of Good Hope or by the Red Sea, and the third with the question of time. The question, *If a merchant in Moscow dines at 3 o'clock P.M. and a merchant in Boston at 2 o'clock P.M., which dines first?* is an ambiguous question. The stickler for precision will point out that the question may be answered correctly " Boston " by those who take " Which dines first " to mean each in his own day, and by those who consider the Boston merchant to dine the day preceding the Moscow merchant, since no day is stated.

[1] From the 1919 test blanks.

However, the intent of the question is plain and Moscow was the only answer accepted as correct. This was as fair in 1919 as in 1845.

It should be noted further that this question and the question about Lakes Erie and Ontario are of a type in which allowance must be made for guessing. There are only two possible answers. Consequently, in judging of the results a score of 50% right and 50% wrong may indicate pure guesswork. This fact, pointed out by the 1845 committee, needs to be kept in mind in judging the results.

ARITHMETIC

The questions in arithmetic proved entirely unsuited to 1919 children, and selection was difficult to make. The abstract examples were of a type almost eliminated from modern texts, while, as has already been stated, the problems were so difficult that practically none of the Boston children of 1845 could solve them correctly. Yet too many people are greatly interested in arithmetic as one of the traditional subjects for it to be omitted. It was finally decided to repeat the five out of the ten questions which the 1845 children were in any way able to answer, more as a means of directing public attention to the important fact that the subject matter of arithmetic is today being continuously modified to eliminate all elements of little direct use in the life of the child, than as fair tests for modern school children.

As has already been mentioned, the average child in the Boston Schools gave two or two and one-half hours a day to arithmetic, for from seven to nine years. This time was evidently spent mainly upon "computational stunts." For instance, the first question, *How much is $\frac{1}{2}$ of $\frac{1}{3}$ of 9 hours and 18 minutes?*, has no life value. (Answers accepted as correct: 1 hour and 33 minutes; 93 minutes; 1.55 hours; $1\frac{11}{20}$ hours.) Such questions do not arise in practical situations. In similar fashion, *What is the quotient of one ten-thousandth divided by ten thousand?* Express answer in decimal and common fractions (Answers accepted as correct: .000,000,01; $\frac{1}{100,000,000}$; one hundred-millionth. Two out of the three answers were required for full credit. Half credit for one.), and *What is the square root of $\frac{5}{9}$ of $\frac{4}{5}$ of $\frac{4}{7}$ of $\frac{7}{9}$?* (Answer, $\frac{4}{9}$ or .44.) are given solely for the purpose of testing the children's power to juggle figures. Modern educational theory holds that work of this type has less educative value than the meaningful, purposeful use of computational processes as means to ends. The test questions are, therefore, of value in arithmetic only as an index of how generally this type of ability has been eliminated from present-day educational objectives. Failure to answer these questions is not an indication of inefficiency in arithmetic.

One of the questions dealt with roods, a measure of land surface no longer even mentioned in our arithmetics. Accordingly it has no value for comparative purposes. On the other hand, the question was repeated in 1919 because (1) there were no other questions which could be used and (2) it offered a chance to test an important type of educational product. In 1845 the children were expected to know their table of land measures, but in the 1919 test the following information was printed on the paper: "A rood is a measure of land no longer in use. There are 40 sq. rods in a rood and 4 roods in an acre." The question thus becomes a test of the ability of the modern children to attack a new situation intelligently when the essential information is supplied. It is not a very good test, it is true; for the form of the question, *What part of 100 acres is 63 acres, 2 roods and 7 sq. rods?* is again a question quite unlikely to arise in the experience of eighth-grade children. The results must therefore be judged from this point of view.

The remaining question, *A sold goods for $1500.00, to be paid for one-half in 6 months and one-half in 9 months. What*

is the present worth of the goods, interest being at 7 per cent?,
deals with a topic very lightly touched upon, if at all, in
present-day schools. This problem is, therefore, also of
little value for purposes of comparison, except to prove the
nature of the change which has been made in the subject
matter of arithmetic.

The answer accepted as correct was $1,457.32. Notice
the following statement, however:

The answers on the papers may differ from this and still be right.
Variations of one or two cents should not be counted wrong. If
the example is worked correctly in principle, and no mistakes in
computation have been made, it should be accepted. Possible
correct answers are:

$1442.44	$1440.75	$1438.92	$1436.89	$1434.08	$1433.40
$1441.09	$1440.41	$1437.57	$1435.43	$1433.74	

An answer is not to be counted wrong, if the dollar sign is omitted.

GRAMMAR

Comparisons in the field of grammar are also questionable,
so radical and complete have been the changes in our view of
the value of grammar. The 1845 committee says, "The
Boston Schools, we think, would be rated very high in comparison with the best schools in the world, on the subject of
technical parsing." Yet today the tendency is steadily to
reduce the emphasis upon grammar, and "technical parsing"
has in many schools completely disappeared. The reason for
this change has been the discovery of a fact clearly voiced
by the 1845 committee:

It would seem impossible for a scholar to take up a stanza of
Childe Harold and parse the words correctly, to perceive, that is,
the connections and relations of the words, and yet fail to feel the
force of the metaphors, or to understand the sense of the whole
stanza; nevertheless, this is sometimes done. Such is the power of
drilling! Such is the effect of close attention to the mere osteology
of language; to bones and articulations, in forgetfulness of the substance that covers, and the spirit that animates them.

In the 1845 tests there were two parsing questions. The simpler was chosen for the 1919 tests. Under the circumstances, the results from this question, *Parse the following sentence, and write a full account of each word: " The wages of sin is death,"* require careful interpretation. The following directions for scoring the questions were given:

Check each point correctly given in the answers and count the number of checks.

OUTLINE FOR SCORING

(1)   (2)   (1)   (2)   (3)
The: Definite article (or limiting adjective) modifies wages.

    (4)   (5)   (6)   (7)   (8)
Wages: Common noun, third person, singular number, neuter gender, nom-
     (9)   (10)
   inative case, subject of verb is.

    (11)   (12)
Of: Preposition, shows relation between sin and wages, forms with sin an
    (13)   (14)   (15)
   adjective phrase, modifying wages.

    (16) (17) (18)   (19)   (20)   (21)
Sin: Common noun, third person, singular number, neuter gender, objective
                 (22)
   (or genitive) case, object of preposition of.

    (23)   (24)   (25)   (26)   (27)   (28)
Is: Copulative verb, third person, singular number, present tense, indicative
       (29)   (30)
   mood, agrees with wages, shows the relation of the predicate noun death
   to the subject wages.

    (31) (32) (33)   (34)   (35) (36)
Death: Common noun, third person, singular number, neuter gender, predi-
      (37)   (38)
   cate nominative after is.

Allow 1 point additional for conjugation of verb, 1 point for each rule quoted, and 1 point for statement that the sentence is of the simple declarative type.

ILLUSTRATION OF SCORING

The following answer is taken from the 1845 report. It should be given a credit of 18 points. The points allowed are listed below.

Wages is a noun 3rd Person Sin Nom to is of Preposition shows the relation between Sin and Wages Sin is a noun 3rd Person Objective case govern by in is is a verb Indc mood Pres tense 3rd person Sin no Nom C after is

POINTS

1. Noun.	10. Objective case.
2. Third person.	11. Govern(ed) by in (of).
3. Sin (singular).	12. Verb.
4. Nom (nominative).	13. Indc (indicative).
5. To is (subject of is).	14. Pres (present).
6. Preposition.	15. Third person.
7. Shows relation.	16. Sin no (singular number).
8. Noun.	17. Nom C (nominative case).
9. Third person.	18. After is.

The grammar test of 1845 was made up also of three questions involving the writing of a type sentence, three requiring the explanation of differences in usages, and five in punctuation. The questions selected from these were as follows:

Write a short sentence containing an active transitive verb and an objective case.

Illustrative answer: I wrote a letter.

Write a sentence containing a neuter verb, a relative pronoun and an adjective in the comparative degree.

Illustrative answer: He, who is wise, grows constantly wiser. (Note in the 1919 tests, neuter was changed to intransitive, as the 1845 term has nearly gone out of use.)

Punctuate the following sentence; correct all the errors you may find in it; and write it out grammatically if you think it to be ungrammatical:

Your brother was there and he said to my sister and i i am tired and must go and lay down to rest me and when he was laying down we tried to lie a vail over his face.

The directions for scoring the above question were as follows:

Your brother was there (1) and he said to my sister and i (2) (3) (4) i (5) am tired (6) and must go and lay (7) down and rest me (8) (9) (10) and when he was laying (11) down (12) we tried to lie (13) a vail (14) over his face.

POSSIBLE CORRECTIONS

1. Insert comma.
2. Change i to me.
3. Insert comma.
4. Insert quotation mark.
5. Change i to cap.
6. Insert comma.
7. Change lay to lie.
8. Omit me.
9. Insert period.
10. Omit and and begin when with cap.
11. Change laying to lying.
12. Insert comma.
13. Change lie to lay.
14. Change vail to veil.

ILLUSTRATION OF SCORING

The following answer is taken from the 1845 report. It should be given a score of 6 points.

Your Brother was there and he said to my Sister and me I am tired and must go and lay down to rest myself and when he was lying down we tried to lay a veil over his face

POINTS

1. Changed i to me.
2. Capitalized I.
3. Changed me to myself.
4. Changed laying to lying.
5. Changed lie to lay.
6. Changed vail to veil.

In the columns of errors, this answer would be charged with six errors in punctuation, as follows:

1-2. Capitalization of brother and sister.
3. Omission of comma after me.
4. Omission of quotation marks.
5. Omission of comma after down.
6. Omission of period at end of sentence.

The final question was:

What is an allegory? and the answer accepted as correct, a statement equivalent to

"An imaginative story told to illustrate a truth."

In this question, as in previous questions, the comparison between 1845 and 1919 is not very valuable. Present-day emphasis on rhetorical analysis is much less than in 1845. The question was used merely to emphasize the change.

There was no test of reading ability in 1845. The nearest
approach to it was a test of ability to define words taken
from the reading material of that day. Here again the results need careful interpretation. The change in educational
theory from 1845 to the present makes simple comparison of
the results almost meaningless, and again the test is most
useful in showing the great change in content and method of
school work. In 1845 the test was a measure of how far the
children understood what they read in the schools; in 1919,
the test measures how far such words occur in the experiences
of eighth-grade children. For they are not taught in the
schools. The comparison of 1845 and 1919 results reveals
the tendency of the changes in educational thinking. A
careful study of the twenty-eight words of the 1845 test lead
to the selection of the following five as suitable for the 1919
comparison. With each word is given also the definition accepted as correct and a number of children's answers that
were regarded as equivalent to the correct answers:

Monotony. Tiresome uniformity.
    (Sameness, no variety, all in one tone.)
Dormant. Being in a state resembling sleep, torpid.
    (Sleeping, sleepy, stupid, inactive, sluggish.)
Infatuated. To be inspired with such ardent passion as to be deprived of
    ordinary judgment.
    (Blinded, without reason, crazy, impressed with some bad notion.)
Misnomer. A name wrongly applied.
    (A wrong name, misnamed, error, mistake.)
Connoisseur. A competent and critical judge.
    (A critic, a judge, a person who understands some particular business
    but does not practice it.)

NATURAL PHILOSOPHY

Two other tests of the 1845 series proved unsuited to the
1919 children, those in astronomy and in natural philosophy.
Neither of the subjects as formerly used is included in the

modern eighth-grade curriculum. A small part of the astronomical knowledge is covered in geography, but under the circumstances comparisons would have little validity. On the other hand, a repetition of the tests would have a certain value in determining whether present-day children without study would know more or less than the 1845 children with study.

From this point of view, the test in natural philosophy was chosen as the more suitable to the purpose. Five questions were selected, all of which in the original test involved the application of a principle as well as some notion of the principles themselves. Answers were accepted as correct on a " common sense " basis. That is, no use of technical terms was required.

The questions and key answers for scoring were as follows :

What is the reason that when a car in motion is suddenly stopped, the passengers are thrown forward?

When the car is stopped, the passengers keep on moving until they, too, are stopped. (Inertia, momentum.)

What is the reason that you can cut a piece of pasteboard or hard substance more easily by holding it close up to the rivet of a pair of scissors, than by holding it near the end of the blades?

The blades have a greater purchase near the rivet. (Because they move through a smaller distance; exert greater power, have greater leverage, etc.)

Which could you stop more easily, a railroad car weighing a ton, going at the rate of ten miles an hour, or a car weighing 100 tons, creeping along at the rate of one-fourth of a mile an hour?

A car weighing a ton.

In building a cistern, should it be made stronger at the top or at the bottom? Why?

At the bottom, because the pressure is greater there. (Weight, force, tendency to break, etc.)

In a small boat which is in danger of being upset, should the passengers stand up, or lie down in the bottom?   Why?

The passengers should lie down in the bottom to make the boat less top-heavy.   (The lower the center of gravity, the less easily the boat is upset.)

The selected test questions, together with essential directions, were printed in the form of an eight-page folder. A folder of directions for scoring and tabulating the results, and proper answers and tabulation sheets, were also prepared.   Copies of all of these are given in the Appendix. It will be noted that the time allowance for the thirty questions of the 1919 tests was 100 minutes, an average of 20 minutes to each subject, and that provision was made for scoring the mistakes in spelling, punctuation, and grammar as in the original tests.

It may be objected that the scoring of papers by teachers in different cities could not be made entirely comparable by such directions and illustrations, and this is probably true. In the original survey such scoring was done by one small group of persons and was therefore probably more reliable than the 1919 scoring.   On the other hand, the precaution was taken in 1919 of having the results from several cities also scored by one group on a strictly comparable basis without radical change in the results.   Therefore, it is probable that the precautions taken were adequate.

It may be further objected that the actual basis of scoring in 1845 is not known.   This also is true.   On the other hand, the statements of the committee are very explicit and further, so many sample papers are published that it was possible to rescore and retabulate these as an aid to establishing a uniform procedure.   When it is remembered that the purpose of the comparison is the discovery of general tendencies, not the reduction of educational efficiency to exact percentages, it will be seen that minor variations are of relatively little significance.

No mention has been made of the writing tests, and no attempt was made to make comparisons. While in the 1845 report mention will be found of the results of the writing test, no record is given of the way the samples were collected and they were scored wholly in subjective terms. Consequently no basis of comparison was established.

Fifty thousand of the 1919 test papers were printed and distributed free. Others were sold at cost. Through the kindness of editors, invitations to take part in the survey were published in many educational magazines. Personal letters were sent to superintendents known to be interested in the scientific study of educational problems.

The response was immediate and widespread. About 40,000 tests were placed throughout the United States, as follows:

ALABAMA

| Centerville | Selma | Mobile | Montgomery |
| | | | Total tests sent to state 580 |

ARIZONA

| Bisbee | Miami | | |
| | | Total tests sent to state 55 | |

ARKANSAS

| Hope | Little Rock | | |
| | | Total tests sent to state 200 | |

CALIFORNIA

Azusa	Benicia	Berkeley	Corcoran
Glendale	Lankershim	Los Angeles	Ontario
Salinas	San Diego	San Francisco	San José
		Total tests sent to state	2,803

COLORADO

| Breckenridge | Fowler | Greeley | Littleton |
| | | Total tests sent to state | 150 |

CONNECTICUT

Ansonia	Danbury	Litchfield	Meriden
Middleton	New Britain	New London	Norwich
Plainsville	Waterbury		

Total tests sent to state   1,496

GEORGIA

Atlanta	Commerce	Covington	Culloden
Macon	Waycross		

Total tests sent to state   347

IDAHO

American Falls	Blackfoot	Genesee	Pocatello
St. Marias			

Total tests sent to state   312

ILLINOIS

Alton	Chicago	Hinckley	Jacksonville
Moline			

Total tests sent to state   1,730

INDIANA

Bluffton	Fort Wayne	Gary	New Albany
Newport	South Bend	Vincennes	

Total tests sent to state   1,385

IOWA

Cedar Rapids	Dubuque	Fairfield	Iowa City
Keokuk	Mason City	Muscatine	

Total tests sent to state   1,375

KANSAS

Altamont	Atchison	Fort Scott	Ingalls
Junction City	Leavenworth	Pittsburg	

Total tests sent to state   735

KENTUCKY

Anchorage	Brooksville	Louisville	Owensboro
Paducah	Richmond		

Total tests sent to state   2,169

LOUISIANA

Shreveport

Total tests sent to state 50

MAINE

| Biddeford | Caribou | Farmington | Foxcroft |
| Monson | Portland | Waterville | |

Total tests sent to state 640

MARYLAND

Baltimore

Total tests sent to state 630

MASSACHUSETTS

Boston	Easthampton	Everett	Fall River
Fitchburg	Granville	Haydenville	Holbrook
Lawrence	Leicester	Malden	Mansfield
New Bedford	Rockport	Wareham	Wellesley
Wenham	Westfield	West Springfield	

Total tests sent to state 6,920

MICHIGAN

Ann Arbor	Birmingham	Detroit	Grand Rapids
Greenville	Holly	Ishpeming	Marine City
Muskegon	Port Huron	S. Ste. Marie	

Total tests sent to state 2,055

MINNESOTA

Duluth Willmar

Total tests sent to state 1,260

MISSISSIPPI

Canton Hattiesburg Louisville Meridian

Total tests sent to state 213

MISSOURI

| Bolivar | Bonne Terre | Boonville | Kirksville |
| Springfield | | | |

Total tests sent to state 535

MONTANA

Great Falls   Polson

           Total tests sent to state   325

NEBRASKA

Beatrice   Fremont   Lincoln   Norfolk
           Total tests sent to state   655

NEVADA

Elko

           Total tests sent to state   30

NEW HAMPSHIRE

Berlin	Claremont	Dover	Goffstown
Gorham	Laconia	Lisbon	Peterboro
Portsmouth	Wolfboro		

           Total tests sent to state   760

NEW JERSEY

Bernardsville	Beverly	Bordentown	Hackensack
Jersey City	Montclair	Passaic	Pennington
Perth Amboy	Plainfield	Ventnor City	Washington

           Total tests sent to state   1,279

NEW MEXICO

Aztec   Albuquerque

           Total tests sent to state   170

NEW YORK

Cortland	Goshen	Lisbon	Mineola
New York	Woodmere		

           Total tests sent to state   1,225

NORTH CAROLINA

Durham   Winston-Salem

           Total tests sent to state   320

NORTH DAKOTA

Dickinson	Ellendale	Fargo	Hankinson
Mandan	Rugby		

           Total tests sent to state   440

Ohio

Freeport	Junction City	Marysville	Norwood
Ohio City	Sandusky	Steubensville	Toledo
Youngstown	Zanesville		

Total tests sent to state   1,155

Oklahoma

Enid	McAlester	Norman	Oklahoma City
Warner	Weatherford		

Total tests sent to state   1,551

Oregon

Ashland	Eugene	North Bend	The Dalles

Total tests sent to state   221

Pennsylvania

Blossburg	Braddock	Easton	Erie
Montgomery	Munhall	Palmerton	Philadelphia
Wyomissing			

Total tests sent to state   1,935

Rhode Island

Barrington	Bristol	Central Falls

Total tests sent to state   183

South Carolina

Camden	Charleston	Ridgeland	Spartanburg

Total tests sent to state   363

South Dakota

Aberdeen

Total tests sent to state   135

Tennessee

Cooksville	Morristown

Total tests sent to state   86

Texas

Austin	Celeste	College Station	Houston

Total tests sent to state   900

UTAH

Provo   Salt Lake City
                              Total tests sent to state   610

VERMONT

Brattleboro   Carleton   Chester   Montpelier
Woodstock
                              Total tests sent to state   405

VIRGINIA

Harrisonburg   Herndon   Lynchburg   Portsmouth
                              Total tests sent to state   752

WASHINGTON

Aberdeen   Bellingham   Centralia   Chehalis
Kalama   Pullman   Seattle   Vancouver
Walla Walla
                              Total tests sent to state   697

WEST VIRGINIA

                Wileyville
                              Total tests sent to state   20

WISCONSIN

Edgerton   Evansville   Horicon   Janesville
Neenah   Oshkosh   Portage   Ripon
Superior   Wausau
                              Total tests sent to state   1,069

WYOMING

Buffalo   Cheyenne   Douglas   Pine Bluffs
Sheridan
                              Total tests sent to state   330
                              Total tests in United States   40,901

The tests were given in May and June, 1919, just before
the close of the school year. However, not all those who gave
the tests sent in returns, and not all the returns sent in were
usable, because of incompleteness of reports or irregularity

in using the tests.   The final tabulations are based upon the unselected returns from about 12,000 children from all parts of the United States and are extensive enough to represent fairly well the conditions as they existed throughout the country at the close of the school year in 1919.

CHAPTER SEVEN

COMPARATIVE ACHIEVEMENTS THEN AND NOW

SCORES in tests have little meaning unless one feels that they are reliable; yet the determination of the degree of dependence to be placed on the results is a difficult matter. The authors have taken such precautions as were available, and have checked the results in a variety of ways. The scores from schools in different parts of the country tell a consistent story. This chapter will give that story, together with the data on which the conclusions are based. However, this does not relieve each reader from the responsibility of turning to the Appendix and from a study of the material presented determining for himself the meanings of the figures there given.

The most important single condition to be kept in mind in reading this chapter is that, notwithstanding the fact that both in 1845 and in 1919 the tests were given to the highest classes in the grammar schools, these classes represent very different sampling of pupils. In 1845 the only pupils examined by the committee were those selected by the schoolmasters as being superior. Thus, of "1251 pupils in the first class" the largest number taking any test was 530 pupils, comprising, as the school committee reports, "the flower of the Boston Schools." Most of the tests were taken by much smaller numbers. Furthermore, for almost all of these pupils this test marked the close of their school education. In 1919, however, the tests were given without selection to all members of the eighth grade who were present. These pupils, however, comprise but the lower third of the group which would have been tested if modern conditions were like those of 1845. For instance, in Detroit in 1919 nearly three times as many pupils per hundred had completed and been promoted from eighth-grade work as in the Boston Schools of 1845; but only the lower 40 per cent of these could be tested, because the superior 60 per cent had already been graduated.

Therefore, the comparison of the test results as presented in the following pages is between the selected best of the 1845 pupils and the unselected lower 40 per cent of the 1919 pupils.

The outstanding conclusions from the repetition of the Boston Tests of 1845 are these: (1) Present-day children tend to make lower scores on the pure memory and abstract skill questions and higher scores on the thought or meaningful questions; (2) the changes which have taken place are general throughout the country; and (3) the efficiency of present instruction, even at its best, although higher than in 1845, is still far from satisfactory. In other words, there are still many unsolved problems in education. Each of these conclusions will be discussed in some detail.

The average per cent of correct answers for the United States in 1919 range from 2 to 95%, for Boston in 1845 from 14 to 94%. The median score in 1845 was 37.5; in 1919, 45.5. In number of questions, the two periods break even, each excelling the other in 15 questions. (Table I, Table II, Fig. 1.)

The significant aspects of the results, however, are the types of questions on which modern children excel or fail. The five questions on which they make the poorest showing are in formal computation in arithmetic. Next come definitions and grammar, with memory questions in history and geography next. On the other hand, the 1919 children do exceptionally well in certain questions in grammar, history, natural philosophy, and geography. Under these conditions and from the point of view of modern theory, the low scores where they appear are as much a sign of progress as are the high scores. For the low scores are made for the most

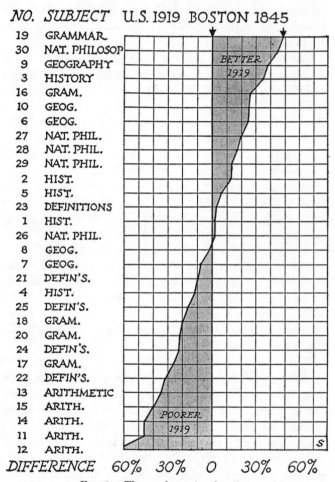

FIG. 1. Then and now in education.

part on material which is of very little value to any one, while
the questions on which the modern children excel are those
which have content and meaning.

A simple illustration will make the situation plain. In
1845, 35% of the children knew the year when the embargo
was laid by President Jefferson, but only 28% knew what an
embargo was. In 1919, only 23% knew the year, but 34%
knew the meaning. In 1845, only 40% of the children knew
whether the nearest route to India is by the way of the Cape
of Good Hope or by the Red Sea, while in 1919, 78% of the
children answered correctly (Fig. 2).

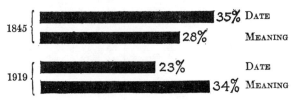

FIG. 2.   Comparison of results of embargo questions.

There are some surprises and disappointments, however.
Only one child in six could solve the arithmetic problem in
" roods," although the full information in regard to the relation of roods to square rods and acres was given on the test
paper.   Only 53% of the 1919 children knew whether Lake
Erie flows into Ontario or vice versa.   On the other hand,
the results on parsing and punctuation were surprisingly
high. In natural philosophy, the 1919 children did much
better without instruction than the 1845 children after study
of a textbook. On the whole, therefore, the 1919 children
must be judged to be more intelligent, more able to think
and to apply knowledge, than the 1845 children, but to have
less control over abstract skills and concepts.

The results from different-sized cities and from different
parts of the country are remarkably consistent.   In no case

TABLE I — PART 1

Boston Tests, 1845–1919, Scores

Comparisons with Cities of Different Sizes

Percentage of Correct Answers by Questions. Results arranged in order of difference between the 1919 scores and those of 1845, the questions on which modern children do more poorly than the 1845 children being put first.

Question No.	Subject	Topic	Boston 1845	Under 5000	5000 to 25,000	25,000 to 100,000	100,000	Total U. S.
12	Arithmetic	Roods	92	13	16	20	14	16
11	Arithmetic	Fractions	94	42	48	49	45	48
14	Arithmetic	Present Worth	48	1	0	3	1	2
15	Arithmetic	Square Root	56	10	10	20	11	15
13	Arithmetic	Decimals	55	17	17	23	15	20
22	Definitions	Dormant	44	13	14	10	17	12
17	Grammar	Trans. Verb	20	52	54	57	53	54
24	Definitions	Misnomer	30	4	55	5	9	6
20	Grammar	Allegory	31	9	7	6	13	9
18	Grammar	Intransitive	45	23	26	28	17	25
25	Definitions	Commission	23	3	6	5	9	6
4	History	Embargo, Yr.	35	16	20	26	26	23
21	Definitions	Monotony	46	33	34	33	45	36
7	Geography	Great Lakes	61	47	51	55	54	53
8	Geography	Europe-Africa	84	85	79	85	81	83
26	Philosophy	Inertia	26	31	28	26	33	28
1	History	Definition	83	86	83	87	82	85
23	Definitions	Infatuated	14	14	16	16	25	17
5	History	Embargo, Def'n	28	30	33	37	37	34
2	History	Colonists	59	37	65	75	76	71
29	Philosophy	Cistern	34	52	50	45	54	47
28	Philosophy	Momentum	27	43	42	46	43	44
27	Philosophy	Levers	29	47	46	47	56	48
6	Geography	Rivers	68	92	94	95	92	93
10	Geography	Time, Moscow	39	62	67	65	57	64
16	Grammar	Parse	32	58	56	59	56	58
3	History	Revolution	36	65	68	70	74	70
9	Geography	Nearest Route	40	82	79	74	75	78
30	Philosophy	Stability	17	70	71	71	67	71
19	Grammar	Punctuate	32	85	70	85	83	80

TABLE I — PART 2

BOSTON TESTS, 1845–1919, SCORES

Comparison by Regional Divisions

Percentage of Correct Answers by Questions. Results arranged in order of difference between the 1919 scores and those of 1845, the questions on which modern children do more poorly than the 1845 children being put first.

QUESTION No.	SUBJECT	TOPIC	BOSTON 1845	STATES					
				East'n	Cent'l	West'n	Coast	South	Total U. S.
12	Arithmetic	Roods	92	18	14	16	15	15	16
11	Arithmetic	Fractions	94	50	49	48	44	45	48
14	Arithmetic	Present Worth	48	0	2	7	1	1	2
15	Arithmetic	Square Root	56	16	14	15	13	13	15
13	Arithmetic	Decimals	55	22	18	21	17	15	20
22	Definitions	Dormant	44	10	11	10	22	11	12
7	Grammar	Trans. Verb	30	59	50	43	49	61	54
24	Definitions	Misnomer	30	5	5	6	7	9	6
20	Grammar	Allegory	31	5	8	24	9	13	9
18	Grammar	Intransitive	45	30	20	21	16	54	25
25	Definitions	Commission	23	5	6	4	8	6	6
4	History	Embargo, Yr.	35	27	19	26	19	21	23
21	Definitions	Monotony	46	32	31	43	45	26	36
7	Geography	Great Lakes	61	54	58	57	41	48	53
8	Geography	Europe-Africa	84	85	77	82	83	85	83
26	Philosophy	Inertia	26	29	30	29	28	24	28
1	History	Definitions	83	89	85	90	77	81	85
23	Definitions	Infatuated	14	16	16	19	24	16	17
5	History	Embargo, Def'n	28	39	33	34	24	32	34
2	History	Colonists	59	74	72	81	64	73	71
29	Philosophy	Cistern	34	49	38	52	50	41	47
28	Philosophy	Momentum	27	45	43	46	45	37	44
27	Philosophy	Levers	29	51	44	47	55	43	48
6	Geography	Rivers	68	95	58	63	91	89	93
10	Geography	Time, Moscow	39	64	61	75	59	62	64
16	Grammar	Parse	32	63	57	46	51	62	58
3	History	Revolution	36	76	65	69	70	65	70
9	Geography	Nearest Route	40	84	78	77	63	72	78
30	Philosophy	Stability	17	71	64	71	75	66	71
19	Grammar	Punctuate	32	86	82	75	67	82	80

TABLE II — PART 1

BOSTON TESTS, 1845–1919, DIFFERENCES

Comparison by Size of Cities

Percentages of Correct Answers by Questions. Results arranged in order of difference between the 1919 scores and those of 1845, the questions on which the modern children do more poorly than the 1845 children being put first.

QUESTION No.	SUBJECT	TOPIC	BOSTON 1845	Under 5000	5000 to 25,000	25,000 to 100,000	100,000	Total U. S.
						CITIES		
12	Arithmetic	Roods	92	−79	−76	−72	−78	−76
11	Arithmetic	Fractions	94	−52	−46	−45	−49	−46
14	Arithmetic	Present Worth	48	−47	−48	−45	−47	−46
15	Arithmetic	Square Root	56	−46	−46	−36	−45	−40
13	Arithmetic	Decimals	55	−38	−38	−32	−30	−35
22	Definitions	Dormant	44	−31	−30	−34	−28	−32
17	Grammar	Trans. Verb	20	−28	−26	−23	−27	−26
24	Definitions	Misnomer	30	−26	−25	−25	−21	−24
20	Grammar	Allegory	31	−22	−24	−24	−19	−22
18	Grammar	Intransitive	45	−22	−19	−17	−28	−20
25	Definitions	Commission	23	−20	−17	−18	−14	−17
4	History	Embargo, Yr.	35	−19	−15	− 9	− 9	−12
21	Definitions	Monotony	46	−13	−12	−13	− 1	−10
7	Geography	Great Lakes	61	−14	−10	− 6	− 7	− 8
8	Geography	Europe-Africa	84	+ 1	− 5	+ 1	− 3	− 1
26	Philosophy	Inertia	26	+ 5	+ 2	0	+ 7	+ 2
1	History	Definition	83	+ 3	0	+ 4	− 1	+ 2
23	Definitions	Infatuated	14	0	+ 2	+ 2	+11	+ 3
5	History	Embargo, Def'n	28	+ 2	− 5	+ 9	+ 9	+ 6
2	History	Colonists	59	+18	+ 6	+18	+17	+12
29	Philosophy	Cistern	34	+18	+16	+11	+20	+13
28	Philosophy	Momentum	27	+16	+15	+19	+16	+17
27	Philosophy	Levers	29	+18	+17	+18	+27	+19
6	Geography	Rivers	68	+24	+26	+27	+24	+25
10	Geography	Time, Moscow	39	+23	+28	+26	+18	+25
16	Grammar	Parse	32	+26	+24	+27	+24	+26
3	History	Revolution	36	+29	+32	+34	+38	+34
9	Geography	Nearest Route	40	+42	+39	+34	+35	+38
19	Grammar	Punctuate	32	+53	+38	+53	+51	+48
30	Philosophy	Stability	17	+53	+54	+54	+50	+54

TABLE II — PART 2

BOSTON TESTS, 1845–1919, DIFFERENCES

Comparison by Regional Divisions

Percentages of Correct Answers by Questions. Results arranged in order of difference between the 1919 scores and those of 1845, the questions on which the modern children do more poorly than the 1845 children being put first.

QUESTION No.	SUBJECT	TOPIC	BOSTON 1845	STATES					
				East'n	Cent'l	West'n	Coast	South	Total U. S.
12	Arithmetic	Roods	92	−74	−78	−76	−77	−77	−76
11	Arithmetic	Fractions	94	−44	−45	−46	−50	−49	−46
14	Arithmetic	Present Worth	48	−48	−46	−41	−47	−47	−46
15	Arithmetic	Square Root	56	−40	−42	−41	−43	−43	−41
13	Arithmetic	Decimals	55	−33	−37	−34	−38	−31	−35
22	Definitions	Dormant	44	−34	−33	−34	−22	−33	−32
17	Grammar	Trans. Verb	20	−21	−30	−37	−31	−19	−26
24	Definitions	Misnomer	30	−25	−25	−24	−23	−21	−24
20	Grammar	Allegory	31	−26	−23	− 7	−22	−18	−22
18	Grammar	Intransitive	45	−15	−25	−24	−29	+ 9	−20
25	Definitions	Commission	23	−18	−17	−19	−15	−17	−17
4	History	Embargo, Yr.	35	− 8	−16	− 9	−10	−14	−12
21	Definitions	Monotony	46	−14	−13	− 3	− 1	−20	−10
7	Geography	Great Lakes	61	− 7	− 3	− 4	−20	−13	− 8
8	Geography	Europe-Africa	84	+ 1	− 7	− 2	− 1	+ 1	− 1
26	Philosophy	Inertia	26	+ 3	+ 4	+ 3	+ 2	− 2	+ 2
1	History	Definition	83	+ 6	+ 2	+ 7	− 6	− 2	+ 2
23	Definitions	Infatuated	14	+ 2	+ 2	+ 5	+10	+ 2	+ 3
5	History	Embargo, Def'n	28	+11	+ 5	+ 6	− 4	+ 4	+ 6
2	History	Colonists	59	+15	+13	+22	+ 5	+14	+12
29	Philosophy	Cistern	34	+15	+ 4	+18	+16	+ 7	+13
28	Philosophy	Momentum	27	+18	+16	+16	− 1	+10	+17
27	Philosophy	Levers	29	+22	+15	+18	+26	+14	+19
6	Geography	Rivers	68	+27	−10	− 5	+23	+21	+25
10	Geography	Time, Moscow	39	+25	+22	+36	+20	+23	+25
16	Grammar	Parse	32	+31	+25	+14	+19	+30	+26
3	History	Revolution	36	+40	+29	+33	+34	+29	+34
9	Geography	Nearest Route	40	+44	+38	+37	+23	+32	+38
19	Grammar	Punctuate	32	+54	+50	+43	+35	+50	+48
30	Philosophy	Stability	17	+54	+47	+54	+58	+49	+54

does the extreme variation amount to more than 10%, and in 70% of the cases the differences are 3% or less. For certain questions the differences between north, south, west, and east seem significant, but at best the differences are small and it is impossible to trace any marked general tendencies. In other words, the tendencies measured by these tests are national, not sectional, tendencies. Educational ideals have changed so completely that even the differences which are known to exist between different parts of the country do not succeed in masking the general nature of the change.

However, in spite of the favorable conclusions drawn above, the tests confirm the results of other educational surveys in proving that much work must be done before the efficiency of teaching may be regarded as satisfactory. For instance, even under our improved conditions only 71% of our eighth-grade children know when and why the American colonists left their mother country; only 70% know when the American Revolution began and who were the allies of the Americans; only 53% could tell whether Lake Erie runs into Lake Ontario or vice versa, in spite of the fact that pure guesswork should yield a score of 50%. The failure on the " rood " example in arithmetic is further proof of the inefficiency of American children in the face of real difficulties which are within the range of their intelligence. American schools have made progress. They are headed away from mere memorization and drill, and are discarding abstract and meaningless subject matter, but they have still a long way to go. Methods of teaching must be modified until the effectiveness of the process is very greatly increased.

The 1845 Survey Committee makes a great point of the many errors made in spelling and punctuation. Very fortunately they reported the results question by question.

Accordingly the attempt was made to secure comparable data in 1919. However, the papers were corrected by many different persons and there are many evidences in the returns that the instructions for scoring were not interpreted by different scorers in the same way. The results are, nevertheless, suggestive and interesting even though their reliability is open to question. For certain cities the papers were scored by paid tabulators under careful supervision and these comparisons are valid, except that the 1919 children wrote many more words in answer to the questions than did the 1845 children, so that the results, to be strictly comparable, ought really to be expressed in terms of errors per 100 words written.   Since this correction cannot be supplied, the obtained results are reported as tabulated below.

COMPARATIVE ERRORS IN SPELLING AND PUNCTUATION

Based on Mistakes in Answers to History and Geography Questions

	BOSTON 1845	U. S. 1919	CITY A 1919	CITY B 1919	CITY C 1919
Spelling					
History . . .	.48	.15	.57	.07	.13
Geography . .	.93	.20	.18	.13	.06
Punctuation					
History . . .	.05	.26	.13	.06	.38
Geography . .	.12	.37	.26	.08	.54

The evidence is reasonably complete and satisfactory that the 1919 children are much better spellers than those of 1845. If the data could be made strictly comparable, it is probable that modern children would make a still better showing. It is possible, therefore, that our present eighth-grade graduates make only $\frac{1}{4}$ to $\frac{1}{3}$ the errors in spelling made by the children of 1845.

In punctuation the evidence is not consistent and the results vary much more widely from school to school, probably on account of the varying standards of the scorers. In the grammar test, there was one question which asked the children to punctuate a sentence, correct all the errors found in it, and write it out grammatically where it was ungrammatical. The scores for the 1845 children were 32% correct, while for the 1919 children the corresponding scores were 80%. On the other hand, in the scoring of the answers to the questions in history and geography, the 1919 children made two or three times as many mistakes in punctuation as in 1845. The explanation is probably to be sought partly in the changing social standard. The tendency today is to make much less of punctuation than formerly. Many of our magazines and periodicals of the highest literary standard, in keeping with the spirit of the times, have deliberately adopted the policy of omitting all punctuation marks not absolutely required by the sense. Teachers reflect public opinion, and extreme care in punctuation is much less emphasized in school now than formerly.

The 1845 committee was greatly distressed by the fact that " there should be so many who try to answer and answer imperfectly ; that there should be so many absurd answers." Accordingly the attempt was made to see whether the present-day children are better or worse in this respect. Account was kept, as in 1845, of the right answers, the wrong answers, and the answers omitted. It does not do, however, to compare simply the numbers of answers wrong, for the chances of wrong answers change with the number of answers right. The method adopted has been to find, for both the 1845 and the 1919 results, what percentage the wrong answers are of the possible wrong answers. For instance, in response to the question, *About what year did the first colonists come to New England ard what were*

the supposed motives for their leaving the mother country?
the 1845 children gave 59 correct answers per hundred, 29
wrong answers, and 12 children per hundred failed to answer.
In 1919, 71 children per hundred gave correct answers, 22
wrong answers, and 7 failed to answer. It is obviously incorrect to compare the 29 wrong answers in 1845 with the
22 wrong answers in 1919 and conclude that the 1919 children are more careful not to reply unless they feel reasonably
sure their answer is correct, because the chances for wrong
answers are not the same at the two periods. In 1845 there
was a possibility of 41 wrong answers $(100-59)$, while in
1919 the possibility was but 29. In 1845 the children gave
71% of the possible wrong answers; in 1919, 76%; and the
ratio is 1.1. That is, the 1919 children gave 1.1 times as
many wrong answers out of the possible wrong answers.

A tabulation of the results for history and geography, according to this method, yields a median ratio for the five
history questions of 1.2, for the five geography questions of
1.4. That is, the 1919 children have a greater tendency to
answer these questions when they do not know the answers
than the children of 1845.

In appraising this result, one must ask one's self whether
it is better for children to know something about a situation
even though that something is not exactly right than it is
to know so little about a situation that they are not able to
make any response. In the history and geography questions
the 1919 children on the whole did better than the 1845
children, and they also on the average gave 1.3 as many
wrong answers out of the possible wrong answers. In the
five definition questions, however, the 1919 children were
asked to define words for the most part entirely outside
their experience, since the words probably do not often,
if ever, occur in their reading. The 1845 children made
a poor showing in correct answers, but, as has already been

noted, the 1919 children made a poorer showing. This was to be expected and does not indicate poorer school work, since the schools no longer even attempt to teach such useless and difficult words to eighth-grade children. The median ratio of wrong answers for the definition questions was .33. In other words, the 1919 children gave only one-third as many wrong answers in a test which was beyond their powers, as did pupils in 1845.

These results taken as a whole, therefore, also indicate plainly the improvement of instruction. More of the 1919 children gave answers to questions (correctly or incorrectly) when they had studied a subject and less when they had not.

Horace Mann quotes with great glee some of the absurd answers to the definition questions. These were taken up by the newspapers of the day and discussed widely. To the authors they seem to have little meaning, except to show that the words were outside the experiences of the children. In the actual definitions given, many interesting and curious analogies and associations can be traced. The following collection of " gems " was taken from a small sampling of 1919 papers and should be compared with those given by Horace Mann. It could be greatly extended.

Monotony. Dismal, gloomy, nothing to do, sad, sound, to much of anything, dull, a pest, continuous, toil, lonesome, weird, about plants, to get a divorce, harmonization, undertone, in fear of something, forever, something we learn, a study which is taken up in college.

Dormant. Willing, lordly, good natured, sad, bold, a large beam, bold, haughty, thrifty, meek, steady, to exult over another person, something with three sides, flat and level, a bedroom, frozen, a crazy idea, one who has been out in a storm, to stand out.

Infatuated. To get angry, to become wet, to soak, not tired or sick, unfit, stupified, to be deep into it, to affect, to be foolish, not tire, soaked with, made foolish, swelling, delighted, worried, grieved, lazy, to be overpowered by some spirit, to coöperate, deceived, interested.

Misnomer. A man who studies about certain things, to like a thing, liking, an error, ill treatment, bad.

Connoisseur. French word for reconnoisance, act of tricking someone, a
business man, a scout used in the army, officer in French army,
one who makes magic, a motor truck, to think, a French scout,
a stern man, a French word meaning "come again," disguise,
to fight for something else, a gentleman.

It is evident from the foregoing that pupils of today are
much like those of 1845.   Their errors and successes are of
the same general nature.   The types of education they receive differ from those of the earlier day, with corresponding
differences in the results.   To appreciate the full significance
of these differences it is necessary to study not only the results but the conditions under which they were achieved.
The succeeding chapter presents such a study.

CHAPTER EIGHT

THE SCHOOLS OF TODAY AND OF TOMORROW

TEACHERS should turn from a consideration of the schools of 1845 to those of the present with feelings of satisfaction and encouragement. Inefficient as our schools have been proved to be, they are nevertheless a great improvement over those of 1845. We have made wonderful progress. We continue to be dissatisfied with achievements solely because our ideals themselves have undergone a similar progressive development. Modern ideals of education involve objectives of so much greater scope and worth than formerly, that our attainments in comparison seem inadequate. Actually, conditions have changed so profoundly for the better that some of the descriptions and comments of the 1845 report seem scarcely credible. No reasonable parent, teacher, or child would think for a minute of wishing to return to such primitive conditions. In the light of these revelations, even the general criticism to which education is at present subjected is seen to be an evidence of progress, and desirable. For it is in itself an indication of the increased estimation in which education is held and a guarantee that still further changes for the better both in ideals and accomplishments will be made in the future.

Few teachers, however, take the time or make the effort to survey present-day educational conditions as completely as the 1845 education has been surveyed in the foregoing pages. Accordingly in this chapter the attempt will be made to give a condensed but comprehensive and comparable report of present conditions, that the changes which have been brought about may be appreciated by all.

We are an individualistic people. In the United States progress is mainly dependent on individual initiative. Each community, even each department within a single school system, in its own way solves what, for it, is the pressing problem of the hour, and in the long run only the fittest solutions survive. Democracies seldom develop centralized organizations with power to collect the gains made by individuals and to transmit them systematically. As a result, education as a whole moves forward slowly. In a country as large as the United States illustrations of every stage of progress may be found, from those which in primitiveness antedate the conditions of the Boston schools in 1845 to those which foreshadow what general educational conditions may be like 50 to 100 years in the future.

In 1845, however, Boston was one of the great cities of the country, and the great cities with their wealth and their resources have always outdistanced the villages and country schools, just as the cities themselves, with their problems of numbers and restrictions of political influences, have lagged behind the private experimental schools whose reason for being is to furnish an objective protest against the sluggishness with which public education sees and responds to changing social needs. It seems wise and just, therefore, to compare the Boston schools of 1845 with a great city school system of the present time. The schools of Detroit have been selected for this purpose for two reasons. The first is opportunistic. Detroit is the city whose schools are best known to the authors and the one for which adequate comparative data can most easily be obtained. The other and basic reason is that Detroit, having recently passed through a period of rapid growth and evolution, probably offers a better and more complete expression of modern ideals and tendencies in public education than any other large American city. It must be remembered, however, that Detroit serves simply as a specific illustration of present-day tendencies; that there is little or nothing in Detroit, which is not either suggested or actually existent wholly or in part in other cities, and that many of the features to be described were put into effect in other cities before they were adopted in Detroit. In similar fashion, in forecasting future development, recourse must be had to private experimental schools, of which the Lincoln School of Teachers College, Columbia University, is the one best known to the authors.

In Boston in 1845, the political influences operating in and through the large school committee were stated by the survey committee to be one of the factors responsible for the lack of progress. In Detroit in 1920, a small school board elected at large on a non-partisan ballot is looked upon by the citizens of the city as the dominant force aggressively bringing about progress. The comparison is the more striking in that for many years school affairs in Detroit were managed by a twenty-one-man political board, elected by wards and adequately illustrating all the evils mentioned by the Survey Committee of 1845. During this period progress was slow, and was effected in spite of the board, not because of it, as has been generally true where similar conditions have prevailed. However, political influence, mismanagement, and resistance to progress at length became so flagrant and notorious that an indignant citizenry forced through the state legislature in 1912 a measure giving the larger cities of the state the privilege of reducing their boards to seven members elected at large for a period of six years, providing a majority of the voters favored the same at a general election. The question was put to vote and approved by the citizens of Detroit, May 7, 1912. In due time the new board was elected. It took office July 17, 1917. An era of unparalleled reorganization, progress, and public interest in education has followed. Similar action, resulting in localization of responsibility for school management in a smaller and presumably better-selected board, has been taken in other cities and seems likely to be adopted quite generally in the future.[1]

The exact details of the organization of the Boston School Committee of 1845 have not been ascertained, further than that it consisted of 24 members, elected each year by wards. However, the contrast between the old and the new, as far as details are known, is objectively presented in the following diagram:

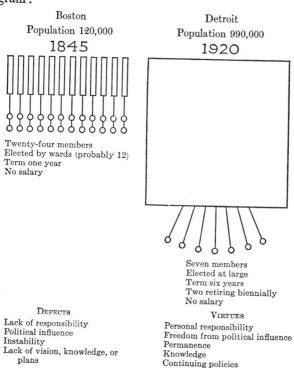

Boston
Population 120,000
1845

Twenty-four members
Elected by wards (probably 12)
Term one year
No salary

Detroit
Population 990,000
1920

Seven members
Elected at large
Term six years
Two retiring biennially
No salary

DEFECTS

Lack of responsibility
Political influence
Instability
Lack of vision, knowledge, or
    plans

VIRTUES

Personal responsibility
Freedom from political influence
Permanence
Knowledge
Continuing policies

FIG. 3.   Comparison of school boards of 1845 and 1920.

[1] The small board was adopted by Cleveland in 1892, San Francisco 1898, Boston 1905, New Orleans 1912, Cincinnati 1913.

In passing it should be noted that the method by which the new board was created is also to be counted as one of the elements of progress. In 1845, Horace Mann, the first state secretary of public instruction in Massachusetts, was battling strenuously against great odds, to bring about an adequate public conception of the importance of education in the life of the state and of the republic. Today, his point of view is universally accepted. State Departments of Education exist in some form in every state in the union. The importance of governmental interest in and control over all education, public and private, is generally recognized and is constantly being strengthened. "The chief business of a republic is education" has become a national slogan, while the subject of free public education is constantly receiving more and more attention in the parliaments of the nations of all the world.

As the desire and the demand for the abolition of war becomes more insistent and universal, it also is more evident that the time will come when the conflicts of nations and peoples will be settled by battles of wit and diplomacy instead of by force of arms; that intelligent control of education will be the factor ultimately deciding national progress and supremacy. In our own country, the struggle of 1845 for the development of adequate state supervision and control has been fought and won; yet today a very similar contest is being refought on a national basis. At the date of publication (1923) the issue is still in doubt. Yet in view of the change in national attitude from 1845 to the present, the creation of a National Bureau of Education, with adequate recognition and authority, would seem to be an inevitable "next step" in our program of national progress.

No proof of the change in public sentiment in regard to the importance of education is quite as striking as the comparison of statistics for then and now. Consider, for instance, the following:

ITEM	BOSTON, 1845	DETROIT, 1921	TIMES LARGER
1. Population, adult	120,000	993,000	8.3
2. Children, school age . . .	25,731[2]	237,592	9.2
3. Membership[1]			
Primary (kg. Gr. 1) . .	8,845	42,259	4.8
Grammar (2–8)	8,193	81,392	9.9
High (9–12)	268	14,083	52.5
College	0	1,422	new
Continuation	0	2,904	new
Adult	0	1,566	new
Private.	2,802	47,707	17.0
Not in school	5,623	46,259	8.2
4. Total budget	$250,000	$31,201,024	125.0 [3]
Teachers' salaries	$127,000	$10,252,354	80.0 [4]
Building and maintenance	$37,400	$20,665,122	241.0 [5]
Interest and other charges	$85,600	$283,548	7.0
5. Assessed valuation	$100,000,000	$1,854,053,580	18.5
6. Per cent of total tax levy .	33%	27%	
7. Cost of living per week, small family — 3	$7.05	$25.50	3.6 [6]
8. Amount raised per capita of population	$2.00	$32.00	16.0
9. Cost per child			
Primary	$4.00	$35.00	8.75
Grammar	$18.00	$85.00	3.61
10. Attendance	85%	91%	

Detroit in 1921 was approximately eight times as large as Boston in 1845, but the school census shows more than nine times as many children of school age. In the interval,

[1] School ages taken as 4 to 16 inclusive in 1845, 5 to 20 in 1921.

[2] Taken from 1847 report, as data were not given in 1845 report.

[3] No allowance made for change in purchasing power of dollar. If such allowance is made (after Burgess), the ratio would be 34.

[4] Caused by increase in number of pupils in school, by decrease in number of pupils per teacher, and increase in amount of professional preparation required.

[5] Probably abnormal, due to resumption of building program following the war.

[6] From *Trend of School Costs*, Burgess, 1845–1920.

" school age " has itself undergone a significant change. In 1845, the age limits were 4 to 16; in 1921, 5 to 20. This probably accounts for the increase in the census figures, and a reliable comparison would probably show a decrease because of the decline in the birth rate. When the comparison is made by departments, however, the differences are striking and the meaning stands out clearly. Of course, reliable comparisons are not possible because exact records were not kept in the old days; but counting " primary " all children found today in the kindergarten and first grade, and as grammar all children in Grades 2-8 (in 1845 children had to be 7 to be admitted to grammar school and the boys had to leave at 14, the girls at 16 [1]), the membership of primary school has increased nearly five times, the grammar school ten times, and the high school more than fifty times since 1845. The small increase in the primary is probably accounted for partly by the decreased birth rate and partly by the fact that in 1845 many older children were probably held in the primary schools because they could not qualify for the grammar school.

The figures tell plainly the story of an increasing percentage of children going to school and of larger numbers remaining in school and for a longer period. The fact that the city of Detroit, in common with many other American cities, now provides for college and continuation courses, for extensive summer and evening schools, and for certain types of training for adults, is a further indication of the general tendency toward more education for all. Such a change in the general educational level of a people is a factor of the greatest social significance.

Even more significant are the comparisons on the basis of money expended. It must be remembered that the purchasing power of the dollar has steadily declined, and that,

[1] See page 14 for requirements for entrance to grammar school.

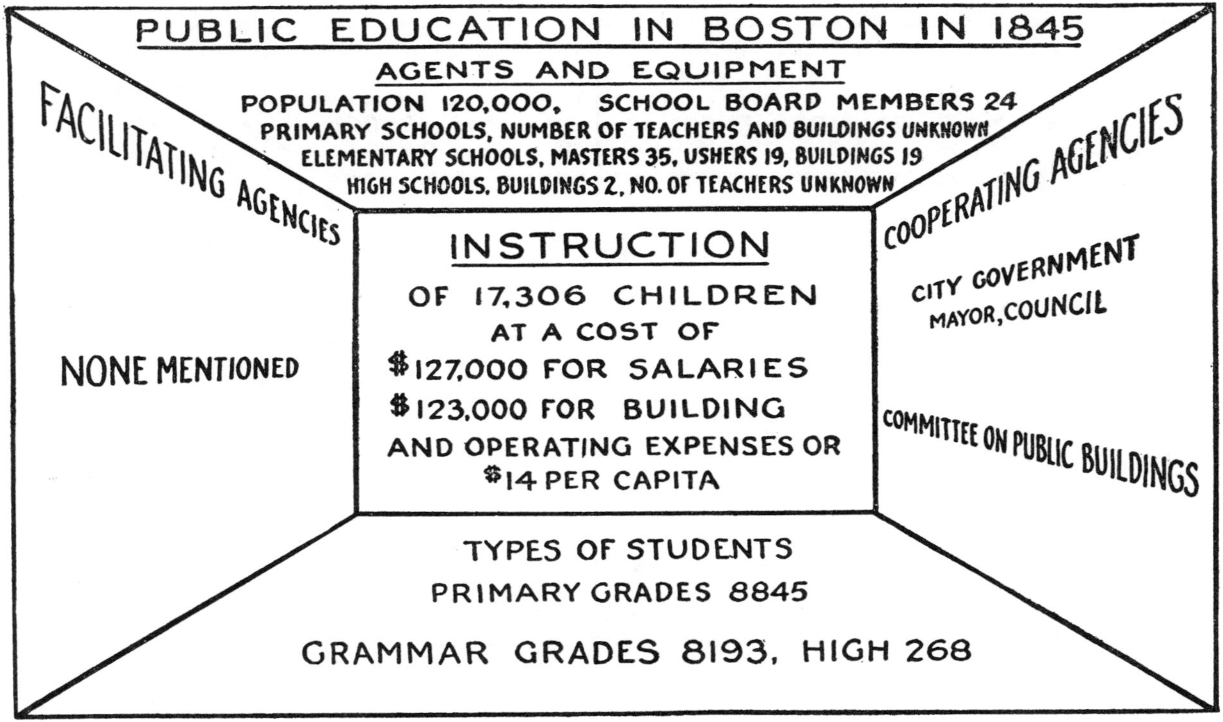

PUBLIC EDUCATION IN BOSTON IN 1845

AGENTS AND EQUIPMENT

POPULATION 120,000, SCHOOL BOARD MEMBERS 24
PRIMARY SCHOOLS, NUMBER OF TEACHERS AND BUILDINGS UNKNOWN
ELEMENTARY SCHOOLS, MASTERS 35, USHERS 19, BUILDINGS 19
HIGH SCHOOLS, BUILDINGS 2, NO. OF TEACHERS UNKNOWN

COOPERATING AGENCIES

CITY GOVERNMENT
MAYOR, COUNCIL

COMMITTEE ON PUBLIC BUILDINGS

INSTRUCTION

OF 17,306 CHILDREN
AT A COST OF
$127,000 FOR SALARIES
$123,000 FOR BUILDING
AND OPERATING EXPENSES OR
$14 PER CAPITA

FACILITATING AGENCIES

NONE MENTIONED

TYPES OF STUDENTS
PRIMARY GRADES 8845

GRAMMAR GRADES 8193, HIGH 268

Fig. 4.

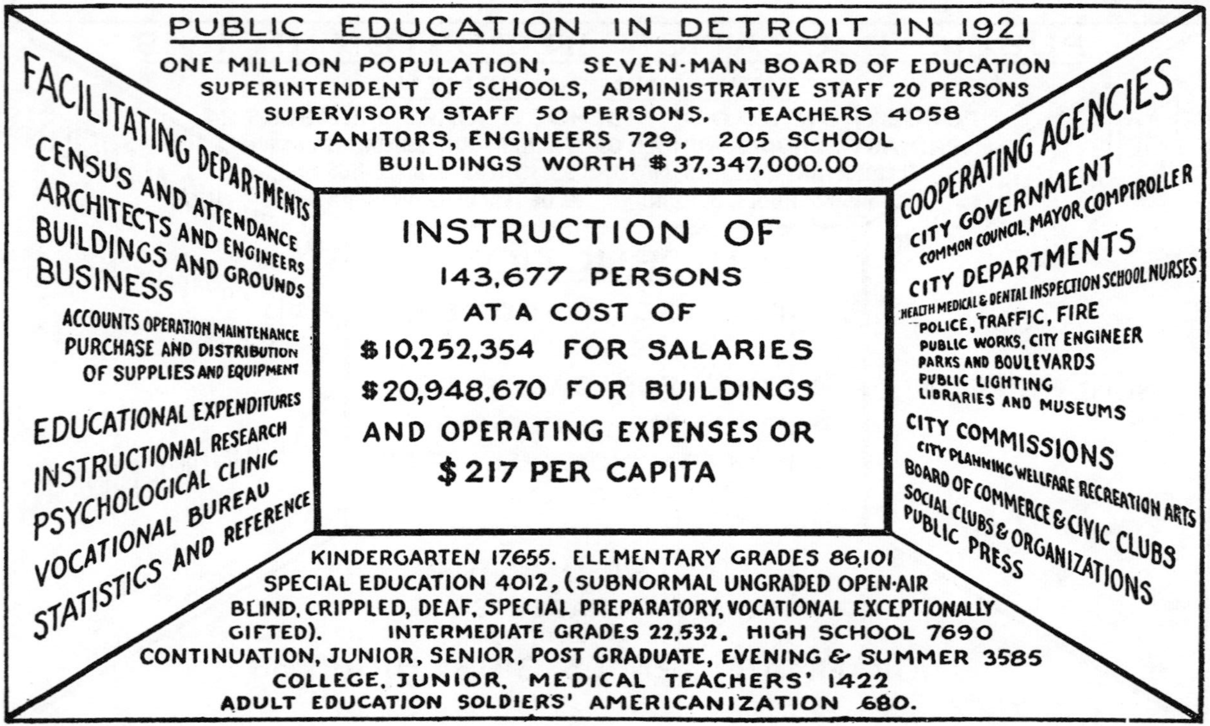

PUBLIC EDUCATION IN DETROIT IN 1921

ONE MILLION POPULATION, SEVEN-MAN BOARD OF EDUCATION
SUPERINTENDENT OF SCHOOLS, ADMINISTRATIVE STAFF 20 PERSONS
SUPERVISORY STAFF 50 PERSONS, TEACHERS 4058
JANITORS, ENGINEERS 729, 205 SCHOOL
BUILDINGS WORTH $37,347,000.00

FACILITATING

CENSUS AND ATTENDANCE
ARCHITECTS AND ENGINEERS
BUILDINGS AND GROUNDS
BUSINESS
ACCOUNTS OPERATION MAINTENANCE
PURCHASE AND DISTRIBUTION
OF SUPPLIES AND EQUIPMENT

EDUCATIONAL EXPENDITURES
INSTRUCTIONAL RESEARCH
PSYCHOLOGICAL CLINIC
VOCATIONAL BUREAU
STATISTICS AND REFERENCE

INSTRUCTION OF
143,677 PERSONS
AT A COST OF
$10,252,354 FOR SALARIES
$20,948,670 FOR BUILDINGS
AND OPERATING EXPENSES OR
$217 PER CAPITA

KINDERGARTEN 17,655. ELEMENTARY GRADES 86,101
SPECIAL EDUCATION 4012, (SUBNORMAL UNGRADED OPEN-AIR
BLIND, CRIPPLED, DEAF, SPECIAL PREPARATORY, VOCATIONAL EXCEPTIONALLY
GIFTED). INTERMEDIATE GRADES 22,532. HIGH SCHOOL 7690
CONTINUATION, JUNIOR, SENIOR, POST GRADUATE, EVENING & SUMMER 3585
COLLEGE, JUNIOR, MEDICAL TEACHERS' 1422
ADULT EDUCATION SOLDIERS' AMERICANIZATION .680.

COOPERATING AGENCIES

CITY GOVERNMENT
COMMON COUNCIL, MAYOR, COMPTROLLER
CITY DEPARTMENTS
HEALTH MEDICAL & DENTAL INSPECTION SCHOOL NURSES
POLICE, TRAFFIC, FIRE
PUBLIC WORKS, CITY ENGINEER
PARKS AND BOULEVARDS
PUBLIC LIGHTING
LIBRARIES AND MUSEUMS

CITY COMMISSIONS
CITY PLANNING WELFARE RECREATION ARTS
BOARD OF COMMERCE & CIVIC CLUBS
SOCIAL CLUBS & ORGANIZATIONS
PUBLIC PRESS

FIG. 5.

because of the suspension of building during the war, 1921 saw an unusual appropriation for new buildings. The total amount expended for education has increased 125 times, although the cost of education is a smaller proportion of the total tax levy now than formerly. Teachers' salaries have increased 80 times, and the amount raised for teachers per capita of population has increased from $1.50 to $10.50. Relatively more of the additional money is expended on the primary grades than on the grammar grades, although the grammar grades have been by no means neglected.

Inexact and general as these comparisons are, they nevertheless tell a story of remarkable progress. Education, and education under greatly improved conditions and on higher levels, is not only offered but accepted by a larger proportion of the total population now than in 1845. Colleges and universities are " swamped " by the flood of students. High school and continuation classes everywhere grow at amazing rates. National warfare is being waged against illiteracy, even in the foreign immigrant. Education is becoming truly universal.

It is difficult even for schoolmen to realize the changes in the magnitude and character of education which these figures imply; in the minds of many citizens the term " education " still simply calls up the picture of an immature young lady hearing a child " recite his A B C's " or perform some other simple and routine task. It is true, the heart of education is instruction, but to arrange for the instruction of millions of persons throughout the year, to manage an army of hundreds of thousands of skilled workers, to provide them with adequate equipment and supplies, to expend a billion dollars in a single year, makes of education a great national business. But its growth to such proportions is less important than the change in the nature of instruction. Learning has come to mean something more than mere memorization. It stands for growth in power and life. Instruction is now specialized and is being adapted to the needs of each type of children.

The diagram presented herewith shows the growth in size and complexity for one city from 1845 to the present day.

The superintendent, as the responsible head of the system, is called upon to be the directive agent in many different types of affairs. He must know how many children of school age there are, and how many must be provided for in the years to come (School Census),[1] and must see that each one within the age limits set by the compulsory attendance law is in school (Attendance Department). He must provide suitable buildings and grounds (Architectural Department, Supervisor of Properties, Architectural Research), and equip them and keep them stocked with necessary supplies (Business Manager, Purchasing Agent, Stockroom, Distributing System). They must be manned by janitors and engineers, and kept clean and in repair (Supervising Engineer). Then the superintendent must provide adequately trained teachers to teach the children, administrators to organize and direct their efforts, and supervisors to plan the educational work of the system and to improve instruction. The pupils themselves must be measured physically, mentally, and educationally, sorted into various classes, groups, and grades, and a special course of study provided for each group (Department of Instruction, Special Education Department, Psychological Clinic, Instructional Research). Machinery must also be set up for determining and keeping records of each child's progress and of the working of the system as a whole (Bureau of Statistics and Reference) and for reporting the same to the public (Publicity). Children must be assisted in the choice of life work and helped to find a

[1] Each year Detroit must provide facilities for nearly as many *new* children as the *total* number of children in the city schools of Boston in 1845.

suitable position (Vocátional Bureau). Teachers must be trained, and continued training provided for those in service (Teachers College). All this requires money, and after a budget has been prepared and the money obtained, it must be expended wisely (Cost Accounting, Department of Educational Expenditures). The morale of the force as a whole must be developed and maintained (Teachers' Organization) and provision made for old age (Pensions). Friendly coöperative relations must be maintained with other city departments and with state and national educational institutions. Take it all in all, education has grown from simple beginnings to an undertaking of astounding size, complexity, and importance.

In the light of the above, it seems strange that the Boston schoolmasters should have waged a controversy for several years against those who believed it was necessary to have a superintendent of schools to coördinate, direct, and assist the educational forces of the city. But it seems even more incomprehensible that the present-day efforts to secure the benefits of coördination, direction, and assistance in national educational affairs should meet with similar opposition.

As has already been stated, in Detroit the new board has been a dominant and aggressive force in inaugurating and making effective better educational conditions. Nine outstanding achievements, each of which represents the adoption or extension of a tendency prominent in the American education of today, may be listed, as follows:

1. Fact basis for action
2. Complete and unified system of municipal education
3. Instructional policy
4. Fixed responsibility
5. Building program
6. Scientific budget
7. Cost accounting

8. Child accounting
9. Publicity

Each merits a brief discussion:

1. Fact basis for action. The development of the scientific study of educational problems has taken place mainly in the first twenty years of the twentieth century. That is, the new era foreseen by Horace Mann in 1845 did not actually begin to materialize until fifty years later. A preparatory development of the basic sciences — experimental biology, psychology, and sociology — and a transfer of scientific ideals and technique from these sciences to education proved to be necessary.

During the first decade of the new century such development and transfer took place. The work of Rice and Thorndike provided suggestions for comparative surveys of different schools and systems on the basis of examinations and statistics given and collected under carefully standardized conditions. The resulting growth of measurement and experimentation in education is one of the marvels of the age. By 1910 the energy of the movement began to express itself in careful studies of the entire school system, and during the second decade of the century the educational survey became the dominating influence. A related development was taking place in industry and commerce. In every field of human endeavor scientific research was paying big dividends, and it was inevitable that in education, too, there should grow up the demand that planning and executive action should be based more upon exact knowledge of facts and less upon individual and dogmatic opinion than in the past. Research bureaus began to be organized in the larger school systems to carry on continuous survey and appraisal of educational endeavor. Intelligent planning on a fact basis is today an accepted ideal.

The first scientific experimentation in the Detroit Schools

began in 1910.   By 1914, a bureau of instructional research was organized and maintained in spite of the opposition and resistance of the board and teachers.   With the coming of the new board, however, the situation completely changed. Exact information was not only welcomed but demanded. The work of the existing bureau was strengthened and expanded.   A bureau of statistics and reference was organized and administrative, building, and psychological research provided for.   One department after another found itself under the necessity of either making surveys to get the facts to support requests for development and extension, or of carrying on appraisal measurements to prove that money allowed had been wisely expended.   Each year the school system holds a two-day meeting of some two hundred administrative and supervisory officers to hear and to discuss certain of the more vital of the experiments and investigations. A copy of the fourth annual program is here presented (pages 111–112) as evidence of working of the scientific spirit throughout the system.   It should be noted that the program consists entirely of scientific studies made within the system, by members of the system, and was presented to the administrative and supervisory agents of the system solely for the purposes of improvement of instruction within the system.

Today the Detroit School System is permeated with the spirit and practical use of scientific research.   More than a million copies of formal educational tests, similar in purpose to those of the 1845 survey, are used during the year, to say nothing of millions more used informally by teachers and pupils alike as a routine form of classroom instruction.   Horace Mann's statement, " We venture to predict that the mode of examination by printed questions and written answers will constitute a new era in the history of our schools," has been more than justified.   A comparison of the current superintendent's report of Detroit with the report of the examining committee of 1845, which was a remarkable document for its day, will make clear to the dullest mind the extent to which the basis of knowing, thinking, and planning in school work has been completely revolutionized since 1845.

2. Complete and unified system of municipal education. In 1845, education meant one thing — book learning, command of the fundamental tools — the three R's, in preparation for life.   There was, to be sure, an English High School and a Latin High School, but these were for the privileged few.   In 1845 but 1.4% of all the children of school age were actually enrolled in high schools.   In Detroit in 1921, 5.9% were enrolled in public high schools, while 2.5% more are found in college, continuation, or other form of adult education. That is, as has already been pointed out, education today is regarded by the public as essential to successful living and more and more opportunities for education are being demanded by the public, and the proportions which education may sometime assume cannot now be foretold.

Ours is the day of wonderful mechanical and industrial achievements.   Our civilization is based upon applied science and upon progressive scientific thought.   Preparation for life involves more than merely learning to read, write, and compute.   It was inevitable that the changing concept of education should give rise to changes in the curriculum.   The struggle between "classical" and "utilitarian" influences has been a long and bitter one, but little by little, at one point or another, the old strongholds have been invaded, and new subjects, new methods of work, new concepts and ideals of education have been making themselves felt.

In the past these changes have usually been unsystematic concessions to changing conditions, grudgingly tolerated and only partially assimilated in either organization or ideal.

PROGRAM

MAY 24 AND 25, 1922

Wednesday, 9:30 a.m.

Chairman
Superintendent of Schools

1. Causes of Failure in High School Studies
   Head of Mathematics Department, Northern High School

2. Does the Study of Latin Help in English?
   Teacher of Latin, Northwestern High School

3. The Effects of Supervised Study
   Assistant Principal, Southwestern High School

4. The Mental Overlapping in School Grades   *Clinical Psychologist*

5. Standards of Promotion   *Assistant Supervisor Reading*

6. Results of Experiment with Practice Tests in Reading
   Assistant Supervisor Reading

7. Distribution of Time in Mechanical Drawing
   Assistant Principal, Hutchins Intermediate School

Wednesday, 1:30 p.m.

Chairman
Dean, Teachers College

1. Comparison of Scores in Midyear, Final, and Initial Tests in Arithmetic
   District Principal

2. Adapting the School Plant to the Curriculum   *Deputy Superintendent*

3. Food Tests   *Supervisor Domestic Science*

4. Tests in Music   *Supervisor of Music*

5. Measurement of Appreciation in Music   *Instructor, Teachers College*

6. Appreciation Tests in Literature   *Assistant Supervisor of English*

7. Results of a Test Measuring Flat-Footedness
   Assistant Supervisor Health Education

Thursday, 9:30 a.m.

Chairman
Director of Languages

1. The New College Entrance Requirement   *Director of Languages*

2. Summary of the Building Program   *Assistant Director of Research*

3. Regulations for Social Activities in Senior High Schools
   Teacher, Western High School

4. The Production Worker and the Schools
   Supervisor Industrial Education

5. Field Work as a Means of Training Student Teachers
   Assistant Dean, Teachers College

6. Effectiveness of Elementary Summer School Work
   Supervisor Evening and Summer Schools

7. The Study of Teacher Rating   *Director of Probationary Department*

Thursday, 1:30 a.m.

Chairman
Deputy Superintendent

1. Distribution of Time in Machine Shop Work
   Head of Manual Training Department, Southeastern High School

2. Age-Grade-Progress   *District Principal*

3. Age-Grade-Progress and Status Ratios   *Assistant Supervisor of Research*

4. Control Elements in Silent Reading
   Assistant Principal, Lingemann School

5. Results of Experiments in Health Instruction in Four Elementary Schools
   Supervisor Health Education

6. Types of Information Collected through Occupational Surveys
   Chief Vocational Information and School Counseling Division

7. Value of Penmanship Certificates as a Means of Motivation
   Supervisor Penmanship

8. Reliability of Physical Examinations by Teachers
   Head of Special Education Department, Teachers College

At one extreme, the kindergarten movement has kept itself apart from regular education. At the other, high schools and colleges have maintained an existence separate and distinct from elementary education. Standards of teacher preparation and recognition for these different institutions have been different, methods and ideals of teaching have been different, and in general the various divisions of public instruction have maintained their ancient conventions as far and as long as they could. Changes have come, not because of but in spite of traditions and conventions.

In Detroit the new board, confronted with the results of surveys of department after department, took an aggressive stand for progress and formally adopted a basic plan of municipal education, which marks the first systematic change in outward form and policy since the system of graded schools was adopted many years ago. This plan is basic in its influence upon all the other actions of the board. It is an expression of the modern conception of education and for many years to come will exert a unifying and directive influence on educational progress throughout the city. The details of changes brought about by this adoption will be discussed in the paragraphs that follow, but in this section will be presented the main outlines of the various divisions.

The central thought of the board's action is that with a population of a million people to support education, it should be possible ultimately for a child born and bred in Detroit to secure, without leaving the city, the main types of educational opportunity which are essential to success and happiness. The board adopted a single educational policy, organized in accordance with the psychological development of the learners into five divisions of educational work.

Type	Age	Function
1. Elementary Schools Kindergarten through Grade 6	Childhood 5–12	Control of fundamentals
2. Intermediate Schools (Junior High Schools) Grades 7, 8, 9	Early adolescence 13–15	Extension of range of experiences. Beginnings of differentiation
3. High Schools (Senior High Schools) Grades 10, 11, 12	Late adolescence 16–18	Continuation and intensification of differentiation
4. Colleges	Adult training 19–32	Specific cultural and vocational training
5. Continuation Education	Maturity	Vocational or cultural assistance in response to specific adult needs

The curriculum of the elementary schools is undifferentiated. In the early grades pupils chiefly gain knowledge, skill, and attitudes, and the educational experiences which are uniformly essential for all. The average child will finish the elementary period of his education at the age of 12, and will have completed those parts of the three R's curriculum which have been conventionally found in grades kindergarten to six. Recent educational experiments make it probable that in the near future the standards of ability attained at the end of the elementary period will approximate closely those which now prevail at the end of the eighth grade. The program for the elementary school represents the best elements of the conventional grammar school, enriched by and founded upon a socialized program of vital activities.

The intermediate school (Junior High School) is a new institution created in recognition of the changes in pupil nature which occur at the beginning of and throughout adolescence. The youth's growing desire for a more varied environment is satisfied by a new organization and by a greatly diversified curriculum, in which opportunity is given the individual to try out for himself a wide range of vocational and cultural experiences. There is provided a series of elective studies which mark the beginning of specialization; but the central core of the intermediate school curriculum is a group of social and scientific studies designed to supply civic information and experiences essential for all. It is expected that ultimately every child in Detroit will finish at least the intermediate school, and in this school are given the minimum essentials of all that is needed for citizenship plus such other education and training as may be required by pupils of various types and levels of intelligence. The intermediate school is an expression of the change from preparation for college as the basis of organization, to preparation for citizenship. It recognizes preparation for further academic training, but only as one of the five major fields of specialization, — commercial, industrial, technical, professional, and home-making.

The educational policy adopted for the lower schools has profoundly modified the high schools, also. The modern general or cosmopolitan high school has in successive grades a smaller and smaller required central core of social and scientific studies and a larger and larger number of elective specialization courses; but the basis of organization, nevertheless, is the central core of citizenship studies, and not, as in the past, preparation for further academic training.

In other words, the elementary, intermediate, and secondary schools are organized about the social and scientific needs and problems of present-day living, a distinct departure from the past. Moreover, they form one unbroken series of educational opportunities, unified in aims, methods, and organization. They look toward the day when every child will complete at least twelve years of educational activity.

One other phase of secondary education merits special comment. Detroit, an industrial and commercial city, has developed also special industrial, commercial, and vocational schools. A technical high school and continuation classes, both for juniors and adults, are features of the educational work of the city that should not be overlooked. Yet here, too, the general policy of the board is having a marked effect. A survey revealed the fact that the technical work was developing independently and overemphasizing utilitarian ends. The same board which brought about a reorganization of high school work in terms of present-day needs and problems exerted its unifying influence on the technical high school to provide for a richer and broader civic training and more fundamental relationship between the various secondary departments and schools.

In the field of college education, no radical reorganization has as yet been attempted, although signs are not wanting that these units also are to be modified along progressive lines. The board has changed the city normal school from a two-year school to a four-year Teachers College, and has put the stamp of its approval upon better training for teachers. It has strengthened and developed the Junior College, and there has been some discussion of the establishment of a Senior College. It has acquired a large site of forty acres on which to erect suitable new buildings. The Medical College has also received attention and support. Law and Engineering Colleges have been mentioned as possibilities. It is evident that ultimately there will be a municipal university, as there are already in several American cities. When it comes it will express in aims and organization the general policy of a complete and progressive school system, organized in terms of present-day needs and unified throughout consistently in terms of aims and methods.

3. Instructional policy. From the point of view of class-

room procedure, the change in policy from 1845 to the present corresponds to the changes in the conception of education itself. The practice in 1845 was memorization, formalized preparation for life. To be sure, Horace Mann and men of similar genius pointed out clearly to their age the inadequacy of training of this type, but it is doubtful that even Horace Mann himself foresaw the development of educational method which has taken place during the last fifty years. The work of Rousseau and Pestalozzi directed attention to child nature and gave rise to a new philosophy which is today transforming classroom teaching. The fall of the doctrine of formal discipline, the discovery of the relation of interest to effort, and the formulation of the psychological laws of learning, have led to developments which have far outrun the prophetic vision of Horace Mann. In American education the new ideas were first given objective expression in the activities of the kindergarten, but have spread rapidly upward through the grades, transforming the teachers' work in its most fundamental aspects.

The changes which have taken place may be summarized, as far as Detroit is concerned, in three general slogans or tendencies, — Socialization, Vitalization, and Individualization. By socialization is meant the carrying on of educational activities in situations which are social both in the sense that they involve group activity with its resultant division of labor, coöperation, and management, and in the sense that they yield life experiences of practical value, rather than experiences which theoretically prepare for life. Vitalization includes the appraisal of the content of the curriculum, the rejection of obsolete or non-functional material, and the retention for training purposes of those elements of maximum value in the social life of the day. By individualization is meant the recognition of fundamental differences in the native capacities and tendencies of children and the adjustment of work in terms of these individual needs. Each merits discussion.

Progress in the socialization of the schools is best shown by the enrichment of the curriculum which has taken place. The diagram [1] on page 119 gives one phase of the interesting story, but one phase only. It shows that today the school attempts to minister to the whole nature of the pupil, not simply to his intellect. Health, manual skill, recreation, æsthetic appreciation, scientific thinking, and moral training have been added to the 3 R's of early days. Even the conventional tool subjects have been completely transformed. Today the best school practices are those made necessary by the life of a democratic community. The tendency is away from the autocratic, academic artificiality of the past. Children read, not as a task, but because the reading serves a real purpose in their lives. The same statement may be truly made of writing and arithmetic. The child who pens invitations to a school play, acts as cashier in the school store, or draws books from the school library is as interested in his work and acts from precisely the same kinds of motives as do his parents. To speak in striking terms, we may say that the modern school has ceased to be a prison and is becoming a childish utopia. It provides him with many opportunities he would not otherwise have, it helps him to form worthy purposes, it aids him in the achievement of those purposes, and finally, its interpretation of his experiences enlarges his vision and adds to the vigor and pleasure of his living. Children arrive early at the modern school and often have to be sent home at night. Enrichment of the curriculum means something more than the mere addition of more subjects to the required list. It means a social revolution as complete and as far reaching as the progress of democracy itself. The table on pages 122–123 exhibits the arrangement of studies in a modern school program.

[1] From *The Detroit Educational Bulletin*, No. 2, 1920.

Expansion of Elementary School Curriculum from 1775 to 1900

1775	1825	1850	1875	1900
				PHYSIOLOGY & HYGIENE
				LITERATURE
			DRAWING	DRAWING
			CIVICS	CIVICS
		HISTORY	HISTORY	HISTORY
	GRAMMAR	LANGUAGE & GRAMMAR	LANGUAGE & GRAMMAR	LANGUAGE & GRAMMAR
READING	READING	READING	READING	READING
SPELLING	SPELLING	SPELLING	SPELLING	SPELLING
WRITING	WRITING	WRITING	WRITING	WRITING
ARITHMETIC	ARITHMETIC	ARITHMETIC	ARITHMETIC	ARITHMETIC
BIBLE	CONDUCT	CONDUCT	CONDUCT	PLAY
	BOOKKEEPING	BOOKKEEPING	NATURE STUDY	NATURE STUDY
	GEOGRAPHY	GEOGRAPHY	GEOGRAPHY	GEOGRAPHY
		OBJECT LESSONS	MUSIC	MUSIC
			PHYSICAL EXERCISES	PHYSICAL TRAINING
				SEWING
				MANUAL TRAINING
1775	1825	1850	1875	1900

On the side of content, vitalization has been an important factor in the program of socialization. In the old days it was thought not to matter much what the child studied so long as he did not like it. The theory apparently was, " The greater the cross the brighter the crown shall be." Subject matter was selected and taught on the basis of its logical value to the adult specialist. Courses were long, heavy, and fantastically complete, that they might bear evidence of the scholarship of their authors. " Cultural " and " practical " were wrongly considered to be opposite in meaning.

The present-day policy of vitalization, however, is completely changing the content of the various subjects of the curriculum. Today, each item of subject matter is being carefully weighed and measured and selection is being made on the basis of vital relationship to the affairs of everyday life. In spelling, for instance, vitalization means the reduction of the course of study from thirty or forty thousand words, many of which were chosen for their difficulty only, to three or four thousand words, every one of which will be used by the child over and over again as long as he lives. In arithmetic it means the elimination of fantastic problems and obsolete methods of work. It means emphasis on present-day applications of arithmetical principles and upon power to use the same as a means to an end. So in every other subject. Not only is the material used in the modern school more and more related to the children's interests and needs, but to an increasing degree its selection has been determined by measures of its social value.

A comparison of the textbooks of 1845 with the best of those of the present day reveals in a striking way the effects of the tendencies which have just been discussed. Illustrations of the older texts are given in Appendix VIII (pages 376–392). In value of content, in attractiveness of appearance, in adjustment to the tastes and abilities of the children for whom they were intended, the change in textbooks is great and far reaching in its influence.

A second change is found in school behavior and methods of control. It is no longer a pedagogical sin for boys and girls to move about the schoolroom, or to laugh in school when the situation is one which gives rise to laughter. To one trained in the rigid discipline of the past, where the one exciting element of a day's work was success in making trouble for the teacher without getting caught at it, the absence of formal order and the apparent relaxation of discipline sometimes seem to be a step backwards. Closer analysis will soon show that movable desks, naturalness of the pupil and teacher relationships, and mutual helpfulness from pupil to pupil are far more productive of self-control and other civic virtues essential to successful social living than prison discipline ever was. The able modern teacher is just as sensitive to " fooling " or " insubordination " as any teacher of old, but she is more human and understands human nature better than did the teacher of 1845. The sour, hatchet-faced, withered spinster and martinet whom the cartoonist of fifty years ago chose as a symbol of the average teacher of that day, has been replaced by a well-trained, social, capable, professionally minded woman, interested herself in the problems of the day and bringing to her classwork the interest and vitality of world affairs.

Proof of the extent of this change and of its consequences is found in the abolition of corporal punishment and the growth of child participation in school management. Today children of every grade from kindergarten through college unite in civic organizations within the school for the control of attendance, of behavior in halls and classroom and on playground, and for care of buildings and grounds. To an increasing degree children are literally setting their own les-

PROGRAM OF SPECIAL ACTIVITIES, 20-SECTION PLATOON SCHOOL

		X		Y				X			Y		
		8:30-9	9-9:30	9:30-10	10-10:30	10:30-11	11-11:30	12:30-1	1-1:30	1:30-2	2-2:30	2:30-3	3-3:30
Auditorium	M	6-2	18-20	4	5-1	17-19	3	8	16-14	10-12	7	15-13	9-11
	T	6-2	18-20	4	5-1	17-19	3	8	16-14	10-12	7	15-13	9-11
	W	6-2	18-20	4	5-1	17-19	3	8	16-14	10-12	7	15-13	9-11
	T	6-2	18-20	4	5-1	17-19	3	8	16-14	10-12	7	15-13	9-11
	F	6-2	18-20	4	5-1	17-19	3	8	16-14	10-12	7	15-13	9-11
Gymnasium	M	10-12	2	16-14	9-11	1	15-13	6-4	8	18-20	5-3	7	17-19
	T	10-12	2	16-14	9-11	1	15-13	6-4	8	18-20	5-3	7	17-19
	W	10-12	2	16-14	9-11	1	15-13	6-4	8	18-20	5-3	7	17-19
	T	10-12	2	16-14	9-11	1	15-13	6-4	8	18-20	5-3	7	17-19
	F	10-12	2	16-14	9-11	1	15-13	6-4	8	18-20	5-3	7	17-19
Literature	M	20	10	18	19	9	17	16	6	14	15	5	13
	T	20	10	18	19	9	17	16	6	14	15	5	13
	W	20	10	18	19	9	17	16	6	14	15	5	13
	T	20	10	18	19	9	17	16	6	14	15	5	13
	F	20	10	18	19	9	17	16	6	14	15	5	13
Science	M	18	12	20	17	11	19	14	4	16	13	3	15
	T	18	12	20	17	11	19	14	4	16	13	3	15
	W	18	12	20	17	11	19	14	4	16	13	3	15
	T	18	12	20	17	11	19	14	4	2	13	3	1
	F	18	12	20	17	11	19	12 Lit.	4	2	11 Lit.	3	
Art	M	14	14	Lit. 12	13	13	Lit. 11	18	18	Lit. 8	17	17	Lit. 7
	T	16	16	Lit. 12	15	15	Lit. 11	10	2	Lit. 8	9	1	Lit. 7
	W	8	6	Lit. 12	7	5	Lit. 11	12		Lit. 8	11		Lit. 7
	T	4	6	Lit. 12	3	5	Lit. 11	10	2	Lit. 8	9	1	Lit. 7
	F	4	8	Art. 12	3	7	Art. 11	20	20	Lit. 8	19	19	
Music	M	4	8	Lit.	3	7	Lit. 1	12	10	Sci. 6	11	9	Sci. 5
	T	14	6	Lit.	13	5	Lit. 1	20	12	Sci. 6	19	11	Sci. 5
	W	14	16	Lit.	3	15	Lit. 1	18	2	Sci. 6	17	9	Sci. 5
	T	16	8	Lit.	13	7	Lit. 1	20	10	Sci. 6	19	1	Sci. 5
	F		6	Lit.	15	5	Lit. 1	18	2	Sci. 6	17		Sci. 5
Library	M	Sup.Study 4	6	Sci. 10	Sup.Study 3	Sup.Study 5	Sci. 9	Sup.Study 12	2	Lit. 4	Sup.Study 11	1	Lit. 3
	T	16	8	Sci. 10	15	7	Sci. 9	10	20	Lit. 4	9	19	Lit. 3
	W	16	Sup.Study	Sci. 10	15	Sci. 13	Sci. 9	12	18	Lit. 4	11	17	Lit. 3
	T		14	Sci. 10			Sci. 9		20	Lit. 4		17	Lit. 3

122

Manual Training	M.	16	16 Sci. 14	15 Sci. 13	Sci. 7	20 18 20	19 17	Sci. 1
	T.		14	Sci. 15 13	Sci. 7	18	17	Sci. 1
	W.		Sci. 16 14	13	Sci. 7	20 18	19 17	Sci. 1
	T.		Sci. 14	Sci. 13	Sci. 7	18	17	Sci. 1
	F.							
Play	M.	8-13	4	6-19	7-18	15	5-14	Sci. 2	2-10	12	1-9	11	20
	T.	8	4	6-15	7	13	5-16	Sci. 2	2	19-10	1-13	9	
	W.	15-13	4-8	6-17	18		5-14	Sci. 2	2-18	10-12	1-17	9-11	20 15
	T.	8	4	6	7		5		2-14	12	1-13	11	15

Work specified in Manual Training Department plus groups from adjacent schools keep these rooms occupied continuously.

Play classes in heavy type are classes in charge of home-room teachers.

NOTE. 1. The above is a program of the special activities of all children for an entire week in a 20-section platoon school, or a school accommodating 20 classes or groups.

2. Each number represents a definite class as shown by the key at the end of the program. Each letter in the key represents the home room, with the respective two groups belonging to it. "X" and "Y" are the two platoons. "X" consisting of even-numbered classes, and "Y" of odd-numbered classes. While classes indicated by odd numbers are in the home rooms, even-numbered or alternating sections are in special departments, and vice versa.

3. The twelve vertical columns represent the half-hour periods for special activities for the entire week. The columns are subdivided into daily periods according to subjects designated at left of program.

4. This form makes possible the tracing of any group through all its respective special activities throughout the entire week.

To illustrate: The special activities of any group in the building for the first period for every day in the week, may be found in the first vertical column at the left of the program; special activities for the following periods are found in succeeding columns.

For example — in the program, Class 20 or an A 6th group is found in the literature room the first period every day in the week; the second period daily, the same group is in the auditorium, and the third period daily, in the science room. At 10 o'clock the group goes to the home room for an hour and a half. At 11:30 school is dismissed, and a luncheon period of one hour follows.

In the afternoon at 12:30 the class reports on Monday and Wednesday for the first and second periods in the Manual Training room; on Friday for first and second periods in the Art room, and on Tuesday and Thursday for the first period it is in the Music room. The second period on Tuesday and Thursday the group is in the Library. The third period daily class 20 is in the Gymnasium.

At 2 o'clock the group reports to the grade room, remaining until 3:30, dismissal time.

KEY

Class No.	Grade	Home Room	Class No.	Grade	Home Room	Class No.	Grade	Home Room	Class No.	Grade	Home Room	Class No.	Grade	Home Room
1	B1 }	J	3	A1 }	I	5	B2 }	H	7	A2 }	G	9	B3 }	F
2	B1		4	A1		6	B2		8	A2		10	B3	
11	A3 }	E	13	B4 }	D	15	A4 }	C	17	B5 }	B	19	B6 }	A
12	A3		14	B4		16	B4		18	A5		20	A6	

123

sons and marking the quality of their success.   The contrast between " self-discipline " and " one flogging every six minutes throughout a six-hour day " tells a story of remarkable progress.   It is not uncommon for more or less mystified parents to give unconscious testimony to the efficacy of modern education.   They come to schools seeking to understand why children like school, and marvel at their growth in intelligent self-control.   However, there are many parents who have still to learn that true discipline can come only from within; that the use of force or physical compulsion is a sign of failure in the development of true character.

By far the most remarkable gain in the seventy-five years that have passed since 1845 is the growing tendency toward individualization of mass instruction.   Public schools have always had to teach children in large masses, and probably always will.   Through the years there has been a slow but steady reduction in the size of classes, yet whether a class numbers twenty-five or forty-five the methods of teaching have been those of " broadside " treatment.   Educational psychology and educational measurement, however, have produced a mass of data, all showing that the most constant trait about human nature is its variability.   As a result, teachers are at last beginning to act on the belief that children differ, and to invent methods of classroom teaching which will enable a teacher to deal with a large group of children and yet allow a child to grow at his own rate and to study in his own way.   This has been made possible by the objective definition of aims in terms of scores in standard tests.   Contrast, for instance, this statement of the standards for admission to the first class of the Grammar Schools with modern statements of similar goals:

STANDARDS AS DEFINED IN 1847 [1]

Before admission to the first class he (the pupil) ought to be able to write sentences and parse, showing the relation of all parts of speech; to write all the words in his reading lessons; to read distinctly and fluently any piece of narrative or didactic prose or verse in his reader and give the meaning of any of the words which occur therein; to give the boundaries of all the states and to draw them readily, from memory, upon the slate or blackboard; and to enumerate the principal productions, natural and artificial, of the different countries, and the principal rivers, mountains, lakes, and towns of each.

STANDARDS AS DEFINED IN 1921

1920 SUBJECT	AUTHOR OF STANDARD TEST USED	NATURE OF TEST USED	SCORES FOR AN AVERAGE EIGHTH-GRADE CLASS
Oral Reading	Gray	Paragraphs of increasing difficulty	Paragraph 8
Silent Reading	Burgess	Paragraphs of simple directions	12 right in 5 minutes
Writing	Ayres	Free choice copying	85 letters per minute with quality 65
Arithmetic	Courtis	Addition of examples each composed of 9 three-place numbers	12 examples in 8 minutes 85% accuracy
Composition	Hillegas	Original story	25 words per minute, quality 75
Grammar	Starch	Grammatical problems	Score 8.3 on Scale B
Spelling	Ayres	Words in list U of spelling scale	84% accuracy

The difference between reading distinctly and fluently and reading paragraph 8 of Gray's Scale in less than 20 seconds with no mistakes is the difference between personal opinion and impersonal scientific knowledge.   In one case the pupil

[1] Highest class, average age fourteen years, corresponding to the present eighth grade.

is dependent upon the teacher's opinion as to whether his efforts have been successful or not. On the other hand he can measure his own performance and determine for himself when he has achieved the standard. Modern teaching devices for developing control of either knowledge or skill use such objective definitions of aim to enable each child to work upon lessons of just the degree of difficulty that constitutes for him the next step of progress and to permit him to grow at a rapid, average, or slow rate, according to his nature and effort.

In 1845 the graded school had not yet been introduced. By 1920 grades in Detroit had begun to lose their value. Inventory measurements are made at the beginning and end of the semester and children are grouped roughly according to capacity and ability. But so great is individual variation that in one semester the most homogeneous group changes to a group of varying abilities. It is rapidly becoming clear that individualization of instruction is the only ultimate solution; that the same general methods which are now used in writing and in certain phases of arithmetic and reading must be extended to include all phases of individual learning.

The efficiency of school work today is low. There is much evidence to show that results secured are vastly better than in 1845, but there is still room for great improvement. In the average school, with standards set so low that approximately two children in ten in each of the various grades have already achieved the standard for their grade at the opening of school, the actual results of teaching effort are only about 40% of the gain necessary for each child to reach standard. Experiments prove that individualization of instruction will ultimately raise the level of efficiency to about 85% of the possible gain. For mass instruction, however, some schools are at present working very nearly at maximum efficiency.

4. Fixed responsibility.   To describe a school system in terms of its best teachers is manifestly unfair.   The real question to be answered is, How far does the average work of the whole system approach the ideal?   It is possible to find in Detroit's army of 4,500 teachers some who represent but very limited advance over the teaching of 1845.   Detroit is unique, however, in its manifestation of consistent and unified instructional policy running through all the actions of the board.   Detroit's unity and progress are not chance phenomena.   It has been made possible by the development of a strong centralized control democratically administered. The organization of the new small board was based upon the recommendations of educational authorities and the experience of other cities.   Specifically Rule II of the Bylaws of the Board of Education states that

II. Superintendent

The Superintendent of schools shall be the Executive Officer of the Board of Education and under its direction he shall attend all meetings of the Board and be granted the privilege of taking part in its deliberations.

1. He shall establish and change boundaries of school districts.

2. He *alone* shall be directly *responsible* to the Board of Education for the efficient operation of all school functions of the Board of Education.

3. He shall have *sole power* to nominate and to assign, transfer, promote and demote or suspend all assistant superintendents, supervisors, principals, teachers and other employees of the Board of Education as hereinafter provided.   All nominations, promotions, demotions, suspensions, assignments, and transfers of employees of the Board of Education which shall be made by the Superintendent shall be reported in writing to the Board at its next regular meeting and shall stand confirmed unless disapproved by the Board by a vote of not less than four members of the Board.   He shall have immediate control of all assistant superintendents, supervisors, principals and teachers.   All directions and suggestions to them with reference to the performance of their respective duties shall come through him.

4. He shall prepare and submit to the Board for approval the several courses of study to be followed, and shall select and recommend to the Board for adoption all textbooks used in the schools. In the preparation of such courses and the selection of such textbooks he shall have the coöperation of other officers of instruction and of such special committees of teachers, principals and supervisors as he may from time to time appoint for such specific purposes.

5. He shall, on or before the first meeting of January, submit to the Board of Education an estimate of expenditure for all purposes of the Board of Education for the ensuing year.

This means that extensive powers are centered in the hands of the superintendent, so that any policy or plan adopted may be effectively carried out. The superintendent, in turn, in choosing his staff, delegates to each one a definite portion of his power and holds that individual responsible for the work of his department. At the same time, the board and the superintendent have set up administrative machinery to provide channels of participation and expression on the part of each group of workers throughout the system.

Centralization of authority to a high degree has always been resisted in America, because it makes possible autocratic use of power for narrow, selfish purposes. On the other hand, distribution of responsibility to a high degree usually produces inefficiency. The success of the Detroit experiment seems to be due both to administrative machinery which provides for democratic participation in administration, and to fixing of responsibility and localizing authority. Such a plan conserves the benefits of the two extremes and permits each to serve as a check upon possible undesirable activities of the other. Therefore a somewhat detailed outline is presented, giving the workings of the plan as shown in two representative divisions.

As in any large organization, which has grown by irregular additions and extensions, all sorts of irregularities and peculiarities exist.   But in the main, as opportunity offers, action is taken consolidating and integrating the organization.   In the account which follows, therefore, no attempt will be made to picture conditions as they actually exist.   Instead, outstanding tendencies will be sketched as illustrations and the reader who is interested in exact detail is referred to the superintendent's annual report.

In general, the work under the direction of the superintendent falls into two major divisions, business and education. Each of these, in turn, has a number of subdivisions.   The organization as a whole is represented in the following figure:

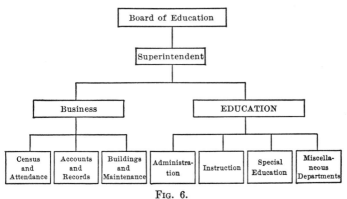

FIG. 6.

The superintendent meets weekly with his administrative staff (composed of heads of departments) to receive reports, make decisions, and issue instructions.   Each head of department in similar fashion holds weekly meetings of his staff.   Systematic coöperation between departments is provided for, as is also systematic gathering of suggestions from the rank and file of teachers.   Free communication and fixed responsibility enable the different departments to compete intelligently in contributing to the progress of the system.

As an illustration of the fixed responsibility and of coöperation between departments, the organization and work of the two departments of administration and instruction will be given in general outline.

Administration is defined as:

that group of activities which deals with (1) the carrying out of policies that provide physical, financial, and educational conditions, under which pupil, teacher, principal, and supervisor may work to best advantage; (2) the provision of channels through which the course of study, general data, and instructions may be quickly and effectually placed in operation; (3) the provision of channels through which information about conditions in the schools may be promptly transmitted to the central office; (4) putting into operation standards of achievement; (5) the preparation of general data and reports; (6) research activities; (7) general publicity.

The general form of organization of elementary, intermediate, high, and college units is best shown by a diagram of the elementary unit.

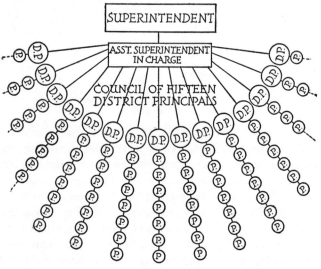

Fig. 7.

Each principal meets weekly with the teachers in his building. The six or seven principals of the schools in a given district meet each week with the principal of the district. The district principal, who himself acts as principal of one of the buildings in the district, also meets weekly with the other district principals and the assistant superintendent in charge. At all of these meetings the problems of the school system are discussed and exchange of ideas and experiences takes place, both from the central administration to the schools and vice versa.

In similar fashion instruction is defined as:

that group of activities which has to do with the actual improvement of instruction as (1) preparation and development of courses of study and bulletins of methods of teaching; (2) examination and recommendation of textbooks; (3) demonstration teaching; (4) institutes and teachers' meetings for the improvement of instruction; (5) personal conferences for the interpretation of methods and of the curriculum; (6) classroom visitation and inspection; (7) setting up standards of achievement; (8) direction and supervision of the training of regular, probationary, and substitute teachers; (8) experimentation and instructional research.

The organization of the department of instruction is as follows:

Through tests and measurement the department studies the workings of the system and discovers possible places of improvement. Through direct experimentation solutions are worked out, the evidence of improvement secured, and the plan presented to the superintendent for his consideration. The superintendent submits the proposed plan with the evidence to the staff of district principals for their study and criticism. When all parties concerned have made their contribution to the plan, it is officially adopted by the superintendent and put into effect. It is also incorporated into the training of all types of teachers and in a short time is in effective operation throughout the city.

The relation between the two departments is a fine example in fixing of responsibility, division of labor, and competitive coöperation.   The story is told in outline in the following simple diagram:

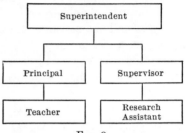

FIG. 8.

It should be noted that each teacher is responsible to her principal and to him alone, that the supervisor has no executive responsibility for the work of any teacher and no administrative authority. Principals receive instructions from one source, the superintendent; and the supervisors have but one person to convince — namely, the superintendent.

Supervisors are specialists whose business it is to know more about their special subject than any one else in the system.   Their work is research and teacher training, not administration.   They are concerned with the improvement of instruction, not administrative appraisal.   They fix standards, but do not administer them.   If a principal or teacher fails, censure comes, not from the supervisor, but from the administrative superior.   If a principal or teacher needs assistance in reaching the adopted standards of efficiency, he may call upon the supervisor, but visits of assistance are wholly a form of service " on call."   Mutual helpful relations are thus established, and each department vies with the other to render the greater service.

Contrast with such a system of organized, systematic effort to administer and improve the schools, the condition

of the Boston Schools in 1845.   Without supervision, other
than meager inspection once a year by the School Committee,
without administrative coördination or control, without even
an efficient internal organization, it is little wonder the survey committee devotes so much space to the need for a city
commissioner or superintendent.   But the time was not ripe.
There was much discussion of the recommendations of the
committee; the Boston *Daily Advertiser* of November 29,
1845, records the fact that the School Committee finally
passed a motion requesting the Common Council to provide
funds for the appointment of a School Superintendent, but
the issue of April 17, 1846, of the same paper also records
the fact that the Common Council voted down the proposal
to elect a School Superintendent, 25 voting against, 15 for,
with 8 absent.   Even the inefficiency revealed by the
survey report had not sufficient weight with the council
to lead them to abolish their double-headed system for the
sixteen independent schools, each operated independently
of all the rest and each officered by two independent and
often warring masters.   They could not see that whether
a system was autocratic or democratic depended upon the
way it was administered.   Even the spectacle of the schoolmasters of Boston combining for the first time to fight Horace Mann, the prophet of progress, did not open their eyes.
Detroit, with a strong centralized organization, democratically administered, provides both for unity of control and
freedom, as well as unity of effort to bring about progress.
The individual agent, be he pupil, teacher, or head of department, has greater " freedom under law " and greater
opportunity to express his genius effectively in constructive
contribution than the Boston masters had in 1845.   Verily,
the schools have made progress in this field, also.

    5. Building program.   One of the persistent problems
in any rapidly growing city is that of maintaining an ade-

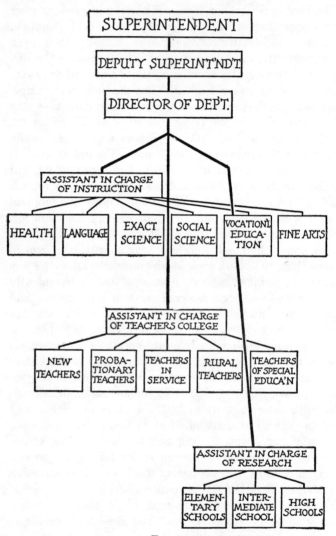

Fɪɢ. 9.

quate building program. In Detroit, during the war, with
the suspension of all building operations, the system fell
rapidly behind, until more than twenty thousand children
were on part time. As soon as the war was over the new
board attacked this problem aggressively and intelligently.
A pupil survey located the children for whom the schools were
to be built, a land survey revealed the vacant lots that were
available, and a school survey brought to light the absence
of past planning. For example, in 1920–21 there were
twenty-three different types of school organizations operating in the city, as shown in the following table. K–8 means
that the building contained grades Kindergarten through 8.

TYPES OF SCHOOL ORGANIZATION, 1920–21

TYPE	No.	PER CENT	TYPE	No.	PER CENT
K–8	66	42.0	8–12	2	1.3
K–6	24	15.3	1–5	2	1.3
K–7	18	10.2	K–1	2	1.3
K–4	8	5.1	K–2	1	0.6
K–4	5	3.2	9–14	1	0.6
K–5	4	2.5	1–3	1	0.6
7–9	4	2.5	K–3	1	0.6
9–12	4	2.5	2–8	1	0.6
1–6	3	2.	3–8	1	0.6
K	3	2.	1,2,4,5,8	1	0.6
1–8	3	2.	2,5,7	1	0.6
7–12	3	2.			

Moreover, the types of buildings which had been erected
were for the most part planned with little relation to the
work to be carried on in them. They conformed in general
type to the first graded school built in Boston in 1848 as
a result of the agitation for better building fathered by Horace Mann. That is, they were square " soap box " buildings
with a room for each grade, and little more. Yet, as has

been shown, the whole character of education had been changing in the interval and there was need for a new type of building adjusted to the instructional policy.

A department of architectural research was organized. The supervisors were asked to aid in formulating standards for each type of room and activity, and a building program formulated which in a few years will completely displace the twenty-three types of school organizations by the three standard types, — elementary, intermediate, and high.

The standard elementary school adopted is a platoon or departmentalized school. The conventional school work in the tool subjects, reading, writing, and arithmetic, is carried on in what are called home rooms; for the socialized work of the newer type made necessary by the changing curriculum, special rooms are provided adapted to the needs of each subject. The school is organized in two departments or platoons. The school day is lengthened to six hours and each platoon spends an hour and a half in the home rooms and an hour and a half in special work each session, there being two shifts a day. The operation of the school program is shown in outline in the following diagram:

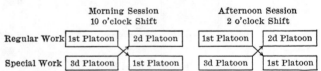

Under this plan the school facilities are in continuous use, and the special teachers are as fully occupied as the home-room teachers.

This plan provides for a greatly enriched socialized program at no increase in cost. The special features found in the standard platoon building for 2,340 pupils are two gymnasiums, 2 auditoriums, 1 library, 4 science rooms, 4 literature rooms, 2 music rooms, 3 art rooms, 1 sewing room,

1 manual training room, and in addition a number of special rooms for the school doctor, physical education department, kitchen, dining room, etc., needed in the operation of a large unit containing such diversified activities.

The plans for a standard elementary school, together with a picture of a completed building, are presented in Figures 10 and 11 (pages 138, 139, and 140).

The specifications for the intermediate and high schools also provide for a building adjusted to a socialized curriculum, as may be seen from the account on page 142 of the accommodations provided.

A further item in the building program should not be overlooked. A survey of school grounds and play space was also made and steps taken to remedy existing conditions. The new buildings stand on adequate grounds and are as splendid in their equipment and appointments as they are in their adjustment to the educational program. At this writing (1923) ten intermediate schools have been authorized, with five in operation, while nearly fifty elementary schools are operating on the platoon plan.

To appreciate what such buildings and such an instructional policy really mean in terms of progress, it is but necessary to turn to Horace Mann's impassioned plea for better buildings and the plans of the structures existing in Boston in 1845. As has already been pointed out, they were for the most part two-room buildings, housing four hundred children, packed tightly into rigid, awkward desks. The diagram on page 141 is taken from a report of this period, in which the Wells School of Boston is held up as a model of school architecture. The contrast speaks for itself.

6-8. Budget making, cost accounting, child accounting. With the rising cost of education, and the growing sensitiveness of the average citizen to the increasing tax rate, there has come a public demand for a more careful scrutiny of educa-

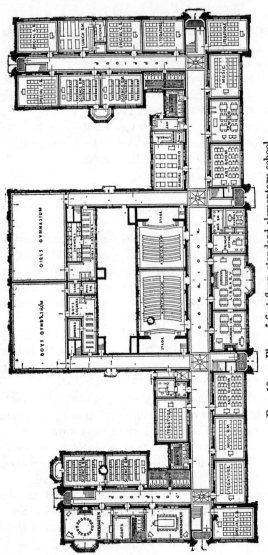

Fig. 10 a.   Plan of first floor, standard elementary school.

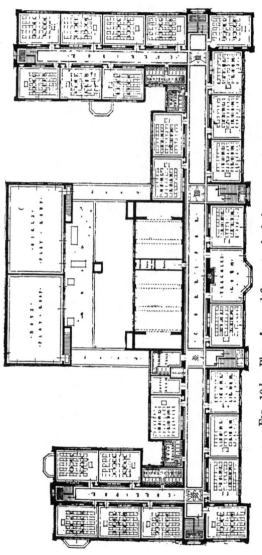

Fig. 10 b. Plan of second floor, standard elementary school.

Fig. 11. A modern standard elementary school.

tion from the business point of view. New buildings, better equipment, and better trained teachers the public accept as desirable, but it has also a deep-rooted suspicion that "professors" are poor business men, and that the money now appropriated could easily be more wisely and efficiently spent. For this reason, in many American cities, two separate departments have been created by the school board, one to deal with the educational administration of the schools, the other to handle all financial and business matters. However, trials of such a plan have not been wholly successful. For the efficient, smooth running of a great business there can be but one responsible head, but one fundamental policy. It seems clear that the ultimate solution of the problem of financing public education must await the coming of the school superintendent who is both a trained business man and a trained and scholarly educator.

An interesting illustration of the efficacy of sound business methods in education is afforded by the action of the new

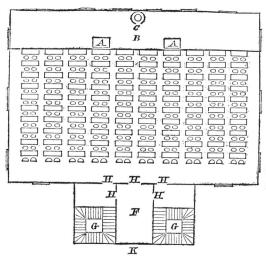

FIG. 12 *a*.   Plan of second story of Wells School, Boston.   The room is designed to accommodate two hundred pupils.   Pupils' desks are double. *A*, *A*, teachers' desks; *B*, platform; *C*, stove; *K*, porch; *G*, *G*, flights of stairs; *F*, small ante-room; *H*, *H*, *H*, *H*, *H*, doors.

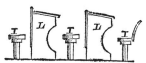

FIG. 12 *b*.   *L*, *L*, end view of pupils' desks; *I*, *I*, *I*, seats.   The seats in the back row are chairs; the others are without any support to the back.

small board of education in Detroit.   Among the members were a railroad president and the auditor of a large electric light and power company.   The mayor of the city was the ex-business manager of a manufacturing company.   The table on page 144 and the graph on page 145 tell an interesting story when properly interpreted.   The table gives the annual appropriation for education in Detroit for the period

STANDARD INTERMEDIATE SCHOOL SPECIFICATIONS

First Floor

1 Machine Shop, 52' x 22'.
1 General Shop, 47' 6" x 22'.
1 Electrical Shop, 38' 6" x 22'.
1 Print Shop, 18' 6" x 22'.
1 Gas Engine Shop (separate building), 65' x 28'.
1 Manual Training Room (wood shop), 52' x 22'.
2 Boys' Toilets.
1 Girls' Toilet.
1 Boys' Showers and Lockers, 80' x 34'.
1 Girls' Showers and Lockers, 80' x 68'.
1 Boys' Plunge, 20' x 45'.
1 Girls' Plunge, 20' x 45'.
1 Boiler Room.
4 Men and Women Teachers' Locker Rooms.
8 Class Rooms, 26' x 22'.
1 Men's Club Room, 54' x 22'.
1 Women's Club Room, 54' x 22'.
1 Medical Dept., 26' x 22' { Dentist / Doctor, 3 separate offices / Nurse
1 Auditorium, 49' x 79'.
2 Storage Rooms.
600 Lockers in Halls.
2 Covered Play Courts, 43' 6" x 49' 6" each.

Second Floor

1 Mechanical Drawing Room, 43' x 22'.
3 Science Rooms, 35' x 22'.
1 Boys' Toilet.
2 Girls' Toilets.
6 Class Rooms, 25' 6" x 21' 6".

1 Teachers' Work Room, 52' 6" x 37'.
1 Administration Dept., 53' x 22' (8 small separate offices for department heads and principals).
2 Student Rooms.
2 Physical Directors' Dept.
1 Boys' Gymnasium, 51' x 80'.
1 Girls' Gymnasium, 51' x 80'.
2 Covered Play Courts, 42' x 50'.
2 Art and Design Rooms, 35' x 22'.
1 Sewing Room, 43' x 22'.
1 Millinery Room, 52' 6" x 22'.
550 Lockers in Halls.

Third Floor

1 Lunch Room, 61' x 62'.
1 Kitchen, 24' 6" x 17'.
2 Cooking Rooms, 43' 6" x 22'.
1 Home Science Room, 21' x 17'.
1 Model Suite, 26' 6" x 22'.
2 Music Rooms, 25' 6" x 22'.
1 Boys' Toilet.
2 Girls' Toilets.
1 Boys' Corrective Gymnasium, 45' x 16'.
1 Girls' Corrective Gymnasium, 44' x 16'.
8 Class Rooms.
8 Consultation Rooms.
1 Library, 50' x 95'.
1 Bookkeeping Room, 39' x 22'.
1 Typewriting Room, 25' 6" x 22'.

Fourth Floor

1 Boy Scout Room, 136' x 24'.

the new board has been in existence and for an equal period of years before the new board took hold.

The first two years of the new régime were spent in becoming familiar with the problem, and many were the stormy sessions held. Detroit had been no better, no worse, than many other American cities. Budgets had been prepared " by guess and by gosh " and cut and passed by the estimators on the same basis. The new board objected and demanded supporting facts. A scientific budget procedure was set up. Not only were the facts secured and used in preparing the budget, but they were put to good use in convincing the appropriating bodies that the budget should be passed. The increases obtained are the more remarkable in that during the same period enormous sums were also spent for new sewers, the building and purchase of municipal street-car lines, and many other civic-improvement projects. However, the gross figures in dollars and cents tell but a small part of the story. Not only have much larger amounts than ever before been secured from the public, not only have far-reaching policies been initiated and a stupendous building program been carried through successfully, but internal reorganizations and adjustments have increased both the value received for money expended, and the more equitable distribution of loads within the system. A new and adequate system of records insures that each year the superintendent's report to the board will account for what has been done with children, supplies, and money, in an objective and understandable fashion; that costs by schools, departments, and subjects shall enable a superintendent to follow intelligently the actual workings of the system and detect and remedy weaknesses and defects before they do serious harm. In a general account of this character, details cannot be given. A comparison of the 1922 superintendent's report with those of ten years ago

Financial Growth of Detroit, and Increase in Money Raised for Education for the Five Years Preceding and Following the Adoption of the Small Board

Year	Total Assessed Valuation	Total City Budget	Total Tax for Education	% Education is of Total Budget	Total Bonds for Buildings and Grounds	Total for Education
1912	456,816,100	9,014,654	2,086,210	23%	585,453	2,671,663
1913	491,324,120	9,877,183	2,223,650	22	823,827	3,047,477
1914	525,856,500	10,267,999	2,578,510	25	1,790,751	4,369,261
1915	558,943,950	13,106,187	2,876,609	22	1,333,485	4,210,094
1916	736,552,960	13,494,144	3,250,919	25	2,226,889	5,477,808
1917	1,176,517,900	16,218,778	3,803,672	21	1,897,624	5,701,296
1918	1,237,238,500	22,010,134	6,137,468	23	*	6,137,468
1919	1,357,971,110	25,086,358	7,442,226	30	*	7,442,226
1920	1,699,149,580	35,086,358	7,904,874	22	2,921,613	10,806,487
1921	1,854,053,580	40,164,706	11,359,967	27	9,172,576	21,532,543

* War years, building operations suspended.

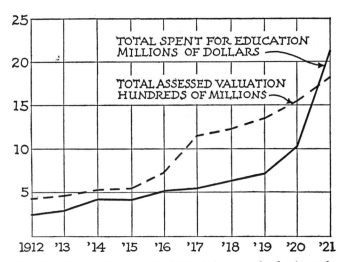

FIG. 13.   Comparative growth of Detroit in assessed valuation and
money spent for education.

will furnish the evidence of the workings of the newer methods, if such is needed. Nor must it be imagined that the
experience of Detroit in these matters is exceptional. In
city after city, the country over, similar attention to the
statistical and financial aspects of educational administration are leading to increased appropriations and to increased
administrative efficiency. The general movement is one
of the marked tendencies of the times. Nothing comparable
to it can be found in 1845, in spite of the proud boast of the
School Committee that Boston spent more money for free
education than any other municipality in the world.

9. **Publicity.** Perhaps no tendency in modern education
is in more marked contrast with the policies of 1845 than
the efforts now made by schoolmen everywhere to keep the
public informed as to what the schools are doing. In the
old days schools followed, they did not lead. In many a

city there have been times when even a parent must secure a special permit before he could enter a school building on a visit of inspection. The reaction of the Boston school masters of 1845 to the criticisms of Horace Mann and their resistance to the inspection of even the duly appointed school committee show quite a different attitude from that implied in the 1922 proclamation of the President of the United States, of a national school week in which parents are urged to visit and inspect the schools. Today, school boards and superintendents not only gladly avail themselves of the public press to keep the taxpayers informed as to the activities and state of the schools; they consciously organize various forms of publicity campaigns, encourage public education and parent-teacher associations, and seize upon every opportunity to appear before various civic clubs, conventions, and other public gatherings. More and more, school authorities are coming to see themselves as the responsible agents of the people in an undertaking in which the people as a whole are vitally interested, and more and more they are taking pains to render an adequate account of their stewardship. Schools are beginning to lead, not follow. It is already evident that a school system can move forward no faster than it can carry the public with it. A well-organized publicity department is essential to progress. On pages 147–150 there are presented the four pages of a publicity letter used for a time in Detroit.

A visitor from another world, reading the comparisons of 1845 with the present, might feel that all the problems in education had been solved and that the millennium had already arrived. However, all that has gone before seems destined to be but the prelude to further and more profound changes in the future. In spite of the wonderful progress that has been made and in spite of the acceleration in the rate at which it is being made, signs are not wanting

DETROIT PUBLIC SCHOOLS

SUPERINTENDENT'S MONTHLY LETTER

Issued monthly by the authority of the Board of Education, City
of Detroit, for the purpose of acquainting the
people of Detroit with their schools

Address all communications to 1354 Broadway

Vol. 1   NOVEMBER, 1921   No. 2

Everyone Helps

EARLY every morning more than 134,000 bright-eyed children leave their homes to receive instruction in the public schools.

Just a little earlier 4,500 teachers are traveling from different parts of the city to teach these children.

Earlier still 500 engineers and janitors have come to heat and make comfortable the buildings for children and teachers.

More than 100,000 parents also play their part. Children are dressed, fed, and started to school.

The public schools exist for the children.

They form a great and complicated system. Their success depends upon the combined efforts of parents, children, teachers, engineers, and janitors. All have an important part in the making of citizens.

FRANK CODY
Superintendent

147

What the School Provides

IT WILL cost $12,553,532.00 to run the schools this year.

Just what do the parents of Detroit children receive for this money?

The schools are in operation 190 days a year and six hours each day. In addition there are the summer and evening sessions. The total number of instruction hours given to pupils amounts to 144,500,000.

For six hours each day 134,600 children are cared for in regular sessions. During all this time parents are relieved of their care. The Board of Education, in its building program, is attempting to provide clean, well lighted, well heated and ventilated buildings for all of these children.

In addition to being cared for they are taught to work, study, and play together. They are given a chance to learn how to be healthy, how to read, write, and figure, how to make things with tools, and how to use their leisure time. All human progress is brought before them.

Their characters and their ideals are being formed. They are trained for citizenship.

It is costing the citizens of Detroit 8.6 cents an hour for each child for this educational preparation for life.

The Teachers

FORTY-FIVE hundred teachers and principals are required to give Detroit children their schooling.

The teacher's work consists of teaching and preparation for teaching. This means from eight to ten hours of work daily.

More than half of the teachers, 2,848 exactly, have had two years of teacher training and 978 have spent four or more years in fitting themselves for teaching positions.

One-quarter of the teachers have served Detroit nine years or longer. Half of them have served three and one-half years.

Detroit teachers are wide awake. They know that education asks more of them in professional training each year.

They know that the schools will go forward only as teachers increase their training and keep up to date.

Every summer hundreds of them go to school, returning in the fall with fresh ideas and new methods.

For the last two winters more than half of the teachers have spent from one to three evenings each week taking courses that would increase the quality of service they give to the children.

Detroit is fortunate in its teachers. In their eagerness to learn and in their willingness to make personal sacrifice for the sake of education, they are striving to give your children the best education in the country.

Your Investment

IF A MAN invests a large sum of money in a business he will be watchful of how that business is run.

The people of Detroit have invested about $230.00 in land and buildings for every child in school.

There are 197 permanent and 38 temporary buildings.

The people are still spending money to provide places for every child and must continue to do so as long as Detroit grows and its citizens have children.

Seats for about 10,000 new children must be provided yearly.

Many of the present buildings are old and each year become less satisfactory as places in which to teach children.

In addition to providing for growth the Board of Education must replace worn-out buildings.

The success of the schools is your business. Take an active interest in them.

Religion, morality and knowledge being necessary to good
government and the happiness of mankind,
schools and the means of education shall
forever be encouraged.—Ordinance
of 1787.

both that the present efficiency of achievement is very
low and that the lay and professional public are even yet
scarcely more than beginning to awake to the real problems in education. The next few paragraphs will attempt
to array the evidence upon which the foregoing statements
are based and to sketch in vague outline the schools of
tomorrow.

No attempt will be made to review the statistical and
educational data which prove the educational inefficiency of the present order. Survey after survey is
filled with irrefutable evidence that from every point of view
great improvements in our present educational system are
possible. The reader who is not familiar with this literature should review it for himself.[1] Present purposes will
be served by pointing out the bearing of the present study
upon such results. They lead to a twofold inference:
(1) Unsatisfactory as present conditions are, they nevertheless
represent great progress over the past.   (2) In view of this
progress, present conditions are or should be a source of
inspiration rather than of discouragement, for they prove
that the application of new instruments and new methods
of appraisal will yield great returns to those men and women
of vision who attack present conditions with optimistic faith
in the possibility of bringing about still further progress.
The present situation spells opportunity, not discouragement,
to those who read aright. Never have the possibilities in
education been so great or the conditions so favorable for
the achievement of those opportunities. The call to service
should thrill the heart and soul of every worker in the educational field and release the energy and power for great achievement. A new day is dawning and the splendor of the com-

[1] See Report of Committee on School Inquiry, New York City, May,
1912; Salt Lake City Survey, 1915; Cleveland Survey, 1916; Gary Survey, 1917; St. Louis Survey, 1917; and some four or five hundred others.

ing light is dispelling the fogs and mists of the past and revealing the path along which progress is to be sought. The pioneers are already blazing the trail. Let us see where that trail leads.

A significant symptom of the growing esteem in which education is held is the creation of great educational foundations and the private financing of all sorts of educational institutions and experiments. A mere inspection of a list of the larger educational foundations and a consideration of the educational power of the money at their disposal is impressive.

ELEVEN GREAT FOUNDATIONS

NAME	WHEN ORGANIZED	PRODUCTIVE FUNDS
Peabody Education Fund	1867	$ 3,000,000
Slater Fund for Education of Freedmen .	1882	1,000,000
Carnegie Institute	1902	22,000,000
General Education Board	1903	53,000,000
Carnegie Foundation	1906	15,000,000
Russell Sage Foundation	1907	10,000,000
Jeanes Foundation	1908	1,000,000
Commonwealth Fund (Partly educational)		Amount not reported
Cleveland Foundation (Partly educational)	1914	" " "
Juilliard Musical Foundation . . .	1920	15,000,000
Laura Spellman Rockefeller Memorial (Partly educational)		73,875,000

To these must be added many millions of dollars more of special endowment or expenditure, all for the improvement of educational procedure. Disregarding entirely the purely commercial private schools, most of which are able to exist solely because the parents of the children who attend are dissatisfied with public education, there are in the United States more than fifty schools whose avowed purpose is experimental modification of existing procedures, with a view to working out practical ways of bettering the educational product. Nor is the movement confined to America alone. It is world wide. " New experimental schools are found in Germany, France, England, China, India, and wherever the drive of our present unrest and confusion has made itself felt." [1] Some of these experiments represent extreme and bizarre modifications of the conventional school, but for the most part, especially in the United States, the goal is a reasonable, scientific experimentation. The following statement from the catalogue of the Lincoln School of Teachers College, Columbia University, is typical of the aim of the movement:

PURPOSE

There is a widespread conviction that education can be improved through the use of critical and experimental methods. The ordinary curriculum, though it already contains a considerable amount of new material derived from modern activities, still retains much that is of doubtful value. Moreover, even under relatively favorable conditions, pupils do not satisfactorily master this material, old or new. Several problems are thus presented: first, how much of the traditional material has actual educational value in modern schools; second, what new materials should be introduced into the schools and how can they be prepared for school use; and, third, how can teaching methods be made more efficient and more economical? Many teachers in various parts of the country are trying to solve these problems, but they are for the most part simultaneously carrying a heavy teaching or administrative routine, so that they are not free to devote themselves to new educational tasks. They lack the time; they lack the strength; the burden of their daily tasks hampers original effort. In the hope, therefore, that a school created for the purpose of attacking such problems may contribute to progressive educational movements, the Lincoln School was established.

In the Lincoln School, the curriculum, since it is in process of development, changes from year to year; but the purpose remains

[1] See Bulletin No. 10, *The New Schools*, by the Progressive Education Association, Washington, D. C.

constant. The aim is to construct a fundamental curriculum which
will be representative of the important activities, interests, and
possibilities of modern life. It is hoped that a balanced combination can be obtained which will include æsthetic, linguistic, social,
industrial, and scientific elements. This is obviously a selective
task. The curriculum cannot be comprehensive in the sense of
containing everything that is important; it can at best select those
fundamental and characteristic activities which are valuable in
themselves and which are likely to encourage the pupil's further
development. From the great range of things worth while the
Lincoln School is thus trying to choose those which promise to be
most effective in developing the pupil's abilities and in bringing
him intelligently into touch with the world in which he lives. It
does not follow that a curriculum of this type when constructed
will necessarily be best for all pupils; but experience with the conventional types of curriculums indicates that a curriculum more
closely related to normal interests and to society's current activities
may effectively serve the needs of large numbers of children.

Although the school is frankly experimental in spirit, purpose,
and method, it adopts as its starting point the best types of approved contemporary practice. In developing from this point,
every precaution is taken, through the use of standard tests and
measures, to secure the best education for each pupil.

Besides subject matter, two other features deserve emphasis.
First, the conditions under which American children grow up
make it very important that they should cultivate self-control and
self-direction. In the hope, therefore, that an effective democratic
discipline may be established, every pupil is given opportunities
to exercise initiative, and at the same time is led to bear the ac-
companying responsibility. Second, American life is not only
individualistic, but coöperative. Every member of a community
must know how to express himself and to take care of himself, but
he must also know how to coördinate his own efforts with those of
his fellows. In school, therefore, the pupil must be made aware
of the needs and responsibilities, not only of himself as an individual,
but also of the student body of which he is a member. To this end
coöperative efforts of various kinds have been encouraged; as-
sembly exercises largely conducted by the pupils have been instituted; boy scouts and girl scouts are given recognized places
in the school activities; a school bank, a school council, a school

employment committee, and a school orchestra have been organized, and school publications are issued.

The school is, therefore, something more than a curriculum made up of modern studies taught in a modern spirit; it is a society of which the pupils are responsible members. The goal is the physical, intellectual, moral, and social training of each pupil.

Generalization based upon the characteristics shown by the experimental schools yield the following statement of tendencies:

(1) The schools of the future will pay far more attention to individuals than the schools of the past. Each child will be studied and measured repeatedly from many angles, both as a basis of prescriptions for treatment and as a means of controlling development. The new education will be scientific in that it will rest on a fact basis. All development of knowledge and skill will be individualized, and classroom practice and recitation as they exist today in conventional schools will largely disappear. The motive for this type of learning will come from the social activities of the pupils both within and outside the school.

(2) On the other hand, the organization and life of the school will be concerned mainly with a series of social activities directed toward the achievement of childish goals as directly related to childish purposes and interests, as the goals of adults are to theirs. There will be only incidental learning from these activities in the sense in which the term has been used in the past, but there will be more important products in terms of interpretation of life experiences, development of initiative, of creative and executive power, of understanding of moral and social relationships, and of learning to live and work on a rational basis as coöperating and responsible members of a social group. Subject matter organized merely as such will almost completely disappear, except for the minimum essentials of knowledge and skill.

Labor on a production basis as opposed to a learning basis will also form a part of each day's program at each level of maturity.

(3) The grade organization and ideas of grade standards will undergo fundamental modifications. Promotion, graduation, and much of the present organization of school and classroom procedure will function differently. The school will become a miniature democratic community, in which right living will be the chief " subject " of instruction. There will be development from one level of ability to another, and promotion from one task to the next highest, but no failures, no lockstep, no restricting classifications. Whatever progress the child makes will be thorough, but at a rate natural to his ability and effort. Levels of development of knowledge and skill will be more objectively and scientifically defined than they ever have been, but it will be by small units of accomplishment and not by whole grades. Individuals will do such work as is most required for their own development. The individual himself, as he matures, will have an ever enlarging share, under guidance, in choosing his activities and taking charge of his own education.

(4) An accompaniment of changed organization and increased attention to individuals will be adequate provision for the optimum educational opportunity for each person. The result of this for children now considered handicapped will be to increase their usefulness and happiness; and at the other extreme the larger capacity of the specially gifted will likewise have its full measure of opportunity.

(5) Some of the experimental schools are country boarding schools, but it is difficult to see how such provisions, desirable as they are, can be made for all children. Indeed, the home needs to be brought more closely into coöperation in the work of education. On the other hand, the necessity for the schools taking over some phases of the parental care

which in the past has been exercised in the home, grows daily more evident. The school today is much more concerned about the health of children than formerly. Medical and dental inspection and care are increasing. More time is spent in health training in school. But no child can be made and kept healthy unless his eating, sleeping, and cleanliness are controlled. Public feeding of children who need it is already an accomplished fact in many cities. School regulations affect home life more every day. The development of the day nursery and the kindergarten or infant school point in the same direction. It seems probable that the schools of the future will control the life of the child more completely than at present and from an earlier age.

(6) The teachers in the schools of tomorrow will be much better trained and correspondingly better paid than those in our present schools. The improvement will be along three main lines: (1) Intellectual. Much greater demands will be made upon teachers professionally than at present. Teaching will be creative, artistic work. (2) Technical. Much greater knowledge of educational science and technique will be necessary. Teachers will need to be thoroughgoing scientists. (3) Cultural. Much greater familiarity with world affairs will be called for. The most important function of education is the interpretation of life and the development of character and spirit. The teacher of the future, at least the controlling masters of education, will need to be persons of broad vision, true leaders in their communities.

Teachers of greater skill, paid larger salaries than at present, will be assigned to those who are beginning their school careers. Much more attention than now will be given to starting children right, and many of our present-day problems will be solved in the kindergarten and early school years.

In the light of recent legislation it seems possible that teachers of the future will be examined as to their social and civic orthodoxy before they are licensed to teach. All schools of whatever character or type are likely to come under public control and supervision. On the other hand, the need for experimental variation will be as fully recognized as the need for standardization, and provision will be made for every reasonable type of experimentation, under conditions which will make for scientific appraisal of the results secured. Scientific research and experimentation will be the recognized source of progress.

One logical consequence of the increasing tendency to demand social and civic orthodoxy of teachers should be the representation of the educational forces of a community on state and legislative bodies. When social education along lines now being attempted in many schools has become general and effective, many of the present problems of government will have been solved. Also, when the schools lead society instead of following, the solutions of many social problems of the day will be worked out in the classroom. One prophet of the future has suggested that government as we now know it will ultimately disappear, to be replaced by a form of organization in which the educational forces will play a determining part. Certain it is that the present educational emphasis upon civic problems is destined to have the most profound and far-reaching consequences upon social life.

(7) From the point of view of organization and administration, the schools of tomorrow are apparently to be more democratic than those of today. The growth of teachers' associations and councils, the demand for teacher representation on board and staff organizations, all point the way toward a new order. It is too soon to tell what these symptoms portend. In general, it is probable that executive

power will pass from one man to a council of experts representing all the interests involved.   The business of education
in the larger units has grown to too stupendous proportions
and has become of too great importance for any one person
to direct it all intelligently, however good his intentions or
great his ability.   It should be emphasized that this problem
is a general social problem, common to all forms of human
endeavor.   It may be solved first in education and the solution spread by means of the schools to industry and politics.

(8) A highly important sign of the times is the increasing
emphasis on adult education.   Its significance lies first in
the proof that society has changed its conception of what
education is, and second, in the possibilities of the development of education which the new conception creates.   In
the past, education was preparation for life.   It was primarily for children.   It terminated at a given time.   The
newer idea of education is that it is an aid to living, a necessity as long as life endures, a never ending activity, a part
of living.   The tremendous and steadily increasing extensions of human knowledge have made a continuous education
along certain elemental lines necessary for even the day
laborer or factory hand.   Industry itself these days maintains schools and expends large sums in the continued education of both its managerial staff and its labor.   Hundreds
of commercial schools and enterprises minister to adults,
while the increasing use of libraries and museums, the development of special columns in our press and magazines, conventions, clubs, and other gatherings of specialists to discuss
the vital problems of their craft, all tell the same story of
increasing appreciation of education by adults.   In the meantime, evening schools for adults, continuation schools, part-
time classes, extension courses, are increasing at an amazing
rate.   Is it too much to predict that in a city like Detroit,
with 750,000 adults and only 250,000 children, adult educa-

tion will in time become the chief division of educational work and child education a minor phase? The increasing cost of the present duplication of informal and unorganized adult educational effort, as well as its gross inefficiency, will in time force all such activities into the hands of school authorities.

As a nation America prides itself on the value it places on free, universal education, but in this, as in so many things, the founders of our country builded better than they knew and better than any except a very few have begun to realize. The backward look from the present to 1845, a survey of the present tendencies in social and educational life, and a very superficial following of those same tendencies to their logical conclusions will cause many to realize how crude and short-sighted all our thinking and planning have been. We have lived from day to day, from hour to hour, we have taken this step or that, not always because of intelligent reasoning and capable planning, but often under the drive of the vision of some heroic soul like Horace Mann, not knowing to what ultimate goal our steps were tending. In the past, progress has been along a winding path, a constant compromise between the desirable and the immediately expedient. We have made progress, great progress, greater even than we have realized, but the future calls for still more strenuous efforts, for greater advances, for more direct progress since the goals are more clearly seen. The contribution of the past to the present is a clearer vision of the possibilities of the future.

APPENDIX ONE

REPORT OF GRAMMAR SCHOOL COMMITTEE

This report is reprinted in full in order that the data and discussions may be available to all who read *Then and Now in Education*.

REPORTS

OF THE

ANNUAL VISITING COMMITTEES

OF THE

PUBLIC SCHOOLS

OF THE

CITY OF BOSTON

1845.

BOSTON

J. H. EASTBURN, CITY PRINTER

1845.

CITY OF BOSTON

In School Committee, September 11, 1845.

Ordered, That ten thousand copies of the Reports of the Annual Examining Committees, be printed for distribution among the citizens.

Resolved, That in ordering the Reports on the Grammar and Writing Schools to be printed and distributed, this Board are not to be understood as adopting or rejecting the views therein contained, or expressing any opinion respecting them. And that this resolution be printed with the Report.

A true copy.

Attest,   S. F. McCleary, Secretary.

REPORT

Of the

SUB–COMMITTEE OF THE LATIN SCHOOL

Made August 5, 1845.

To the School Committee of Boston.

The Sub-Committee of the Latin School, respectfully report that they examined said School on the 24th ultimo, and found it in its usual good condition.

The whole number of pupils was 139.

Average attendance in July,   126.

EDWARD WIGGLESWORTH,
WILLIAM HAGUE,
THEOPHILUS PARSONS,
J. I. T. COOLIDGE.

Boston, August 5, 1845.

REPORT

Of the

SUB–COMMITTEE OF THE ENGLISH HIGH SCHOOL,

Made August 5, 1845.

The Sub-Committee of the English High School, respectfully report,

That they visited the School on four different days in the month of July, for the purpose of making the Quarterly and Annual Examinations. They examined the School in its several departments, and were impressed with the thoroughness and accuracy manifested by the scholars generally in their various studies. In Algebra and Geometry, especially, there was great proficiency, and the only thing in which there appeared any deficiency was the pronunciation of the French language, entire accuracy in which can of course be obtained only from a French teacher. The result of the examination has satisfied the Committee that the School maintains the high character which it has long held; and although they are far from intimating that there is no further room for improvement, they are fully of the opinion that this Board and the Public have no reason to be dissatisfied with its present condition.

All which is respectfully submitted.

ALEXANDER YOUNG,
AURELIUS D. PARKER,
WINSLOW LEWIS,
SAMUEL G. HOWE,
EZRA PALMER, JR.

Boston, August 4th, 1845.

CITY OF BOSTON

In School Committee, May 6, 1845.

Ordered, That Messrs. Parsons, Howe, and Neale be a Committee to make the annual examination of the several Grammar Schools, and report at the quarterly meeting in August.

Attest,   S. F. McCLEARY, Secretary.

To the School Committee of the City of Boston.

Gentlemen:

Your Sub-Committee, appointed for the purpose of making the Annual Examinations in the Grammar Department of all the Schools, have attended to their duty, and submit the following

REPORT:

A single glance at the nature of the work assigned to us, shows its extent and importance. There are nineteen Public Grammar and Writing Schools in the City of Boston; sixteen being divided into two parts, with two masters independent of and unconnected with each other; and three others, the Lyman School at East Boston, the New South in the extreme southern section of the City, and the Smith School, set apart for the instruction of colored children, being organized as single Schools, with but one master, who superintends the writing, as well as the grammar department.

It has long been the custom to appoint an Annual Committee to visit and examine the Writing Department in all these Schools, and another to visit and examine the Grammar Department, and for each to make a separate report. It was, however, found to be impossible to do any thing like justice on the examination, for Committee-men could not be found who could give the time necessary to examine over 7,000 children. A few years ago it was ordered, that the Annual Committee might limit their examination to the first class in each School; and it was under this order that your Committee was appointed. But although we were to examine only the first class in nineteen schools, still the task was a very difficult one, for we were expected to judge of the real and comparative merits of the whole School; because long custom, — the common law of the Committee, — required us to attend to many points of inquiry not especially named in the order.

The School Committee has no way of obtaining a condensed and comparative view of the condition of all the Schools, except through the Reports of its Annual Committees; and it does not obtain these until more than half the year for which it is chosen has expired. It was in view of the great importance of the subject, that your Committee, anxious to do all that could possibly be done towards a thorough and satisfactory examination of the Schools, resolved to adopt, in addition to the usual mode of oral examination, the plan of submitting to the scholars a series of printed questions on all the subjects studied in the Schools. These questions were so graduated that the simpler could be understood and answered by any children of common sense and ordinary attainments, while the more difficult would tax the powers of the best of our scholars without being quite beyond them. For instance, in Geography, the first question was, What are the principal lakes in North America? Another was, Upon which range of mountains is the line of perpetual snow most elevated above the ocean; the Rocky Mountains of North America, or the Cordilleras of Mexico?

Most of the questions might be answered by children who are familiar with the text-books used in our Schools; all of them by children to whom those text-books had been fully and familiarly explained by good teachers.

It was our wish to have as fair an examination as possible; to give the same advantages to all; to prevent leading questions; to carry away, not loose notes, or vague remembrances of the examination, but positive information, in black and white; to ascertain with certainty, what the scholars did not know, as well as what they did know; to test their readiness at expressing their ideas upon paper; to have positive and undeniable evidence of their ability or inability to construct sentences grammatically, to punctuate them, and to spell the words. One of the papers prepared was a list of words to be defined, all of them taken from the reading book used in the class; another was a set of questions upon Geography; another upon Grammar; one upon Civil History; one upon Natural Philosophy; one upon Astronomy; one upon Whately's Rhetoric, and one upon Smellie's Philosophy.

No School had studied Smellie, or Whately, and therefore none could be examined in these; * fifteen declined to be questioned on

* These studies are permitted, but not required.

Astronomy, six upon Natural Philosophy, and two upon History; all of the Schools were examined in Geography, English Grammar, and Definitions.

Our plan of proceeding was as follows. In order to prevent the children of one School from having an advantage over those of another by ascertaining what the questions were to be, they were privately prepared and printed; then, without any previous notice, each member of the Committee commenced at 8 o'clock in the morning with one School, and spread before the first division of the first class the printed questions in geography. The maps and books were put out of the way; the scholars were placed at a distance from each other, so as to prevent communication by whispers; they were told that they would have one hour to answer the questions, and that they should not lose time in trying to write handsomely, as the chirography would not be taken into account. Then they were set to work. Notwithstanding all that was said about their being taken by surprise, about their being unused to such a mode of questioning, about their inability to express what they knew in so short a time, we found that in a few minutes they were all busily at work; all adapted themselves to their new circumstances with that readiness which characterizes our countrymen, without embarrassment, and, generally, they had exhausted their power to answer before the hour expired.

At the end of the hour, the Committee-man gathered up his papers, and went as quickly as possible to the next School, remained there an hour, and then proceeded to a third. After the noon intermission, the Committee commenced again and visited three more Schools; thus each Committee-man finished the examination in geography of six Schools, and the three finished all the Schools in the City. The next day we took the questions on another subject, and thus finished the whole.

We were sorry to feel obliged to adopt these and other precautions, which seemed to imply a suspicion upon our part, that attempts might be made by individuals to defeat the object of the examination, and to take an unfair advantage of any knowledge which might be obtained of the nature of the questions; and we are still more sorry to say, that the result has proved those precautions to have been necessary, though not exactly for the reasons we had anticipated. During the noon intermission, the boys, for instance, who attended a School which had been examined, may possibly have communicated to their playmates, who attended a

School which had not been examined, some of the words which were to be defined. This may have occurred in a very few instances, and might have been generally the case had we allowed a night to intervene. But boys are generally honest, and careless too; and perhaps not ten availed themselves of the knowledge so gained. We were pained, however, to find, that, though many of the masters cooperated with us, some did not.

We extended our examination into some of the Schools in the neighboring towns and states, and gained much useful information from them. But we include only the Dudley School in Roxbury among our returns. We examined this first, and were certain that neither master nor scholars knew any thing beforehand of our questions. Of those examined afterwards, there was some doubt, and we therefore omit them.

With regard to the Schools in the City proper, we believe, that upon no one subject except definitions, was a knowledge of the questions obtained by the scholars of any School previously to their being presented by the Committee; and even in regard to definitions, very little advantage was gained by any one School. Fraud ever carries a suspicious front; the natural language of a cheat can be detected even in his mode of writing; and the unfairness in one School was discovered by a glance at the written answers. But in almost every set of answers obtained from the Schools, there is internal evidence of honesty; — honest ignorance, and honest error, as well as honest accuracy. Those masters, or others, who may attempt to undervalue the accuracy or importance of these returns, for the sake of saving the character of particular Schools, will sink all the Schools low indeed; for if, with the aid of a previous knowledge of the questions, the answers are so very unsatisfactory, what must they have been if no one had meddled with a trial which was designed as a fair one, and which certainly was as fair for one school as for another?

But we repeat the assertion, that, to the best of our knowledge and belief, the statistical returns which we submit will present the fullest and the fairest means for judging of the real merits and de-merits of our Schools, and of their comparative rank, which have ever been embodied so as to be within the reach of any but actual examiners of the Schools. We may say this safely, because it is perhaps the only statistical information which has ever been so em-bodied.

We may remark here that there were, in some of our lists of

printed questions, typographical errors of spelling, punctuation and
grammar, which were discovered too late for correction; and that
in many Schools the scholars were directed to correct such errors,
as a part of their exercise.

We now proceed to consider the statistical returns.

The first feeling occasioned by looking over these returns is that
of entire incredulity. It is very difficult to believe that, in the
Boston Schools, there should be so many children in the first classes,
unable to answer such questions; that there should be so many
who try to answer, and answer imperfectly; that there should be
so many absurd answers; so many errors in spelling, in grammar,
and in punctuation. If by any accident these documents should
be destroyed, we could hardly hope that your faith in our accuracy
would induce you to believe the truth if we told it. But the papers
are all before you, each signed by the scholar who wrote it.

The whole number of pupils present in the Schools on the days
when we examined, was 7526; the whole number offered for examination, — a number comprising the flower of the Boston Public
Schools, — was 530; their average age is about thirteen years,
six months.* The whole number of questions put to them

In Geography, — was 31
Definitions, ... 28
Grammar, ... 14
History, ... 30
Natural Philosophy, ... 20
Astronomy, ... 31
Making a total of 154 questions.   154

To these there should have been 57,873 answers, if each scholar
had been able to answer; but there were only 31,159, of which only
17,216 were correct in sense, leaving unanswered 26,714. The
31,159 answers contained 2,801 errors in grammar; 3,733 errors
in spelling; and 35,947 errors in punctuation. Some of the errors
in punctuation were of no great consequence; for instance, in enumerating the rivers or lakes of a country, the scholars often omitted
to put commas between the names; and a large proportion of the
errors arose, doubtless from mere haste. But punctuation is

* In the Girls' Schools, the average age of the scholars examined is about
14 years.

very much a matter of habit, and if the children had been accustomed to punctuate carefully, they would not have failed so egregiously.

These results are surprising, when it is considered that the answers were very short — some merely an affirmation or a negation in one word. They would, however, have been more so, had we rigidly adhered to the rules of criticism, and set down every answer as incorrect which was not faultless; but we have put the most lenient construction upon the answers, and whenever it appeared that the scholar had any tolerable idea of the subject, we have recorded his answer as correct. If we had put down as correct only those answers which were perfect in regard to sense, to grammatical construction, to spelling and to punctuation, the record would have been very short.

But no generalization of this kind can give an idea of the true state of the case; let us therefore descend to particulars, and take up each subject; and first that of Geography.

There were 31 questions, — some very simple, some rather difficult, — but not one which well-taught children, of fourteen years of age, should not answer. To these questions, which were put to 487 children of our first classes, there should have been 15,097 answers; but 5,233 were not answered at all; 4,671 were answered incorrectly, and only 5,193, — or about one third of the whole number, — were answered correctly; while the answers contained 63 errors in grammar, 1,759 errors in spelling, and 14,025 in punctuation.

The careful observer will learn, by looking over our tables, the general system of instruction pursued in our schools; namely, that of verbal or book knowledge; and by comparing one School with another, he will see what masters vary most from the usual routine, and teach most thoroughly. Generally speaking, the questions which would be asked by one who teaches from books, as the names of the principal lakes, rivers, etc., are answered correctly; but take such a question as this, Do the waters of Lake Erie run into Lake Ontario, or those of Ontario into Erie? — and 287 answer correctly, while 130 answer incorrectly. Now, if we take into consideration what is unquestionably true, that many of those who did not know, answered by guess, and that they were just as likely to guess right as wrong, much the largest proportion of our best scholars could not tell which way the waters run, in spite of all the fame of Niagara!

To the question: What is the general course of rivers in North
and South Carolina; and in Tennessee and Kentucky? — pretty
correct answers were given; but to the next question: What is the
reason that the waters of these four contiguous states run in opposite directions? — only 128 showed by their answers that they
had ever thought of the reason; 308 did not answer at all; and of
the 51 incorrect answers, most were as vague as the reply of one
scholar, who said, that these waters run in opposite directions because it was the will of God!

To the question, What is meant by the line of perpetual snow, —
only five per cent of correct answers was given; and to the question, Upon which range of mountains is the line of snow most
elevated above the ocean, the Rocky Mountains of North America,
or the Cordilleras of Mexico? — only nineteen per cent answered
correctly, notwithstanding it is a question with which guessers
were as likely to go right as to go wrong.

The highest percentage of correct answers, in geography, in the
Boston Schools, was forty-six per cent, in the Winthrop School.
The lowest, excluding the Smith, was eighteen per cent in the
Otis. The percentage in the Dudley School,* Roxbury, was
fifty-five.

The verbal examination which followed in geography, confirmed
the opinion which would be drawn from the answers to the printed
questions. In a few schools, the children seem to have been taught
orally, and upon correct principles; but generally they were lost
when taken out of the common routine of questions. They could
bound states and countries; name capitals, capes, and mountains;
enumerate rivers, lakes, and bays; and answer a series of questions
put by the master, of half an hour's duration; but, questioned as
to the drainage of countries, their capacities for commerce, the
causes which direct streams and determine the force of water, —
their want of comprehension of these and similar subjects, showed
plainly, in almost every school, that they had learned geography
as if it were only a catalogue of names of all the divisions of
water, from ponds up to oceans; of land, from towns to
empires.

In reviewing the answers to the questions upon History, the same
conclusion presses upon us as on examining the questions on the

---

* We consider the Dudley School a fair sample of the best schools in our
neighborhood.

other subjects. The scholars have, for the most part, learned to recite the words of the text-book, without having had its spirit illustrated, and without having been accustomed to think about the meaning of what they had learned. A list containing thirty questions was submitted to 438 scholars, and certainly there is hardly a question which any child of thirteen, who had studied history, should not answer; nevertheless, instead of the 13,140 answers which should have been given, there were only 5,933; of which only 3,567 were correct; 2,366 were incorrect; and the answers contained 206 errors in grammar, 629 errors in spelling, and 824 in punctuation.

To questions such as these, — What is history? What are some of the sources of history? — the answers were correct and full, because they were in the text-book; but to the questions, What was the period of the Commonwealth in England? and, Who was the most distinguished character in it? only 63 answered correctly; 80 answered incorrectly; and 295 did not answer at all. To the question, At what period was the present federal constitution adopted, during, or after the war of the revolution, and how many States adopted it at its formation? only 139 answered correctly; 190 answered incorrectly; and 109 could not answer it at all.

But the answers to the following questions show most undeniably, that in many schools, nothing but the words of the books are learned, and that these are often learned without understanding their meaning. First came the question, When was the embargo laid by President Jefferson, and when was the non-intercourse act substituted for it? To this many scholars could answer correctly, while they could not answer correctly the question which came soon after, viz.: What is an embargo?

We would here remark, that in judging of the schools by the statistics of answers, care must be taken to compare the number of the class who answered with the total number in the school; as a master who, out of a school of 400, presents a class of 50 for examination, will not have so high a percentage of correct answers as one who presents only 25.

A careful judge will also discriminate between the questions, and award most credit to those schools which give a high percentage of correct answers upon questions involving principles rather than facts. This will be illustrated by comparing the answers of some schools to the two preceding questions. In one school, the Adams,

15 out of 20 answered correctly as to the date of the embargo, while only one of them could tell what an embargo meant.   In another, the Hawes, 13 out of 17 knew about the date of the fact, but only 4 could tell what the fact was, — what the word embargo means — and 6 gave an incorrect definition of it.

On the other hand, in the Bowdoin School, only 15 out of 42 knew when the embargo was laid; but 29 out of the 42 defined it correctly.   In the Brimmer School, where 6 knew the date of the embargo, 13 could define it correctly.

Now this is a case illustrative of that to which we shall often allude; — the practice of teaching the name of the thing rather than the nature of the thing.   It is worth positively nothing to know the date of an embargo, if one does not know what an embargo is.   Nay, it may be worse than nothing, because some erroneous idea will be attached to it, as must be the case in the minds of those scholars who defined embargo to be "a duty."

In history, the written answers show the Adams school to be highest, having a percentage of 59 of correct answers; and the next to be the Bowdoin which has a percentage of 48.   The lowest is the Phillips, which has only 8 per cent of correct answers, and the next above it is the Otis, which has 9 per cent.   The Dudley School in Roxbury has a percentage of 42.

In the oral examination which followed, the scholars generally did better, and it is probable that there is more of oral explanation in this branch than in any other.

But the most striking results are shown in the attempts to give definitions of words.

There were twenty-eight words selected from the reading book, which the classes have probably read through during the year, and some probably more than once.   Some of these words are the very titles or headings of reading lessons; some of them occur several times in the book; and yet, of the 516 children who had these questions before them, one hour, not a single one defined correctly every word; only 47 defined half of them; and 39 could not define correctly a single one of the whole 28 words.   It is true that some of the words are not in common use, and are what are called "hard words," but these are the very kind of words which should be explained to our upper classes; — as for the easy words, they learn them in conversation.   Take the word "infatuated;" this is not a rare or an uncommon or a difficult word; nevertheless, only 62 out of 516 children answered it with any correctness.

"Panegyric" is not a very uncommon word, yet only 87 out of 516 answered it correctly; while the approximations of many, as calling it a "strong medicine," "a universal medicine," etc. showed how they were misled by the resemblance of the word to other words.

"Misnomer" is not a very uncommon word, yet only 160 out of 516 defined it with any correctness.

Some of the answers are so supremely absurd and ridiculous, that one might suspect the boys of attempting to jest with the Committee, were it not that there are marks of honest attempts to trace analogies between words which they did know and words which they did not. Many of the children were probably set upon the chase after their meanings for the first time, and it was not strange if they should make great mistakes.

People may think that it is unreasonable to expect children to define such words as "Thanatopsis," and a few others which will be seen in the tables in the appendix; and masters may say they have explained the word, but their scholars cannot remember it. But here is a very important principle in question. The masters wish to have their children pronounce correctly every word in the Reader; they tax the memory of their pupils, and it yields every thing that is demanded; the scholars will not fail to remember how the eleven letters should be pronounced when so arranged as to make t h a n a t o p s i s; they would expect an instant rebuke if they hesitated at it or mispronounced it. Now if the memory suffices to recall the sound, why should it fail to recall the meaning? Will any one say that it is easier to remember the exact pronunciation of French or German words, than their meaning? Or can any one explain why 86 per cent of the scholars in one School, the Bowdoin, should define the word correctly, while not one pupil in three other Schools, (Mather, Phillips, and Smith,) and not 26 per cent in half a dozen other Schools, could define it correctly, without admitting what we have stated elsewhere — that the powers of the pupils are taxed in their greatest effort in those branches of study in which they are most likely to make a show.

But waiving all reasoning, we admit that Thanatopsis, (like some other words selected,) is a rare and difficult one, and it would not have been chosen, were it not the heading of one of the lessons in the Reader, and the name prefixed to one of the most beautiful gems in the whole collection of American poetry.

The Eliot School (the highest) gives 55 per cent of correct an-

swers; the Phillips School (the lowest) gives 8 per cent; the Dudley *
School gives 45 per cent.

Eleven Schools were examined in Natural Philosophy. The first
division of the first class in these Schools, we gave printed papers,
containing twenty very simple questions, and required answers to
as many of them as could be written down in one hour.

As a general thing, the answers are better than in the other
branches, as might be expected, for the subject is one which is in itself very interesting, and it almost necessarily requires the masters
to seek for illustrations out of the text-book. But even here there is
too much teaching by rote, as will be seen by the tables. To the
question: What do you understand by the centre of gravity of
bodies? — 195 out of the 279 answered correctly. To the next:
Define momentum, — 133 out of the 279 answered correctly. But
to the question: If a grindstone should suddenly split in pieces
while whirling rapidly around, would the pieces fall directly to the
ground or not? — only 63 out of the 279 answered correctly; and
to the simple question, which involves an important principle:
Whether a pound of water occupies most space when liquid or when
in the state of ice? — 151 out of the 279 answered wrong, and 55
answered not at all.

In natural philosophy the highest percentage is in the Bowdoin
School, 36 per cent; the lowest in the Johnson School, 12 per cent;
the Dudley School gave 36 per cent.

The last subject was that of Astronomy, in which thirty-one
questions were put; varying from those of the simplest nature,
such as, — What is the radius of a circle? — up to questions about
tides, change of seasons, etc.

In only four out of the nineteen Schools had astronomy been
studied. In these 104 scholars were offered for examination.

The same peculiarities were observed here as in the other studies,
— a more familiar acquaintance with the text-books than with the
principles involved, — although a remarkable deficiency of knowledge, even upon subjects defined in the books and of essential importance, was observable. For instance, not one scholar answered
the question: What is the altitude of a heavenly body? Only six
scholars answered correctly the question: How many times does
the moon revolve about the earth in one year? To this simple

* The Reader from which these words were taken is not used in the Dudley
School.

question : At what angle is the axis of the earth inclined to the plane
of its orbit? — only 10 answered correctly; 19 answered incorrectly, and 75 did not answer at all.   To the comparatively unimportant question of — How many secondary planets are there in
our solar system? — 77 out of the 104 answered correctly; while,
to the question about the causes of the change of the seasons,
only 23 answered correctly, 22 answered incorrectly, and 59 did not
answer at all.

Out of the whole number of questions in astronomy, 977 were
answered correctly, 634 were answered incorrectly, and 1,613 were
not answered at all.   The answers contained 38 errors in spelling,
47 in grammar, and 869 errors in punctuation.

One general inference to be drawn from an examination of these
answers is that it is difficult for our scholars to learn to spell correctly, without being more in the habit of writing than they now are.
Scores and hundreds of errors, of the most palpable kind, have been
committed in their written answers, by children who would spell
the very same words correctly, if they were called up in the usual
way, and had the words pronounced aloud to them.   The principle
is the same as that by which they are trained to read words correctly, which they do not understand.   The visible form of the word
suggests the idea of the audible sound by which it is to be expressed ;
in spelling aloud, the audible sound recalls the visible form, or the
arrangement of the letters ; but if called upon to arrange the letters, or to spell without the aid of the sound, or of the spoken word,
that is, if called upon to write, they are very apt to go wrong.

With regard to Grammar, it is rather more difficult to form a
correct idea of the acquirements of the scholars from the statistics
in our tables than with regard to other studies.

Scholars differ very much from each other, with regard to the
conciseness of their mode of parsing ; and undoubtedly some who
answered only a small percentage of the questions, would have
answered nearly all of them if time enough had been allowed.

The Boston Schools we think would be rated very high in comparison with the best Schools in the world, on the subject of technical parsing.   It would seem impossible for a scholar to take up
a stanza of Childe Harold and parse the words correctly, to perceive, that is, the connection and relations of the words, and yet
fail to feel the force of the metaphors, or to understand the sense
of the whole stanza ; nevertheless, this is done sometimes.   Such is
the power of drilling !   Such is the effect of close attention to the

mere osteology of language; to the bones and articulations, in forgetfulness of the substance that covers, and the spirit that animates them.

The whole number of questions in grammar was 14; — some being merely requisitions to write a simple sentence, containing an active transitive verb and an objective case; and others being sentences which contained false syntax to be corrected.

To such questions as, When do you use a instead of an? What is the difference between an active and a neuter verb? the answers were almost all correct. To the question: What is the difference between an ordinal and numeral adjective? 134 answered correctly and 88 incorrectly; and 234 not at all.

The first sentence which contained false syntax to be corrected, was written out correctly by 138 of the whole number 456; incorrectly by 187, and not at all by 131.

But the answers to the questions in grammar are the best proof that scholars may parse technically, and point out the relations of words, their mood, tense, case, person, number, and gender; and yet, in the very sentences which they make use of to express these relations, and in quoting rules in justification of what they write, be continually making blunders; and may parse their sentences grammatically, in the most ungrammatical language. The whole number of answers given was 4,183, and these contained 962 errors in spelling, 2,247 errors in grammar, and 8,980 errors in punctuation.

The highest percentage of correct answers upon the whole number was in the Adams School, being 61 per cent; the lowest, (saving always the Smith School,) was in the Otis, 15. In the Dudley School it is 51 per cent. It is to be remembered, however, here as elsewhere, that allowance is to be made for the number of the class examined in proportion to the total number in the School; including this element in the calculation, the Adams will not rank so high.

There is one painful reflection forced upon the mind by the answers generally; and this is that while in some Schools the scholars seem to be conscientious, and do not answer questions about which they are ignorant; in others they appear to be perfectly reckless, and put down answers quite at hazard, in the hope of hitting upon something that may pass for an answer. This shows an habitual carelessness in giving answers, or a want of that nicely-trained conscientiousness, which deters from trying to appear what one is not.

There is another sad reflection suggested by these answers. They show beyond all doubt, that a large proportion of the scholars of our first classes, boys and girls of fourteen or fifteen years of age, when called upon to write simple sentences, to express their thoughts on common subjects, without the aid of a dictionary or a master, cannot write, without such errors in grammar, in spelling, and in punctuation, as we should blush to see in a letter from a son or daughter of their age. And most of these children are about finishing their School career; they are going out into life; some to learn trades; some to assist their mothers in the house; the larger part never to receive any supplementary education; and how, we ask, are they, by and by, to write a letter that they would not be ashamed to exhibit?

But there is a still more melancholy consideration, which is, that, if the first class, — if the children who have, during a year, enjoyed that special care and attention which our teachers give to the upper classes, go out imperfectly instructed, what must be the case with the hundreds and thousands of the children of our less-favored citizens, whom necessity forces to leave the schools without even reaching the first class! We know that the value of the services of most of our ushers would be underrated by proportioning it to their salaries; and that great injustice would be done to the many excellent instructresses, by supposing their work, as assistants, to be worth to the scholars only one-sixth the work of the masters, — but, if there be anything like justice in the low rate at which the City remunerates their services, those who receive their instruction alone, must go out from the schools but very poorly taught.

There is, however, in the papers which we lay before the Committee, evidence that such a state of things needs not continue for ever. That evidence is to be found in the papers written by the first classes in our best schools, and especially in those written in some of the neighboring schools, — schools kept at much less expense than our own, — kept by masters not superior to our best ones, and which produce better results, because they have a better organization, and a more effective supervision.

We do not recommend the table of rank which we have prepared, and which is annexed to the appendix, as affording a precise estimate of the merits of the Schools. It is based upon the comparative amount of correct answers given to our questions; and even if it were a perfect demonstration, instead of an approximate estimate of the comparative intellectual acquirement of the scholars, still we would not have it considered as an absolute test of the merits of the schools.   Far be it from us to consider intellectual activity and intellectual acquirement as alone worthy of consideration. Since the world will have it so, let such rewards as medals, prizes, parts, etc., be bestowed upon intellectual strength, as the wreath in olden, and the championship in modern times, have been awarded to mere physical strength; but let us look to the cultivation of the religious sense, the supremacy of conscience, the duty of self-culture, the love of knowledge, the respect for order, — let the presence or absence and measure of these be taken into account, before we say which school is first or which is last.   Upon this we shall not decide, but simply remark that, tried by these standards, some Schools that now stand high would stand low, and some that are not conspicuous would be in the foremost ranks.

Besides this examination by printed questions, the Schools were also visited, and examined, as we have already said, orally.   Putting these two methods together, the following are the results.   But we cannot refrain from saying, that after all the labor we have undergone, we still feel that we have not a complete or perfect knowledge of our Schools, and we give these results only as an approximation to the truth; the nearest that we could reach, and perhaps the nearest that can be reached without a far better supervision than our present system permits.   We wish the following to be regarded only as a comparative view of the Schools, and not as a statement of their absolute worth.

LYMAN SCHOOL, — Mr. Bowker.

This School is rather above the average, in the amount and character of the instruction.   The relations between the master and the pupils seemed to be satisfactory.

ELIOT SCHOOL, — Mr. Sherman.

We found the reading of average quality, but wanting in animation.   The instruction in all the branches appeared to be too technical, and limited to the words of the text-books.   There was a want of life and energy in this School.   The order appeared to be good.

HANCOCK SCHOOL, — Mr. Adams.

The moral tone of this School was very good; but intellectually it scarcely reached the average of girls' Schools. The instruction seemed too much confined to the books. The reading was quite correct, but rather monotonous.

ENDICOTT SCHOOL, — Mr. Allen.

The reading was good. In Geography, the scholars were quite imperfect; no use was made of the globes. The history was confined to that of the United States; but with this, as it stands in the text-book, the scholars were familiar. The grammar was much too technical.

MAYHEW SCHOOL, — Mr. Swan.

There was an appearance of activity and general intelligence in this School. The relations between the master and the scholars seemed to be kindly. In the written examinations, the scholars did not appear so well as in the oral.

BOWDOIN SCHOOL, — Mr. Andrews.

This school we place decidedly at the head of our Schools for girls. The reading was particularly good; clear, distinct and graceful. We could not but notice the excellent relation which seems to subsist between Mr. Andrews and his scholars. It is equally honorable to him and to them; and we think we are justified in attributing to it much of their excellence in all the branches of study. After making all proper allowance for the composition of this School, and for the length of time during which scholars remain in it, it must still rank very high. Some branches are not introduced here which are studied in some other Schools.

BOYLSTON SCHOOL, — Mr. Baker.

Reading not very good; rather careless and inaccurate. The instruction generally too technical, but still above the average. The order among the boys is not very good. Allowance here should be made for the location of the schoolhouse, and for the inconvenience of the edifice; still we must recommend to Mr. Baker a greater attention to discipline. We were pleased with his kindliness of manner, and should be glad to see him at the head of a girls' School.

THE ADAMS SCHOOL, — Mr. Barrett.

This school seemed to us somewhat characterized by a want of energy and activity. The reading was indifferent and lifeless; but in many of the branches of study we saw evidence of considerable proficiency. Some allowance must be made for the fact that only the required studies are introduced; this will lower the school a little in the rank which it occupies in the table.

FRANKLIN SCHOOL, — Mr. Field.

The instruction here, although quite too technical, still seemed rather above the average, on the oral examination, particularly in physical geography. We thought we saw too great a difference between the best scholars and the others.

JOHNSON SCHOOL, — Mr. Parker.

There appeared to be much activity in this school, and the pupils manifested much earnestness in their studies. The prevailing, — almost universal, — fault exists here also. The instruction, where not limited to the words of the book, appears to embrace little more than is absolutely necessary to some comprehension of the printed text. But, upon the whole, we are disposed to place this among our best schools.

WELLS SCHOOL, — Mr. Walker.

The instruction in this school seemed to us rather too technical and narrow, with the exception of grammar. In this important branch the girls were well instructed. The reading indicated great care and labor, but not, we think, perfectly good taste. Some of the pupils certainly read extremely well; but in too many instances the reading was affected and theatrical.

HAWES SCHOOL, — Mr. Crafts.

The first class of this school was remarkably small. We have here to complain of the common fault of narrow, verbal, technical instruction; and we were by no means satisfied with the relations between the master and the scholars.

MATHER SCHOOL, — Mr. Stearns.

If we judged of this school only by the oral examinations, we should place it much higher than it stands in the tables. The instruction given seems to cover less ground than in some of the schools, but is very good. The moral tone of this school appears to be excellent, and we regard it, in this respect, as among the very best we have.

WINTHROP SCHOOL, — Mr. Williams.

This also is among our best. The master is zealous, and contends successfully against adverse influences. By directing his efforts, and particularly those of his assistants, still more toward the development of the understanding of his pupils, so as to secure their comprehension of what they study and learn, he will remedy the principal defect in his school, and make it yet more useful.

BRIMMER SCHOOL, — Mr. Bates.

The excellent master of this School has not been in it quite long enough, to produce all the good effects which may be expected from his methods and principles of discipline and instruction; but we regard it as entitled to praise, and as of much promise. The boys of the first class have an uncommon degree of familiarity with the history of the day, and a general intelligence, which was perfectly obvious to the Committee, but of which no record can appear in our tables.

OTIS SCHOOL, — Mr. Shepard.

We were not pleased with the condition of this School; but it has been very recently established, and the master is fully entitled to a longer probation before any opinion is formed against him.

NEW SOUTH SCHOOL, — Mr. Hyde.

This small and recently established School exhibits evidence of zeal, industry and kindness on the part of the master, and justifies the hope of his success.

PHILLIPS SCHOOL, — Mr. Green.

This school is among those which appeared much better on the oral than on the written examination. Its condition is also lower, from the fact that it has been the subject of much change quite recently; but we place it among our best schools.

SMITH SCHOOL, — Mr. Forbes.

In regard to the Smith school, we have come to the conclusion that it is not only in an unsatisfactory, but in a deplorable condition. The attainments of the scholars are of the lowest grade; a few can read aloud from the first class reader, but cannot understand any other than the simplest passages. Their chattering about grammar shows only the power of their memories to retain the names of things which they do not understand; and their knowledge of geography is nothing but the faculty of repeating imperfectly names of states, towns, rivers, etc. There are certain parts of physical and political geography which we supposed might be made most interesting to colored children, those relating to the West India Islands, the condition of the colored race in Cuba, Jamaica, Hayti, etc.; the colonies in Africa, the condition of the natives, etc; but the scholars of the Smith school seemed to know nothing about them. They supposed Cuba to be smaller than Massachusetts, knew little or nothing of the other islands, and though one or two had heard of the emancipation act, the class knew nothing about it. They had only the most crude and vague notions of history; and, as for mathematical geography, astronomy, or natural philosophy, the master declined any examination.

But the intellectual deficiency which prevails in this school is not its worst feature; there is a want of discipline; an indifference to verbal requests for order, which indicates the frequency of appeal to more stirring motives; a want of respectful attention, and many indefinable but clear indications of a low moral tone.

Your Committee are aware, that there are many circumstances to be considered before blame should be laid on any individual, for the present low state of the school; they are aware of the difficulties in obtaining a good average attendance, and they will not say that another individual could at once inspire the colored population with more interest in the school, could secure a more punctual attendance, or could awaken the faculties and interest the attention of the scholars. But they do believe that there is good sense enough among the parents, and intellect enough among the children, if fairly enlisted in the subject, and directed by a zealous and discreet friend, to create a school which shall reach at least to the rank now attained by one half of the city schools.

It is to be regretted that the present incumbent has not more faith in the desire of the colored population for the education of their children, and in the capacities of the children themselves; for we fear that, without much faith, and even some enthusiasm, no great harvest can follow the teacher's labors. We think this school calls loudly for improvement.

It will be noticed that we have spoken of Schools; but it may be well to remind the Board, that our duty and our examination were so far confined to the Grammar departments, that our observations must be taken as relating to them chiefly, and in some respects exclusively.

We have noticed, in some schools, a bad demeanor towards the scholars, and evidence of unrestrained and ill-regulated temper. We are aware that zeal often puts on the aspect of severity, and that this is better than the indifference which is so easily mistaken for kindness. But we regard self-command, a consistent and uniform demeanor, and a manner marked by habitual gentleness and refinement, as of the very greatest importance; and, for our girls' Schools particularly, we should demand good manners, and a gentlemanly appearance and deportment, as absolutely indispensable. We therefore regret the more the defect in these respects, which is but too apparent and too undeniable in some of the Schools. We do not give the names of these schools or masters, after the distinct expression of the wish of the Committee that they should be withheld.

It will be noticed, that we find in most of our Schools, a narrow and merely technical instruction. It appeals to the memory quite too exclusively. And if it leaves the text-books at all, it is only so far as is absolutely necessary for the purpose of explaining them. Assuredly this needs not to be. For instance, geography, when taught as it should and may be taught, in connection with the simple principles of climatology, and other kindred sciences, becomes one of the most important studies, even for children. They may be made to conceive the grand image of the globe, with its continents and islands, its oceans and lakes, swinging unsupported

in space; spinning round upon its axis, while it rushes forward in
its orbit, and ever preserving such exact, yet changing relations
to the sun, as to receive light and heat in due proportion, in all its
various parts; and working out with daily and yearly precision
the changes of morning, noon, and night, summer, autumn and
winter. They may see in the infinite variety of its surface, the
wondrous wisdom of Him who made it for man's tenement; the
great ocean surrounding the land, and pushing forward its kindly
arms into the interior to invite the nations to commerce; the
mountain ridges, connecting earth with sky, and drawing down
the genial fluid, which, flowing in every direction, now leaps over
the rocks and lends to man its tireless strength to do his work, now
spreads out into mimic seas, and now bares its bosom to the cleav-
ing keel as it slowly rolls through the valleys, and fertilizes the
land on its way to the ocean.

Descending to particulars, the pupil should attend to the hydrog-
raphy of the country and to the great subject of drainage; he
should note the boldness of the promontories, the situation, breadth
and volume of the rivers, the depth of the bays, the number of the
harbors, and the facilities for anchorage, and protection from
storms; the directions of the mountain ridges; the great features
of the surface and the soil; the location of the great beds of coal,
and other mineral treasures; he should have explained to him the
immense effect which these and other similar circumstances have
had, and ever must have, upon the climate and fortunes of nations,
and even upon the physical and mental characteristics of our race.
If few of these things are in our text books, they should be in the
teacher's mind, and he should direct attention to them at every
recitation. But, compared with this, what do we usually find in
most of our Boston Schools?   A set of dry definitions, which convey
no vivid idea; a long catalogue of names of rivers, lakes, seas, and
oceans; of mountains, capes, and islands; states, cities, and capitals;
words, words, words! husks without the grain!

Some of our scholars could commence with Maine, and name every
river running into the ocean, without missing a navigable stream;
but if you ask them why the Mississippi flows southward with
sluggish current, and unvarying width, for a thousand miles, while
the northern waters run in a different direction, spread out into
vast expanses, rush through narrow passes and over steep preci-
pices, to seek the ocean through the St. Lawrence, — if asked, we
say, the reasons of such phenomena, they will stand in mute amaze-

ment, and their masters will perhaps complain of the unwonted severity of the examinations.

There can be no reason why children should not commence the study of geography as they do any other study, with its elements; instead of which, we place an account of the solar system before them, on the first page; and begin to teach the geography of their own country by saying that America is 9,000 miles long, before they know the dimensions of their own city, or indeed how much a mile is. Another striking point in our mode of teaching geography, is the vague and imperfect idea which our children form of the relative positions of different countries upon the globe. They are told indeed that the earth is a sphere, and occasionally they use a small globe, and perhaps solve a few problems upon it. This however is but rarely, while every day they study their maps, and have before their eyes a flat surface. Their first thought of China, for instance, is that of an extended portion of the earth's plain, lying far away to the east of us, and not as on the other side of the globe. Hence it is that our scholars almost invariably gave the wrong answer when they were asked; — Which is the longer, a degree of latitude, or a degree of longitude measured elsewhere than upon the equator.

It is in vain that the masters may protest against this, and insist upon it now, as they did insist upon it at the examinations, that their scholars must know, for they have had it explained to them. We doubt not it may have been explained, and well explained; but what is one, or five theoretical explanations of the spherodity of the earth, compared to the daily and hourly evidence of their maps. The best practical teaching of the fact would be to lead a class to a neighboring height, on some pleasant afternoon, after School, and to point out to them the sails of a ship as they appear above the horizon before its hull; — but how many classes of Boston boys have been so taught? Another, and a most glaring fault, is the ignorance of our children respecting the relative extent of different countries. Your Committee have very often been told, in the oral examination, that Ireland is longer than Madagascar; some classes have patriotically maintained the superiority in size of Nantucket over Jamaica, and stoutly asserted that Massachusetts is larger than Cuba, and this in schools where geography had been studied faithfully in the usual way.

The masters may protest against the supposition, that their scholars do not know that maps are projected upon different scales, and do not make allowance in judging of the comparative sizes of countries; they may say, as they have said to the Committee, we have explained this matter, and the scholars really understand it. We do not doubt that they think so; nor do we doubt that the masters can conduct an examination, and ask many questions that the Committee asked, and obtain correct answers where we obtained incorrect or vague ones; but the examination will be in this wise: "Boys, which map is projected upon the larger scale, — that of the British isles, or that of Asia?" and the correct answer will be shouted by all the class. "Which is the longer — Ireland or Madagascar?" — and quick as a report after a flash will come the response, — "Madagascar." "Why do you think so?" — says the master: "Because it is upon a smaller scale," — shout the boys, with a readiness that impresses the spectator with an idea of their intimate acquaintance with geography. But let this lesson get cool, and let the boy some time after read in a newspaper some mention of Madagascar and of Ireland, and he will involuntarily picture to himself Ireland as larger, if not longer than Madagascar; and Massachusetts as larger than St. Domingo, because he has had the two before his eyes a thousand times, and has always seen the smaller one forming the larger picture.

It is difficult, with our present system of teaching, to obviate these errors, which seem less the fault of the masters than of the mode pursued; but they can be obviated by a very simple method, and that is by having in every school, and constantly before the eyes of the pupils, a globe so large, that all the principal countries and islands may be clearly represented, and so highly colored as to be seen distinctly from any part of the room. This should be the constant standard of reference; it should be looked at during every lesson; and it would gradually stamp upon the minds of the scholars such a vivid, lively image of the spherodity of the earth, of the relative positions and sizes of continents, of oceans, and of seas, as would never be effaced. We hesitate not to say that it is impossible to teach even physical geography well without a globe; nevertheless, we have the avowal of many of our masters, that they never use one unless for mathematical geography or for astronomy.

It is true, the globes which are provided for our Schools are very small, and very imperfect; and we would most earnestly recommend to the Committee to procure for each School a globe, of at least four feet in diameter, on which shall be represented, in relief, if possible, an outline of all the great natural and civil divisions of the earth.   An order for a number of these globes would be executed in Germany, or in France, where such beautiful relief maps are made, at an expense which is unworthy of consideration compared with the immense benefit to be derived from them.

We would also recommend the use of blank globes, upon which the pupils can draw with crayons the great circles, the parallels and meridians, and the outline of countries. We have alluded to the advantages of drawing maps, and we may observe here, that all these advantages would be realized by drawing upon a globe, — as far at least as representing large sections of countries.

Near them, upon the walls of the school-room, should be large outline maps, with the different countries all represented upon the same scale;   and there should be a constant practice of sketching countries upon the black-board, and frequent exercises in map-drawing.

With these additional aids for the master, and additional exercises for the scholar, our children would not be perplexed, as their parents often are, to know the dimensions of different countries, with their bearings from each other.   They would not be perplexed by being asked whether New Holland is smaller than the United States or larger; or whether it may be sooner reached by a line drawn southeast from Boston, or by one drawn southwest.

The examinations in grammar, like those in geography, have discovered, that there is in the Schools generally too strict an adherence to the rules in the text-books, without a sufficient acquaintance with the principles of language.   The great object of grammar is to enable the scholar to speak and write with correctness and propriety.

It includes a knowledge of the formation of words from their elementary parts — the mode in which one word is derived from another, as well as a clear and distinct idea of each and every word, according to the usage of the best authorities.   It embraces also a knowledge of the classification, arrangement, agreement, government and mutual dependence of words when joined in construction.

To attain this object, the pupils must be able not only to give the true relation of each word in a sentence, but must be able to supply ellipses, rectify false constructions, and in a word, to analyze the sentence into its clauses, adjuncts, and phrases, and show their mutual relations and dependencies.

To accomplish this object, the method pursued in most of the Schools, is, to drill into the memory of the pupil all the definitions and rules of the text-book, before he has learned their power and application, and then set him to parsing. Thus the memory is burthened with unintelligible rules, and the mind fettered with a cumbrous machinery, which the annoyed and tasked scholar knows not how to employ.

There is another method adopted in some of the Schools, which is more reasonable and better adapted to the end proposed; and that is, to teach the pupil to construct his own sentences, and to learn the use of words and the meaning of definitions and the applications of rules, during the process of construction. Suppose him entirely unacquainted with grammar. Let him first learn the definition of a noun. Let him then be required to give examples of nouns. These may be written upon the board. Let him next learn the definition of a verb, and be required to attach a verb to any of the nouns written upon the board, as "the bird flies." He has now made a sentence in its simplest form. Let him next learn the definition of an adjective, and learn its use and application at once, by attaching some appropriate adjective to each noun upon the board. Let the teachers question him as to its influence on the noun, until he can readily form a sentence containing an adjective, a noun, and a verb. He may next learn the definition of an adverb and be required to attach some adverb expressive of time, place, circumstance, or manner, to each of the verbs on the board.

In the same manner let him, as he commits to memory the definitions of gender, number, case, mood, tense, etc., learn at the same time to apply them to examples written by himself or the teacher. The next step is to teach the pupil to attach an object to a verb, and thus learn the distinction between the objective and nominative cases, transitive and intransitive verbs.

Let him then, after learning the definition of a preposition, attach to the verb or noun, a preposition, and its object, thus "the bird flies through the air," and then explain the relation of the whole phrase "through the air" to the verb. The next step is to construct compound sentences, and make the proper distinction between the principal and dependent clauses with their connectives.

In this way the pupil's memory is not cumbered with a variety of rules and definitions, while he is unacquainted with their use and application.

The scholar may now take sentences already formed, and learn to analyze them into their various parts. Then, by uniting the two processes of constructing and analyzing, the pupil, under the guidance of a skilful teacher, will necessarily, and with pleasure to himself, become acquainted with the principles of grammar.

This process required on the part of the teacher and pupil, labor and patience and perseverance; but it has this recommendation, that the mind is exercised, and every step taken is an advance toward the accomplishment of the object.

Of all the branches taught in our Schools, reading seems to receive the greatest attention on the part of the masters. The attainments of the pupils in this branch are incomparably higher than in any other. Your Committee apprehend, indeed, that in some Schools too high value is attached to it, and that time and labor are spent upon it to the neglect of other studies.

The art of reading well is a beautiful and important one; but it must not be forgotten that it is a means to an end, and not the great end itself. The first object in teaching reading should be, to make the scholar so familiar with the arbitrary visible signs of things and ideas, that a single glance at a sentence shall make him acquainted with its full meaning; he must be able to dispense with the aid which is necessary to those unfamiliar with the signs of moving his lips, or saying to himself the words he looks upon. The second object should be, to enable the learner to enunciate those signs correctly, distinctly and euphoniously, — in short, to read aloud. Now it is very easy to learn the first part of the art without learning the second, as is illustrated in the common remark that one can read French, but cannot speak or pronounce it; but it is very hard, if it be not impossible to attain the second part without the first — to pronounce the signs, without understanding their meaning; yet some of our Boston masters, by their art and perseverance, and by the extraordinary powers of imitation and memory in their pupils, do approach success even in this, which is somewhat like being able to pronounce correctly an unknown tongue.

Your Committee have sometimes been amazed to find that pupils could read, with tolerable emphasis, tone and feeling, whole stanzas, of which they did not understand the metaphors, the leading ideas, or the principal words.

Much as has been said by former Committees, much as has been written in every treatise on education, about the importance of teaching scholars the meaning of every word they read, we believe the lesson has not been learned by all our masters, much less by their pupils; and we fear it never will be learned while the present inefficient and imperfect mode of superintendence and examination is continued.

The first and great object, then, of learning to read, — an understanding of the language, — is often sacrificed to the second, — euphonious enunciation of sound; and for this there is great temptation held out to the masters and great inducements to the scholars. Every casual visitor of a School must hear a reading lesson, but only a few venture to question the readers; every Committee must hear the class read, whether they have time to examine in grammar or not.

Your Committee would by no means undervalue the importance of the elocutionary part of reading. They would not have the masters overvalue it, as some do, but surely not all, judging from the careless and slipshod reading of their classes. There is the greatest possible difference in this respect in our Schools; a difference that could hardly exist under good supervision.

We should venture to offer some remarks upon the other branches of study pursued in our Schools, if we had space for them. If it is thought that we insist too strongly that the children should understand what they study, and if it is said that this cannot be perfectly accomplished, we answer, that we do not demand the impossible. But much more is done in this way in some Schools than in others; more should be done in all; and those who have not had some opportunity of witnessing actual results, would be surprised at the degree to which the understanding of children may be developed, and the facility with which they may be made to comprehend the facts and rules they learn, by vigilant, skilful and persevering efforts.

Upon the whole, the Committee have, reluctantly, come to the conclusion that the Grammar Schools of Boston have not the excellence and usefulness they should possess. Our citizens manifest their strong desire, that their children should have the best possible education, by a very liberal expenditure for this purpose; and it is certain that their children have not this education. We cannot but believe, for we see, that other Schools are better than most of ours; and that the majority of our Schools are further below the best that we have, than any thing in the peculiar condition of the scholars, or other similar causes can explain. And your Committee do not think they should discharge their duty, if they did not suggest some, at least, of the causes which seem to them to operate unfavorably upon our Schools.

The first of these causes may be found in the constitution of the School Committee. Numerous, chosen without concert, in many different parts of the city, offering to those of its members who cannot turn it to their pecuniary benefit, no motive but the mere love of usefulness to induce them to remain long in office, it is necessarily, an uncertain, fluctuating and inexperienced body. The duties which its members ought to discharge, are burdensome, and would require great labor, and occupy a large portion of our time. The duties which we do perform, though quite as much as can be expected or ought to be asked of men who give to these duties only their leisure, and give it without compensation, are but a very small part of those which lie upon us.

Nor is it possible for us to perform even these as they should be performed. The Schools are divided among Sub-Committees. Each Sub-Committee consisting of three members, the whole number for the nineteen Grammar Schools, is fifty-seven. And as only twenty-four members serve on the Sub-Committees, it is obvious that each member must serve on two Schools, and nine must serve on three. The Sub-Committees are required to visit each School, at least once a quarter   We do full justice to their actual labors, when we assume that this rule is complied with, that the required visit occupies a whole day, which is employed in a careful examination of a School of 400 or 500 children. Now, not to dwell at present upon the necessary insufficiency of so brief an examination, we would ask attention to one inevitable result from this practice. It is, that all the School are not examined by any Sub-Committee, as each member confines himself to his own two, or at most three Schools. Of the annual examination, we will speak presently. That which is made by the regular Sub-Committees, never, by any possibility, subjects all the Schools to the same standard. It never ascertains their comparative merits. It provides no means by which improvements that are of great service in one School, may be adopted in another; none by which the example of one School may be made profitable to another; and the greatest and most unnecessary difference may remain for years, in Schools almost in sight of each other. In fact, no one man, and no Sub-Committee, is ever required or expected to know the actual condition of all the Grammar Schools in Boston.

It may be said that the Annual Examining Committees do this. We know something of the toils which these Committees must undergo, if they discharge any tolerable part of their most important

duties. We know what we have done ourselves, and at what expense of time and labor. We have inquired diligently into the
doings of our predecessors, and examined the records they have
left. And we say quite enough when we assert, that the labor of a
faithful Sub-Committee has very seldom exceeded a full day to
each School, spent in its careful examination. This seems to be
the most ever asked, or expected. Now, let us compare what is to
be done, and the time in which it is to be done. There are two
Committees, of three each; one to examine the Writing department, and one for the Grammar department. These Committees
are to ascertain the whole condition of the School, and all the particulars which make up this whole, — the proficiency of the scholars
in each department; the methods of instruction in each branch
of study; the discipline and motive-powers relied upon; the character, demeanor and abilities of the masters, ushers and assistants,
and this so well as to judge whether their defects or errors are cur-
able, and if so, by what suggestions or advice most effectually;
the state of the schoolroom, its furniture and apparatus; — all
this and more, in one day, or if the two Committees act in concert,
and divide their labors between them, in two days. It is obviously impossible. Indeed, by a regulation of the School Committee, the Annual Examining Committee now confine their attention
to the first class in each School. This regulation was found to be
necessary, because, if the Examining Committees attempted to do
more, they did nothing; but its effect has been to confine the labors
of many masters, quite too much to the first class.

These examiners are, by a long usage, new men every year,
which makes any thing like systematic and continuous observation
out of the question; and the Reports of successive years show a
discrepancy which we cannot otherwise explain.

Indeed, if any more proof is wanted of the utter inefficiency of
the old mode of examination, we hope they who ask it, will look
for it in a comparison of the Reports of the Annual Visiting Committees for different years. One Committee will infer from an
examination that a particular School is wanting in discipline, and
its scholars deficient in a knowledge of geography, while they rank
high in the other branches; another year, another Committee
report the order good, and the attainments in geography high,
while in all the other studies the scholars are very deficient. Such
discrepancies occur, for instance, between the successive reports
of the Rev. Mr. Hague, and Mr. Hillard; and we mention these

names, because these gentlemen are so well known in this community, that we may safely say, it is impossible for the School Committee to have their work done by better men.

The Reports are often at entire variance with each other, as would naturally be expected where men of different tastes, different capacities for examining Schools, or in different frames of mind, examine the same School under different circumstances. Sometimes the mere state of the weather may have an effect, both upon the class and upon the Committee-man; a close and sultry afternoon, in midsummer, may render an examination tedious and unsatisfactory, which, in the clear, bracing air of morning would have been lively and satisfactory to both parties.

Our citizens seem to have built up an extensive establishment of Schools, to tax themselves annually for their support to the amount of more than two hundred thousand dollars, and then to leave them without any thing like adequate or appropriate supervision. What other great interest of the city is so uncared for? What other great expenditure so unwatched? It is, we repeat, impossible that the present School Committee should perform this work of supervision. But while it constitutes, as in fact it does, the Board of Education for the City, and is therefore supposed to do this work, it protects and perpetuates defects, by preventing that personal examination by parents, which might, in some degree at least, be given, if it were supposed to be needed; — thus verifying the saying of Jeremy Bentham, in his argument in favor of individual responsibility, that a Board is but too apt to become a "Screen."

How, then, would we remedy this? Not by a change in the School Committee itself; for the constitution of this Board, for some purposes, is admirable. Its members come fresh from the people, every year; and being chosen from all the Wards, they represent all the wants and interests which should be provided for, and all the opinions and feelings which should be consulted. The excellent elements for a Board of Education which we now possess, we would retain, — adding those which are wholly wanting; and these are permanence, personal responsibility, continued and systematic labor. This we would do, by adding to the officers of the city, one whose duty it should be to watch over the Schools; to know the exact condition of every one, in all particulars; to bring the lagging forward; to suffer no defects to become prescriptive, no abuses to be indurated by time; to acquire and to impart such information as shall bring all our Schools to that degree of excellence which our citizens not only have a right to demand, but without which they have no right, in justice to themselves and to their children, to be satisfied. This should be his business, — his whole business; and he should be adequately paid. Although chosen annually, like our masters, his tenure of office, like theirs, would be permanent, if he discharged the duties of his office acceptably; and if he did not, another should be chosen in his stead. We think also that he should be chosen by the City Council, and be amenable in part to that body and in part to the School Committee, under a system of duties which can easily be arranged, when it shall be time to go into these details.

It is easy to bring a certain class of objections against this measure. Many interests will be assailed and endangered by it, and therefore much influence will be exerted against it. The numerous objections which lie against all new propositions will of course be worked as hard as they will bear. Thus, — it will be liable to abuse, — as if there were any thing on earth that is not. It will add to our expenses; but it can be shown that the cost of such an officer can be saved many times over by the good he may do, and by the actual expenditure he may save. We are unwilling to enter into details on this subject, for they would carry us much too far. But there is one thing we would suggest. The cost of books lays now a heavy burthen upon many parents. A competent School Commissioner might have charge of a Book Depository. Contracts could easily be made, by which the books would be cheaper than they are, and they could be sold to scholars at their cost, or with only the slight addition necessary to pay the rent of a cheap room and the wages of a clerk. The Commissioner would also see that they were so manufactured as not to come to pieces quite so soon as at present; and a boy, who had taken care of his book, might, when he had done with it, leave it at the Depository, and receive the half price paid by some scholar obliged to study economy. By these means alone, the Commissioner would save more than his salary, and he would save this money for those upon whom an unnecessary expense presses most heavily. But, it will be said, there may be favoritism, and management in the choice of masters to answer a particular purpose, and in the introduction of books to help somebody's pocket, and so forth and so forth. The answer is, — there may be all this now. In the one case we have a Board of twenty-four men, not paid for any labor, who share a responsibility, which, thus broken into fragments, presses on no one; and

who must, on the common principles of human nature, be supposed to be made willing to hold this office by every variety of
motive, from the highest and purest love of usefulness, down to a
mere personal purpose of coining its privileges and opportunities
into dollars and cents. In the proposed case, we have one man,
paid, under contract, before the eyes of the public, regularly reporting every thing that he does under his own name, and liable to
lose his livelihood if he goes wrong. The question is, — in fact
it is the only question, — under which system are abuses least
likely to creep in, and most likely to be detected and removed,
when they have found entrance?   The experience of other great
cities may help us to answer this question. In our peculiar organization we stand alone, and the important functions resting elsewhere upon a School Commissioner are by us very imperfectly
provided for. It may be added, that such an officer might supply
a link between the School Committee and the City Government,
which is now wanting. For some purposes, the official Presidency
of the Mayor would seem to form this connection, but in reality
it does not. That officer is burdened with duties of very great
amount and very great variety; and he can only go from one to
another, dividing his time and attention among them all.

Another defect in our Schools, which operates upon them injuriously, is that which gives to each school two heads. There
are in each,* one called a grammar master, who teaches grammar and
certain other branches, and one called a writing master, who teaches
writing and also some other branches. Those two masters are both
masters, and equal masters, with equal pay, no difference in rank
or authority, neither having exclusive control or responsibility.
It is certainly proper for those who respect the common sense of
mankind, and the common usages of all time, to say that a system
which is so distinctly opposed to both, is, upon the face of it, objectionable, and ought not to be retained, unless strong arguments,
arising out of peculiar circumstances, justify it as an exceptional
and peculiar arrangement. But there are no peculiar circumstances, and we know of no strong argument. This subject has
been frequently and earnestly debated in the School Committee
in times past; and perhaps most of the views of it which can be
presented have been considered and discussed. We do not deny,

---

* There are two exceptions; the Smith School for colored children, and
the school at East Boston. The new South school is not yet fully organized.

— for it is certain and obvious, — that there must have been powerful motives, or interests, or influences, of some kind, which could have caused the adoption and continuance of so strange an arrangement; and they might have taken the appearance of strong reasons, or have given that appearance to weak ones. Of these we have nothing to say; and of the arguments in its favor, we can only remark, that we are wholly unable to perceive their force. Indeed, the only one which we have heard, of any weight, is this : — the departments of writing and arithmetic being very important, require that we should secure the most competent instructors, and we can do this only by giving to such instructors the same pay, and the same rank, and the same power, that we give to the grammar masters. Now, to say nothing of the contradiction of this argument by the notorious fact, that inferior men are very often chosen to this office, the argument itself is, in our estimation, very feeble. That writing and arithmetic should be taught just as well as they can be taught, we hold ; and we hold this principle just as firmly as it can be held by any person. But we cannot see why either writing or arithmetic can be taught any better because the person who teaches them has just the same power, and just the same compensation, that another person has who teaches something else. Boston is not the only place in which the value of writing and arithmetic has been discovered; it is not the only place where these things are well taught; and we cannot see why it should be the only place where an opinion should prevail, that they cannot be well taught unless every school has two heads.* They should be well taught, and for that purpose we should give the instructors money enough, and authority enough to secure competent persons, and enable them to do their work; and having done this, whatever we do more, is without reason and against reason. If it be true, as only the School Committee of Boston ever supposed, that writing and arithmetic cannot be taught unless the teacher is head of the school, then let him be the head, — but not one of two heads. For if it be contended that there is a precise, mathematically exact equality between the branches which are taught by one of our masters and those taught by the other, that the equilibrium cannot be disturbed without violence, and that neither master can be the responsible head of the School without

* A similar double-headed system was adopted in Salem for a time, but is now abandoned.

detriment and injustice, — we have only to say, it may be so, it may have been reserved for the School Committee of Boston to make and to apply this most singular discovery; but we are rather of opinion, that this wonderful equality is more apparent than real, and seems to exist only because the balance which weighs this matter does not turn quite so freely as might be desired.

But the positive and practical objections to this arrangement are very great. In the first place, two masters, are no master; and it is strictly true, that there is no master in our grammar schools. No master, who has the authority, who lies under the responsibility, can perform the duties, and sustain the relations, and effect all the good results, which belong to the office of a schoolmaster. We hold this office in high respect; for we would respect every man in his own position, and in the discharge of his duties; and respect that position according to the value of those duties. And judging by this standard, who is entitled to more respect, to a more affectionate regard by the whole community, than the faithful and useful schoolmaster? But not merely because he teaches, from books, or otherwise, certain branches of knowledge. This is the smallest thing he does, if he does all that he should, all that he may do. When Providence in its mercy gives us children, we receive from its hands these germs of human life, and with them the solemn duty of watching over them, of training them in their growth, and so preparing them in the morning of their lives for the hours of noonday toil, that the various uses and employments of life may be discharged by the men and women who are to follow us, in such wise as to promote their own good, and the good of mankind. We feel the burden of this task, and we call upon the schoolmaster to aid us; we tell him to stand in the place of the parent; we put in his hands a large part of our authority; we lay upon his shoulders a heavy portion of our own responsibility. Whoso enters our schoolrooms, and is able to see there only feebleness and imperfection, and the day of small things, forgets, or is incapable of knowing, that, in the immature and slight-seeming Present before him, there lies an indefinite Future. There are the men and women of a time that is near at hand; there is the nation of the coming age. Within those walls are a large part, — no man can say how large, — of the influences that are to set their seal upon that nation, to form its character and determine its destiny. There is the beginning of Education. And the end of it is not when as men and women they take their places in society; but afar off, in the distance of Eternity, these never-ending influences go on; and every step of their eternal progress is colored and qualified by this beginning.

It is in this respect, that the personal relations between the master and the child are of the utmost importance. If the child learns that he has a master who is to be obeyed, whose every rule and every act are for his good; if he finds there kindness, firmness and consistency, if he knows that the experience of today will help him tomorrow, because he is under no changeful domination; if he gradually, — always with some difficulty and after some conflicts, — learns to understand and acquiesce in the rule under which he lives, and to rejoice in it because it is kind, and well adapted to bring out and cultivate the good that is in him and make him happy, while its firmness and stability give him the feeling of security, and if habits of order, of intelligent self-government, of obedience in freedom, thus grow up in him, — then he is acquiring, what will be more useful in the coming ages, — and after all coming ages, than all that was ever put between the covers of a book, even if he were able to put all that in his memory.

But how is it possible that relations like these should exist, in any good degree, where there is in fact no master? where the child is today under one government, and tomorrow under another, or rather passing from one to the other every half day; where the idea of unity has given way to that of diversity; and where, instead of unvarying consistency, there is only constant change? The two who are called masters must both feel this. Both may be good, and experienced, and intelligent; but if they are both men, each must be himself, each must have his own way of thinking, and feeling, and acting, and governing, if he have character enough to be fit for his place; and it is as impossible that the ways of the two should be one, as it is that two men should stand in one place. Both must feel this difficulty; and they must feel it as an insurmountable obstacle to the establishment of proper relations between themselves and the children under their joint care. And if the longing desire for that which every good schoolmaster must feel to be the greatest good of the school, should induce either of them to strive for this great end, the obvious impossibility of reaching it will come home to him every day, and compel him to desist. The School will quietly fall down to a low level, and there things will rest.

This must happen, but too often, even if we suppose the most favorable case possible, and that is, the union in one School of two

good masters, both desirous of acting upon their scholars by the
highest motive-powers; but let us suppose what is far more likely
to happen, what actually does happen, — the union of two masters
of opposite characters, opposite views and opposite modes of government.   In the morning, the grammar master comes in among his
scholars, and commands their respect by those peculiar appearances
which high moral worth, united with intellectual power, ever stamp
upon the outer man.   He wins their confidence and affection by
his paternal solicitude, and his genial smile; he fixes their attention
by presenting each subject of study in a new and interesting light;
and he gradually fills the School with an atmosphere of love, which
begins to subdue the most turbulent and refractory spirits.   The
children go away almost with a feeling of regret, and assemble again
in the afternoon with hearts half softened towards authority; but
what a change is there!   The master is one who has mistaken his
vocation; he may try to look as a master ought, but he cannot;
the animal nature predominates in his composition, and he cannot
suppress its natural language.   It flashes from his eye, it speaks
in every motion, and inspires distrust and dislike; he opens his
mouth, and his harsh voice grates upon the ear, confirming the first
impression; his directions assume, (involuntarily, perhaps), the
tone of command which will evidently be enforced by the physical
power at hand.   Human nature revolts at this, and thenceforward
the boys are insensibly but certainly arrayed against the masters;
the beautiful harmony between the ingredients of the moral atmosphere of that School is broken by the invasion of base fear, and
thenceforward discord reigns.   The master becomes discontented
and fretful; the boys become distrustful and hypocritical.

Now it is easy to see how the unwise conduct of the one master
may counteract the kindly influence of the other, and, perhaps, drive
him from his chosen system; but who can tell the effects which
dwelling three hours every day in an atmosphere of fear, of hypocrisy
and of eye-service, may have upon the tender minds of boys.   We
can calculate the effects upon the body, of an undue proportion of
carbonic acid gas in the air; but who will tell the effects upon the
character, of a vitiated moral atmosphere?

It is a fact of some significance in this connection, that the masters, as the Schools are now organized, do not really have much to
do with either the instruction or the discipline of the lower classes,
and in most cases positively nothing to do with their moral training.   Our Schools are not only double-headed, but they are triple-

headed, — if not quadruple-headed. Each of the masters is nominally the responsible head of his own department; but he confines his attention almost entirely to the upper class, and leaves his usher and his assistants to manage the lower as they can.

In some Schools, the masters, in reply to the printed questions of the Committee, say they have but sixty under their personal care; and it is a fact, beyond all question, that some of them do nothing, and know nothing about the instruction of the lower classes.

All nations, in all ages, have seen the great principle more or less clearly, that, in every School, there must be an acknowledged and responsible head. Hence, always and everywhere, under every form of government and every kind of civilization, the School has been a place where authority, discipline and order were to be found; and that kind of order which implies of necessity unity and consistency of government, and can exist only where there is one master. The name Master, or one of exactly equivalent meaning, has been given to this office in all languages. We believe that this unity of government in Schools has been almost a universal fact,* and is so at this moment, with the exception of our own City. The School Committee of Boston must have supposed that all states and nations, and all past ages were in an error, which they alone had discovered and corrected. This is certainly possible; but it does not seem to us probable. On this question the School Committee may have been wiser than the whole world and the whole past, but we think not; and when the time shall come, — and it cannot be long delayed, — for us to adopt a system better conforming to universal usage, to common sense and obvious right, we have little doubt that experience will satisfy us or our successors, that we have changed for the better.

Indeed, the result of our long and minute examination of our own Schools, and those of other towns and states; the result of deep reflection and sober thought, is, that the School system of our own City, is wrong in the principle of its organization, inefficient in its operation, and productive of little good, in comparison with its very great expense.

Holding honestly this opinion, and believing that no half way measures, no temporizing policy, nothing short of radical reform

---

* The neighboring town of Charlestown furnishes the only other instance within our knowledge of strictly double-headed Schools.

will cure these evils, and enable the children of the City to receive a proportionate benefit from the large sums which the fathers of the City annually invest for them, we feel bound to suggest a plan so extensive in its nature and thorough in its operation, that we should have shrunk from the bare contemplation of it, three months ago, as many to whom it is addressed, for the first time, will now shrink.

Most of the School Committee, and most of our fellow-citizens, have been so long accustomed to the present organization of our Schools, that its extraordinary character does not, perhaps, strike them. Perhaps few have examined this organization, in comparison with that of other Schools of high standing. Let us look at it, therefore, as though it were not our own. Take one of our boys' Schools, for instance : here are 500 children, from seven up to fourteen or fifteen years of age, who are to be taught reading, writing, grammar, arithmetic, geography, etc. How do we divide them, and organize the School? We divide them by a perpendicular line, into two classes, — not according to age, not according to acquirement, but according to the principle of making two separate and independent Schools, of equal age and acquirement, with two independent masters, each having equal jurisdiction; one being master of one half all the morning, the other of the other half ; and then exchanging in the afternoon. Thus in sixteen Schools we have thirty-two independent rulers, each on a salary of $1500, and sixteen vicegerents, or ushers, each upon a salary of $600.

We have alluded, elsewhere, to some of the evils of this arrangement; many others may be seen by a close examination of the workings of our Schools, of which the only ostensible benefit is, that it affords comfortable places and salaries for persons otherwise, perhaps, out of employment.

Now suppose, instead of this, that we should divide the scholars horizontally, or according to their age and acquirements, — placing the older or more advanced half in the upper room, and the other half in the lower room ; the whole to be under the general care and superintendence of a head master, whose immediate sphere of duty, however, should be in the upper room, in the care and instruction of the older children. The lower room, with the younger children, should be under the care and instruction of a female teacher and her assistants ; for all reason, and modern experience, show us that women are, by nature, better fitted than men to teach and train young children.

As it will be necessary to have a head master of the highest character and acquirements, and as his responsibilities, both in and out of the School would be greater than at present, the actual salary might be increased.

In order to secure the most capable and accomplished women for teachers in the junior department, it would be necessary to pay at least $400 per annum; and thus we might keep at home those superior teachers who now go to the South and West to get higher salaries than they can get here.

By this simple and feasible plan we should obtain higher kinds of services and have better schools; while by substituting one lady for one master, and even two female assistants for one usher, we should save the salaries of sixteen masters at $1,500, and of sixteen ushers at $600, being thirty-two persons, to whom we now pay $33,600, and have in their place forty-eight competent female teachers, to whom we should pay only $14,400, thus making a clear saving of $19,200 per annum in the item of salaries, excepting only what might be allowed by way of increase of the masters' salaries.

Will any one venture the assertion that we cannot find women of energy enough to take care of and teach a school of boys under twelve years of age, with a head master in the same building, to be called upon in any emergency, in the face of the fact that all over the civilized world, such things are done? Or in face of the fact that at this moment, in our Boston Schools, hundreds of boys are so managed; for we have said the head master usually leaves the management and care of the younger boys to his female assistants, and often knows not and cares not what she does with them.

Will any one venture the assertion that a grammar master cannot teach writing and arithmetic as well as the other branches, in face of the fact that all over this country, and in Europe, it is done? Or can this be said, in face of the specimens in writing, taken from the Dudley School in Roxbury, which are so decidedly superior to those of our own schools? Yet they are from a school taught by one master, and at much less expense than ours.

It may be said that this plan has been tried before in the Boston Schools and failed; but the fact is not so, and even if it had been so, we trust that good influences would now be brought to support the plan, and sinister influences would be counteracted, so as to prevent its failure. The former feeble attempt at reform was made when great comparative ignorance and indifference about Public Schools pervaded the community, and when interested individuals exerted an influence which might now be palsied by a newly awakened public interest.

But the old attempt was not what is now proposed. That lowered the writing masters from their rank, and made of them mere subordinates, at a small salary; and it thus introduced into the Schools themselves an element of destruction. To expect schools to succeed in such hands was to expect a miracle. That attempt failed mainly because a sense of duty to the public did not stifle the appeals for sympathy from a few individuals; and because war was waged upon it by those who availed themselves of the ignorance and indifference of the public upon the subject, to work its destruction.

There was a great clamor raised then, and there would be a greater clamor raised now, should the Committee entertain the present proposal, although it be simpler, more efficacious and more economical, for it is not possible to discontinue so many offices, even though they may be supernumerary, without being disturbed by the protestations of thirty-two incumbents and their connections to the third and fourth generation, and their circles of friends.

If such a simple and demonstrable plan of saving fifteen or twenty thousand dollars annually, and yet having better schools, was ever defeated, we trust this could not be now done, in the face of accumulated knowledge and reviving interest in the community.

Your Committee have considered, not this plan only, but some others which have been from time to time suggested. But they represent this only, because after the fullest examination and deliberation, they are convinced that it is the best.

The attention of the School Committee and of the public, has been directed of late to the subject of corporal punishment. There has been a strong desire to diminish this in amount, and put it under such regulations as may leave its usefulness unimpaired, and lessen its mischiefs. This is well; but there is always danger in any thing which partakes of the nature of reaction. It is easy to feel, and to excite, a morbid and mischievous sensibility on the subject of punishment. We are delighted with the beautiful instances of individual scholars, or of some excellent Schools, where moral motives are all that are used, and all that are needed. But we must not forget, that upon this as on all other practical subjects, the wise man aims at what is possible, and does not lose the good upon which he may lay his hand, in a vain effort after that which is unattainable. Nor must we forget, that if our Schools are to be places where human

beings shall be taught and trained, there must be discipline, restraint, and positive authority. He who hopes for an escape from this
necessity, knows nothing of human nature. He has not learned the
most universal law of human life, who does not know that every
man, from his cradle to his grave, errs and sins, and suffers the punishments by which Providence would restrain, instruct and reform
him. It is thus the man learns, and so must the child learn to become a man. Doubtless moral motives are infinitely higher than
merely sensual motives; and for that very reason they are less
adapted for some masters to use, and some scholars to feel. Nor is
the effort to substitute the one for the other without its danger. A
blow with a ferule may give less pain, and do a far less permanent
injury, than an exposure to disgrace, or an appeal to self-esteem
and the love of approbation; for these may crush one kind of temper, and excite in another and make habitual, feelings that will
render it selfish, useless and miserable. It is still true, however,
that moral motives are far higher than those appealed to through
the sense of bodily pain, and it may well be the earnest endeavor
of the Committee and of the schoolmasters, to bring down corporal
punishment to its minimum, and enlarge as far as may be the domain
of moral discipline. But if all perceive the propriety of doing this,
and all aim to do this, their success will be very different. Experience shows that there are masters who know how to dispense
with the rod and others who do not; and that those who possess
this knowledge are generally, in other respects, most successful as
teachers.

We are forced to believe that there has been a gross abuse of the
power of corporal punishment; but in consequence of the late order
of the Committee, and of the direction of public attention to this
subject, the abuse is much diminished. There is little danger of its
revival, nor is there, in the actual condition of our Schools in this
respect, any thing to call for or justify alarm or excitement. There
is room for improvement; but that improvement can only be
effected by temperate and just opinions, deliberately formed, resting
upon a clear understanding of facts and possibilities, and contented to advance slowly, or what may seem slowly to the enthusiastic. Undoubtedly there are some persons who look upon the rod
as if it had a magic power, as if chaos must come again, if it were
abandoned and forgotten. They quote the saying of Solomon, as
if it contained all his wisdom, and regard the rod as if it must ever
be the chief instrument of education. Possibly there may be some

persons in our own Schools whose minds are inclined too much in this direction; but the regulations of the Committee and the power of public opinions, will, we hope, break the force of the blows, and save the little victims from outrage.   If we have such persons among our masters, we would not turn them away, if they are good men, and good masters in other respects, and are restrained by any means or motives from doing too much "execution" in their Schools.   At least, we would not send them away, until we have given them the fullest opportunity for reform and improvement.   We would let them stay, and hope they would become wiser, nor would we content ourselves with merely hoping, for we would try to help them.

We have spoken of this subject, not only because it happens just now to receive much attention, but because it is itself of the utmost importance.   And while we do not propose, nor deem it our duty, to go into a full consideration of this interesting topic under all its aspects, we ask permission to state one other view of it, which has much weight with us.   It is that which regards corporal punishment, as peculiarly unsuited to our own Schools, and to a system of education for this country.   In Prussia, for example, where it is, however, almost disused, if the child, from its cradle, were taught to obey and to be good, only by the constant terror of immediate corporal punishment, the habits of mind and of character which would be formed in this way, would be well suited to the influences and circumstances that would surround him when he went forth to the duties and employments of adult life.   There, too, he finds a master over him, and a master who holds a heavy rod in a hand always uplifted.   He is still subjected to laws, which he did not help to make, which he need not reason about, to which he must yield a blind and unreflecting obedience, because they have the power to compel this obedience by prompt and certain punishment.

In this country, when the boy escapes from school, he never hears the word Master again.   He is free; free for good or for evil.   He sends his neighbor, or goes himself, to make all the laws which bind him; and if he does not like them, it is right for him to say so, and to use proper means to effect their change or repeal.   Unless he sinks down to absolute crime, he scarcely comes in contact with penal law, or knows what legal restraint means.   Nine tenths of the lives of nine tenths of our citizens are passed with no sense whatever of coercion or compulsion, beyond that which may come from social usages, or their own sense of interest or right.   And what must be the condition of him who comes into such a life as this, with no habit and no idea of self-government, beyond that which he could derive from corporal punishment? The great end of the education of a child, is to fit him to become a man; and so far as this end is concerned, his education has utterly failed. He must begin now, when the impressible years of childhood are passed, to learn all that is most necessary for him to know; and under what influences, what temptations! A man who knew that his child was destined to an occupation, in which he could earn his bread only by the use of his right hand; if, during his whole childhood, he bound that hand to his body, and permitted every other limb to grow and strengthen, would act wisely in comparison with the parent or schoolmaster who seeks to prepare a child to become an American citizen, by no better discipline than that of corporal punishment.

We are, indeed, willing to confess that we dislike the habitual use of corporal punishment, for many reasons, but we object to it, principally because it is addressed to that kind of fear, which is not only not curative in its nature, but is degrading. It may keep boys still, it may make them obey; but it never makes them esteem order; it never makes them really respect authority; it never makes them love him who imposes it.

We have referred principally to the habitual use of corporal punishment in our boys' Schools, for we are ready to say of him, who, in this age and city avows, that he cannot teach our girls without resort to blows, that he cannot so use the respect, the docility, and the affectionate temper, which characterize the many, as to subdue the perversity of the few, he is not yet fit for the high vocation of teacher.

We cannot but think, that the endeavor to avoid corporal punishment in our schools, would induce our masters to resort to other powers for the maintenance of order; and as the change would be under the awakened attention of the community, and of the Committee, it could hardly fail to be an appeal to higher motives. We shall not suggest any method to be adopted, but content ourselves with making a few further remarks upon the present, or rather the passing system.

It will be found upon examination that, in most of the cases where severe injury has followed corporal punishment in our schools, the offence was very trifling, and no great severity intended when the master began to strike. Moreover it is beyond all question that in the majority of the cases of corporal punishment and other kinds

of punishment in our schools, it is inflicted for violations of arbitrary rules of discipline, — for whispering, for disorderly conduct,
arising perhaps from mere physical uneasiness, and it is equally
certain that the fault in most cases, is as much that of the School,
as of the scholar.   Whoever will go into our Schools, at any hour of
the day, will find a large portion of the scholars unoccupied by any
study; they may have a book before them, but as its contents are
insipid, or perhaps incomprehensible, but nevertheless to be committed to memory, and as there is no master immediately over them,
they do not study. Now, to expect boys full of young life and pent-up
vigor to remain motionless, like soldiers upon duty, is to expect
that which is impossible; oftentimes the best boys, — the boys who
will make the ablest and best men, — will manifest their uneasiness
in a way to bring down a punishment.   We say that in such cases
the fault is as much that of the school, as of the scholar; and as a
general rule, when children under ordinary circumstances are idle,
or disorderly in school, we hold this fact to be prima facie evidence,
either of incapacity in the master or of faulty organization of the
School; — there are too many in the class; or they are retained too
long at one study; or the air of the school is vitiated; or the seats are
irksome; or the mode of instruction is bad; something is wrong.

The natural love for mental exercise is so great, the variety of objects which may be held up to interest the different mental faculties
is so inexhaustible, and it is so easy to kindle the enthusiasm of a
class and make it extend even to the dull, that, as we believe, the
ferule or the spur of emulation is seldom or never necessary to
quicken it.   We appeal to all who have been idle in School, and how
few have not, we appeal to all teachers to say, whether, when an
interesting event in history is well told, when the manners and customs of a strange country have been vividly depicted, when a
striking experiment in natural philosophy is performed, when a
mimic creation is going on upon the black-board, and islands, continents and mountains are opening into view beneath the rapid
touches of a good draftsman, is there an idle or mischievous scholar
among those who comprehend it?   It will be said that it is as impossible to keep up the attention of scholars for any length of time,
as it is to hold out a weight, by the extended arm.   Exactly so! and
when that moment comes it is time to change the subject or give
a recess.

Surely any man aspiring to be a teacher, can claim the attention
of ten boys, by the interest he will throw into his lessons, without

whip or spur; another will so enchain twenty, another fifty, let each one do all he can do well, and attempt no more; the rest of the School can be well governed by assistants. It will be said, that this is mere theory; we point to thousands of Schools in Europe, to scores in our own neighborhood, every whit as difficult to manage as ours, in every respect as well disciplined and as well taught. It will be said that children must be coerced to study some subjects which are too dry and hard to be of themselves interesting: we reply, let the text-books for these studies be as interesting as possible, and let the time for studying them be postponed to a later period of the pupil's school life, to the period when his moral sense is developed, and when he understands the value of time. We know very well that the rod cannot be given up at this moment in our Schools, organized as they are, without substituting some other equally objectionable mode of discipline, but this is not because our children are worse than others, nor because the thing is impossible, but because our schools are labor-saving machines, because an ordinary man, (and surely all our teachers are not extraordinary men,) must, and will take the shortest and easiest course, which is that of coercion, by the fear of physical pain or discomfort; and because we have not enough of female assistance of the highest character. Before we say this cannot be done, let us organize our Schools aright, and give them proper female assistants, of whom there are more than enough that nature has fitted for teachers, to take the place of those incumbents who cannot manage children without a constant and habitual appeal to the lowest motives.

On this subject of corporal punishment, and indeed on many others, your Committee have sought for light and aid from the masters themselves, and have given to each a series of printed questions, in which they were invited to express fully their opinions on many points connected with the welfare of the Schools.

On the question, whether in their opinion corporal punishment has increased or diminished since the passage of the resolution requiring that each case be recorded, most of the masters have preserved a remarkable silence, or evaded the question; — only four come out and say frankly that it has diminished. Now this is remarkable, because the fact of its diminution is becoming notorious, and your Committee have learned from other sources that this diminution is a very material one.

In reply to another questions: Do you think that the true interest of your scholars has been promoted by the passage of the

resolution? the masters generally answer with an unqualified
No. One only says that it has been promoted.

Your Committee feel bound to say that all they can learn on this
subject convinces them that the more radical measure of abolishing
corporal punishment altogether, would have been premature and
probably injurious to the Schools; and that it requires great vigi-
lance on the part of the School Committee and the friends of the
scholars to prevent the resort to worse measures than blows, by
those who are incapacitated by nature from governing by higher
means; and great attention too on their part as friends of the masters, that they may be encouraged and supported in the attempts
at reform, which we believe are honestly made.

Your Committee would fain digress here a moment, and allude to
what seems to them perfectly obvious, and yet is difficult of proof;
— the want of a feeling of manly independence, and of fearless
frankness, on the part of the masters. We were everywhere, as
your representatives, treated with great respect and deference.
But in the reply to many of our oral and printed questions, there
very generally seemed to be an excessive reserve. The masters
evidently are very desirous of obeying implicitly, and in some
cases blindly, every wish of the General Committee; but they
seem to fear a secret power which may govern them and the
Committee too.

This is very unfortunate, for the Committee never can accomplish
its high purpose, without the hearty coöperation and the full confidence of the masters. For want of this, the wisest measures that
can be devised in this room, will be productive of very little good
in the schoolroom. Your Committee endeavored to meet the masters as gentlemen and friends; and would be equally surprised and
pained to learn that any thing on their part inspired that feeling of
restraint and reserve, and that indisposition to coöperate with us
in an honest endeavor to find out the true condition of the Schools,
which certainly were obvious among a few of them. For instance,
we would gladly have gone into the important subject of text books,
and we gave to each master among our printed questions the following: Can you suggest any improvement in the text books studied
in our Schools?

Most of the masters declined answering this question; those who
did answer, touched it as one would handle the edge of a very sharp
instrument; and the only full, free and valuable communication
was given by an energetic and able master, after assurance that no

public use would be made of it! Such a state of things ought not to be. It is discreditable to this Committee, and injurious to the masters and to their Schools, to have them placed in such relations, that they dare not express their honest opinion of any text book, used in any department of instruction, let who will own the copy-right.

But to return to the subject of corporal punishment. If it can be abolished only by increasing the gloom of that atmosphere which hangs like a pall over some schoolhouses, where the iron face of authority is the central source whence emanate the fear and distrust that chill the young and timid into unnatural sobriety; if for blows upon the hand there must be blows upon the soul, then we say, give back the rod to the master.

If to adults are given all the property and all the authority in the world, to children is given the heritage of happy hearts, every generation that comes along, proclaims its careless joy by their happy faces and gladsome frolics; and thus through the whole warp of humanity, runs a beautiful thread of happiness, which we may trace back to the great source of all love and all good. We would not that this thread should be needlessly broken for a moment; and we prefer that the few reckless and turbulent spirits should be kept in subordination by the rod, rather than that a whole School should be held under severe restraint.

Or if the other great motive-power in our Boston Schools, must be increased; if emulation must, even more than it now does, produce envyings and jealousies and strife; and the contented indolence of the many who early find that they cannot succeed; again we say, rather give back the rod. But we do not believe that this is necessary; abundant experience has proved that Schools as large, and as difficult of management as ours, can be governed by an appeal to higher motives than a fear of pain; and we will not believe that the children of Boston are less alive to appeals to their sense of duty, — to their self-respect, — to their love of knowledge, than the children of the most favored city in the world. Nor do we believe that men cannot be found, soon, if not now, competent to the task of guiding and teaching our children by appeals to high motives; for we know that some such are to be found among our present masters. Give them associates who will not try to pull them down to their own inferior level, — give them smaller classes and more assistants, — give them more models, — maps, — apparatus and means of illustration, and above all give them more active and visible sympathy and respect, and every School in Boston will be as one or two are now, a place to which children delight to resort.

We cannot forbear repeating the remark, that we render the highest respect to the faithful teacher and his most useful profession. There is no station higher and more honorable than that occupied by the guides and guardians of youth. The profession of the teacher has a direct influence upon the most important interests of society; it is felt most essentially in the formation of individual character, and in its ultimate effects and consequences, it is coextensive with its existence of the soul itself.

In order adequately to fill this high station, and meet these weighty responsibilities, something more is requisite than mere scholarship. A thorough acquaintance with the various branches of study, taught in our Schools, although indispensable, is yet only a part of the teacher's qualifications.

Much depends upon his moral character. If he is known to be a good man, governing himself by correct principles, and acting habitually from a high sense of duty, he will have the respect and confidence of his pupils. His character will give weight to his instructions, and inspire the youth under his care with motives to study and to good behavior, such as can be supplied from no other source. But if a teacher is reckless of principle, and incapable of controlling his own temper; if he is not seen to be himself in subjection to the authority of conscience, and of God, no other means which he can employ will make him a good disciplinarian. He cannot govern his School. He may, by hard words and harder blows, impose temporary restraints upon the pupils; but their characters are unchanged, except from bad to worse.

The efficiency of the teacher depends essentially upon the interest he feels in his scholars. There is a great difference in this respect among instructors, everywhere. Some appear to have no higher object in view, than simply to go through with their required task. If they teach what is demanded by law, and are with their pupils during the hours assigned in the regulations, they are satisfied. They have apparently no further interest in those immortal minds whose training for this world, and for the future, is in a great measure committed to their agency. Such men are influenced by selfish and mercenary motives, and whatever may be their other qualifications, are unfit for duties, of which they know not the worth.

Is there not some light thrown upon the duties of a school-master, by the analogies which connect this office with that of a minister of religion? He should be the known and fast friend of those who confide themselves to his instruction. He should be acquainted with the scholars, should visit them at their home, and show an affectionate, parental interest in their welfare. Surely he may be likened to a clergyman in this; that his power depends not more upon the intelligent performance of his public and required duties, than on the thousand attentions that are prompted by the law of love. The secret of his success consists in knowing those with whom he deals; their individual peculiarities, the influences by which they are surrounded, their habits of thought and action, and in being able to sympathize with them where sympathy is most grateful and most useful. The schoolmaster must toil for many hours of many days, and must have his hours of rest and recreation. We do not ask of him to visit all the homes of his pupils. But occasions sometimes occur, when visits like these would be practicable and most beneficial. Something of this is now done, but more might be done, and would be eminently useful.

In things like these, we think there is room for improvement in our Public Schools. There is too great a distance between the teacher and the pupils. Some of the masters reside out of the city, and never see their scholars except in the schoolroom, and know little or nothing of the influences which are bearing upon them in private life. Instead of that free and confiding intercourse which has so powerful an influence upon the warm and generous hearts of youth, the teacher is seen or heard of, loved or feared, only as "the master."

The efficiency and success of the teacher, it may be said, depends very much upon the character of the scholars. If they are dull and unamiable, ungrateful and stupid, his efforts are all lost upon them. But the old proverb is true in reference to teachers, as well as clergymen, "Like priest, like people." The teacher, after all, may make his own School. It follows very closely the model of his own character.

If he is competent to his profession, and feels that interest and enthusiasm in it which he ought to feel, he will of necessity infuse life and vigor into his pupils; and as to the love, gratitude and confidence of his scholars, these are obtained only by paying the price. He must deserve them. Let him cherish a deep interest in their welfare, and show by patient attention to their mental and moral culture, in season and out of season, that he seeks their good, and he cannot fail to touch a spring from which shall gush forth emotions of gratitude and love. Let him give himself wholly to his work. Let the pupils have the full benefit of his intellectual resources, and ever feel when in his presence the refreshing influence of a kind and honest heart, and his words will drop upon them like the rain, and distil as the dew. He will thus rise to the elevated and dignified level of his profession, and the blessing of thousands that are ready to perish will come upon him. Our Schools, under such a guardian-ship, would be what they ought to be, so many centres of a healthful moral influence; — the salt of the earth and the light of the world.

Finally, we would deprecate the conclusion, that we have, in our desire to find out and reform the errors and deficiencies of our Schools, overlooked their excellences, which are many and various. All honor to the city which so generously upholds them; all honor to our predecessors who have stolen time from the severe labors of the day, and from their hours of rest at night, to watch over and improve them; all honor, and all praise, — aye! the highest and sincerest, to those masters who have heretofore labored, or now labor, with steadfastness and zeal, — giving their time, their love, their life, to a cause which they regard as the noblest to which a mor-tal can devote himself, — the moulding and training of immortal spirits!

These are not words of hollow pretence; these are not merely feelings got up in the closet; we have, during our long and severe labor, been often cheered by the thought that the Schools we were examining were worthy of more than we could do for them; and we have formed acquaintance with masters whom we must ever respect and esteem. That many of our Schools are far better than they once were, we well know, and gladly acknowledge. But the knowledge that there are such improvements, has only made us look to the possibility of farther progress, and resolve to do all in our power to leave for our children Schools as much better than the present, as the present are better than those of olden time.

THEOPHILUS PARSONS,
S. G. HOWE,
ROLLIN H. NEALE.

APPENDIX TWO
REPORT OF COMMITTEE ON WRITING SCHOOLS

The Committee, who were directed to make the annual examination of the several Writing schools, respectfully

REPORT:

That they have given the subject committed to their charge the attention which its importance seemed to demand.

They have visited all the schools, now numbering nineteen, and have endeavored from personal examination to learn their present condition, and to ascertain how far this branch of our system of instruction answers the just expectations of the public.

By the present organization of the schools, five are exclusively for girls, six for boys, and eight for girls and boys. The girls are allowed to attend from seven years of age till the next annual exhibition after they shall have arrived to the age of sixteen. The boys leave two years earlier. Sixteen of the schools are divided into two departments, called the Grammar and Writing departments, between which the pupil's time is equally divided. Practically these divisions constitute separate schools, for each has its distinct teachers, and each is perfectly independent of the other. The only claim which the two departments have to any connection, is in the fact that the same pupils are half of the time in each, and are half of the time absent from each, and that both departments are called by the same name. In the Lyman, New South, and Smith schools, this division has not been made.

These schools possess various degrees of merit. Some are of a high order, and do credit both to the teachers and the taught. Others are of a different class, and, in the opinion of the Committee, do not possess the character and standing which the citizens have a right to expect from all their schools, so liberally sustained, and so important to the well-being of society. This difference arises in some cases from local circumstances beyond the control of the teachers, and in others, from the zeal, capacity or efforts of the teachers themselves. Some of the schools, — such as the Otis and New Smith, — have been lately organized, and have not as yet any distinct character given them by their present teachers. They are composed chiefly of pupils taken from other schools, and from them we learn the present state of public instruction in the city, rather than the progress which they have made under their present instructers. The zeal and capacity which the masters in both of those schools exhibit, will, it is believed, in a proper time, give them a high character, and gain for them a large share of public favor. The committee were required to examine the first class only, and in most cases they limited their inquiries to this class. This is composed of children between the ages of eleven and sixteen. It is believed that the average age of the first class in all the schools is about twelve or thirteen years. The first division of this class, which generally comprises from one-fifth to a quarter of the whole, average about fourteen years. The studies pursued are Arithmetic, Algebra, Geometry, Writing and Bookkeeping. The rules of the Board also require instruction to be given in pen making. Since, however, the introduction of steel pens in all the schools, this has become less necessary, and with the exception of two or three, no instruction whatever is given in this once necessary department of a writing school. It is believed, however, that until the use of steel pens shall have become universal, it would be expedient and desirable for each writing master to give instruction in pen making to those of his first class, who may require it. Algebra and Geometry are not made necessary studies by the rules, but are permitted in such cases as are thought expedient. For this reason Algebra is studied in only about two-thirds of them, and Geometry in only two, viz.: the Hancock and Bowdoin.

From thirty minutes to one hour each day is devoted to writing by all the pupils of each class. In most of the schools one hour is spent in this way. Printed or engraved copies are generally used, though in many cases, for the younger children, they are written by the teacher. Writing books and pens are furnished by the teacher, and paid for by the pupils at a fixed price. This is believed to be general. The writing books are furnished the pupils at a price varying from six to twelve cents each, and the pens are provided for two or three cents per month.

The city supplies all the schools with ink. In several of the schools "Root's" system of writing has been introduced, and, so far as the Committee could learn, has been attended with good success. The best experiment in this system was seen at the Brimmer school, which, in this branch of instruction, the Committee place at the head of the schools.

In forming an estimate of the relative rank of the several schools in writing, the Committee confined themselves wholly to the specimens offered by the first class. The highest mark given by them was 12, and the rank assigned to each in this branch, is as follows:

Eliot	. . . .	10
Endicott { Girls	. . . .	12
{ Boys	. . . .	7
Hancock	. . . .	10
Mayhew	. . . .	6
Otis	. . . .	6
Wells	. . . .	9
Bowdoin	. . . .	11
Smith	. . . .	4
Phillips	. . . .	9
Adams	. . . .	6
Boylston { Girls	. . . .	12
{ Boys	. . . .	9
Franklin	. . . .	9
New South	. . . .	5
Brimmer	. . . .	12
Johnson	. . . .	9
Hawes	. . . .	8
Mather	. . . .	10
Winthrop	. . . .	9
Lyman	. . . .	10

So far as relates to the writing in the schools, the committee have no suggestions to make.

It is not desirable to have entire uniformity in the mode of instruction in all of them. It is believed to be better to leave each teacher to adopt such improvements, from time to time, as he shall judge expedient. Much must be left to his own judgment, and his instruction must be varied according to the capacity and acquirements of the learner. The present mode of furnishing pens and writing books seems as free from objections as any which could be adopted. It is necessary to have uniformity in the books of each school, and it is also necessary to have those of a proper quality. Neither of these objects could be obtained, if each pupil purchased his book wherever he pleased. The masters purchase them cheaper by the quantity, and selling them as they undoubtedly do to their pupils at cost, they are obtained at a much less price than single copies could be purchased at the stores. It is necessary to continue this system, or else have all the books purchased of some individual at a fixed price, under a contract made by the City. The latter plan would take some labor, from the masters, but its advantages would hardly compensate for the increased trouble which it would give the pupils.

The Committee commenced their examination early in June, and continued the same, from time to time, to the middle of July. In Arithmetic, they examined the pupils by submitting printed questions for their solution, and also by propounding questions orally. Before, however, they state the result of that examination, they propose to give, in detail, certain facts and statistics relative to each school. They begin with the

ELIOT SCHOOL

This school is located in North Bennett street — was established in 1713 — has connected with it 470 boys. Its present master has been in the school 20 years. During the last six months, 215 pupils have been admitted, and 177 discharged, owing chiefly to a change in the limits of the districts. Eighty pupils belong to the first class. Twenty-seven study Book-keeping, but none study Algebra or Geometry. The first class have been "through the first thirty-seven articles in Emerson's Third Part." The school house has no recitation rooms. The pupils are younger than in several of the other schools, and appear to have made greater progress in writing than in arithmetic. In Book-keeping their acquisitions seem to have been very limited.

ADAMS SCHOOL

Was established in 1717, and is located in Mason street. It has connected with it 420 boys. The building in which the school is kept is badly situated, has no recitation rooms, and is wholly unfit for the school. Seventy-two constitute the first class, a part of whom have gone through the Third Part of the Arithmetic. None study algebra. The present teacher took charge of the school in December, 1833. Several changes have been made in it during the last six months. Sixty-three of the first class have been discharged and seventeen admitted.

FRANKLIN SCHOOL

Is located in Washington street, and was established in 1785. It is a school for girls, and has 411 belonging to it. The first class consists of 40. Eleven have been through Bailey's Algebra, and nine study Book-keeping. The first class have been through the

Third Part of the Arithmetic. The present master has been connected with the school seven years. This school has been somewhat broken up the last year by reason of the School House having been burned.

MAYHEW SCHOOL

Is located in Hawkins street, and was established in 1803. It is a school for boys — has 373 pupils. The school house is inconvenient, and has no recitation rooms. There are fifty-four in the first class. Eighteen study Algebra; none Book-keeping. The first class have been through forty chapters of the Third Part of the Arithmetic. The present master has been connected with the school since December, 1833. Since September last, 120 have been discharged from the first class and sixty admitted.

HAWES SCHOOL

Was established in South Boston in 1811, and has 424 boys and girls connected with it. Twenty-four study Book-keeping, and none Algebra. The first division of the first class have been in Arithmetic nearly through the Third Part. The present teacher has been in the school ten years.

BOYLSTON SCHOOL

Was established in 1819, and is located on Fort Hill. It is open for both boys and girls, and 547 now belong to it. Nineteen study Algebra, and twenty-two Book-keeping. There are 101 in the first class, the first division of which have gone, in the Third Part of the Arithmetic, to the one hundred and eighty-first page. The present master has been connected with the school four and a half years. The School House needs recitation rooms.

BOWDOIN SCHOOL

Is a school for girls: was established in 1821, and is located in Derne street. At present, 511 belong to it, and there are 113 in the first class. Seventy-five study Algebra, twenty-five Geometry, and sixty Book-keeping. The present master has been connected with this school twenty years, and has been a teacher in the Public Schools of the City thirty-five years. About 150 pupils have been discharged from this school within a few months, to go to other Schools.

HANCOCK SCHOOL

Was established in 1822, and is located in Hanover street. Five hundred and forty-nine girls belong to it, one hundred of whom are in the first class. Thirty-eight study Algebra, thirty-eight Geometry, and fifty-one Book-keeping. The present master has been in the School twenty-one years. The school House is inconvenient, and has no recitation rooms. Within a few months, and at the time of the organization of the Otis School, about one fifth part of this school was changed.

WELLS SCHOOL

Is situated in McLean street, and was established in 1833 : was changed, last spring, from a boys' and girls' School, to one exclusively for girls. Four hundred and forty-five now belong to it, and seventy-seven are in the first class. Thirty-five study Algebra and Book-keeping. The first division have been through the Third Part of the Arithmetic. The present master has been in the school seven years.

JOHNSON SCHOOL

Was established in 1833, and is situated in Tremont street. It is exclusively for girls, and has connected with it 504. Twenty-seven study Algebra, and thirty Book-keeping. There are one hundred and thirteen in the first class. The present teacher has been connected with the school about four years.

WINTHROP SCHOOL

Was established in 1836, and is situated in East street. Five hundred and fifty-three boys and girls belong to it. Eighty-one constitute the first class. Twenty study Algebra and Book-keeping. The present master has been connected with the school since 1841.

LYMAN SCHOOL

Is situated in East Boston, and was organized in 1837. Three hundred and sixty boys and girls belong to it. Forty-one belong to the first class. Twenty-eight study Algebra. This school is under the charge of one master, an usher and three female teachers. A division of the school into distinct departments has not been adopted. The present master has been connected with the school eight years. Many changes have taken place in it, and during the past year about three hundred have joined, and two hundred have left it.

ENDICOTT SCHOOL

Is situated in Copper street, and was established in 1840. The present master has been connected with the school five years. It is for both boys and girls. Five hundred and eighteen belong to it. Eighty-one belong to the first class. Twelve study Algebra. The school has suffered a good deal the past year by a change of pupils.

MATHER SCHOOL

Was established at South Boston in 1843. Four hundred and eighty-five boys and girls belong to it, of whom fifty-nine are in the first class. Eleven study Algebra, and eight Book-keeping. The present master has been connected with the school since its organization.

BRIMMER SCHOOL

Was organized last year, and is located in Common street. It is a school exclusively for boys, and the number now belonging to it is 532. Nineteen study Algebra and Book-keeping. The present teacher has been connected with the school since its organization. The master instructs some of the pupils in Drawing, out of school hours. Forty constitute the first class.

PHILLIPS SCHOOL

Is situated in Pinckney street, and has 454 pupils. It was established last year. The first class in arithmetic have gone nearly through the third part. The present master took charge of the school in November last. It has been a good deal changed since that time by reason of making the Wells school a girls' school.

OTIS SCHOOL

Is situated in Lancaster street, and was first opened the present year. Four hundred and seventeen boys and girls belong to it. None at present study Algebra. The master instructs several of the older pupils in Drawing, after the usual school hours. There are thirty-seven in the first class.

NEW SOUTH SCHOOL

Is a school for boys, and is at present kept in the vestry of the Suffolk Street Chapel. One hundred and thirty-six belong to it. It has been established but a short time, and is under the control of a master and two female assistants. A new school house is now in process of building in Concord street for this school.

SMITH SCHOOL

Was instituted in 1812, and is designed for the instruction of colored children of both sexes. At the time of the examination, 163 belonged to it. The average attendance since the first of April last has been 109. This school is under the instruction of a master and two female assistants. It is divided into four classes. Twenty-seven are in the first class. Four half days each week are devoted to writing and arithmetic. Of the first division of the first class only five were present, whose average age was twelve years and four months. There seemed to be but few pupils present more than ten or eleven years of age. The present master has been connected with the school eleven years.

The Committee do not hesitate to say that they were disappointed in this school. With but two or three exceptions the pupils had not gone beyond the simplest questions in oral Arithmetic, and on examination they seemed to be unable to answer any thing but the plainest propositions. The school is in a low condition, and does not appear to be answering the objects for which it was instituted. There are, no doubt, great difficulties in the management and instruction of this school, arising from causes which do not affect any other school in the city. The children leave early and as soon as they are able to obtain employment. Those best educated and most capable usually go first.

They often, too, join the school at an advanced age, and without much previous education or discipline. They are inconstant in their attendance, oftentimes tardy, and in many cases exceedingly inattentive to their studies. It is evident that in a school of this character, other and greater efforts are required in its management than in the other city schools. It may not be made to compete with the other schools, yet it is believed that it can be much elevated, that its usefulness may be increased, and that it may be placed on such a footing as to answer the just expectations of its benevolent founder, as well as the rightful claims of the colored population.

The Committee do not deem it their duty to go into a discussion of the causes of the present state of things in this school. Evils do exist which must and ought to find a remedy. The school is not what it ought to be, nor is it what it is believed it can be. The particular measures which shall be adopted for its elevation and improvement, the Committee are not prepared to point out, but will leave them to be devised and adopted by a community always generous in its means to educate and improve its members.

The written examination in Arithmetic was adopted in all the schools except the Smith. It was limited to the first division of the first class, which varied in numbers from four to twenty-six. The Committee prepared ten questions for solution, on a variety of subjects, and caused them to be printed on a single sheet, leaving between each a sufficient blank space to enable the pupils to record the process of solution. The same questions were submitted to all the schools, and the pupils were required to lay aside their books and slates, and work out the process on the paper itself. One hour and ten minutes were allowed them, at the expiration of which all the papers were returned to the Committee, whether the questions were solved or not. It was not expected that any considerable number could work out all the sums in so short a time, but it was thought expedient to propose such questions that even those who had made the greatest advancement might find employment during the allotted period. It was also intended to have these questions embrace such a variety of subjects as to require a pretty thorough knowledge of the whole science of arithmetic to give the right answers to them all.

The whole number of children belonging to the schools at the time of the examination was 8,243, of whom 308, comprising the best scholars in each school, were examined in this manner.

Two hundred and eighty-nine gave a correct answer to No. 1; two hundred and eighty-two to No. 2; one hundred and seventy to No. 3; nine to No. 4; none to No. 5, though one hundred and twenty-six gave the same answer, viz.: six months, which is nearly correct; two to No. 6, both of whom belonged to the Mather School; one hundred and forty-seven to No. 7; none to No. 8; one hundred and seventy-four to No. 9; and one, — Miss Frances A. Lathrop, of the Hawes School, — to No. 10. A considerable number gave different answers to No. 4, but only nine gave the correct one, two of whom belonged to the Adams School, one to the Johnson, and six to the Winthrop. It will appear that the most successful schools were the Wells, Lyman, Winthrop, Mather, and Bowdoin.

The average number of sums correctly solved by each pupil in the Wells and Lyman is four and six-tenths; in the Winthrop four and four-tenths; in the Mather, four and five-elevenths; and in the Bowdoin, four and two-nineteenths.

The Committee do not wish to be understood to say that the result of this written examination is a perfectly correct index of the standing of the several schools. It is only one mode of ascertaining that fact. It is certain and conclusive so far as it goes, and, if the character of a school depended upon the actual capacity of its pupils to solve questions of this nature, it would be a certain test. The Committee prefer, however, to judge of the value of instruction in the school, in part from other evidence. There are so many causes in operation which give some of our schools an advantage over the others, without any merit or demerit of the teacher, that it would be unjust to hold the masters of all the schools alike responsible for actual results. They should be responsible for only what they have and what they do or neglect. The master of a school lately organized or composed of new pupils, who exhibits a zeal and capacity in his vocation, who inspires in his pupils a love of learning and makes the schoolroom the place to which they like to resort, even though he cannot exhibit in them any great progress, deserves as much credit as the master of the best school in the City, and is in a fair way to bring his school into the first rank. This remark will apply to several of the schools, which have been organized within a few years. They have not at present so high a standing as some of the older schools, yet it is believed that equal credit is due to their teachers, and that instruction equally valuable and fitting is given to their pupils. In some cases, the new schools seem to have gone beyond the older ones. The Committee have ranked the Mather above the Hawes, and the Brimmer above the Johnson. They were much gratified with the instruction in the Winthrop, Phillips, Lyman and Endicott, all of which, gave ample evidence of the zeal, fidelity and capacity of their teachers.

Of the girls' schools, the Bowdoin undoubtedly takes the first rank. Its pupils have made greater progress than in any other, and a greater number of them attend to the higher branches of Algebra and Geometry. The average age is believed to be greater than in any other school in the City. One hundred and forty-three compose the first class, more than half of whom study algebra and many of them have become well acquainted with its principles. Due credit is to be given to the teachers, yet it is believed that injustice would be done to other schools, if its superiority was not attributed in some degree, to other causes than their capacity and fidelity. Next to this school stand the Wells and Franklin, and then follow the Hancock and Johnson.

Of the boys' schools, the Committee give the Brimmer the first rank. Next to this, they place the Phillips and Eliot. After these comes the Adams, and then the Mayhew.

Of the mixed schools, the Boylston is at the head.

Of the comparative rank of the several schools, the Committee have said all they think necessary. Improvements may be made in them all, and in a City which has always been distinguished for its generous efforts in the cause of popular education, it is not becoming to lag behind, and follow at a distance and with reluctant step, the modern movement in this great cause. The preëminence of Boston in a matter so philanthropic, so just, and withal so economical as the education of the whole people, must be preserved. To promote this object, there is no lack of appropriations. The City give all that can be reasonably asked, and more than any other City in the world in proportion to its means. More than two hundred thousand dollars were paid last year for the support of schools and the building of school houses, of which about one hundred and twenty thousand were paid in salaries to instructors. During the present year appropriations have been made for similar purposes to the amount of $212,600. Of this, $127,000 are appropriated to the payment of salaries. Add to this the interest on the amount expended in school houses and owned by the City, and the whole expense paid by the City for schools and school houses the present year will exceed $250,000, being an amount equal to one third of the whole City tax. With such generous appropriations for popular education what cannot be effected? Let this amount be economically expended in schools properly organized, with able, efficient and zealous teachers, rejoicing in the duties and labors of their honorable and responsible profession, and inspired with a love of promoting the moral and intellectual progress of their race, and such an advance would be made in popular education in our City, as not only to bring joy to the heart of the christian and philanthropist, but to make even the money calculator proud of the preeminence, the intellect, and moral power of our people.

It has been said by one of our own distinguished citizens, that the influence of New England in our widely extended country must hereafter depend, not on its numbers, but on carrying forward and extending our system of popular education, in developing the intellect and promoting the moral character of the whole people. Of the truth of this there can be no doubt, and equally true is it that the past influence of New England has depended on the same cause; that to this are due her early triumphs in sustaining and extending her settlements, her successful vindication of her rights, and above all, her preservation of a truly republican government.

The Committee do not intend to say any thing in derogation of the present masters of our schools, but, on the other hand, to the meritorious efforts and success of many of them, they cheerfully bear testimony. There are some cases where they think there is a want of the proper spirit, as well as the proper faculty to teach. Such, however, are exceptions, and are not very numerous.

Much of the improvement in the schools necessarily depends on the teachers. Elegant school houses and princely appropriations do but little without the teacher, who has a sufficient capacity and a proper spirit. If we employ a teacher whose efforts are to be limited to the use of means necessary to retain his place and get his salary, not much can be expected from him beyond that. He may get his salary, but he does not earn it. Nay, he does greater injustice than that. He deprives those committed to his charge of the benefit of that instruction, which, by accepting the office, he pledged himself to give. He commits a double wrong, — in the first place to the public, and in the second place by doing an irreparable injury to his pupils. Upon the teachers must, in a great degree, depend whether the pupils shall confine their acquisitions to the letter and rules of the text book, or whether they shall understand the principles of the studies they pursue.

In this respect there is a most striking difference in our schools. In some the pupils seem to understand what they have studied, and to know how to apply it to the cases which may arise; in others they can repeat rules with great fluency and accuracy, answer printed questions in arithmetic, while the book is before them, and, in fact, recite all their lessons in the book in a manner which would seem to do them great credit. When, however, these landmarks are thrown aside, and they are called to the black board and requested to answer questions not found in the book, and for which they have no prescribed rules, they come to a dead stand, and lose the whole skill which before they apparently exhibited.

It seems to the Committee that this latter mode of instruction is quite too prevalent in some of the schools; that the pupils learn rules rather than principles, and that the text books are made quite too much their guide. It is believed that no school can be very successful while this plan is adhered to, that a good and sufficient education will not be acquired by keeping within the pages of text books, and that no person can be a successful teacher without constant instruction in the principles and application of the studies pursued.

The Committee are satisfied that improvements should be made in several of the school houses. All should have proper recitation rooms, and there would be much less interruption if the large school rooms were divided into two or three apartments by movable partitions. There should also be a much greater supply of blackboards. In many of the schools there is but one, and that a small one. If they were more generally provided, the teachers would use them more, and this would be attended with the most beneficial results. The City should provide all the necessary instruments for the teacher, so that on this head he shall have no excuse.

There is another topic for the improvement of the schools which the Committee beg leave to refer to the consideration of this Board. Each of the schools is divided into two departments, or in other words into two schools. Unless there is an advantage in this system of greater weight than its manifest disadvantages, it ought to be abolished. It is an anomaly in the school system of this Commonwealth, and exists hardly beyond sixteen of the Grammar and Writing Schools in Boston. It is exceedingly expensive, and more so than it need be. This is worthy of consideration, and should not be allowed unless its advantages are manifest. The Committee are not aware what are the arguments of the advocates of the present system. They can see no substantial good arising from it, while on the other hand, it is attended with great inconvenience and evil. Every pupil who attends these schools attends two schools, at the same time. He has two masters, under whose influence he is acquiring an education. One he visits in the forenoon, and the other in the afternoon. If he neglects one, the other knows nothing about it. One may instruct him in rules, the other in principles. One may adopt one course of conduct towards him, and the other a different course. One may deal in corporal punishment, and the other govern by the use of other means. The pupil always makes a comparison between them, and is very likely to entertain towards them different feelings.

But the great difficulty in the system is a proper distribution of studies between the two departments. By the present rules nothing but Writing and Arithmetic is required in the writing department. Some may avail themselves of the study of Algebra, Geometry and Book-keeping, but they are few, and are confined to the most advanced pupils. One half of the time is given by all the rest to Writing and Arithmetic, and this without any regard to sex, age or acquirements.

The girl at seven and sixteen gives the same time to these studies. From one half to an hour in each day is devoted to Writing, so that two hours or two hours and a half are set apart for arithmetic during the seven or nine years that the pupils may remain in school. The rules give the masters no discretion in this matter, and the child who studies nothing but oral Arithmetic, and who, in fact, can learn nothing except during the recitation, is compelled to spend two or two and a half hours in this way. The Committee do not doubt that the older pupils may spend this time in the study of Arithmetic profitably, but they believe that with the younger it is not only partially lost, but tends to weary and disgust them.

By a late vote of this Board, Geography and Natural Philosophy are hereafter to be added to the studies of the Writing Department. Of the expediency of this, there is a difference of opinion among the masters, and it may well be doubted whether it will not give that department more than its proportion of studies. It will be exceedingly advantageous to the younger pupils in that department, and will give them employment in an agreeable study, during the time that is now partially lost, and so far as they are concerned, it is desirable. Whether it will be so to the older pupils, remains to be seen.

In the schools exclusively for girls or boys, a division is made into classes, according to their attainments in one or the other department, and if the principle be rightly carried out, there must be frequent changes from one class to the other. The higher classes belong to one department, and the lower classes to the other, and all influence of the one on the other, whether for good or evil, is wholly lost. In the mixed schools a different rule prevails. In them the boys constitute one department, and the girls the other, — so that there is a first class of boys as well as of girls in each, and the master in each department is compelled to repeat his course of instruction every day. Many of the evils would be avoided by abolishing this system, and establishing in its stead a system which has for each school but one head master, who should be responsible for the instruction, management and discipline of the whole school. Let the school then be divided so as to give him all the older children, whom he should instruct in all the branches taught in the schools, and to each of whom he should give such attention as should be thought for their good.

Such assistants might be employed to take charge of the younger classes as the condition of each school required. In the girls' schools, and perhaps in all, the services of several male teachers might be dispensed with, and in their stead females could be employed as assistants, who, it is believed, would be equally, if not more efficient and successful teachers of the young.

Your Committee cannot refrain from saying a few words on the subject of medals, as prizes for scholarship, etc. Much has been written for and against the principle of emulation as an incentive to diligence and intellectual developement, and it would seem from the fact that prizes are multiplying in our schools, through the munificence of individuals, that competition is the acknowledged principle of our school system, that it constitutes its life as it does of business. Your Committee cannot but express their regret if the fact is as it appears. They could wish the whole plan abolished, as presenting low and unworthy motives, where the noblest only should govern, and where the noblest, if presented, would be found the most powerful; and as introducing rivalries, jealousies and heart burnings, not only into the schools, but into families and social circles. It would need only that one should attend an examination for the awarding of medals to be convinced of the essential evils of the system.

To witness the anxiety, the feverish excitement of mind and body, preventing frequently the most meritorious scholars from doing justice to themselves, the crushing sense of a false shame at a mistake or temporary absence of memory; the starting tear of a modest, worthy and diligent girl at the forced consciousness of her inferiority in the eager race, would lead all of any sensibility, as it has your Committee, to deprecate the system, and to pray it may be no further extended by private or public bounty, but curtailed in every possible manner, if it may not be utterly abolished.

The schools suffer severely from the inconstant attendance of the

pupils.   The absence each day is about one fifth of the whole school.
Parents and guardians should consider this subject, and endeavor
to secure if possible a more regular and constant attendance.   The
good order and management of the school, as well as the progress
of the pupils must be very seriously affected by so great an amount
of absence.   The Committee know no remedy for this evil, except
by an appeal to the parents, and by making the school a more agreeable place for children.

The Committee have referred to most of the topics which seem
to require consideration.   They submit their recommendations and
opinion with diffidence, and with no other view than to promote the
good and growth of our system of public instruction.   They believe
it is capable of great improvement, and though they may differ with
others in the means which shall be adopted, yet they will yield, to none
in their ardent wishes for the attainment of so desirable an end.
They have acquired a new interest in our public schools, by the
somewhat laborious examinations which they have been required
to make, and they hope and trust that the system of popular education, first established in our Commonwealth, and steadily sustained
even in the most trying periods of her history, will be improved until
every child in the country is educated, and made capable of using
for the best purposes, the powers which God has given him.

WILLIAM BRIGHAM,
J. I. T. COOLIDGE,
HIRAM A. GRAVES.

APPENDIX THREE

EXTRACTS FROM "THE COMMON SCHOOL JOURNAL"

The editor of *The Common School Journal* was Horace Mann. In the following extracts only his comments have been quoted. Copies of the tests, tables, etc., given elsewhere in this Appendix have been omitted.

THE
COMMON SCHOOL JOURNAL

Vol. VII.   Boston, October 1, 1845.   No. 19.

BOSTON GRAMMAR AND WRITING SCHOOLS

(We commence, in the present Number of the Journal, the publication of copious extracts from the late Reports of the Annual Examining Committees of the Boston Grammar and Writing Schools. To prevent misapprehension, it should be premised, that there are *five grades of Public Schools in the city of Boston,* — *namely, the Latin, the English High, the Grammar and Writing, the Intermediate,* and *the Primary.* The Reports from which we are about to quote, relate to the Grammar and Writing Schools only. In but few instances before, has any Report of the examining committees of these schools been published. In no instance before, have these schools ever been subjected to a thorough, scrutinizing examination, — and to such an examination as would make their condition known to the public, as well as to the committee. Such an examination they have this year received; and their actual condition, as to present proficiency and ability, is now made known to the world. This condition reveals, with inevitable accuracy, the motive-powers by which they have been governed; for, other things being equal, the proficiency made by pupils will always be greater or less, according to the elevated or the degrading character of the motives by which they are governed, and incited to study.

Many circumstances conspire to place these Reports of the committees among the most remarkable, as well as the most instructive and admonitory of all our school documents. The high character of the committees who conducted the examination; the mode of examination, at once thorough, and perfectly fair and impartial, the labor and care expended in reducing the results of the examination to a tabular form, so that the common eye can compare them, and determine at a glance the relative standing of each school; the astounding character of the results themselves, and the consequences, in regard to a change of teachers, to which they have already conduced, together with the admirable suggestions and doctrines, laid down in their pages, on many of the most important topics that pertain to our schools; — all these, and other considerations, combine to give an extraordinary degree of importance to these Reports, and to commend them to the attentive perusal, not only of those parents immediately interested in the city schools, but of the whole people of the State. — Ed.)

Having now completed our extracts from the Report of the Committee on the Grammar Schools, and also our abstract of the Tables, we find the whole subject too deeply freighted with interest and instruction to allow us to pass it unnoticed. In order that our remarks may stand in immediate connection with the subject to which they refer, we postpone, until another opportunity, the consideration of the facts contained in the Report of the committee on the Writing department.

In the first place, not the city of Boston only, but the whole State, and the cause of education generally, are under a vast debt of obligation to the committees who assumed, and who have carried through, the labor of this novel mode of examination. We call it novel, because, although such a plan of examination is common in Europe, and has been partially adopted in some places in this country, yet we have seen nothing, on this side of the Atlantic, so thorough and complete, and embracing, in one view, so large a number of schools and of scholars, as the Boston committees' Reports. We venture to predict, that the mode of examination, by printed questions and written answers, will constitute a new era in the history of our schools. There is a variety of reasons which give it a decided superiority over any and all other methods, — some of which we proceed to notice.

1. It is impartial. It is impartial, not in a limited, but in a very extended application of that term; for it submits the same question not only to all the scholars who are to be examined, in the same school, but to all the schools of the same class or grade. Scholars in the same School, therefore, can be equitably compared with each other; and all the different schools are subjected to a measurement by the same standard. Take the best school committee man who ever exposed the nakedness of ignorance, or detected fraud, or exploded the bubbles of pretension, and let him examine a class orally, and he cannot approach exactness, in judging of the relative merits of the pupils, by any very close approximation. And the reason is apparent. He must propound different questions to different scholars; and it is impossible that these questions should be equal, in point of ease or difficulty. A poor scholar may be asked a very

easy question, and answer it. A good scholar may be asked a very difficult one, and miss it. In some cases, a succeeding scholar may profit by the mistake of a preceding one; so that, if there had been a different arrangement of their seats, the record would have borne a different result of plus and minus. The examiner may prepare himself beforehand as carefully as he pleases, and mark out the precise path he intends to pursue, and yet, in spite of himself, he may be thrown out of his course by unforeseen circumstances. But when the questions are the same, there is exactness of equality. Balances cannot weigh out the work more justly. So far as the examination is concerned, all the scholars are "born free and equal."

Suppose a race were to be run by twenty men, in order to determine their comparative fleetness; but instead of bringing them upon the same course, where they should all stand abreast and start abreast, one of them should be selected to run one mile, and then a second, starting where the first one stopped, should run another mile, and so on until the whole had entered the lists; might it not, and would it not so happen that one would have the luck of running up hill, and another down; that one would run over a good turnpike and another over a "corduroy"? Pupils required to answer dissimilar questions, are like runners obliged to test their speed by running on dissimilar courses.

Again, it is clear that the larger the number of questions put to a scholar, the better is the opportunity to test his merits. If but a single question be put, the best scholar in the school may miss it, though he would answer the next twenty without a blunder; or the poorest scholar may succeed in answering one question, though certain to fail in twenty others. Each question is a partial test, and the greater the number of questions, therefore, the nearer does the test approach to completeness. It is very uncertain which face of a die will be turned up at the first throw; but if the dice are thrown all day, there will be a great equality in the number of the different faces turned up.

In fine, the method adopted by the committees, was not merely impartial, — for this is only an adjective, — but it was the noun substantive, Impartiality itself.

2. This method is far more just than any other to the pupils themselves. It may be said that this is only a corollary from our preceding position. It is, however, something more. Suppose, under the form of oral examination, an hour is assigned to a class of thirty pupils, — this gives two minutes apiece. But under the

late mode of examination, we have the paradox, that an hour for thirty is sixty minutes apiece.   Now it often happens that a sterling scholar is modest, diffident, and easily disconcerted under new cir-cumstances.   Such a pupil requires time to collect his faculties. Give him this, and he will not disappoint his best friends.   Debar him from this, and a forth-putting, self-esteeming competitor may surpass him.   In an exercise of two minutes, therefore, the best scholar may fail, because he loses his only opportunity while he is summoning his energies to improve it ; but give him an hour, and he will have time to rally and do himself justice.   It is one of the principal recommendations of this method, indeed, that it excludes surprise as one of the causes of failure, and takes away the simula-tion of it as an excuse.

3. The method under consideration is the most thorough.   To give out two or three questions on the whole subject of grammar, or geography, for instance, or to require the solution of a single question in arithmetic, resembles not a little the device of that Scholastikos in the fable, who, wishing to sell his house, carried a brick to market as a specimen.   It is true the brick gave some in-dication about the house, as a single answer may do about a pupil's knowledge of a study ; but both a discreet purchaser and a discreet examiner would like some additional information.

4. The new method prevents the officious interference of the teacher.   Nothing is more annoying to a good examiner than to be interrupted by the teacher.   It sometimes happens that when an examiner has brought a pupil or a class to a test-question, — to a point that will reveal their condition as to ignorance or knowledge, — the teacher bolts out with some suggestion or leading question that defeats the whole purpose at a breath.   We would look with all possible lenity upon teachers who take such a course ; for we perceive the vehemence of the temptation under which they labor. When the pupils of their favorite class, and perhaps in their favor-ite study, are in danger of being sunk in the abysses of their own ignorance, how natural it is for a kind-hearted and quick-feeling teacher to wish to throw them a rope.   But such interference is unjust, not to say ungentlemanly.   The case supposed is the very juncture where the teacher should abstain from intermeddling, though he should be obliged to thrust his pocket-handkerchief into his mouth, or put his head out of the window.   Of what use to ex-amine a school, if each boy and girl is to be like Punch and Judy in the puppet-show, and to be told by another the things they are

to say? While, then, we respect the feelings which prompt the teacher to interfere with the course of the examination, we consider it a great point gained, to prevent the mischief of their indulgence. Now where a school is examined by written or printed questions, distributed on the instant, by the examining committee, questions of which the teachers themselves are as ignorant as the pupils, — they must, perforce, look on at their leisure. Though they writhe in anxiety, yet their ill-judged kindness can do no harm; their improper suggestions are excluded. They are obliged to reflect that the day of probation has passed; the time for trial and judgment has come.

5. And, what is not inferior in value to either of the preceding considerations, it does determine, beyond appeal or gainsaying, whether the pupils have been faithfully and competently taught.

All pupils of average ability, who have been properly taught, should have a command, not merely of the particular fact, or the general statement of a truth or principle, but also of its connections, relations and applications; and every faithful examiner will strive to know whether they possess the latter as well as the former species of information. Text books contain a much greater proportion of isolated facts, and of abstract principles, than of relations and applications. This is the circumstance which gives pertinency and significancy to their distinctive appellation, — text books. They are books containing texts. These texts the teacher is to expound. Each one of them should be the foundation of a discourse, or of a series of discourses. This is teaching. Hearing recitations from a book, is not teaching. It has no claim to be called by this dignified and expressive name. It is the exposition of the principle contained in the book; showing its connection with life, with action, with duty; making it the nucleus around which to gather all related facts and all collateral principles: — it is this, and this only, which can be appropriately called teaching. All short of this is mere journey-work, rude mechanical labor and drudgery.

Now the method of examination lately adopted by the Boston School Committee, settles the question as definitively, what kind or quality of instruction has been given by the masters, as it does what amount or extent of proficiency has been made by the pupils. A pupil may most faithfully commit the whole of one of our grammars to memory, and yet know nothing more of the science of English Grammar, than a parrot, who has been taught to say "Pretty Poll," knows of the power and copiousness of the English language;

or he may con Geography and Atlas, till he can repeat every line in the one and remember every island speck in the other, and yet have no distinct conception of anything beyond the visible horizon. A child may know, — as any child unless it be an idiotic one does, — that water will run down hill, and yet never be led to embrace the truth, that it is mountain ridges and table lands that give descent and direction to the course of rivers. Nay, because he has faithfully learned the fact that the upper part of a map represents the north, he may conscientiously deny that the waters of Lake Erie run into Lake Ontario, because, as he holds his map before him, it looks as though they must, for that purpose, run up hill. A child may know how to spell from a spelling-book, and yet, when put to the twofold operation of writing and spelling, he may bring vowels and consonants into very strange juxtapositions. Or he may be introduced to ten thousand English words, and not know the real meaning and use of more than five hundred of them.

We repeat, then, that this method of examination tests, in a most admirable manner, the competency or sufficiency of the teaching which the pupils have received; for, as a workman is not taught any art or handicraft, until he can execute it, so a child is not taught any principle until he can explain it, or apply it. Where children of ordinary abilities have been continuously and for a long time under instruction, any deficiencies, of the kinds above specified, are not to be laid to their charge, but to that of their instructers. How should pupils know what lies beyond the text books, or what is necessary in order to understand the text book, unless they have been taught it? The case is different, we acknowledge, with regard to children who attend school irregularly, or for short periods only. In such cases, it would be unjust to hold the instructer responsible for their deficiencies.

6. There is another point, in which every faithful committee man has a deep interest, which is not merely subserved, but secured by the mode under consideration. It takes away all possibility of favoritism, and all ground for the suspicion of favoritism. A most unpleasant, and generally, we doubt not, an unfounded accusation, is sometimes brought against examiners; — namely, that they are guilty of partiality in putting out questions; that they visit the iniquities of fathers upon children, by selecting difficult questions for the child of an adversary or opponent, and reserving the easy ones for the children of friends. Now, in its practical mischiefs, the next worst thing to their committing so unjust an

act, is the suspicion that they have committed it. Either the fact or the suspicion greatly impairs the value, if it does not defeat the object of an examination. We have known instances where it would have been far better that there should have been no examination at all, than to have the cry of injustice raised, and the feelings of the district exasperated against committee men. But by putting the same questions to all, not only the odious offence of favoritism, but even an indulgence of the suspicion of it, is excluded.

7. We shall mention but one more point of superiority possessed by the method under consideration over all others. When the oral method is adopted, none but those personally present at the examination can have any accurate or valuable idea of the appearance of the school. By hearing the questions asked and the answers given, they may form a notion, more or less correct, of the attainments of the pupils, and the readiness with which they can command them. But all the information which approaches authenticity is confined within the walls of the schoolroom. Whoever is not there, and is not there at the time, too, must rely upon rumor for his opinions. Not so, however, when the examination is by printed questions and written answers. A transcript, a sort of Daguerreotype likeness, as it were, of the state and condition of the pupils' minds, is taken and carried away, for general inspection. Instead of being confined to committee and visitors, it is open to all; instead of perishing with the fleeting breath that gave it life, it remains a permanent record. All who are, or who may afterwards become interested in it, may see it. The school, during successive years too, can be compared with itself, in order to determine whether it is advancing or retrograding; or whether it has improved under one teacher, while it deteriorates under another. It is true that the committees, from year to year, under the old method, may make known their opinion, — they may write it out and publish it; — but different committees will have different standards of excellence; and thus it is quite possible that a school may have a brightening reputation, while in reality it is running down, and a waning one while it is improving. If every man's foot is to be taken as twelve inches long, it becomes an important question by whose foot we shall measure. So of the different standards of judging in the minds of different men.

Another remark falls appropriately under this head. Where the questions are all printed and preserved, their character as to ease or difficulty can be seen. Should the questions be too difficult for children of the age and opportunities of those examined, equitable abatement can be made for their failures. If, on the other hand, the questions are simple, and yet the children blunder, the censure must fall upon them with proportionate severity. If the scholars fail to answer, with promptitude and correctness, such questions as are found in the books, they must bear a portion at least of the dishonor; but if they answer from the book accurately and readily, but fail in those cases which involve relations and application of principles, the dishonor must settle upon the heads of the teachers. Whether one or the other, whether more or less of either, cannot be sufficiently known, unless the character of the questions is known. This important knowledge can be obtained only when the question can be inspected; that is, only when the written method of examination has been employed.

In closing our remarks upon their mode of examination, we doubt not the committee will be willing to listen to a suggestion which we respectfully make, in relation to it. The suggestion, however, has reference rather to the next year's examination, than to that of the present year. But we presume, that since the present experiment has so clearly demonstrated the superiority of the written over the oral method of examination, no committee will ever venture to relapse into the former inadequate and uncertain practice.

For future examinations, then, we would suggest a plan which, while it will very much abridge the labor of the committee, will present their results in a more tangible form. As at present organized, the different schools differ considerably from each other in the number of their pupils; and we see, by referring to the tables appended to the report, that the proportion of the school submitted to this method of examination, differs greatly in different schools; — varying, in Geography, from .04 to .09 per cent; in Definitions, from .04 to .11; in Natural Philosophy, from .03 to .09, and so forth. Now, the less the proportion of scholars examined, in a particular school, the better ought the results of that examination to be, in order to make it equal any other school where the proportion examined was greater. No one, without looking at the Tables we have prepared, can duly estimate the vast apparent advantage which some teachers have gained over others; by the smallness of the number in the class belonging to their schools, which was examined. But the casual reader will never stop to estimate the result of the compound ratios, to be embraced in the comparison of one school with another; and, indeed, when different schools are to be compared together for a series of years, it would make a somewhat complicated problem. To obviate this difficulty, and to make easy, a b c work of the whole matter, we would suggest that a certain percentage of pupils should be taken for examination from each school; and the same percentage in all the schools. For instance, if there are 500 scholars in a school, let 100, or 20 per cent, be taken; if there are 400 in the school, let 80 be taken, — different numbers, but the same percentage; — and then the result will be as intelligible, and as easily compared, one part with another, as a column of ordinals.

We mention 20 per cent because we observe by the Reports that, in some schools and in some important studies, only a very small proportion of the school was submitted for examination. In English grammar, the highest proportion examined in any school was only nine per cent; and it appears by the Report of the committee on the Writing department, that although there were 8,343 children in the schools at the time of the examination, only 308 were examined, — considerably less than four per cent. Now, every honest master will rejoice to have the temptation forever taken away from himself and his associates, of submitting only a few, — a select number, — of his scholars for the examination. He will rejoice to have the temptation forever removed of preparing four or five per cent of his school, — Brag Scholars, as they call them at the west, — while he neglects the rest. Besides, if so small a number is taken, many, if not most of the children of poor parents, will leave the school before it will come their turn to be examined in this critical way; and therefore the force of the temptation to neglect this class of children, — who should rather be the special objects of the teacher's care, — will be greatly enhanced.

Further remarks upon these important Reports appear in later publications of the Journal, from which the statements on subsequent pages are taken.

Having now made copious extracts from the late Reports of the committees who were appointed to examine the Boston Grammar and Writing Schools; and having, in the last number of the Journal, presented our views respecting the excellences of the method adopted by those committees, — a method which we trust will be copied in other parts of the State and country, — we proceed to submit some observations on the results of that examination. That the facts disclosed by the Reports, have spread through the city a general and deep feeling of sorrow and mortification, no one will

be so presumptuous as to deny.   Sad indeed would it be, if this feeling should die away without producing a reform.

We have no wish to blazon abroad the defects of these schools;
but if this occasion should not be made use of, for admonition and
warning, the calamity of their present condition would not only
be gratuitously suffered, but it might be perpetuated for years to
come.   If there is anything in the institutions of the city, or in the
character of its inhabitants, to which we have always referred with
a feeling of exultation, it is the heartiness and the bounteousness
with which our noble system of Free Schools has been sustained
by the popular voice.   In no city in the world, has there been one
half so much pecuniary liberality for the maintenance of Common
Schools, as in the city of Boston.   In no city in the world, have the
generous appropriations made in behalf of the schools, been seconded and advocated by the citizens with so great a degree of unanimity.   In no city in the world, have the wealthy and the children
made so little clamor or opposition, in regard to that great fundamental principle of Republicanism, — that the property of the
country must secure the education of the country.   It is an extraordinary fact that, for the last six or eight years, the annual
appropriations of money for the support of Public Schools, in the
city of Boston, with its eighty thousand, its one hundred thousand,
or its one hundred and twenty thousand inhabitants, has constantly
kept in advance of the appropriations made by the Parliament of
Great Britain, in behalf of Popular Education, for all England, with
its sixteen, seventeen, and now, as it is supposed, its eighteen millions of people.   When the Parliament granted £20,000 for all England, Boston granted more than $100,000.   When the Parliament
rose to £30,000, Boston had risen to more than $150,000; and now,
when the Parliament, in spite of the opposition of lords and bishops,
has strained itself up to £40,000, the appropriations of the city of
Boston are more than $212,000.   By far the largest item in this
expenditure is for the Grammar and Writing Schools.   The salaries
of all the teachers of the Primary Schools, where there are about
8000 children, are less, in the aggregate, than $30,000; while the
salaries of the teachers of the Grammar and Writing Schools, where
there are but about the same number of children, amount to more
than $77,000.   With some half dozen exceptions, the salaries paid
to the Grammar and Writing Masters, are the only competent
salaries paid to public school teachers, in any part of the Commonwealth.   And we devoutly hope the time may never come when

these salaries shall be less. It is true that there is an immense disproportion between the salaries of these masters, and the average paid to the male teachers in the Commonwealth, — the latter being at the rate of $32.11 only per month, while the former is at the rate of $125 per month, — almost four times as much, besides including all their vacations, and paying for them as for term time. The disproportion is still more flagrantly impolitic and unjust between the salaries paid to the masters and those paid to the female teachers of the city, — the former receiving six times as much as the latter. Still, if this unjustifiable inequality is to be diminished, let it be done, we say, by raising the compensation of the other teachers, and not by diminishing that of the masters so much as one penny. These views respecting the salaries of the Boston masters, we have always maintained, and we can imagine no combination of circumstances, within the range of probability, which will induce us to abandon them. When, some years ago, a reduction of these salaries was seriously threatened, we acted with all promptitude and earnestness, in endeavoring to avert so disastrous a measure, and though we may have had no influence in warding off the attack, we have at least the satisfaction of having striven to do so. But, in return for the generous salaries paid to the masters, a generous education should be given to the children. The money is not raised to be squandered upon place-holders, but, by a glorious alchemy, to be transmuted into intelligence, good feelings and good habits. It surely was not to be expected beforehand, that, in other towns, whose teachers were receiving a far inferior compensation, and where an improved system of schools had been but recently organized, the pupils would be found to be far superior to the pupils in the Boston Schools. Yet such is proved to be the fact; and it has filled the intelligent citizens of Boston, — those who have the interests of the schools most deeply at heart, and who are not blinded or biased by any mercenary or sinister motives, — with amazement and grief. The Report of the Grammar committee, from which we have quoted so largely, leaves no doubt of the humiliating fact. The committee have not sent out their conjectures, or their opinion merely, — had they done so, it would have been denied and denounced by acclamation, — but they have presented the data from which the fact is deducible with mathematical certainty. The same printed questions were submitted to several schools in the vicinity of Boston that were submitted to the Boston schools; and the committee have placed on file the answers received from one school in the contiguous town of Roxbury; so that the results may be compared, by any one who has the interest or the curiosity to do so. If the mode of examination were new, it was as new in the one case as in the other. If any allowance is to be made, because the children were taken by surprise, the children of the schools out of the city are as much entitled to that allowance as those in it; — nay more, because the former were examined by strangers, — by persons coming from another place, where the schools had enjoyed a high reputation, — and therefore it would be natural that they should be somewhat alarmed and disconcerted. A tabular view of the answers received by the committee from the Dudley School, in Roxbury, has been incorporated into their Report; and respecting this school, the committee say, "We consider the Dudley School a fair sample of the best schools in our neighborhood." How then does a "fair sample" of the "best schools" out of the city compare with the Grammar Schools in it? A few facts will answer the question. In Geography, the highest per centage of correct answers in any of the Boston Grammar Schools, was 46 per cent; the lowest, (excluding the colored school, where it was only 11,) was 18 per cent. The per centage of correct answers in the Dudley School, in the same study, was 55 per cent, — an excess of 37 per cent over the lowest of the Boston schools for white children, and of 9 per cent over the highest.

In History, two of the Boston schools excelled the Dudley, while fifteen fell below it, — some of them not giving one quarter of the per centage of correct answers which was given by the Dudley School.

In Definitions also, two of the Boston schools gave a higher per centage of correct answers than the Dudley, but fifteen a lower per centage. And it is to be remarked, that the words selected for definitions in the Boston schools were taken from the reading books used by the children in these schools; whereas, in the Dudley School, a different reading book was used. This demonstrates a vast difference in the general intelligence of the readers.

In Natural Philosophy, not one of the Boston schools gave a higher per centage of correct answers than the Dudley; one only gave the same per centage; sixteen gave a less one!

But, without dwelling longer upon details, the startling result of a comparison between the Boston schools, and a "fair sample" of the "best schools" of the same grade out of the city, is this: If the mean of the merits or comparative excellence of the Boston schools be represented by the decimal fraction .0769, the merits of the Dudley School must be represented by the fraction .1544; — that is, the average rank of the Boston schools is not quite one half that of the Dudley School!

Without attempting a full explanation of this astounding fact, we would observe, that we do not attribute it wholly to the incompetent teaching of the masters. There are two or three efficient causes in producing this sad result, for which they are not responsible.

1. We would first notice, as one of these causes, the organization of the schools into two departments, with a separate and independent head over each. In one department, there is a Grammar Master, (so called,) who has the sole charge of orthography, reading, grammar, geography and history to which, if he pleases, he may add natural philosophy and astronomy; and, in the other department, there is a Writing Master, (so called,) who has charge of arithmetic and hand-writing, with perhaps a little of algebra, geometry, and book-keeping. The children pass from one master to the other each half day.

A system which gives two heads to one body, is, at least, unnatural. Nature rarely exhibits such a production in the whole animal kingdom; and when she does, all mankind, by common consent, call it monstrous. A phenomenon of this kind, too, is as rare in civil society, as in the works of creation. Survey the history of civilized man, and how few the instances where two heads have been given to the same body, whether that body were social, civil or military. Any such system or plan, therefore, may be considered as being repugnant to the common sense of mankind, — as it is clearly contradictory to all the analogies of nature. Can any reason be given in favor of two heads for a school, which would not be equally persuasive and convincing in favor of two presidents for a college, or two governors for a Commonwealth? No navies sail with two admirals; no armies march with two commanders. When Rome tried this, she lost the battle of Cannae.

But the argument does not stop with such generalizations. A close inspection reveals objections of a formidable character. It has become a proverb, that when responsibility is divided, it is diminished; that is, if we understand it, the sum or aggregate of responsibility felt by its several sharers, will be less than that felt by a single one of them, were the whole of it stringently fastened upon him. As the reason of this exists in human nature, its results may be considered as certain and uniform. If one man can shift the blame or the penalties for neglect upon another, one of the great inducements to fidelity is removed. The mass of men will perform labor to save themselves, — to save their own character or their own office, — which they will not perform to save the office or character of another. Hence, whenever responsibility can be shifted, the motives to exertion and fidelity are weakened.

Let us suppose two heads to a school, each of whom is held responsible for certain prescribed studies, and for those only. In the first place, we would observe, that it is almost as preposterous to divide and separate the Common School studies from each other, and to carry forward one set in one room and under one instructer, and another set in another room and under another instructer, as it would be to divide a tree or a plant into its two halves, and to cultivate each half in different gardens and under different horticulturists. Many of the studies are so connected together that they cannot be torn assunder without fatal injury to each. Suppose, for instance, that chirography is assigned to one department, and English grammar, or, more comprehensively, the English language, is assigned to another. Chirography embraces the mechanical formation of letters in writing a coarse or a fine, a plain or an ornamental hand. Spelling, punctuation, the proper capitalizing of letters, with the construction of sentences, come under the head of Written Language. As soon as a child can write legibly, he should be put to writing simple sentences from memory, or from dictation ; and, as a part of this exercise, he should be taught spelling, syllabication, punctuation, the rules for capitalizing both prose and poetry, etc. Whoever is responsible for the whole instruction of a child, in both hand-writing and language, will attend to all these things together. He will not accept of beautiful hand-writing, deformed by errors in spelling, etc. ; nor will he accept of correct spelling, in a hand with difficulty legible. Being interested in all, he will, at the same time, aim at perfection in all. But if responsible only for a part, he will, unless he be a very extraordinary man, attend mainly, or only, to that part for which he is responsible. Of course, the pupil's attainments will be diminished as the teacher's instructions are withheld. Now, is it wise to place two teachers in a position, where one of them may say, "I am not responsible for any violation of the rules of orthography and grammar, provided they are committed in a fair and legible hand ; " and where the other may say, "It is my duty to teach spelling, grammar, etc., but whether the laws of language are obeyed in a hand-writing that any one can read, belongs, not to my department, but to that of another." The truth is, in teaching any one of these branches, all the connected ones should be kept constantly in view. In composition, the elegance, or, at least, the legibility of the hand-writing should be regarded; and in hand-writing, it is a wicked waste of time to confine children, year after year, to copy-books. After a certain stage has passed, — and that not a very late one, — hand-writing should be made the common and everyday means of acquiring and reducing to practice, a knowledge of orthography, syllabication, punctuation, capitalizing, and the construction of sentences. The late examination of the Boston Grammar and Writing Schools, has demonstrated for the thousandth time, — though perhaps more fully than ever before, — that children who have been kept in their copy-books until they can write a fair and legible hand, will, if required to write down sentences of their own construction, produce the most illegible and disgraceful scrawls. We hesitate not to say, that in all the schools of Massachusetts we have ever visited, we have never seen so great a proportion of disreputable specimens of hand-writing, and of errors in spelling and punctuation, as in the children's answers, now on file in the office of the city clerk. It is evident from an inspection of these that the kindred exercises in hand-writing and in written language had not been properly combined in one exercise. Had this been so, the errors in grammar, in punctuation and in spelling, would not have amounted to thousands and tens of thousands, in the answers of only five hundred children.*

Not only are there the strongest reasons against this violent severing of the studies, and making one master wholly responsible for one part, and another for another part of kindred subjects; but if the subjects must be divided at all, the division made in the Boston Grammar and Writing Schools is a most unfortunate one. Handwriting should go with orthography, punctuation, grammar, (in its limited sense,) and composition, wherever these may go, because it is one of the most important aids and concomitants in the acquisition of them all. It bears a much closer relation to them than to geography, or even to arithmetic. And yet, in the absurd distribution of studies between the two departments, hand-writing has been put with arithmetic, while the latter has been separated from natural philosophy and astronomy.

* The errors in grammar were 2,801; in spelling, 3,733; and in punctuation, 35,947.

Let us give one more illustration of the impolicy of taking, from a single head, the general responsibility of superintending all the common branches. One department of geography is closely allied to mathematics; history is indissolubly connected with geography; and geography and chronology have been called the two eyes of history. Now, if there must be a division in the school, and a separate head placed over each department, mathematical geography would belong more appropriately to the Writing department, and physical and political geography to the Grammar department. But this would lead to the dividing of geography itself; and thus, subjects having a mutual and natural relationship and dependence would be estranged from each other to their common detriment. We remember once asking a master whether he did not illustrate a certain geographical topic so and so. His reply was, "That belongs to the other department." In children so taught there will be a blank stripe running all along through their minds, where the two departments approach each other.

It is well known that division of labor increases manual skill and dexterity. It is as well known that it diminishes the capacity for generalization and arrangement. Hence the practical rule has been this: Division of labor as much as possible among work-men, but as little as possible among head-men. Look over England and our own country; — places where the sagacity of men has been most sharpened; and, in all business operations, has not a single man always been put at the head of affairs? Even the Facher system recognizes this principle, for there, too, one responsible person is placed at the head. Some very wise men, — Bishop Potter among the number, — have objected even to this system, because of its too great subdivision of labor among the assistants.

But the natural consequences of an equal division of responsibility and of authority are far more disastrous in a moral than in an intellectual point of view. We hold that the office of a school teacher will never become what it ought to be and what it may be, until the teacher considers himself, to a very great extent, responsible for the exemplary conduct and the correct moral department of his pupils. We care not how promptly or perfectly children may recite in the schoolroom, if, when we follow them into the street or the play-ground, we hear profane language from their lips or witness the evidences of a quarrelsome disposition in their actions, or observe a harsh and unkind bearing of the great towards the small, of the old towards the young, or of the strong toward the weak.

Where such vices exist, the school has not accomplished one of its highest purposes. And where children have been for a succession of years under the same teacher, and still are found to be profane or obscene, unkind towards equals or tyrannical towards inferiors, the facts point to a deficiency, on the part of the teacher, in the discharge of his moral duties. But, where there are two teachers, how can the responsibility be fastened upon either? Now, and for a long time to come, even in Massachusetts, the school teacher must be a school missionary. He must be familiar with the poorest house and the poorest family in his district. If a child is idle, or mischievous, or refractory, in school, the teacher must visit his parents out of school. Their coöperation in reforming their child must be sought, not merely by words, but by acts of kindness and interest; and these solicitations must be so importunate that the most unjust parent will be constrained to yield to them, — if from no higher motive, yet, like the unjust judge, to be rid of the importunity. A schoolmaster cannot work upon the six-hour system, nor upon the ten-hour system; but he may think himself fortunate, if, in preparing himself to meet his pupils and in preparing his pupils for the school, he is not obliged to work as many hours in a week out of school as in it. While society remains as at present, every teacher has a sort of parochial duty to perform. He is to explain to the ignorant members of his district, the benefits and the blessings of education, and he is to win over the parents to become his allies in the government of his school. His zeal must compensate for their indifference; his fidelity for their neglect. To instruct the beautiful, the affectionate, the bright-minded, the grateful, would be unalloyed delight. But to take an unclean, ill-dressed, ill-mannered, ill-tempered child, and to work up an interest in it, to love it, to caress it, and to perform a double measure of duty towards it; — this draws upon all the resources of conscience, virtue and religion. Yet, in the eye of true benevolence, of Christian duty, such children are the dearest of objects, — the first to be attended to, the last to be forgotten. Wherever teachers have been guided by such a principle, and animated by such a spirit as this, — and we have known many such, — all obstacles to progress have stood aside, all difficulties in government have vanished.

Now, in which system, — the double-headed or the single, — will such a state of things, or an approximation to such a state of things, be most easily secured? The faithful teacher, under the single-headed system, will feel all the responsibility, and will also enjoy the whole reward of his labors. Under the double-headed system, each one will feel, at most, but half the responsibility; and he will know, whatever labors he may perform, or sacrifices he may make, that his colleague, however neglectful or selfish, will be an equal sharer in their benefits.

These are some of the natural consequences of such a division of a school. Its obvious tendency is to reduce the attainments of the pupils. It is doubtless one reason for the present deplorable condition of the Boston Grammar and Writing schools. So far as this cause has been operative, the masters should be absolved from responsibility for their condition, and for their great inferiority to other schools in the neighborhood.

2. Neither would we hold the masters wholly responsible for the prominent rank which Emulation holds in their schools, as one of the incentives to study. This motive-power is incorporated into the system in which they work, and all that they can do is to mitigate its evils, by their administration of it. Yet we believe it to be one of the causes for the average low character of the schools. Not only the reason and philosophy of the thing, but actual experiment, in a vast number of cases, has demonstrated that the average standing of a school, even in an intellectual point of view, will be degraded by the use of emulation, — that is, by mating the children against each other, to study for a prize. If one or a few children make greater progress, under its sharp goadings, many will be discouraged, and will make less. Hence many teachers, who once plied this motive to the uttermost, have abandoned it; and we have never heard of a single instance where any one, who had made a full and fair trial of both methods, has chosen to continue or to resume it. But until the views of the school committee shall be changed, the masters must continue to suffer for the evils of a system they are required to administer.

3. But, in the third place, no one can look carefully into the details of this examination without discovering an accumulation and redundancy of evidence in support of the declaration made by both of the committees, that the children have been superficially taught. There is a painful superabundance of proof, that the children have experienced but little of the highest, and indeed the only valuable kind of instruction, — an indoctrination into principles. For the benefit of other schools, and for the warning of other teachers, in the State, we proceed to point out a few particulars.

Take, for instance, the question in geography, "On which range of mountains is the line of perpetual snow most elevated above the ocean, — on the Rocky Mountains of North America, or on the Cordilleras of Mexico?" — and it appears that only 91 pupils answered the question correctly; while 154 answered it wrong, and 242 did not answer it at all, being either ignorant of the meaning of the terms used, or unable to form any conclusion respecting the fact. Now this precise question may never have been put to the classes before, and we should not feel disposed to blame a teacher, even if it could be proved that he had never propounded this particular question to his scholars. But, that children who have professedly studied geography for years, and who have recited in anything but the most parrot-like manner, should not have discovered the principles which would lead them inevitably to the correct decision of such a question, is wholly inconceivable. That less than one in five, less than 20 per cent, — of the flower of the Boston Grammar schools, should have been ignorant of the true answer to such a question, and ignorant also of the principles which would conduct them to it, almost transcends credibility. It proves conclusively that the great majority of the children must have committed to memory the names of the zones, without any adequate conception of the different temperatures belonging to each; that all their recitations about the sun's altitude and declination, must have been unconnected with any idea of the calorific effects of his more or less vertical rays, and that the varieties of climate and of vegetation, of cold and of heat, had never been considered in connection with their natural causes.

Take another almost incredible case. One question was, "Do the waters of Lake Erie run into Lake Ontario, or the waters of Ontario into Erie?" This was answered correctly by 287, but incorrectly by 130, and 72 did not know which way they run. Yet this was one of the questions for guessing, and one where an ignorant child would be as likely to guess right as to guess wrong. Now, independently of the world-wide renown of Niagara, one grand idea, which, in teaching the geography of North America, should no more be omitted than the name, North America, itself, would have prevented this exhibition of ignorance and error. Ten minutes' explanation respecting the great central table-land of North America, from whose four vast slopes, the four great rivers flow onwards towards the four cardinal points of the compass, — ten minutes' explanation, we say, of this great fact, given in so graphic a manner that the children should see these grand declivities as plainly as they can see the four sides of the hip-roof of a house; and then, the tracing down of the course of the waters in each direction, until they are lost in their respective oceans, — would have made it impossible for any child, even of the most moderate capacity, to have ever committed such a blunder. Any child, even of ordinary powers, is capable of conceiving this grand scene, if it be vividly described to him, shown upon the maps, and pictured out upon the blackboard; and having once conceived it, he never can forget it. It will then only be necessary to commit to memory the names of the great lakes, in their order from west to east, which can be learned as easily and remembered as tenaciously as the order of the letters in the alphabet. But if the lakes are considered only in connection with the States which they bound, or within whose limits they lie; if the learner does not draw them upon the black-board, and never sees them drawn upon the black-board, it is no wonder that their names should be confusedly in his memory, and that, notwithstanding all the fame of Niagara, he should make the waters run up hill, or be ignorant of the fact that there is any running water there.

If any of the children were led into the error, because, when they look upon a suspended map, or upon an atlas held upright before the face the water would apparently run "up" on the map, if it should run north; — if any of the children, we say, were led into the error for this reason, it would argue more imperfect teaching still.

Commonly, in our geographies, the rivers and mountains are classified and described separately. But this is a great mistake. They should always be taught in connection. The course and rapidity of rivers depend upon the face of the country, upon its mountain ranges and table lands; and therefore mountains and rivers should always be associated together. They are not arbitrary facts, but the latter are necessarily dependent upon the former. In teaching the natural features of any great portion of the solid surface of the globe, such as North America, or Europe, or Asia, as soon as the boundaries and the latitude and longitude have been defined, the great mountain ranges and table lands should be brought into view, and then the rivers. In this great frame-work, the position of the different nations, cities, &c., should be respectively assigned to them. If this were done, such a mass of mistakes as are exposed by this Report, could never be committed.

Take another fact stated in the committee's Report, which, if it were not authenticated by the testimony of men whose honesty and intelligence are above suspicion, and if an inspection of the answers on file did not corroborate every word of the statement, we should be inclined to pronounce a libellous misrepresentation of the Boston schools. The committee, after asking the two questions, "What is the general course of the rivers in North and South Carolina?" and "What is the general course of the rivers in Kentucky and Tennessee?" inquire, in the next question, "What is the cause of the rivers in these four contiguous States running in opposite directions?" And what is the result of the answers given by the first division of the first class in the Boston Grammar Schools, to a question which seems almost too simple to be put to any child over ten years of age? It is this: 130 answered correctly; 61 answered incorrectly, and 308, — more than three fifths of the whole number, — could not answer the question at all! One child said the rivers ran in those opposite directions, "because it was the will of God," — a remarkably easy method of answering questions in physical geography, natural philosophy, astronomy, chemistry, or anything else; and one which would save philosophers an immense amount of labor.

A still more striking proof of ignorance and uncertainty, in the minds of the pupils, was brought to light by the two following directions: "Name the rivers running eastward into the Mississippi." To the first of these, 254 correct replies were made, 220 incorrect ones, and 13 scholars made no reply. To the second, the correct replies were 109, the incorrect 355, and 23 made none. Take the two together, and the majority of the incorrect replies over the correct ones is two hundred and twelve, not including the 36 who did not risk a reply. Now we can conceive of but one mode of teaching which could be followed by such a result; and that mode is, that the States and territories through which, or along the boundaries of which, the Mississippi and its branches run, were taken up, one by one, and those parts only of the rivers which were connected with the State or territory under consideration, were brought into view. In this way, it is true, that when all the States and territories should be gone over, all the rivers would be brought into view; but they would be brought into view as sections and fragments only, and no bond of connection would exist between them. Weeks, if not months, would have elapsed between the first recitation on the subject and the last; and, in the mean time, much of what had been committed to memory would have been forgotten. But suppose, when the subject of the Mississippi valley should be first introduced, and before a single State on either bank of the great "Father of Waters" should be named, the teacher should take the child, in imagination, to the mouth of that river; suppose that, by the use of the map, the blackboard, and by vivid descriptions, he should lead the child to conceive of the Mississippi, as the trunk of a vast tree thousands of miles in length, with branches on each side, some of them thousands of miles in extent, and all as a single object, — stretching from the great central table land of North America to the Gulf of Mexico; on the eastward reaching to the Alleghanies, and on the westward to the Rocky Mountains; — suppose the child, we say, were once made to embrace this, in one grand conception, and then to learn the names of all the tributaries, in their order, from south to north, he could no more forget them than he could forget the fruit tree, where he has been accustomed to go and regale himself with fruit.

Another requisition was made by the committee, and doubtless it was intended to ascertain whether the children had been taught a mere mass of isolated and unconnected facts, or whether they had been let to string these facts upon a principle, so that, when they should take hold of the string in any one place, they could command its whole length. The answers show in a painfully conclusive manner that the facts had never been so filed, or arranged, on any string. The direction was this, "Name the rivers, gulfs, oceans, seas and straits, through which a vessel must pass in going from Pittsburgh, in Pennsylvania, to Vienna, in Austria." The result was that only 35 out of 487 gave a correct reply; 118 gave a wrong one and 334 did not attempt so difficult a navigation. During the last years of the study of geography, no inconsiderable part of the exercises should be made up of questions like the above; and we can hardly conceive that the identical direction above quoted should not have been given to more of the children in the schools, than the number that were able to meet it.

Perhaps the most striking illustration of an ignorance of all principle, developed by the Report, consists in the answers to the question, "What do you understand by the line of perpetual snow?" The result was, that only 25 answered correctly, 160 answered incorrectly, and 302 confessed ignorance. If we were to put a parallel or equivalent question, it would be, "What is the line of perpetual ignorance?" and the answer would be, "Where principles cease to be taught." Where children are so ignorant of the principles on which temperature depends, it ceases to be a wonder that they should say, as a number of them did, that cotton is a production of New England.

We will give but one more illustration on the subject of geography. The pupils were directed to "draw an outline map of Italy." It is obvious that no other country in the world could have been selected, so easily depicted, as Italy, upon slate, paper or blackboard. We should have said beforehand, that every child in all our schools above the Primary, must have heard that Italy is shaped like a boot and spur; and also that the mind of every child must have been so agreeably and vividly impressed with the similitude that no amount of lifeless teaching would ever efface the image. Is not map-drawing taught in the Boston Grammar Schools? Does any professional teacher, at the present day, pretend to teach geography without drawing maps himself, and insisting that all his pupils shall do so? Does not every competent teacher know that there can be no adequate security that a child understands physical and political geography, unless he can produce, from his own mind, and through his own fingers, the outlines of countries and boundaries of nations? When we see a pupil draw the map of a country, sketch its mountains, trace its rivers, dot down its cities, &c., from memory, we know that he has an image of them in his mind; but this knowledge we can never fully possess until we find that he is able to do so. Hence the committee required one outline map to be drawn, and selected the easiest case possible from among all the countries in the world. The result we give in the committee's own words:

"Each scholar was required to sketch on his paper an outline of Italy, and many attempted it, but of the whole number (500,) only seventeen made a drawing which could have been recognized as a representation of Italy by one who did not know what the scholar was trying to do. In the Dudley School, (Roxbury,) more than 50 per cent, of the scholars drew such an outline as could be recognized."

More than 50 percent. in a Roxbury school against less than 4 per cent. in the Boston schools! We have seen the original drawings themselves made by the Boston children; and surely nothing even of barbarian rudeness can surpass them. Any boot made after the similitude of many of these outlines of Italy, must be designed for a club or a cloven foot, and the spur would be as appropriate on one side as on the other. In one instance, the toe of the boot points towards the east, as though it menaced an assault upon Greece or Asia Minor. In another case, the scholar has made a pair of shanks and feet, with the toes pointing inward, like the limbs of those unfortunate cripples, who, when they walk, lift one foot over the other !

But we must close our remarks on the subject of geography ; — a beautiful study, equally useful and interesting to all children, when properly taught. While we express our keen regret that the children who have now left the Boston schools have gone out so ignorant of its first principles, we would also express our firm conviction, that, in consequence of these exposures, the children who are hereafter to follow them, will be more competently taught.

But the most extraordinary, and we may add, frightful ignorance, was exhibited in regard to Definitions. Here, in this most important branch of an intellectual education, ignorance was the rule, and intelligence the exception.

To test the knowledge of the children in regard to what they had read, the committee selected twenty-eight words, — not from the dictionary, nor from books with whose contents the children were not familiar, but from the reading books used in their own schools, — from books which many of them had read for years, and parts of which they had committed to memory. A portion of the words were common and simple ones; another portion were in less general use, and a few of them (as "thanatopsis," which means "a view of death,") are not found in any common dictionary. This last class, there was a special propriety in selecting. Not being in the dictionary, but being important words and found in the reading books for schools, if the children do not learn their signification while at school, when will they ever learn it ?

We feel bound to say, that to suffer children to read without understanding what they read, is one of the most flagrant cases of incompetent teaching. The proper pronunciation of words, according to the standard of the best speakers, is a desirable accomplishment. Distinct enunciation, the length of sounds, the pitch and power of the voice, should be attended to by all teachers; but the signification of the words, — the meaning of the author, — is primary, is principal, is indispensable. Whatever else is omitted, this must be attended to. There can be no compromise here. However outlandish or brogue-like, the voice; however slovenly or slip-shod the enunciation; the sense of the author must be sought out and brought out, and made the sure possession of each pupil. The elocutionary part of reading is but its body, the intellectual part is the soul, and the former without the latter is only a dead mass of matter. It would be painful to find that a teacher had abandoned his children, and had spent his time in fitting up a hundred of Maelzel's automata, which could be made to utter words by the turning of a crank; but it would not be half so deplorable as to find living minds, with faculties all hungering and thirsting for information, with powers capacious of old thoughts, and capable of originating new ones, — to find such minds turned into automata, and made to utter pages of words, month after month, and year after year, with no proper conception of their beauty, their wisdom, or their truth. It is not enough, that children should understand four words out of five, or nine words out of ten, or ninety-nine words out of a hundred; for, if they do not understand the fifth, the tenth, or the hundredth word, they may lose all the soul of whatever they read. No one thing at the present day, draws so broad a line of demarcation between the competent and the incompetent teacher, as the intelligence or the ignorance of their pupils, in regard to the meaning of what they read.

But we need not enlarge here. Whoever has read the pages of this Journal, from its commencement, knows with what earnestness, with what unweariable importunity, we have dwelt upon this point. Committees and teachers, through the country, have seconded our endeavors, until such a change has been effected that we believe there is hardly a school in any of the country towns of the State, where, if the same proportion of the advanced classes should be taken, they would not appear better, if subjected to a similar examination, than the Boston schools have done. Soon after the report of the committee was made, a few of the definitions given by the children were published in some of the city papers; and, of course, they were read, more or less, in different parts of the State. So extraordinary were they, so improbably ridiculous and absurd, that we know they were regarded by many persons as a fiction, a jeu d'esprit, got up by some wicked wag to caricature the Boston schools. The only proof of their genuineness consisted in the fact, that they were worse than any mortal could have invented. Sheridan, in the character of Mrs. Malaprop, fell infinitely short of them. Here follow a few of these wonderful Definitions:

Monotony. — Change of names, Thick-headed, — Thick-headed, — A plant, — Is a word which means a variety, Music, — Time, — A study, — Scene, — Silent, — Musing, — Discord, — A song sung by one person, — Alone, from the Latin word, monoo, alone, — The bones of human animals, — Sameless, — Motion, — Monitory, — Cold, ceremonious, — Indifference, — Motion, — Smoothness, — Soothments, — A moaning noise,

— Dolorousness, — Moaning noise, — Pleasant, — Silence, — Silence, — Silence, — Many, &c. &c.

Panegyric. — A curious man, — Satire or a satiric poem, — Show, — A kind of Fear, — Fright, — Criticising anything, — Prayers, — Prayer, — Prayer, — Prayers, — A great pill, — Physic, — Sensual emotion, — A sudden shock, — A strain satirical, — Exercises, — Gymnastics, — Magic, — Quick, — Strict law, — Madness, — Letters, — Furious, in a violent manner, — A show in which the actions of persons now dead are represented, — Wonder, — Terror, — Without much sense, — Medicine, — Custom, — Some strange feat, — A cure for all evils, — Panic struck, — Writing by sounds, (Phonography?) — Startling, — Startling, — Startling, — Remedy, — Anything for a cure, &c. &c.

Evanescence. — Soft or mild, — Everlasting, — Unchanged, — Ever existing, — Something which exists after death, — Goodness, Kindness, — Bounty, — Bounty, — Bounty, — All goodness, — Kindness, — Goodness, — Goodness, — Goodness, or Highness, — The smell of anything is called its evanescence, — Mankind, — Man, — Purity, — The body of a person enduring long after death, by reason of being embalmed, — Everlasting, — Everlasting, — Everlasting, — Everlasting, — Everlasting, — Everlasting, — Everlasting, — The work of God, — The spirit of a thing, — An odor or a perfume, — Supreme, — What will never fail, — Immortality, — Smell, — The works of God, — Flesh, — Perfume, — A state we are in when the consumption or absent minded, — A sweet smelling essence, — Man, — A beautiful scene, — Not decay, — It means the power of doing a thing, — Greatness, — Immortality, — Sweetness, — That which never decays, — Never decaying matter, — Sweetness, — Beautiful, — Overflowing — Sweet smell, — In motion, — In motion, — Order, — Hard, — The highest, — Ever present, — Fruit, — Sweetness, — Breath of heaven, — Froth, — Ever present, — Sweetness, — Omnipotence, — Omnipotent, — Ever present, — Head one, — Immortality, — A mortality, — Immortality, — Immortality, — Immortality, — Immortality, — Immortal, — Not to be avoided, — Mortality, — Flesh, — Immortality, — Death, — Immortality, — &c. &c.

Connoisseur. — Lover, — People who write funeral services, — A juryman, — A rich merchant, — A person who composes requiems, — A stranger from places unknown, — A poet, — A requiem for the dead, — A picture, — Soldiers, — A wealthy gentleman, — One who has everything that he wants that money can procure, — It is the name of some foreign person, — Some great personage, — A great personage, — A great person, — A person of importance, — A look out, — Governor, — One that is dead, — A person who corrects letters, — A name by which Frenchmen are called, — A piece of money, — A journey, — One who spies, — A gentleman, — A kind of brigands, — Is a name applied to some nation, — Friend, — A soldier, — Ambassador, — &c. &c.

Infatuated. — Filled with air, — Charmed, — Bound up, — Bound up, — Charmed, — Charmed, — Charmed, — Charmed, — Charmed, — Renewed Force, — Renewed Force, — To have your attention taken up by anything means that you are infatuated with the idea, — Delighted, — Being very much pleased with anything, — Drunk, — Induced, — Filled with, — Pleased, — Delighted with, — Exhausted, — Enraged, — Not fatuated, — Not fatuated, — Taken up with, — Not fatuated, — To deprive, — Taken up with; absorption, — Triannical, — &c. &c.

Sphinx. — Monarch, — Person who held some office in old times, — Ancient pyramids of Egypt, — An ancient pyramid of Egypt, — A pyramid in Egypt, — A pyramid in Egypt, — A pyramid in Egypt, — A pyramid in Egypt, — An ancient pyramid in Egypt, — Ancient pyramid in Egypt, — A fabled bird, — A pyramid in Egypt, — A pyramid in Egypt, — A sphinx is an animal about 1½ feet in height, and about 3 in length, — A fairy, — Some kind of a bird, — A king, — A ruler, — Funny, — A species of bird, — The lady of the lake, — A person of fame, — Goddess, — One of nine muses, — A spirit, — A pyramid, — An animal, — A person's name, — One of the Muses, — A celebrated orator, — A woman in old times who was shaped like a horse, — A goat, — A monument in Egypt built in the form of a man's head and neck, — A monarch, — A monument in Egypt built in the form of a man's head and neck, — A being in existence, — The sphinx is a mountain in Egypt with a virgin's head carved on the top, — A spirit, — A pyramid, — An image supposed to have been constructed by the ancients, — Hideous monster with three heads, &c. &c.*

Misnomer. — Truth, — A reality, — Wonder, — Wonderful thing, — A hoax, — A name, — A true thing, — A name, — A name, — A name, — A person who makes an arrow, — A person who makes an arrow, — A name, — A name, — A name, — A name, — A name, — A story not authenticated, or a story the truth of which is doubtful, — A story the truth of which is doubtful, — A fabulous thing, — Means a soldier or people, — Was an ancient writer, — The real one, — Humbug, — Humbug, — A mistake, — Humbug, — Cheat, — Cheat, — Having no name, — A true story, — Something great, — Something that never existed, — A thing that never was, — Bad, — A drawn name, — False, — A strange thing, — Wrong story, — A fable, — A lie, — Belonging to several places, or claimed by several places, — A falsehood, — Accident, — Something bad for which we are corrected, — No name, — Fiction, — Fictitious, — A wrong action, — A wise man, — A namesake, — Namesake, — A false indictment, — A namesake, — A false indictment, Not true, — Namesake, — True thing, &c. &c.

* Suppose, on the occurrence of the word, Sphinx, in the reading lesson, the teacher had turned to the black-board, and drawn the figure of " A monster having the face of a virgin and the body of a lion," and had required some of the scholars to do the same, would the greater monsters of these definitions ever have been born?

Hades. — A poet, — Is a place beneath the earth where it was supposed the kings of Babylon were conveyed after death, and where they retained their rank, — One of the nine Muses, — One of the nine Muses, — One of the nine Muses, — One of the nine Muses, — Ancient city, — The name of a town, — Something that grows, — A sort of weed, — A town, — The god of the devils, — A city, — Thought, — I should think that it was a statute, — Grass, — Earth or spirit, — An author's work or novel, — &c. &c.

We need not say that these are among the worst specimens, for who can conceive anything worse than these? We might take each of the twenty-eight words submitted to be defined, and give specimens equally ridiculous and pitiable. Computation shows that there were only 3,511 correct definitions, while there were 3,025 incorrect ones, and, in 7,912 cases, they were not defined at all; that is, no attempt was made to define more than one half, and only a little more than one half of the attempts which were made, succeeded. And these, too, were words taken from a reading book used by the scholars. Well might the committee exclaim, that they had "Sometimes been amazed to find that pupils could read, with tolerable emphasis, tone and feeling, whole stanzas, of which they did not understand the metaphors, the leading ideas, or the principal words"! In what condition are these children to read the Bible, or to hear a sermon? In what condition are they to read an essay, or a speech, on any instructive subject? In what condition are they to sound the depths of any mind that is worth sounding? With what advantage can they listen to any useful conversation, or lecture? How can they read any valuable work with profit or edification, when they are incapable of understanding one fourth part of the words which are above the style of common conversation? What intellectual resources have they, unless in miserable gossip, or in more miserable novel-reading? Let teachers, everywhere, take warning from this exposure; and hourly, let them put the question to their pupils which Philip put to the man of Ethiopia, "Understandest thou what thou readest?"

After all, the thing most to be lamented in these answers, is the recklessness with which they seem to have been given. Many of them appear to have come, not merely from a vacant but from a distempered mind. Any vague association, any floating fancy, any crude notion stirred up in the mind by the excitement of the occasion, must have been made welcome. How little do they indicate the power and the habit of thinking. Where is the evidence that the minds of the children had been trained to precision and exactness of thought? To be unable, through ignorance, to give an answer, is bad enough; but the fool-hardiness which jumps after an answer in the dark, which seizes anything at random, and offers whatever it seizes, as the thing inquired for, is the worst form of error. If a teacher is bound to train a child's conscience to the duty of mastering all the knowledge he can, he is not less bound to the duty of teaching him never to pretend to knowledge, in cases where he is ignorant.

Before leaving this topic, we ought to say, that there is a very great difference between the schools, in regard to their success in defining the words propounded. In one school, one of the most difficult of the words was correctly defined by 86 per cent. of the scholars examined. In three other schools, the same word was not defined by a single scholar. There is a great difference also in regard to the conscientiousness manifested by the scholars, in abstaining from a pretence of answering, where they were ignorant. We might name two or three of the schools, where, though there was not a great number of correct answers, there were but comparatively few incorrect ones; — doubtless because the scholars had been led to perceive, that ignorance, bad as it is, is not so bad as an error; and that cheating by false pretences is as inexcusable in regard to knowledge as it is in trade.

The result of the examination in Arithmetic, appears in the Table contained in the Report. Ten questions were submitted for solution to 308 scholars, out of 8,343, who then belonged to the Writing department. Some of the questions hardly required a dozen figures for their solution; and the most difficult of them only required such a degree of knowledge as may be obtained from any common arithmetic. An hour and ten minutes were allowed to each scholar, to perform the operations. Had all the questions been correctly solved, there would have been 3,080 correct answers. There were, in fact, but 1,074, or only a fraction more than one third. Such a result repels comment. No friendly attempt at palliation can make it any better. No severity of just censure can make it any worse. Who of all the boys in the Boston Grammar and Writing schools, shall hereafter be city assessors, when not one of them can tell what tax shall be levied on a hundred thousand dollars, when all the necessary conditions are given, with perfect precision and clearness? Who of all the boys, aye, or girls either, shall cast the interest on a note, either as borrower or lender, when not one of them knows that there is any difference between the

value of a note for $200 payable in six months, and the value of
two notes of $100 each, — one payable in three and the other in
nine months !

We have said above that we did not think the masters wholly
responsible for this deplorable state of things. We believe that
a part of these deficiencies has resulted from the use of low motive-
powers; and one of these powers, — that of Emulation, of the
mating of each scholar against all his classmates, — is enforced
upon the teachers by the system in which they work. Though
the use of this incentive may make a few brilliant scholars for
exhibition, yet a large majority of each class will soon find that
a competition with their better endowed fellow-pupils, or with
those who can receive assistance at home, is hopeless, and will
therefore abandon all efforts at rivalry, in despair; and the consequence will inevitably be, that when an average of the attainments of the class is taken, — as must be done in a written examination — the general conditon of the whole will be degraded
by it. So far, let the Masters be absolved.

But there is another motive, — that of Fear, excited by the use
of Corporal Punishment, — which it seems now to be admitted
on all hands, has been employed to a most pernicious extent, in
some of the schools. We do not refer so much to extreme cases,
where surgical operations have become necessary, in order to save
life or limb, — as to that general condition of mind, either of
intense and disabling alarm, or of reckless hardihood and defiance,
which is generated through the school, when corporal chastisement,
like a grim Minister of Terror, stands forever at the teacher's right
hand, and its aid is perpetually invoked to overcome all the evils
of the schoolroom. The abuse of this instrumentality had become
so flagrant, and, at last, so notorious, in these schools, that, at the
close of the year 1844, the school committee passed the following
order, — in hope that the fear of publicity and its consequences
would effect a reform, which an appeal to reason and conscience
had been unable to achieve.

"Ordered, That it shall be the duty of the several Masters and
teachers in the public schools, in the immediate charge of this
Board, to keep a record of all inflictions of corporal punishment,
— subject to the quarterly examination of the sub-committees;
— the record to give, as exactly as may be practicable, the nature
of the offences, the age and sex of the pupil, the instrument employed, and the degree of severity used; — by corporal punish-

ment being understood all inflictions of physical pain; — said record not to be preserved beyond each quarterly examination."

The committee for examining the Grammar department refer to the effect of this order and they speak of the diminution of the punishments which had been already occasioned by it, as "a very material one." But some of the quarterly reports of the sub-committees, who have this matter more especially within their cognizance, present the change which has taken place, in this respect, in a very striking and gratifying light. Although sufficient time has not yet elapsed for the order to produce its full and natural results, yet it is proved to have been highly salutary, in promoting a much-needed reform. We cannot tell, with exactness, the extent of the reduction in punishments, between the last three months preceding the passage of the order, and the first three months after the punishments were required to be recorded. One would naturally suppose, however, that it would be much greater, than between the first three, and the second three months, after the restraint of publicity was imposed. And yet we learn from the quarterly report of the sub-committee on the Johnson school, for August last, that the diminution of corporal punishments in that school, for the months of May, June and July, as compared with those inflicted in February, March and April preceding, was 84 per cent. — eighty-four, — in the figures; — and this was found so far from producing any injurious effect upon the discipline of the school, that the committee declare they had not known it to be better than at that time, especially in the Writing department (Kept by Mr. Joseph Hale.) Here then, after the unknown reduction, between any three months, in the year 1844, and the months of February, March and April, in 1845; we find a further reduction of 84 per cent., between the three last named months, and the following ones of May, June and July, — and all this without any unfavorable effect upon the discipline of the school. Does not this prove beyond all denial or cavil, that 84 per cent. of unnecessary punishment had been inflicted, during the first quarter after the record was required to be kept? — while we know not how much greater a per centage of gratuitous suffering there had been, during the months and years previous to that time. We concur sincerely in the commendations bestowed by the committee upon the efforts that had led to so gratifying a result. Let those efforts be continued; let the school be brought more and more, as doubtless it may be, within the influence of humane and Christian principles, and we doubt not, that, before a long time has elapsed, there will be a reduction of another 84 per cent. upon the amount of punishment still inflicted.

We refer to this case with more satisfaction, because it furnishes a signal proof of the soundness of the doctrine for which we have always contended; — namely, that, if the right to use corporal punishment be not taken away from the teacher, he can govern his school, if he has any competency for his office, with but a rare resort to it; and that, other things being equal, the less he uses it, the greater will be the proficiency of his pupils. The Writing department of this school is set down by the examining committee, in their Report, as the lowest of all the girls' schools in the city, — a stigma, from which nothing will be so likely to relieve it, as the amelioration in its discipline which has been so happily commenced.*

We concur in both the commencing and the closing sentiment of the following passage, taken from the Grammar committee's Report: "We are forced to believe that there has been a gross abuse of the power of corporal punishment; but in consequence of the late order of the committee, and of the direction of public attention to this subject, the abuse is much diminished. There is little danger of its revival, (especially, since a portion of the Masters have failed to be reëlected, on account, as it is supposed in regard to some of them, of the severity or frequency of their punishments,) nor is there in the actual condition of our schools in this respect,

---

* Since the above was written, the sub-committee of the Johnson school have made their quarterly report for November. We copy the following passage from it with unalloyed delight, and would join our congratulations with those of the sub-committee at the truly glorious revolution which has been effected.

"A steady and perceptible improvement in the discipline of the school has been shown, and this manifest improvement is the more gratifying to the committee from the fact that it has been brought about without the aid of corporal punishment which now exists only in name. Not a blow has been struck in the Grammar department since last June; and in the Writing room, the teacher has substituted other modes of correction, (principally, detention after school,) which appear to have more than answered the end of the appliances, the places of which they have taken. Whether the result is attributable wholly to this change or not, it is still an undoubted fact, and one which has been observed by all the members of the committee, that, with this change, a very perceptible improvement in good order, in advancement in studies and in the relation between teacher and pupil, has been most obvious."

anything to call for or justify alarm or excitement. There is room for improvement; but that improvement can only be effected by temperate and just opinions, deliberately formed, resting upon a clear understanding of facts and possibilities, and contended to advance slowly, or what may seem slowly to the enthusiastic."

Before leaving this whole subject, — so full of painful interest and of valuable instruction, — there is one point which we cannot, in conformity with our views of duty, pass over in silence. We have no doubt that the Boston school committee, as a body, intend to observe the laws of the Commonwealth, by virtue of which they hold their honorable offices; and yet, there is one respect, in which they act systematically in contravention of the law of the State. The statutes declare that the school committee "shall ascertain, by personal examination, the literary qualifications and capacity for the government of schools," of all the teachers whom they may employ. This injunction is imperative. It contains no qualification; and it admits of no qualification. No exception, in regard to any school committee, or any school teacher, can be engrafted upon it. Yet, in the appointment of Masters for the Grammar and Writing schools of Boston, this salutary provision of the law is disregarded. As it respects those teachers who have been in the public service for years, perhaps the committee may say, that, by their quarterly and annual examinations of the schools, they do, virtually though indirectly, examine the teachers, and thereby bring themselves within the spirit of the law. But in regard to all new appointments, no such defensive allegation can be made. The reasons for a "personal examination" of all new teachers, according both to the letter and spirit of the law, are far stronger in the city of Boston than in any other part of the State. Where the compensation is so high, (high, we mean, as compared with that paid in other places, for we should rejoice to see it higher for all competent teachers,) competition will be keen; and where competition is keen, we must expect that some admixture of unworthy means and motives, will enter into the canvass. Now it is obvious, that where teachers are appointed without the "personal examination" required by law, and where either the applicants or any portion of the committee are governed by motives extraneous to the merits of the case, there will not be, and there cannot be, the highest degree of security, that the most worthy candidates will be selected to fill the vacant places. We venture to suggest, therefore, that when a vacancy occurs in the city schools, the fact should be extensively made known, by advertisements or otherwise; a day for examination should be appointed, and there should be a public Concursus, — a coming together, — of all who wish to enter the lists as competitors for the office. First, — the moral character of all those who apply, should be established by the most indubitable evidence. Then their literary qualifications, — both absolute and relative, — should be investigated by an actual trial, covering not only the whole ground of Common School studies, but all those collateral attainments which every teacher of the Boston schools ought to possess. All this should be done by direct question and answer. A subject should then be given out, embracing some point or points connected with the management and government of the schools, and each candidate should be required to write a composition upon it, on the spot. Other topics should be propounded, and each applicant requested to speak extemporaneously, for five minutes, or other definite period of time, upon the one assigned to him. In particular, should their ability to draw be inquired into; and they should be required to draw maps on the black-board. The examination should be public. It should embrace such exercises as would enable the committee to observe the manners, personal appearance, deportment, &c., of each candidate, and his powers of expressing himself both in writing and in oral discourse. In a word, the leading features of each applicant, both as a gentleman and a scholar, should be brought out, and then the committee should make the decision, under all their solemn responsibilities for the welfare of the children, and by the aid of all the light reflected from the examination. This and this only, would be a full compliance with the requisitions of the law.

We have the means of knowing that such a mode of examination would produce two very important changes. It would induce many persons to apply for teachership in the Boston schools, who do not now apply; and it would prevent many from applying, who, under the present system, will urge their claims with the greatest pertinacity. We know many honorable and high-minded teachers, who consider it a degradation to go round from door to door, to solicit a teachership in the Boston schools, but who would not hesitate to enter the lists where merit and not favoritism should sit as umpire between the competitors. On the other hand, who does not know that the lucrative and honorable station of a mastership in the Boston schools, has been sought for, in some instances, by persons who relied more on the partiality of friends, or the efficacy of the selfish motives they could arouse in some member of the committee, than on their own personal merits or fitness for the office; and who would as soon have put their heads into Nebuchadnezzar's furnace as to have entered an arena where their merits were to be weighed with those of others, in an even balance.

Suppose a member of the school committee, — and we take the supposition from fact and not from the imagination, — should make overtures to a teacher in another town, to apply for a mastership in one of the Boston schools, and should engage to second the application; but before the conversation should close, suppose this same school committee man should propose to the teacher, that, before leaving the town where he was then employed, he should cause the aforesaid committee man's books to be introduced into the schools of that town; — does not every one see that the person thus dishonorably approached, must either comply with the suggestion made to him; or, if he should become a candidate for the place, without such compliance, that he must encounter the opposition of the suborner, whose selfish purposes he had disappointed?

An examination such as the law requires, conducted in the manner we have above indicated, would prevent the prostitution of one of the highest offices in the land, to base and sinister purposes.

But we must abstain from further comment on this eminently valuable Report, and the extraordinary condition of the schools which it discloses. We could not have said less, for it would have been traitorous to the cause we have espoused, not to set up beacon lights along the perilous coast where the hopes of so many parents, and the prospects of so many children have been wrecked.

In closing then, we would adjure all teachers, throughout our state and country, to adopt and introduce high motives, as their main reliance, in the government of their schools; for they will never be able to obtain a full tale of work from children who are governed by low ones. We would exhort them also to teach all things thoroughly, however apparently slow may be their progress; for such is the only right and conscientious course, and, in the present inquiring state of the public mind on the subject of education, a contrary course will assuredly have its day of retribution.

As to the schools which have been the subject of this examination and Report, we are sure that a better fortune awaits them. The day of improvement has dawned, — has already arisen. Proofs already exist that the next examination will find them greatly in advance of their condition at the last. For ourselves, although the Boston Grammar and Writing schools have been, for years, sequestered, as it were, from the great movement of reform which has reached the schools in all other parts of the State, we could desire no greater honor or pleasure than to coöperate, in any way in which our humble faculties and willing spirit may be made serviceable, in advancing them to that preëminence which they ought to possess. If a reform is effected, then let the past be forgotten; or let the year 1845 be remembered only as the bound or starting-post, whence an honorable progress is to be reckoned, from year to year, throughout an indefinite future.

APPENDIX FOUR

THE 1845 TESTS

HISTORY
GEOGRAPHY
ARITHMETIC
GRAMMAR
DEFINITIONS
NATURAL PHILOSOPHY
ASTRONOMY

* Question 1. What is History?

Question 2. What are some of the uses of History?

Question 3. Enumerate some of the sources of History.

Question 4. What nations are among the first mentioned in History?

Question 5. For what were the Egyptians distinguished?

Question 6. For what were the Phoenicians distinguished?

Question 7. Who was the founder of Babylon, and about what period did he live?

Question 8. Who was the founder of the Persian empire?

Question 9. Who were some of the most distinguished orators and poets of Greece?

Question 10. Who was the founder of Rome?

Question 11. What was the character of the early government of Rome?

Question 12. Can you mention the names of the Roman Emperors?

Question 13. Can you give any account of the feudal system?

Question 14. What were the purposes of the Crusades?

Question 15. In what century was the great French Revolution, and who were some of the characters who figured in it?

Question 16. What nation ruled Britain at the commencement of the Christian Era?

Question 17. Who were the Saxons, and how came they to invade Britain?

Question 18. What do you understand by the Norman Conquest?

Question 19. What was the period of the Commonwealth in England, and who was the most distinguished character in it?

* Question 20. About what period did the first colonists come to New England, and what were the supposed motives for their leaving the mother country?

Question 21. How long did they continue subject to the mother country, and what were some of the assigned reasons for throwing off her government?

* Question 22. When did the war of the American Revolution commence, and who were the allies of the Americans?

Question 23. When was the great Federal Constitution formed, during or after the war of the Revolution, and how many States accepted it at its formation?

* Question 24. About what period was the embargo laid by President Jefferson, and non-intercourse substituted for it?

Question 25. About what period did the last war between Great Britain and the United States commence, and what were the causes assigned by the Americans for its declaration?

* Question 26. What do you understand by an embargo?

* Asterisk signifies that the question was used in the 1919 tests.

Question 27. How many more members are there now, in the Senate of the United States than there were at its first adoption?
Question 28. What was the result of the invasion of Canada by the Americans in the last war?
Question 29. What is Chronology?
Question 30. What are the eras the most used in Chronology?

Arithmetic

* 1 — How much is $\frac{1}{2}$ of $\frac{1}{3}$ of 9 hours and 18 minutes?

* 2 — What part of 100 acres is 63 acres, 2 roods, and 7 rods?

* 3 — What is the quotient of one ten thousandth, divided by ten thousand? Express the answer in decimal and vulgar fractions.

4 — A stationer sold quills at 10s 6d per thousand, by which he cleared $\frac{1}{3}$ of the price — but the quills growing scarce, he raised the price to 12s per thousand. What per cent would he clear by the latter price?

5 — Suppose A owes me $100 due at the end of 3 months, and $100 due at the end of 9 months, and he agrees to give me a note for $200 payable at such a time that its present worth shall be the same as the sum of the present value of the two first mentioned notes. How long after date must this note be made payable?

6 — A man has a square piece of ground which contains one quarter of one acre and a quarter, on which are trees, which will make wood enough to form a pile around on the inside of the bounds of the land 3 feet high and 4 feet wide. How many cords of wood are there?

* 7 — A sold goods for $1,500, to be paid for one half in 6 months, and one half in 9 months. What is the present worth of the goods, interest being at 7 per cent?

8 — A merchant in New York where interest is 7 per cent gives his note, dated at Boston, where interest is 6 per cent for $5,000, payable at the Merchants' Bank, Boston, on demand. Thirty days after the date of the note demand is made. A year after demand $200 are paid on the note. What sum remains due at the end of two years from the date of the note?

* 9 — What is the square root of $\frac{5}{9}$ of $\frac{4}{5}$ of $\frac{4}{7}$ of $\frac{7}{9}$?

10 — The City of Boston has 120,000 inhabitants, half males, and its property liable to taxation is one hundred millions. It levies a poll tax of $\frac{2}{3}$ of a dollar each on one half of its male population. It taxes income to the amount of $50,000, and its whole tax is $770,000. What should a man pay whose taxable property amounts to $190,000?

Geography

Question 1. Name the principal lakes in North America.
* Question 2. Name the principal rivers in North America.
Question 3. Name the rivers running eastward into the Mississippi.
Question 4. Name the rivers running westward into the Mississippi.

Question 5. Name the states which lie upon each bank of the Mississippi, and their capitals.

* Question 6. Do the waters of Lake Erie run into Lake Ontario, or the waters of Ontario into Erie?

Question 7. Which is most elevated above the level of the sea, Lake Superior or Lake Huron?

Question 8. Write down the boundaries of Lake Erie.

Question 9. Quebec is (according to your maps) 4° 40' north from Boston; Ithaca in New York, is 5° 30' west from Boston. Which place is farthest from Boston?

Question 10. What is the general course of the rivers in North and South Carolina?

Question 11. What is the general course of the rivers in Kentucky and Tennessee?

Question 12. What is the cause of the rivers in these four contiguous states running in opposite directions?

* Question 13. Which is most accessible in its interior parts, to ships and to commerce, Europe or Africa?

Question 14. Name the empires of Europe.

Question 15. Name the kingdoms of Europe.

Question 16. Name the republics of Europe.

* Question 17. What is the nearest route from England to India,— by Cape of Good Hope, or by the Red Sea?

Question 18. What do you understand by the line of perpetual snow?

Question 19. On which range of mountains is the line of perpetual snow most elevated above the oceans, on the Rocky Mountains of North America, or on the Cordilleras of Mexico?

Question 20. The city of Mexico is in 20° of N. latitude; the city of New Orleans is in 30° of N. latitude. Which has the warmest climate?

Question 21. Name the rivers, gulfs, oceans, seas and straits, through which a vessel must· pass in going from Pittsburg in Pennsylvania, to Vienna in Austria.

Question 22. On which bank of the Ohio is Cincinnati, on the right or left?

Question 23. What are the principal natural and artificial productions of New England?

Question 24. Over what continents and islands does the line of the equator pass?

Question 25. What parts of the globe have the longest days?

* Question 26. If a merchant in Moscow dines at 3 o'clock, P.M., and a merchant in Boston at 2 o'clock, which dines first?

Question 27. Name the countries which lie around the Mediterranean Sea.

Question 28. What countries lie around the Black Sea?

Question 29. What rivers flow into the Black Sea?
Question 30. Name the principal ports of Russia on the Black Sea, on
the White Sea, and on the Gulf of Finland.
Question 31. Draw an outline map of Italy.

WORDS TO BE DEFINED

* 1.	Monotony	15.	Aërial
2.	Convocation	16.	Sphinx
3.	Bifurcation	17.	Rosemary
4.	Panegyric	18.	Thanatopsis
5.	Vicegerent	19.	Monody
6.	Esplanade	20.	Anthology
7.	Preternatural	21.	Pother
8.	Forum	* 22.	Misnomer
9.	Evanescence	23.	Zoönomia
10.	Importunate	24.	Maniacal
* 11.	Infatuated	25.	Hallucination
12.	Kirk	26.	Machiavelli
* 13.	Connoisseur	27.	Madrigals
* 14.	Dormant	28.	Hades

There are two or three of these words, as Thanatopsis, Zoönomia, etc.,
which, being in the reading lessons, the scholars would meet with, and not
being in the Dictionary, they would not be likely to understand unless the
masters taught them their meaning.   They are, therefore, a better test than
words which may be found in the dictionary, of the endeavors of the masters to secure on the part of the children, an understanding of what they
read.   It is so obvious, as hardly to need the authority of the best instructors
and of all good writers on Education, that the habit of reading without understanding and without knowing whether one understands or not, is easily
formed and confirmed, and is most injurious; while the pupil who never
passes a word without knowing whether he understands it, and inquiring into
its meaning if he does not, has acquired a habit of mind, which will be almost
sufficient, of itself, to insure constant improvement.   The difference amongst
our Schools, in this respect, is very great.   Thus, in the Bowdoin School,
taught by Mr. Andrews, thirty-seven girls out of forty-three defined "Thanatopsis" correctly; and in some other Schools, not one.

GRAMMAR

1. Parse the following sentence, and write a full account of each word: —
Withhold not good from them to whom it is due.
* 2. Parse the following: — The wages of sin is death.
* 3. Write a short sentence, containing an active transitive verb, and an
objective case.

* 4. A sentence containing a neuter verb, a relative pronoun, and an adjective in the comparative degree.
  5. A sentence, with the verb to comfort, in the passive voice, potential mode, perfect tense, 2nd person plural.
  6. In what cases do we use a instead of an?
  7. What is the difference between an active and a neuter verb?
  8. The difference between ordinal and numeral adjectives?
* 9. What is an allegory?
* 10. Punctuate the following sentences; correct all the errors you may find in them; and write them out grammatically if you think them to be ungrammatical:
  Your brother was there and he said to my sister and i i am tired and must go and lay down to rest me and when he was laying down we tried to lie a vail over his face.
  11. I shall come to see you this afternoon unless it rains.
  12. Vain man thou presumest too much neither the lion nor the tiger will bow their necks to thee.
  13. To be or not to be that is the question.
  14. The property of such rules are doubtful.

Natural Philosophy

  1. What is the difference between Natural History and Natural Philosophy?
  2. What is the difference between Zoölogy and Geology?
  3. Define the attraction of gravitation, attraction of cohesion, and chemical attraction or affinity?
  4. What do you understand by the centre of gravity of a body?
  5. Define momentum.
* 6. What is the reason that when a coach in motion is suddenly stopped, the passengers are thrown forward?
  7. What is the rate of velocity of falling bodies?
  8. How much farther will a body fall in ten seconds than in five?
* 9. What is the reason that you can cut a piece of pasteboard or hard substance, more easily by holding it close up to the rivet of a pair of scissors, than by holding it near the ends of the blades?
  10. Why is it that when you skip a stone over the surface of water it does not sink the first time it strikes the water, since it is heavier than the water?
* 11. Which could you stop most easily, a railroad car weighing a ton going at the rate of 10 miles an hour, or a car weighing 100 tons, creeping along at the rate of ¼ of a mile an hour?
  12. Explain the hydrostatic press.
  13. What is specific gravity?
  14. How high can you raise water in a common pump, with a single box?

15. How high can you raise quicksilver by the same contrivance?

* 16. In building a cistern should it be made stronger at the top or at the bottom? Why?

17. If a grindstone should be suddenly split in pieces, while whirling rapidly around, would the fragments fall directly to the ground, or not? Explain the principle.

18. Is a stage coach with baggage upon the top, more liable to be overset than the same coach with the baggage hung under the axletree? If so, why?

* 19. In a small boat which is in danger of being overset, should the passengers stand up, or lie down in the bottom? Why?

20. Which occupies the most space, a pound of water when liquid, or when in the state of ice?

ASTRONOMY

Question 1. What is the radius of a circle?

Question 2. What is the arc of a circle?

Question 3. How many degrees are there in the quarter of a circle?

Question 4. Which circle contains the greater number of degrees, the equator or arctic circle?

Question 5. What do you understand by the terms zenith and nadir?

Question 6. What is the horizon?

Question 7. What is the axis of the horizon?

Question 8. What is a vertical circle?

Question 9. What is the altitude of a heavenly body?

Question 10. What is the azimuth of a heavenly body?

Question 11. Has the earth the greatest velocity in the rotation upon its axis, or the revolution around the sun?

Question 12. In the diurnal revolution of the earth, who are moved with greatest velocity, the inhabitants of Mexico or of Boston?

Question 13. What difference will there be in the velocity with which the inhabitants of the above named cities are moved in the annual revolution of the earth around the sun?

Question 14. Suppose one man is on the top of a mountain, another at its foot, and a third in a deep cavern, — all on the same parallel of latitude, — which will pass through the greatest space in one revolution of the earth upon its axis?

Question 15. Which moves with the least velocity?

Question 16. At what angle is the axis of the earth inclined to the plane of its orbit?

Question 17. Suppose the angle of the earth were perpendicular to the plane of its orbit, what effect would it have upon the order of the seasons?

Question 18. Explain the causes of the change of seasons.

Question 19. How many times does the moon revolve around the earth in one year?

Question 20. How often does the moon revolve upon her axis?
Question 21. Why is it that we see only one side of the moon?
Question 22. What causes an eclipse of the moon?
Question 23. What causes an eclipse of the sun?
Question 24. How many primary planets are there in our solar system?
Question 25. How many secondary planets?
Question 26. How many satellites has Jupiter?
Question 27. How many satellites has the earth?
Question 28. Which way does the earth move around the sun, from east to west, or from west to east?
Question 29. What is the principal cause of the tides?
Question 30. What do you understand by neap tides?
Question 31. What do you understand by the transit of a planet?

APPENDIX FIVE
REPRESENTATIVE ANSWERS, 1845

EXPLANATION OF THE TABLES

Table I is given as a fair specimen of the standing of our best or medal scholars. It is known that in the first class of each school, there are six medals awarded annually to the best scholars in each school, except in the case that there are no scholars "much advanced in improvement." The scholars of the Smith school for colored children, receive no medals; the Otis and New South are excluded on account of their not being fully organized; from each of the other schools (with one exception) the name of one medal scholar of the present year was taken at random, from the list printed in the newspapers, all being unknown to the Committee except two or three. The answers written by these fifteen medal scholars to questions about History, are printed carefully from their papers, exactly as they spelled the words, and punctuated the sentences, and used capitals or small letters.

Table II contains the answers given by the same fifteen medal scholars to the questions in Definitions. These two tables, of necessity, present the best aspect of the schools, for they are the answers by the best scholars in the first class.

Table III is made by taking from a school which has more than a medium rank, the answers to questions in Natural Philosophy, written by five scholars of the first class, first division, including one medal scholar; and they are supposed to present a fair specimen of the mode in which the average of the scholars express themselves on paper.

Table IV contains the answers of the same scholars to questions in Grammar.

But in order to allow every one to judge for himself, there is still another table, No. V, made up by taking from one of our girls' schools the answers given by the ten first scholars, according to the alphabetical order of their names. Side by side with this are the answers written to the same questions by the ten first scholars in alphabetical order, in a girls' school in a neighboring town.

Specimens should have been given of the method of drawing maps, but this would have caused much delay and expense. Each scholar was required to sketch on his paper an outline of Italy, and many attempted it, but of the whole number, (500) only seventeen made a drawing which could have been recognized as a representation of Italy by one who did not know what the scholar was trying to do. In the Dudley School more than 50 per cent of the scholars drew such an outline as could be recognized.

The specimens of map drawing, from some of the city schools, are very creditable; but few of the scholars can sketch a representation of the outline of a country without having a map before their eyes for a pattern.

All mention of names of schools or of scholars has been omitted on these last tables for obvious reasons, but the original papers, written by the scholars, are carefully preserved, and are at the service of any one.

TABLE I

SHOWING THE ANSWERS GIVEN TO QUESTIONS IN HISTORY BY
ONE MEDAL SCHOLAR FROM EACH SCHOOL

1. WHAT IS HISTORY?

No. 1. History is a narrative of past events.
2. History is a narrative of past events.
3. A narrative of past events
4. History is a narrative of past events
5. Is a record of past events
6. A narrative of past events.
8. History is a narrative of past events.
9. History is the facts which took place in Ancient and Modern times.
10. A naritive of past events
11. Is a narrative of past events.
12. I have not studied it
13. A narrative of past events
14. History is a narrative of early events.
15. History is the narration of past events.
16. History is a narative of past events.

6. The Egyptians.
9. Rome Greece
10. Egypt percia Babylon
10. Greece, Rome,
11. Have not studied this
12. I have not studied it.
13. Asia Minor Greece
14. England & France
16. Egypt, Babylon Persia. Assyria, Greece, Rome

5. FOR WHAT WERE THE EGYPTIANS DISTINGUISHED?

No. 3. I have not studied
5. For architecture
6. For literature, science and knowledge of the arts.
9. Civilization and Literature
12. For Arts.
13. Never studied it
14. For worshipping Idols or false gods.
15. For the Arts

4. WHAT NATIONS ARE AMONG THE FIRST MENTIONED IN HISTORY?

No. 2. Egyptians,   Phœnicians,
3. Babylonians,   Grecians, Romans,
4. I never studied it
5. The Egyptians, Phœnicians, Persians, Grecians, Romans I believe are among the first.

6. FOR WHAT WERE THE PHŒNICIANS DISTINGUISHED?

No. 2. They were distinguished for glass, purple, and coinage.
3. I have not studied
4. I never studied it
6. for ware
12. I have not studied it,
13. Never Studied it
16. for the invention of Glass

NOTE. — In some schools it was found that the scholars had not studied those parts of the textbook on History referred to in some of the questions, and they were directed where that was the case, to say so.

7. WHO WAS THE FOUNDER OF BABYLON, AND ABOUT WHAT PERIOD DID HE LIVE?

No. 3. I have not studied
4. I never studied it
5. Nebadeanezar
6. Nimrod.
9. Nimrod
12. Have not studied it.
13. Never Studied it
16. Nimrod. not long after the dispersion of Babel

8. WHO WAS THE FOUNDER OF THE PERSIAN EMPIRE?

3. I have not studied
4. I never studied it
6. Cyrus.
12. I have not studied it.
16. Cyrus the Great

9. WHO WERE SOME OF THE MOST DISTINGUISHED ORATORS AND POETS OF GREECE?

3. I have not studied
4. I never studied it
12. Do
13. Demosthenes Aristotle Cicero
16. Simonides Demosthenes, Euripides

10. WHO WAS THE FOUNDER OF ROME?

2. The foundation of Rome was attribute to Romulus, leader of a band of shephards.
3. Romulus
4. Romulus and Remus
5. Romus and Romelius
6. Julius Ceasar
9. Romulus, and Remus
12. Have not studied it.
16. Romulus

11. WHAT WAS THE CHARACTER OF THE EARLY GOVERNMENT OF ROME?

3. vicious
4. I never studied it
5. it was the best ever known
9. Tyranical
12. I have not studied it
16. Never studied

12. CAN YOU MENTION THE NAMES OF THE ROMAN EMPERORS?

No. 2. Romulus and Remus. Numa Pompilius. Servius Tullias. Ancus Marcius Tullias Hostillias.
4. I never studied it
5. Ceasar
12. I have not studied it.
16. Augustus Ceaser Tiberius Nero, Claudius Caligula Galba Titus Vespasian, Domitian Nerva Trajan

13. CAN YOU GIVE ANY ACCOUNT OF THE FEUDAL SYSTEM?

No. 3. I have not studied.
5. No Sir
12. Have not studied it.
16. The feudal Sistem had its origin from among the barbarous nations the Goths Huns & Vandals etc., but it is supposed to have received its earliest improvements from the Lombards

14. WHAT WERE THE PURPOSES OF THE CRUSADES?

No. 1. For the delivery of Jerusalem.
2. Never studied
3. I have not studied
4. They wished to visit the holy City
5. I believe they fought for their religion, they were cruel in their dispositions
6. To rescue the Holy Land from the power of the Saracens.
9. To rescue the Tomb of christ from the Heathen nations
12. Not studied.
16. To recover the sepulchre of our Savior from the Mohametans

---

15. IN WHAT CENTURY WAS THE GREAT FRENCH REVOLUTION, AND WHO WERE SOME OF THE CHARACTERS WHO FIGURED IN IT?

No. 2. Never studied
3. in the 17th century Robespierre & his associates
4. I never studied it
5. in the 18th century Napoleon Louis Phillippe.
6. In the 18th century.
8. In the 17th century. Generals Washington, Wolfe and Montcalm
12. Have not studied it.
14. 18 century. Bonaparte, La Faette & Duke of Orleans.
16. 18 century Napoleon Wellington Blutcher

16. WHAT NATIONS RULED BRITAIN AT THE COMMENCEMENT OF THE CHRISTIAN ERA?

1. The Romans
3. Saxons
4. Roman
5. Saxons
6. The Saxons.
9. The Christian era was the time when the Saxons invaded Britain and Became the masters
12. Have not studied it.
13. Rome
14. romans.
16. Rome

---

17. WHAT DO YOU UNDERSTAND BY THE NORMAN CONQUEST?

4. The period in which William the conquerer took possession of Britain
5. A war with the Norwegians.
6. The conquest of England by william of Normandy
8. The time when William the conqueror, ascended the throne, in 1066
12. Not studied it.
13. the time Britain was concord by William the Norman
14. They were conquered by William I
16. Edward the Confessor dying without children bequeathed the crown to William Duke of Normandy who resolved to maintain his claim by force of arms. He raised an army of 6000000 men, and defeated Harold with

an equal army in the battle
of Hastings

---

18. WHAT WAS THE PERIOD OF THE
COMMONWEALTH IN ENGLAND,
AND WHO WAS THE MOST DIS-
TINGUISHED CHARACTER IN IT?

No. 1. Oliver Cromwell.
 3. 1550. Oliver Cromwell.
 6. 1670 Oliver Cromwell
 7. 1653. oliver Cromwell
 12. Have not studied.
 13. 1648 The most distinguished caracter was Cromwell
 14. In the 18th century. Cromwell
 16. 16 century. Cromwell

---

19. ABOUT WHAT PERIOD DID THE
FIRST COLONISTS COME TO NEW
ENGLAND, AND WHAT WERE
THE SUPPOSED MOTIVES FOR
THEIR LEAVING THE MOTHER
COUNTRY?

No. 1. On account of religious
 persecution carried on in
 England. 1607
 2. They came to escape from
 religious persicution Dec.
 22, 1620
 3. 1620
 4. Dec. 22. 1620. They were
 persecuted on account of
 their religion
 5. in 1620. 1623 1634 1635
 they came here to enjoy
 civil and religious liberty
 6. In 1620. on account their
 religion.
 8. 1620. On account of religious persecution

9. About the 15th century
 Because they wanted to
 enjoy a more free and religious liberty.
 10. 1606 They came here with
 the idea of obtaining
 wealth.
 11. In 1620 on account of their
 religious persecution
 12. 1607. Came here to enjoy
 their religion Being driven
 from England by Religious
 Persecution.
 13. A settlement was made in
 1620. at Plymouth by 101
 puritains the motives for
 leaving the mother country
 was that they might enjoy
 religious liberty
 14. 1620 they left on account
 of Religious persecutions
 15. About 1600 Their motives
 for leaving the mother
 country was that they
 might enjoy freedom both
 civil and religious.
 16. About the time of protec-
 torate of Cromwell, on
 account of religious persecution

---

21. HOW LONG DID THEY CONTINUE
SUBJECT TO THE MOTHER
COUNTRY, AND WHAT WERE
SOME OF THE ASSIGNED REASONS
FOR THROWING OFF HER GOV-
ERNMENT?

No. 1. From 1607 to 1776. The
 taxing of them.
 3. till 1775
 4. about 150 years The mother
 Country taxed them and
 laid duties on all articles
 of commerce and passed

laws which the Americans did not like to obey.

5. until the 1776 There reasons were that the mother country tried to raise a revenue

6. Until July 4th 1776. — taxes were imposed on the merchandise by the British.

8. If the war had been waged by G. Britain on their account it was because they were useful to her

9. Between the 17th and 18th centuries The taxes imp^sed on them

11. 1620 until 1763 because she taxed the colonies and would not let them send representatives to parliament.

12. Dont Know.

13. From the first at Jamestown in the year 1607 to the declaration of Independance in the year 1776 (reasons) taxations without representation

14. till 1775 because they imposed on them duties on Tea, Coffee, Clay sugar, Painters colors etc.

15. They claimed the right of taxing themselves till the revolutionary war.

16. nearly two centuries. the Mother country began to assert her sovereignity over them and to interfere in their civil concerns and duties were laid on goods imported from West India Islands as did not belong to Great Britain

22. WHEN DID THE WAR OF THE AMERICAN REVOLUTION COMMENCE, AND WHO WERE THE ALLIES OF THE AMERICANS?

No. 1. The French.
    2. The French. 1775.
    3. About the year 1776
    4. 1774 the French
    5. 1775
    6. The French.
    8. In the 17th century
    9. 1775 The French
    10. 1600
    11. 1775 French,
    12. 1775 the French
    13. The war commence in the year 1775
    14. 1776 Allies France
    15. In 1775
    16. in the year 1775 The French

—————

23. WHEN WAS THE PRESENT FEDERAL CONSTITUTION FORMED, DURING OR AFTER THE WAR OF THE REVOLUTION; AND HOW MANY STATES ACCEPTED IT AT ITS FORMATION?

1. After the war. All the States except two.

3. After the war II

4. During the war 13 states accepted it

5. after the war all the states except Rhode Island and Georgia

6. After the war. Eleven. There were 13 all but two accepted it.

8. In 1788. After the Revolution. 11 States accepted it

9. In 1788 13 states

10. All but two During the war
11. after the war of the revolution 13 States
13. after the Revolution in the year 1788
14. after the Revolution II
15. 13 States. After the revolution
16. After

---

24. ABOUT WHAT PERIOD WAS THE EMBARGO LAID BY PRESIDENT JEFFERSON AND NON-INTERCOURSE SUBSTITUTED FOR IT?

1. After the war of the Revolution
3. 1809
4. I never studied it
5. 1807 or 9
6. 1809
7. 1807
8. December, 1807
9. In 1809
10. 1809
11. 1807
13. 1807
14. 1809
16. 1807 December

---

26. WHAT DO YOU UNDERSTAND BY AN EMBARGO?

1. Prohibition to sail
3. stop our trade
5. a protection
6. Restriction on trade.
9. Duty to be paid on vessels entering the waters from which an embargo
10. Put to trade
11. Stopping the trade with other Countries
13. not to let the vessels go out of port

14. a prohibitation to pass a stoppage of trade
15. A duty laid on certain goods
16. A prohibition to Never Studied

---

27. HOW MANY MORE MEMBERS ARE THERE NOW IN THE SENATE OF THE UNITED STATES THAN THERE WERE AT ITS FIRST ADOPTION?

1. 30
3. 26 more
4. I never studied it
5. twice as many
8. 15 more including Iowa and Florida
6. 28, if Florida comes in, if not 26
14. 32
16. Never Studied

---

28. WHAT WAS THE RESULT OF THE INVASION OF CANADA IN THE LAST WAR?

1. The French northern possessions in American confirmed to Britain and the Americans experienced a release from the calamities which they had experienced from the French and Indians.
3. unsuccessful
4. I never studied it
5. unsuccessful
6. Canada was ceded to England.
8. Took fort Erie, and Bridgewater
9. They were defeated

14. unsuccessful to the Americans.
16. Never studied

---

29. WHAT IS CHRONOLOGY?

  2. Never studied
  3. science of computing time
  4. I never studied it
  5. is a table containing some of the principal events & dates under which they happened.
  9. The dates of a country taken in one view

11. a tabular view of History
12. Science of time and study of dates
14. doctrine of time & dates
16. Never Studied

---

30. WHAT ARE THE ERAS THE MOST USED IN CHRONOLOGY?

  2. Never studied
  3. I have not studied.
  4. I never studied it
  9. The Christian Era
12. the eras of the delug
16. Never Studied

NOTE. — The answers to 1, 3, 17, and 25, being generally very long, are omitted.

TABLE II

Showing the Answers Given by One Medal Scholar from Each School in the City

DEFINITIONS

1. Monotony

No. 1. Sameness.
    2. Sameness
    3. Sameness.
    4. is a slow manner
    5. Undisturbed silence, or a sameness of manner, with no variety.
    6. Soothments.
    7. Dullness.
    8. Unvaried
    9. Sameness
    10. All in one tone.
    11. Readind without on the same tone of voice
    12. Same tone of voice
    14. Sameness, without variation
    15. Stillness.

No. 13 did not answer.

---

2. Convocation

No. 1. Business.
    2. an assembly
    3. An assembly.
    4. the act of bringing about
    5. A collection.
    6. Pray
    8. Assemblage
    9. An assembly
    10. To install.
    11. The act of calling together
    12. To convert
    15. something that is not heavanly

Nos. 7, 13 and 14 did not answer.

3. Bifurcation

No. 1. The place where two rivers meet.
    2. I do not know
    3. The forking of any thing.
    4. projecting out in the form of a fork
    5. To go from
    7. Fork of a River.
    8. Transmigration of birds
    9. Division
    10. Where two rivers branch out.
    11. Turning of a stream from its course
    12. Meeting of two things
    15. Washing

Nos. 6, 13, and 14 did not answer.

---

4. Panegyric

    1. A poem
    2. I do not know
    3. I do not know.
    4. Eulogy.
    6. Startling
    8. Terror
    9. Whim, notion
    10. I do not know
    12. Hystorick Life of a person
    15. Crasy

Nos. 5, 7, 11, 13, and 14 did not answer.

---

5. Vicegerent

    1. A person who does some business, or work for another one.

2. a ruler.
3. Independent
4. Ruling in stead of another
6. Head One
8. Agent
9. One invested with power from the head
10. A commander.
11. A shairer in power
12. Representative
13. When any thing knows itself, or knows its power
15. Captain

Nos. 5, 7, and 14 did not answer.

6. ESPLANADE

1. A Portico.
2. a walk
3. Platform
4. A level Space of land
6. Archway
7. A body of people.
8. Lawn in front of a house
9. A place to walk on the outside of a castle
10. A walk.
11. A garden before a house
12. Battlements of a fort or a castel
13. The Front of a house.
15. a platform

Nos. 5 and 14 did not answer.

7. PRETERNATURAL

1. Something more than natural, some higher power.
2. Irregular
3. Not natural
4. not natural.
5. Not natural.

8. More than human
9. Not Natural
10. Before the time.
11. more than natural
12. Something unnatural
13. Extraordinary.
14. External
15. something natural

Nos. 5 and 7 did not answer.

8. FORUM

No. 1. A large hall
2. a public place
3. A Roman pulpit.
4. a place for speaking in Rome
6. Market
8. Stage or Platform
9. A public house in Rome like Faneul Hall
10. A body of people.
11. A large space within the cittey of Rome
12. A large ampi Theater
15. a platform which surrounded the Roman capitol

Nos. 5, 7, 13, and 14 did not answer.

9. EVANESCENCE

No. 1. Sweetness.
2. Immortality
3. I do not know.
4. something that passes away
6. Ever Present
8. Shortness of duration
9. Smell
10. Odor
12. Vanishing
13. Anything that is in motion
14. Unsubstantial, Vanishing

Nos. 5, 7, 11, and 15 did not answer.

10. IMPORTUNATE

No. 1. Harrassing, Asking for the same thing often
2. Urgent
3. Impatient.
4. a desire for any thing
5. Imploring.
6. One Important
7. Desirous of knowing something.
8. Persevering
9. Plagueing
10. To tease.
11. Earnest
12. to ask a question
14. Entreating.
15. to ask

No. 13 did not answer.

------

11. INFATUATED

No. 1. Blinded
2. I do not know
3. Blinded
4. without reason
6. Not Fatuated
7. Crazy
8. Deluded
9. One that has wrong notions and is very ardent in their course
10. Impressed with some bad notion.
11. excited to envy
12. Believing a thing that no argument can induce him to alter.
15. inspired

Nos. 5, 13, and 14 did not answer.

------

12. KIRK

No. 1. A Church.
2. A Church
3. Church
4. a Scottish name of Church
5. The House of a Scottish Minister.
6. Country Church
8. Residence of a minister.
9. Minister
10. A church.
11. A Church
12. Towns in Scotland
15. Capitol

Nos. 7, 13, and 14 did not answer.

------

13. CONNOISSEUR

No. 1. A person who understands some particular business, but does not practice it.
2. A critic
3. Lover of any art.
4. one that is not acquainted with any art
6. Critticin
7. A man that composes music
8. A critic or Judge
9. A man of rank.
10. One who spys.
11. A Judge
12. A Judge of a Critic
15. Governer

Nos. 5, 13, and 14 did not answer.

------

14. DORMANT

No. 1. Still. Silent
2. Sluggish
3. Sleeping
4. Sleepy
5. Stupid
6. Adored.
8. Inactive
9. Without life

10. Still
11. Sleep
12. Supid
14. Inactive
15. Selfish

Nos. 7 and 13 did not answer.

---

15. AËRIAL

No. 1. In the air.
2. relating to the air
3. Relating to the air.
4. something pertaining to the air.
6. Airy
8. In the Air
10. Of wind
11. relating to the wind
12. Flying in the air
15. belonging to the air

Nos. 5, 7, 9, 13, and 14 did not answer.

---

16. SPHINX

No. 1. A King — A Ruler
2. An Image
3. A woman's head, formed of stone, in the Arabian desert.
4. a Egyptian Image
6. Statue
7. An animal made of Stone.
8. A Muse
9. Was an image which had the body of a lion and the head of a virgin
10. A woman in old times, who was shaped like a horse.
11. A fabulus being in Egypt
12. A Statue
13. Image in Europe,

Nos. 5, 14, and 15 did not answer.

17. ROSEMARY

1. A flower,
2. A Rose
3. A flower which blooms in winter.
4. relating to marriage
6. Flowers that bloom in winter
7. A place where there are a great many flowers.
8. Sort of Berry, which grows in the West Indies
9. A flower
10. A flower
11. relating to flowers
12. A Flower
13. Flowers.
15. an herb

Nos. 5 and 14 did not answer.

---

18. THANATOPSIS

1. The dwelling of the Dead.
2. Nature
3. Vision of death.
4. relating to death
5. A view of Death. Thoughts on Death.
6. A view of Douth
7. It is the name of a piece in Reader, but I dont know the definition of it.
8. View of death
9. A sight of Death
10. I do not know
11. pertaining to death
12. A vision of Death

Nos. 13, 14, and 15 did not answer.

---

19. MONODY

1. A song written by one person.
2. Lament

3. A Lament
4. very slow
6. Song
9. Epataph
10. I do not know
11. Mornful Song
12. Bewailing of a friend
15. Sameness

Nos. 5, 7, 8, 13, and 14 did not answer

20. ANTHOLOGY

2. I do not know
3. I do not know
6. anciantness
9. Record
10. A science
11. science
12. a description of Birds
15. the study of fishes

Nos. 1, 4, 5, 7, 8, 13, and 14 did not answer.

22. POTHER

No. 2. Noise
3. A tumult.
4. a bird
6. Noise
9. Talk, Nonsense, vain rabble
10. A noise.
11. noise.
12. Interfearing
13. Great noise.
15. Noise

Nos. 1, 5, 7, 8, and 14, did not answer.

22. MISNOMER

No. 1. A wrong name
2. A wrong name,
3. A wrong name.
4. a wrong name,

6. Name sake
7. A thing that never was.
8. Error or mistake
9. Misnamed a wrong name
10. I do not know
11. misnamed
12. A Story not authentacated
13. Mistake
14. Error
15. a falshood

No. 5 did not answer.

23. ZOÖNOMIA

No. 2. Account
3. I do not know what Zoönamia means.
4. works
6. Journal
9. Record of cases
10. Memorandum
11. Zoönamia is a collection of animals
12. Book of Records

Nos. 1, 5, 7, 8, 13, 14, and 15 did not answer.

25. HALLUCINATION

No. 2. Mental delusion.
3. Derangement.
4. evivles of man
6. Crazy mind
9. out of mind
10. A. maniac

Nos. 1, 5, 7, 8, 11, 12, 13, 14, and 15 did not answer.

26. MACHIAVELLI

No. 2. I do not know
3. The name of an author.
4. novel
6. novel
10. I do not know

11. A philossophical book
12. Book of plays

Nos. 1, 5, 7, 8, 9, 13, 14, and 15 did not answer.

---

27. MADRIGALS

No. 3. Songs
    4. Songs
    6. Any good
   10. Songs
   11. A book of Hymns
   12. Fassions

Nos. 1, 2, 5, 7, 8, 9, 13, 14, and 15 did not answer.

28. HADES

No. 2. I do not know
    3. The Greek name for Hell.
    6. Spirits
    9. Hell.
   10. A town.
   11. Hell from beneath is moved because of thee
   12. a part of Hell
   14. Greek word which means the Infernal regions
   15. Hell

Nos. 1, 4, 5, 7, 8, and 13 did not answer.

TABLE III

[The following Table is made up by copying exactly the written answers to questions in Natural Philosophy, by five scholars of the first division, first class, in one of the schools, which ranks above mediocrity. The two preceding Tables show the answers of our choice medal scholars: this and the following will show answers of scholars, neither the highest nor the lowest. No. 1, was a medal scholar, — fifteen years old; the average age of the others is fourteen years.]

NATURAL PHILOSOPHY

I. WHAT IS THE DIFFERENCE BETWEEN NATURAL HISTORY AND NATURAL PHILOSOPHY?

No. 1. Natural Philosophy is that science which treats of the powers and properties of natural bodies, their mutual action on one other, and the laws and operation of the material world.

No. 2. Natural History is a narration of past events. Natural Philosophy treats of the natural laws and effects of Macheneary

No. 3. Did not answer.

No. 4. History is a narration of past events Philosophy is the science which treats of the powers and properties of natural bodies their mutual action on one another and the laws and opperations of a meterail world

No. 5. Natural History treats of beasts and birds. Natural Philosophy treats of the heavenly bodies such as the sun, moon, stars, and comets.

II. WHAT IS THE DIFFERENCE BETWEEN ZOOLOGY AND GEOLOGY?

No. 1. Did not answer.

No. 2. We have not attended to them.

No. 3. I do not understand it.

No. 4. We have never studied it.

No. 5. We have never studied them

III. DEFINE THE ATTRACTION OF GRAVITATION, ATTRACTION OF COHESION, AND CHEMICAL ATTRACTION, OR AFFINITY.

No. 1. The attraction of gravitation is that which causes bodies at a distance to approach each other. The attraction of cohesion is that which unites the particles of a body.

No. 2. The attraction of gravitation causes bodys to approach each other. The attraction of cohesion causes the particles to approach each other we have not studied chemesterty.

No. 3. Did not answer.

No. 4. Gravitation causes bodies to fall towards the centre. Cohesion is that which unites the particles of a body.

No. 5. The attraction of gravity is that which causes bodies at a distance to approach each other. The attraction of cohesion binds the particles of a body together. I do not know what chemical attraction is.

IV. What do you understand by the centre of gravity of a body?

No. 1. The point about which all parts of the body balance each other.
No. 2. That part round which all bodies ballance each other.
No. 3. The point round which all parts of the body moves.
No. 4. The centre of gravity of a body is the parts around which all parts balance each other.
No. 5. It is the point about which all parts of the body balance each other

V. Define momentum.

No. 1. It is the force which a moving body would strike against another body.
No. 2. Is the force which one body would strike against each other
No. 3. I do not understand it
No. 4. Momentum is the part around which all parts move.
No. 5. I do not understand it

VI. What is the reason that when a coach in motion is suddenly stopped, the passengers are thrown forward?

No. 1. Did not answer.
No. 2. On account of the momentum of bodies
No. 3. because the center of gravity is not supported.
No. 4. because the centre of gravity is not supported
No. 5. I do not know.

VII. What is the rate of velocity of falling bodies?

No. 1. It is in proportion to the force with which they are thrown
No. 2. Is in proportion to thur density
No. 3. In proportion to there Density
No. 4. It is in proportion to their density
No. 5. I have never learned it.

VIII. How much farther will a body fall in ten seconds than in five seconds?

No. 1. It will twice as far if the velocity be the same.
No. 2. Twice as far
No. 3. twice the distance.
No. 4. Twice as far
No. 5. Twice as far

IX. WHAT IS THE REASON THAT YOU CAN CUT A PIECE OF PASTEBOARD OR HARD SUBSTANCE, MORE EASILY BY HOLDING IT CLOSE UP TO THE RIVET OF A PAIR OF SCISSORS, THAN BY HOLDING IT NEAR THE ENDS OF THE BLADES?

No. 1. Because the nearer the power is applied to the end of the lever most remote from the fulcrum the greater is the advantage gained.

No. 2. A pair of scissors is a lever of the first kind the revet is fulcrum the points is the power and end in hand is the weight so it will be cut more easily near the revits

No. 3. Did not answer.

No. 4. beceause

No. 5. I do not understand this question

X. WHY IS IT THAT WHEN YOU SKIP A STONE OVER THE SURFACE OF WATER IT DOES NOT SINK THE FIRST TIME IT STRIKES THE WATER, SINCE IT IS HEAVIER THAN THE WATER?

No. 1. Did not answer.

No. 2. I dont know

No. 3. Did not answer.

No. 4. dont know

No. 5. I dont know.

XI. WHICH COULD YOU STOP MOST EASILY, A RAILROAD CAR WEIGHING A TON, GOING AT THE RATE OF 10 MILES AN HOUR, OR A CAR WEIGHING 100 TONS, CREEPING ALONG AT THE RATE OF A QUARTER OF A MILE AN HOUR?

No. 1. A car weighing 100 tons.

No. 2. A Car of a 100 tons.

No. 3. A railroad car weighing a ton.

No. 4. Did not answer.

No. 5. One weighing 100 tons.

XII. EXPLAIN THE HYDROSTATIC PRESS.

No. 1. It is constructed on the principle that whenever water is confined in a vessel, and a pressure is exerted on the surface, a pressure to an equal amount will be transmitted over every square inch of the surface, of the vessel in which the water is confined.

No. 2. I cannot

No. 3. Did not answer.

No. 4. dont know

No. 5. In the hydrostatic press any quantity however small may be made to balance another quantity however large.

XIII. What is specific gravity?

No. 1. It is the relative weight of a body compared with that of another body.

No. 2. It is a term given to expriss the relative weight of different bodies of eaqual dinsities

No. 3. Did not answer.

No. 4. Specific gravity is the term eused to show the weight of equal quantities of different bodies

No. 5. It is a term used to express the relative weight of equal quantites to different bodies

XIV. How high can you raise water in a common pump, with a single box?

No. 1. 32 inches

No. 2. I dont know

No. 3. Did not answer.

No. 4. dont know

No. 5. 32 inches

XV. How high could you raise quicksilver by the same contrivance?

No. 1. Did not answer.

No. 2. I dont know

No. 3. Did not answer

No. 4. dont know

No. 5. I do not understand it

XVI. In building a cistern should it be made stronger at the bottom, or the top? Why?

No. 1. At the top; because their is more weight above it.

No. 2. At the bottom because a greatir weight will well come upon the bottom

No. 3. Did not answer.

No. 4. dont know

No. 5. At the bottom If it were not the water would leak away.

XVII. If a grindstone should be suddenly split in pieces, while whirling rapidly around, would the fragments fall directly to the ground, or not? Explain the principle.

No. 1. Did not answer.

No. 2. The fragments would fall to the ground on account of the attraction of gravitation

No. 3. Did not answer.

No. 4. The fragments would fall to the ground because the attraction of gravitation Causes bodies to fall to the ground.

No. 5. They would not.   I do not understand the principle.

XVIII. Is a stage coach, with baggage upon the top, more liable to be overset than the same coach with the baggage hung under the axletree? If so, why?

No. 1. It is the centre of gravity is not supported

No. 2. Becaus when the baggage is upon the top the center of gravity is not supported

No. 3. Did not answer.

No. 4. The baggage upon the top, because the baggage on the axletree would be heavier so that it could not overset.

No. 5. I do not understand it.

XIX. In a small boat which is in danger of being overset, should the passengers stand up, or lie down in the bottom? Why?

No. 1. The passengers standing up. because the centre of gravity is most firmly supported

No. 2. They should lie down in order to support the center of gravity.

No. 3. Lie down, then the center of gravity is supported.

No. 4. Lie down, because it does support the centre of gravity.

No. 5. They should lie down in the bottom.   Because if they lie down in the bottom there is not so much danger of their falling out.

XX. Which occupies the most space, a pound of water when liquid, or when in the state of ice?

No. 1. A pound of water when liquid

No. 2. Water when liquid.

No. 3. when liqide.

No. 4. A pound of water when liquid

No. 5. When liquid.

TABLE IV

[Written answers of the same five scholars to questions in English Grammar.]

I. PARSE THE FOLLOWING SENTENCE, AND WRITE A FULL ACCOUNT OF
EACH WORD : — WITHHOLD NOT GOOD FROM THEM TO WHOM IT IS DUE.

No. 1. Withhold is a verb present Withhold preterit Withhold imperfect
participle Withholding perfect participle Withheld irregular Active transitive Imperative mood Subject ye or you second person plural number.
Not Adverb manner qualifys Withhold. Good common noun Adjective used
as a noun objective case and governed by Withhold. From is a preposition
and governs them i shows the relation between Good and them. To is a
preposition and governs whom it shows the relation between whom & them,
It is a personal pronoun it third person Singular number Neuter Gender
Nomitive case to is. Them is a personal pronoun third person Singular
number objective and governed by from, whom is a relative pronoun third
person neuter gender Singular number governed by to. Is, is a verb present
Be or am preterit was imperfect participle being perfect Been irregular
Neuter verb Iendecitive mood present ense third person Singular number and
agrees with it Due is a adjective common adjective belongs to it

No. 2. Withhold, Verb, Imperative Mood, Present Tense. Second Person.
Singular Number, Agrees with Thou
  Not. Adverb. Added to Withhold
  Good. Adjective Added to Things
  From. Preposition Shows Relation between Things & Them
  Them. Personal Pronoun Third Person Singular Number Objective Case
Governed by From
  To. Propposition Relation between Them & Whom
  Whom. Relative Pronoun Third Person Singular Number Objective Case
Governed by To
  It. Personal Pronoun Third Person Singular Number Nominative Case
to Is
  Is. Verb Indicative Present. Third Person Singular Agrees with It.
  Due. Adjective
No. 3. Withhold is a verb — Withhold Withheld Withholding Withheld
Irregular Nueter Verb Imperative Mood Present tense Second person Singu-
lar and Agrees with Thou understood. Not is an Adverg of manner and
relates to Withhold — good is an Adjective represents its noun third person
singular Objective case and governed by Withhold — from is a preposition
shows the relation between Withhold not good them to Whom it is due —
them is a pronoun third person plural number Objective Case and governed
by from —
No. 4. Withhold is a verb; an Active Transitive verb; Potential mood
present, 2d person singular, and agrees with thou understood. Not is an
Adverb and is added to withhold. Good is a noun, 3d Person singular,

neuter gender, Objective case and is governed by withhold. From is a Preposition shows the relation between good and them. Them is a pronoun third person, plural, and is governed by from. To is a preposition, shows the relation between them and it. Whom is a relative pronoun, 3d person, plural, objective case and is governed by to. It is a pronoun, 3d Person singular, nominative to is. Is is a neuter verb present and agrees with it. Due is an Adverb, added to, is.

No. 5. Withhold is a verg. irregular newter Withhold. Withheld Withholding. Withheld Imperitive Mood Present tense 2d Person Singular agrees with thou understood. Not adverb adverb of Manner and added to Withhold good is an adjective represents its noun. 3d, Plural Number Nominative case after Withhold from is a Prepersition Shows the relation between Good and Them. Them is a pronoun 3d Person Plural number objective Case and governed by from to is a preposition Shows the relation between them & Whom Whom Pronoun 3d person Sin No Objective Case govern by to it is a Pronoun, 3 Person Singular no Nom Case to is

II. Parse the following sentence: — The Wages of Sin is Death.

No. 1. The is a definite article. Wages is a common noun Nominative case to is — third person Singular number neuter gender, of is a preposition governs Sin Shows the relation between Sin and Wages. Is a verb present be or am preterit was imperfect participle being perfect participle been Iregular Nueter verb indicitive mood present, third person Singular number. Death is a noun third person Singular number nominative case after is.

No. 2. The. Article Added to Wages
Wages. Noun Third Person Singular Neuter Gender Nominative Case to Is Of. Preposition Shows Relation between Wages & Sin
Sin. Noun Third Person Singular Number Objective Case Governed by of Is Verb, Indicative Present Third Person. Singular Agrees with Wages Death. Noun. Third Person Singular Nominative Case after is.

No. 3. The is an article limits wages wages is a noun 3d person singular number Nueter gender Nommative Case to is — of is a preposition shows the relation between The Wages — sin is death — sin is a noun third person singular number Nueter gender Objective Case and governed by of — is as a verb third person singular number Indicative mood present tense and agrees with wages —

No. 4. Wages is a noun, 3d person singular, neuter, nominative case to is, Is is a neuter verb, present, Indicative, and agrees with wages. Of is a preposition, shows the relation between wages and sin, Sin is a noun 3d person, singular, objective case, and governed by of. Death is a noun, 3d person, singular, nominative case after is,

No. 5. Wages is a noun 3d Person Sin Nom to is of Preposition shows the relation between Sin & Wages Sin is a noun 3d Person Objective case govern by in is is a verb Indic mood Pres tense 3d person Sin No Nom C after is

III. WRITE A SHORT SENTENCE CONTAINING AN ACTIVE TRANSITIVE VERB, AND AN OBJECTIVE CASE.

No. 1. Parse the following sentence
No. 2. James & I went in the Country
No. 3. John Struck Charles
No. 4. I love you
No. 5. Wm Struck me

IV. WRITE A SENTENCE CONTAINING A NEUTER VERB, A RELATIVE PRONOUN, AND AN ADJECTIVE IN THE COMPARATIVE DEGREE.

No. 1. the days are longer now than what they used to be
No. 2. He who is Sick if is not Careful will be Sicker
No. 3. Who is better than him
No. 4. She was the prettiest girl, that I ever saw.
No. 5. What was that Better than this

V. WRITE A SENTENCE WITH THE VERB TO COMFORT IN THE PASSIVE VOICE, POTENTIAL MODE, PERFECT TENSE, 2D PERSON PLURAL.

No. 1. ye or you may be comforted
No. 2. Did not answer.
No. 3. Did not answer.
No. 4. You might have gone to comfort her
No. 5. You may have seen me before you came to comfort me.

VI. IN WHAT CASES DO WE USE A INSTEAD OF AN?

No. 1. A is used before words beginning with A consonant and an is used before words before
No. 2. When the word begins with a Consonant
No. 3. Where the following begins with a consonant —
No. 4. Before consonants, (except the words beginning with silent letters)
No. 5. When the fowlering begins with a consonant.

VII. WHAT IS THE DIFFERENCE BETWEEN AN ACTIVE AND NEUTER VERB?

No. 1. Active verb is a verb which expresses an action and has some person or thing for its object. Neuter verb is a verb which expresses neither action nor passion but simply being or state of being.
No. 2. An Active Verb expressive an action An Neuter verb expressive a State of Being
No. 3. One expresses an action and the other a state of being
No. 4. One expresses an an action and the other a state of being
No. 5. Active verb expresses an Action
Newter verb expresses neither action nor passion but Simply being or state of being

VIII. What is the difference between ordinal and numeral adjectives?

No. 1. ordinal adjective are such as first second third adjective of order numerel adjective is one that a definite number one two three

No. 2. Did not answer.

No. 3. Did not answer.

No. 4. An ordinary adjective is a common epithet or adjective denoting quality. A numeral adjective is one that expresses numerical value

No. 5. Numeral adjective is one that expresses a definite No Ordinal adjective is one expresses a definite No No difference

IX. What is an allegory?

No. 1. I never studied it

No. 2. Did not answer.

No. 3. A tale founded on fiction

No. 4. An assertion founded on fiction

No. 5. Did not answer.

X. Punctuate the following sentences; correct all the errors that you may find in them; and write them out grammatically, if you think them to be ungrammatical.

Your brother was there and he said to my sister and I I am tired and must go and lay down to rest me and when he was laying down we tried to lie a vail over his face.

I shall come to see you this afternoon unless it rains.

Vain man thou presumest too much neither the lion nor the tiger will bow their necks to thee.

To be or not to be that is the question.

The propriety of such rules are doubtful.

No. 1. Your brother was there and he said to my sister i am tired and must go and lay down to rest me and when he was laying down we tried to lie a vail over his face.

I shall come to see you this afternoon if it Does not rain

No. 2. Your brother was there and he said to my sister and I I am tired and must go and lay down to rest me and when he was laying down we tried to lie a vail over his face.

No. 3. Your brother was there and He said to my sister and myself i am tired and must go and lay down to rest me and when he was laying down we tried to lie a vail over his face.

No. 4. Your brother was there, He said to my sister and myself I am tired I must go and lie down to rest myself and when he was lying down we tried to lay a veil over his face.

I shall go to see you this afternoon if it does not rain

Vain man thou presumest too much, neither the lion or the tiger will bow his neck to thee.

To be or not to be, these are the questions

The propriety of such rules is doubtful.

No. 5. Your Brother was there and he said to my Sister and me I must go and must go and lay down to rest myself and when he was lying down we tried to lay a veil over his face

I, shall go to see this afternoon unless it rains

Vain man thou presumest to much neither the Lion nor the Tiger will bow their necks to thee

To be or not to be is the question.

The propriety of such rules is doubtful.

TABLE V

[Showing the exact answers given to thirty-one questions in geography by ten scholars, taken in alphabetical order from a girls' school in Boston, and a girls' school in Roxbury, the average of their ages being about the same.]

I. NAME THE PRINCIPAL LAKES IN NORTH AMERICA.

City School

Scholar.

No. 1. Superior. Michigan. Huron. Erie. Ontari.

2. Superior, Huron, Michegan, Erie, Ontario, Slave, Great Bear,

3. Superior, Huron, Erie, Michigan, Ontario,

4. Slave, Great Bear, Winnepeg

5. Superior, Huron, Erie. Ontario Slave. Lake of the hills. Great Bear.

6. Superior-Huron-Erie Ontario Slave Michegan.

7. Superior, Huron, Michegan, Erie, Ontario, Winnepeg.

8. Superior, Huron, Erie, Ontario, Slave.

9. Superior, Michigan, Huron, Erie, Ontario Winnepeg, Athapescow, Slave, Great Bear, Lake of the Hills.

10. Lake Superior Lake Ontario Lake Erie Lake Huron Lake Champlain.

Dudley School, Roxbury

Scholar.

No. 1. Lakes Superior, Michigan, Huron, Erie, Ontario, Champlain, Winnipeg, and Great Bear Lake.

2. Great Slave Athabasca Winnipeg Lake of woods Superior Erie Ontario Champlain Michigan Great Bear Huron George

3. Lake Superior, Michigan, Huron, Erie, Ontario, Great Slave, Bear Winnipeg, Champlain, Lake George.

4. Lake Superior, Ontario, Erie, Huron, Champlain, Michigan, George, Grand, Oswegee, Winepiesego, Black.

5. Slave, Great Bear, Winnepeg, Superior, Huron, Erie, Ontario, Champlain Athabasca, George, Tulo Buenaventura, Red, Itasca, Michigan.

6. Lake Superior, Lake Huron, Erie, Ontario, Michigan Champlain

7. Lakes Erie, Huron, Superior, Michigan, Ontario Great Bear, Great Slave, lake of the woods, Rainy lake Nigeraugua, Champlain.

8. Superior. Huron Ontario Erie Michigan Great Bear Great Slave Athabasca Nicaraqua Winnipeg, Champlain.

9. Lake Superior, Michigan, Huron, Erie, Ontario, Great Slave, Great Bear, Winnepeg, Rainy, Red, Lake of the Woods, Itasca, Chesuncook etc.

10. Superior, Michigan, Huron, Erie Ontario, Great Bear Slave, and lake of the Woods.

II. Name the principal rivers.

City School

1. Mississippi. Missouri. St. Lawrence Columbia.
2. Mississipi, Missouri, Arkansas, Red, Tennessee, Columbia, Merrimac, Hudson, Delaware,
3. Mississippi, Missouria, Ohio. Arcansas St. Lawrence
4. Mississippi, Mississpuri, Oregon
5. Mississippa. Missoura. St. Lawrence. Rio del norte. Collumbia. Severn.
6. Mississippi Nelson Mississouri Sant Lawrence
7. Mississippi, Missouri, St. Lawrence, Columbia, Severn, Colerado.
8. Mississippi, Missouri, St. Lawrence, Columbia, Severn, Colorado.
9. Penobscot, Kenebec, Androscoggin, Hudson, Deleware, Potamac Missisipi, Missisouri, St. Lawrence, Arkansas, Red, Ohio, Columbia, Ria Del Norto.
10. Missisippi River Missouri River Ohio River Delaware River Connecticut River Kennebec River.

Dudley School

1. Mississippi, Missouri, Ohio, Arkansas, Red, Del Norte, Colarado St. Lawrence, Oregon and Mackenzie.
2. Mississippi Missouri Ohio Tennessee Kentucky Penobscott Kenebeck Merrimack Connecticut Hudson Susquehannah Deleware Altamaha Potomac James Great Pedee Roanoke Red Arkansas Desmoines Rock Lewis Clarke Platte Wisconsin Detroit Savannah St. Johns Illinois Pearl
3. Mississippi, Missouri, Ohio, Hudson, Potomac, Susquehanna, Red, Mackenzie, St Lawrence, Connecticut, Savannah.
4. Mississippi Missouri Ohio Savanah Santee St. Lawrence Tennessee Alegany Alabama Catawba Ocmulgee Big black
5. Mississippi Missouri Lewis, Clarks, Androscoggin, Connecticut, Hudson, St. Lawrence, Red Platte Roanoke Tar, Neuse Lumber Yadkin, St. John Me. Arkansas Ohio Rio del Norte, Colorado.
6. Mississippi, Missouri, Arkansas, Ohio, Kentucky, Tennessee.
7. Mississippi, Missouri Arkansas, Red Hudson, Connecticut, Ohio, Tennessee, Kentucky, St. Lawrence Susquehanna, La Platte Rio del norte.
8. Mississippi Missouri Ohio Red Arkansas, St Lawrence, Cumberland. Alabama Susquehannah Mowhawk. Hudson. Nuse. Tar. Alleghany Monongahela Savannah. Colerado. Rio-del. Norte. Platte.
9. Mississippi, Missouri, Ohio, Arkansas, Red, Connecticut. Kentucky, Platte, Osage Yellow etc.
10. Mississippi, Missouri, Ohio, Arkansas, St. Lawrence, Tennessee, Kentucky, Yellow stone, and Colarado.

III. NAME THE RIVERS RUNNING
EASTWARD INTO THE MISSIS-
SIPPI.

City School

1. Tennessee, Cumberland.
2. Missouri, Arkansas, Red
3. Missouria, Arcansas, Red,
4. Ohio, Illinois
5. Ohio
6. Not answered.
7. Ohio,
8. Tennessee, Cumberland,
9. Illinois, Ohio, Kentucky.
10. Ohio River, Tennesee River Cumberland, Kennytucky River

Dudley School

1. Missouri, La Platte, Konza, Red, Arkansas.
2. Wisconsin Illinois Ohio Platte Kansas
3. Missouri, Red, White
4. Missouri Yellow-Stone Red
5. Missouri, Red, Arkansas
6. Ohio, Arkansas
7. Missouri, Red, Des Moines, Arkansas.
8. Missouri, Red, Arkansas.
9. Missouri, Arkansas and Red.
10. Arkansas, Missouri, Red.

IV. NAME THE RIVERS RUNNING
WESTWARD INTO THE MISSIS-
SIPPI.

City School

2. Ohio,
3. Ohio, Cumberland, Tennessee
4. Red, Arkansas
5. Missoura
6. Not answered.
7. Missouri, Arkansas,
8. Red, Missouri,
9. Missisouri, Arkansas, Red.
10. Missouri River Red River Arkansas River.

Dudley School

1. Ohio Yazoo, Big Black, St Francis.
2. Missouri Arkansas Red Desmoines Platte Great fish
3. Ohio, Illinois, Yazoo, Black
4. Ohio, Tennessee, Black stone.
5. Ohio Kentucky Illinois.
6. Red Miszouri,
7. Ohio. Tennessee,
8. Ohio.
9. Ohio, Kentucky, Illinois
10. Ohio, Tennessee, Kentucky,

V. NAME THE STATES WHICH LIE
UPON EACH BANK OF THE MIS-
SISSIPPI, AND THEIR CAPITALS.

City School

1. Did not answer.
2. On the west bank lie Missouri the capitol of which is Jefferson Arkansas Capitol, Little Rock. On the west, Illinois, capitol, Springfield, Kentucky, Frankfort capital
3. Illinois. Capital. Springfield. Missouria. Capital. Jefferson. Arcansas. Capital, Little Rock, Mississippi. Capital Jackson. Tennessee. Capital Nashville. Kentucky. Capital. Frankfort.
4. Mississippi — Jackson Missourri — Jefferson Arkansas Little Rock Louisianna New Orleans Illinois Springfield.
5. Did not answer.
6. Louiseanna Mississippi Missourri Arkansas New Orleans Jackson Jefferson Little Rock
7. of Maine, Augusta. of N. Hampshire, Concord. of Vermont, Montpelier, of Massachusetts, Boston. Rhode Island, Provi-

dence and Newport. Connecticut, Hartford and New Haven, N. York, Albany N. Jersey, Trenton. Pennsylvania, Harrisburg. Delaware, Dover. Maryland. Annapolis. Verginia, Richmond. N. Carolina, Columbia. Georgia Millidgeville. Alabama, Tuscaloosa. Missisippi, Jackson, Missouri, Jefferson City. Louisianna, N. Orleans, Tennesee, Nashvile

8. of Maine, Augusta

9. Louisiana, N. Orleans Missisouri, Jefferson city, Arkansas, Little Rock, Tennesee, Nashville Kentucky, Frankfort, Missisipi, Jackson

10. Missisouri. Capital, Jefferson City. Louisiana. Capital, New Orleans. Kennytucky. Capital Frankfort Tennesee Capital Nashville Arkansas Capital Little Rock

Dudley School

1. Louisiana, Mississippi, Tennessee Illinois

2. Illinois Tenesee Kentucky Mississippi Texas Arkansas The capital of Illinois is Springfield of Tenesee is Nashville of Kentucky is Frankfort of Mississippi is Jackson of Arkansas is Little Rock of Texas is Washington

3. Illinois, Capital Springfield, Kentucky, capital Frankfort, Tennessee capital Nashville, Mississippi, capital, Jackson, Louisiana New Orleans, Arkansas, capital Little Rock, Missouri, capital Jefferson City.

4. On the east bank are Illinois, Tennessee, Mississippi, the capital of Illinois is Springfield of Tennessee is Nashville of Mississippi is Jackson. On the west bank are arkansas, Missouri Louisiana, the capital of Arkansas is Little Rock of Missouri Jefferson City of Louisiana is New Orleans.

5. Louisiana Capital, New Orleans — Mississippi, — Jackson — Tennessee, — Nashville — Kentucky — Frankfort Illinois — Springfield. Missouri — Jefferson city — Arkansas — Little rock.

6. Tennessee Kentucky Missouri Arkansas Nashville Frankfort Andianapolis Little Rock

7. Illinois, Kentucky, Tennessee, Mississippi Louisiana Missouri, Arkansa. Capital of Illinois is Vandalia, of Kentucky is Frankfort of Tennessee is Nashville, of Mississippi is Jackson, of Louisiana is New Orleans, of Missouri is Jefferson-City, of Arkansa is Little Rock;

8. Mississippi. Jackson. Tennessee. Nashville. Missouri. Jefferson City Louisiana. New. Orleans. Kentucky. Frankfort. Indiana. Springfield

9. Indiana Indianapolis Illinois Springfield Tennessee Nashville Kentucky Frankfort Louisiana New Orleans

10. Indiana. Cap. Indianapolis. Missouri. Cap. Missouri. Arkansas. Cap. Little Rock, Louisiana. Cap. New Orleans. Mississippi. Jackson

VI. Do the waters of Lake Erie run into Lake Ontario, or the waters of Ontario into Erie?

City School

1. Did not answer.
2. Did not answer.
3. The waters of Ontario into Lake Erie
4. Did not answer.
5. Ontario into Erie
6. Lake Ontario into Lake Erie
7. Lake Erie into Lake Ontario
8. Did not answer.
9. Into Lake Ontario.
10. Did not answer.

Dudley School

1. The waters of Lake Erie run into Lake Ontario.
2. The waters of Lake Erie run into Lake Ontario.
3. The waters of Lake Erie into Lake Ontario.
4. The waters of lake Erie into Ontario.
5. Lake Erie into Lake Ontario
6. The waters of Lake Erie run into Lake Ontario.
7. Those of Lake Erie flow into Lake Ontario
8. Those of Lake Erie into those of Lake Ontario
9. The waters of lake Erie run into Lake Ontario
10. The waters of Lake Erie run into Lake Ontario.

VII. Which is most elevated above the level of the sea, Lake Superior or Lake Huron?

City School

1. Did not answer.
2. Did not answer.

3. Lake Superior
4. Did not answer.
5. Superior
6. Lake Superior
7. Lake Superior
8. Lake Superior
9. Lake Superior
10. Lake Superior

Dudley School

1. Lake Superior.
2. Lake Superior.
3. Lake Superior.
4. Lake Superior.
5. Lake Superior.
6. Did not answer.
7. Lake Superior
8. Lake Superior
9. Did not answer.
10. Lake Superior.

VIII. Write down the boundaries of Lake Erie.

City School

1. Did not answer.
2. Lower Canada, New York
3. Did not answer.
4. Did not answer.
5. North by Canada
6. Did not answer.
7. Did not answer.
8. Did not answer.
9. N. York. Pennsylvania. Ohio.
10. North by Upper Canada, east by New York south by Ohio west by Michegan

Dudley School

1. Did not answer.
2. On the north by Canada on the east by lake Ontario and New-York, On the south by New York, on the west by Michigan.

3. Bounded on the north by Canada, on the east by New York and Canada, on the south by New York and Pennsylvania, on the west by Canada.
4. It is bounded on the North by Canada, on the East by Lake Ontario and New York on the South by New York, and on the West by Lake Huron and New York.
5. on the North by Canada, south by New York, Pennsylvania, and Ohio.
6. Did not answer.
7. North by Canada, East by N York, south by Pennsylvania & Ohio, west by Michegan.
8. On the North by Canada on the East by New York On the South by New York an Pennsylvania West by
9. On the north by Canada South by New York Pennsylvania and Ohio
10. Is bounded on the north by Canada, on the south by Ohio, on the east by Lake Ontario and the west by ——————— Niagara River.

IX. QUEBEC IS (ACCORDING TO YOUR MAPS) FOUR DEGREES AND FORTY MINUTES NORTH FROM BOSTON; ITHACA, IN NEW YORK, IS FIVE DEGREES AND THIRTY MINUTES WEST FROM BOSTON. WHICH PLACE IS FARTHEST FROM BOSTON?

City School

1. Did not answer.
2. Quebec

3. Itaca
4. Quebec
5. Did not answer.
6. Alike
7. Did not answer.
8. Did not answer.
9. Did not answer.
10. Ithica New York

Dudley School

1. Quebec.
2. Quebec.
3. Ithaca.
4. Ithica.
5. Ithaca.
6. Ithaca
7. Quebec.
8. Ithaca
9. Ithaca
10. Quebec.

X. WHAT IS THE GENERAL COURSE OF THE RIVERS IN NORTH AND SOUTH CAROLINA?

City School

1. Did not answer.
2. S, East
3. They flow south East
4. South East
5. East
6. South East
7. South
8. South east
9. South East
10. East

Dudley School, Roxbury

1. East or South east.
2. South East
3. South East.
4. South East.
5. South East.

6. Nearly South
7. South East and East
8. East and South East
9. South East
10. Easterly or South. Easterly

XI. WHAT IS THE GENERAL
COURSE OF THE RIVERS IN KEN-
TUCKY AND TENNESSEE?

City School

1. Did not answer.
2. Did not answer.
3. North West
4. Did not answer.
5. West
6. Did not answer.
7. Did not answer.
8. Did not answer.
9. N. West
10. West

Dudley School, Roxbury

1. West.
2. North
3. Did not answer.
4. North East.
5. South west.
6. West
7. west and North West,
8. West
9. North West
10. Westerly,

XII. WHAT IS THE CAUSE OF THE
RIVERS IN THESE FOUR CONTIG-
UOUS STATES RUNNING IN OPPO-
SITE DIRECTIONS?

City School

1. Did not answer.
2. Did not answer.
3. Did not answer.

4. Did not answer.
5. Did not answer.
6. Did not answer.
7. Did not answer.
8. Did not answer.
9. Did not answer.
10. Did not answer.

Dudley School

1. Because there are mountains
between them.
2. The difference of their elevation
3. North westerly.
4. They commence and run
5. The elevation between.
6. situation of the mountains in
which they rise.
7. because the land is higher in
the interior of the country
where these rivers rise
8. They are surrounded by mountains and rivers always flow
down hill.
9. Did not answer.
10. Because they take their rise
in the Allegany mountains,
and they are on opposite sides
of the mountains.

XIII. WHICH IS MOST ACCESSIBLE,
IN ITS INTERIOR PARTS TO
SHIPS AND TO COMMERCE, EU-
ROPE OR AFRICA?

City School

1. Did not answer.
2. Europe.
3. Did not answer.
4. Europe.
5. Did not answer.
6. Europe.
7. Did not answer.
8. Did not answer.

9. Africa.
10. North and south Carolina

Dudley School

1. Europe.
2. Europe.
3. Europe.
4. Europe.
5. Europe.
6. Europe.
7. Africa.
8. Africa.
9. Europe.
10. Europe.

XIV. NAME THE EMPIRES OF EU-
ROPE.

City School

1. Did not answer.
2. Russia, Austria Prussia,
3. Russia Austria Turkey
4. Birman
5. Russia. Austria Turkey
6. Did not answer.
7. Did not answer.
8. Russia.
9. Russia, Austria, Prussia
10. Russian Empire, Austrian Empire Turkish Empire.

Dudley School

1. Russia, Austria, Germany,
Turkey.
2. Germany
3. Russia, Austria, Turkey,
Greece
4. Austria, Prusia, Italy, Russia
5. Russia. Austria. Prussia.
Turkey. Poland.
6. Austria Russia
7. Russian empire, Austrian
empire, Great Britain.

8. Russian   Austrian   Turkish,
British
9. Rusia Austria Prusia Turkey
10. Austria, Prussia, Russia.

XV. NAME THE KINGDOMS OF EU-
ROPE.

City School

1. Did not answer.
2. Great Britain France Spain
3. England. France Spain. Great
Brittian
4. Sardinia, Saos.
5. Great Brittian. France Spain,
6. Did not answer.
7. Did not answer.
8. Denmark.
9. Great Britain
10. France Spain Great Britain

Dudley School

1. Great Britain, France, Spain,
Portugal, Italy, Prussia Denmark, Sweden, Norway.
2. Prussia   Denmark   France
Spain
3. France, England, Spain,
Portugal, Germany, Italy.
4. France, Spain, Portugal, Norway, Sweden, Great Britain
5. England Ireland Scotland.
France Spain German States
6. France Spain Portugal
7. France Spain Portugal Itily,
Greece, Denmark.
8. Norway   Sweden   Denmar
Holland   Belgium   France
Spain Portugal, Italy, Germany, Prussia, Greece
9. England France Spain Portugal Denmark Saxony Han-
over Belgium
10. Italy. France, Spain, Great
Britain, Portugal.

XVI. Name the republics of Europe.

City School

1. Did not answer.
2. Did not answer.
3. Did not answer.
4. Did not answer.
5. Switzerland
6. Did not answer.
7. Did not answer.
8. Did not answer.
9. Saxony, Wurtemburg
10. Germany Italy

Dudley School

1. Switzerland.
2. Switzerland
3. Switzerland
4. Greece Switzerland
5. Switzerland
6. San Marino
7. Switzerland, Some of the German States
8. Switzerland
9. Switzerland Cracow
10. Switzerland

XVII. What is the nearest route from England to India, by the Cape of Good Hope, or by the Red Sea?

City School

1. Cape of good hope.
2. Cape of Good Hope
3. Did not answer.
4. Cape of Good Hope
5. By the Cape of good hope
6. Did not answer.
7. Did not answer.
8. by the Cape of Good Hope
9. Cape of Good Hope
10. Did not answer.

Dudley School

1. By the Red Sea
2. By the cape of Good Hope
3. By the Red sea.
4. By the Red Sea.
5. By the Red Sea.
6. By the Cape of Good Hope.
7. by the red sea
8. By the Red Sea
9. By the Red Sea
10. By the Red Sea

XVIII. What do you understand by the line of perpetual snow?

City School

1. Did not answer.
2. Did not answer.
3. Did not answer.
4. Did not answer.
5. Did not answer.
6. Did not answer.
7. Did not answer.
8. Did not answer.
9. Did not answer.
10. Did not answer.

Dudley School

1. The height where snow is always found.
2. Did not answer.
3. I do not know.
4. I do not know.
5. Those places covered with snow during all the year
6. The place which separates those parts which are covered with perpetual snow from warmer countries.
7. the place where the ground is covered with snow every season of the year

8. That mountains are covered with snow.
9. Places covered with snow all the year
10. The line beyond which is perpetual snow.

XIX. ON WHICH RANGE OF MOUNTAINS IS THE LINE OF PERPETUAL SNOW MOST ELEVATED ABOVE THE OCEAN, ON THE ROCKY MOUNTAINS OF NORTH AMERICA, OR ON THE CORDILLERAS OF MEXICO?

City School

1. Did not answer.
2. Did not answer.
3. Rocky Mountains
4. Did not answer.
5. Did not answer.
6. Rocky
7. Did not answer.
8. Did not answer.
9. Did not answer.
10. Did not answer.

Dudley School

1. The Cordilleras of Mexico
2. On the Rocky Mountains
3. Rocky.
4. I do not know,
5. On the Rocky Mountains
6. On both the same —
7. Rocky Mountains
8. Rocky Mountains
9. On the Rocky
10. Cordilleras.

XX. THE CITY OF MEXICO IS IN 20 DEGREES OF NORTH LATITUDE; THE CITY OF NEW OR-
LEANS IS IN 30 DEGREES OF NORTH LATITUDE. WHICH HAS THE WARMER CLIMATE?

City School

1. Did not answer.
2. Did not answer.
3. Did not answer.
4. Did not answer.
5. New Orleans
6. New Orleans
7. New Orleans.
8. Did not answer.
9. The city of Mexico
10. New Orleans

Dudley School

1. New Orleans.
2. Mexico
3. Mexico.
4. Mexico
5. Mexico.
6. Mexico.
7. Mexico.
8. Mexico
9. Mexico
10. Mexico.

XXI. NAME THE RIVERS, GULFS, OCEANS, SEAS, AND STRAITS THROUGH WHICH A VESSEL MUST PASS IN GOING FROM PITTSBURG, IN PENNSYLVANIA TO VIENNA, IN AUSTRIA.

City School

1. Did not answer.
2. Did not answer.
3. Did not answer.
4.
5.
6. } Did not answer.
7.
8.

9. Atlantic Ocean, Mediterranean Sea, Gulf of Venice, Strait of Gibraltar, Alleghany river
10. Did not answer.

Dudley School

1. Down the Ohio, Down the Mississippi through the gulf of Mexico, Across the Atlantic ocean, through the straits of Gibraltar, through the Mediterranean Sea I can conduct it no farther.
2. Did not answer.
3. Susquehanna, Delaware, Danube rivers, Atlantic ocean, gulf of Tarento, Mediterranean sea and Black sea, straits of Giberalter and Dardanelles.
4. I do not know.
5. Did not answer.
6. Susquehannah river Deleware Bay Atlantic, Mediterranean Sea
7. Ohio River Mississippi River, Gulf of Mexico, Atlantic Ocean, etc.
8. Did not answer.
9. Did not answer.
10. The Ohio River, Gulf of —— Atlantic Ocean, Mediterranian sea, straits of Gibralter.

XXII. ON WHICH BANK OF THE OHIO IS CINCINNATI; ON THE RIGHT OR THE LEFT?

City School

1. Did not answer.
2. Did not answer.
3. Right
4. Did not answer.
5. Right
6. Did not answer.
7. Did not answer.
8. Did not answer.
9. Right
10. Right

Dudley School

1. The right.
2. On the right,
3. Right Bank.
4. On the right bank.
5. Left
6. Right
7. Right
8. Right
9. Right
10. On the right bank.

XXIII. WHAT ARE THE PRINCIPAL NATURAL AND ARTIFICIAL PRODUCTIONS OF NEW ENGLAND?

City School

1. Did not answer.
2. Did not answer.
3. Did not answer.
4. Did not answer.
5. Did not answer.
6. Grass Wheat
7. Did not answer.
8. Did not answer.
9. Hemp, Barley, Oats Flax, Tobacco, Cotton, Rice, Sugar.
10. grass

Dudley School

1. Wheat, rye, barley, apples, pears, peaches, nuts, all sorts of artificial productions.
2. Did not answer.
3. Wheat, rye, corn, apples, pears, peaches, plums,
4. Wheat, Potatoes, Corn, Oats, and Barley.
5. Did not answer.
6. Wheat, Corn, Rye
7. Grass Wheat Corn, Rye, Potatoes, Cotton and woolen Goods Paper, etc.

8. Granite. Marble. Slate. Cotton and linen goods woolen goods. Paper, Glass
9. Did not answer.
10. natural productions are gold and silver, copper and coal. Wheat, corn, rye & potatoes.

9. North America Africa & Oceanica
10. Africa and West India Islands. and the East India Islands Asia,

---

XXV. WHAT PARTS OF THE GLOBE HAVE THE LONGEST DAYS?

City School

1. Not answered.
2. Not answered.
3. Not answered.
4. Not answered.
5. Not answered.
6. Not answered.
7. Not answered.
8. Not answered.
9. Not answered.
10. Those south of the equator

Dudley School

1. The polar regions
2. The United States
3. Temperate Regions.
4. Parts near the Poles.
5. Those situated near the equator.
6. The Poles
7. those parts at the poles
8. Frigid Zones
9. Did not answer.
10. The Temperate Zonees.

XXIV. OVER WHAT CONTINENTS AND ISLANDS DOES THE LINE OF THE EQUATOR PASS?

City School

1. Did not answer.
2. Did not answer.
3. South America Africa
4. Did not answer.
5. South America. Europe. Asia Madagascer
6. Africa Holland Madagasca
7. Did not answer.
8. Did not answer.
9. The continent of N. & S, America, Africa, and the Islands of Sumatra, Borneo Celebes.
10. Did not answer.

Dudley School

1. South America, Africa, Australia,
2. The eastern & Western continents Sumatra Borneo Celebes
3. South America, Africa, through the islands of Borneo, Celebes, Java,
4. America, Africa, Australia,
5. America. West India Islands Europe Asia Africa Ocianica
6. South America, Africa,
7. South America, Africa, Sumatra, Formosa, Borneo,
8. South America, Africa Borneo Sumatra

XXVI. IF A MERCHANT IN MOSCOW DINES AT 3 O'CLOCK, P.M., AND A MERCHANT IN BOSTON AT 2 O'OCLOCK, P.M., WHICH DINES FIRST?

City School

1. Did not answer.
2. Did not answer.
3. Did not answer.
4. Did not answer.
5. Did not answer.
6. Moscow

7. Did not answer.
8. Did not answer.
9. Did not answer.
10. The merchant in Boston

Dudley School

1. The merchant in Moscow.
2. The merchant in Moscow.
3. Merchant at Boston.
4. Moscow
5. Did not answer.
6. The merchant of Moscow
7. The merchant in Moscow.
8. Merchant in Moscow.
9. Did not answer.
10. The merchant in Moscow.

XXVII. NAME THE COUNTRIES WHICH LIE AROUND THE MEDITERRANEAN SEA.

City School

1. Did not answer.
2. Greece, Italy
3. Did not answer.
4. Did not answer.
5. Italy
6. Italy, Turkey
7. Europe, Africa, Asia
8. Did not answer.
9. France, Italy Turkey, Spain
10. France Spain Italy

Dudley School

1. Spain, France, Italy, Turkey, Barbary, Egypt.
2. Spain France Italy Turkey Greece Morooco Algiers Tunis Tripoli Egypt
3. Spain, France, Italy, Turkey, Greece.
4. Barbary, Spain, France, Italy.
5. Spain, France. Italy. Turkey. Morocco Algiers Tunis Tripoli Great Desert

6. Spain, France, Italy, and Greece
7. France, Spain, Itily Greece,
8. Spain. France. Italy. Greece. Morrocco. Egypt. Tripoli. Turkey in Asia.
9. Did not answer.
10. Spain, Portugal, Italy, Turkey, Egypt, Morocco Tunis, and Tripoli

---

XXVIII. WHAT COUNTRIES LIE AROUND THE BLACK SEA?

City School

1. Did not answer.
2. Turkey
3. Did not answer.
4. Did not answer.
5. Austria Turkey
6. Did not answer.
7. Did not answer.
8. Did not answer.
9. Russia, Austria
10. Turkey and Russia

Dudley School

1. Turkey Austria Russia.
2. Russia Turkey Greece
3. Turkey and Russia.
4. Russia, and Austria.
5. Russia, Turkey
6. Russia, Prussia and Austria.
7. Russia, Turkey, in Europe Turkey in Asia.
8. Russia, Turkey in Europe and Turkey in Asia.
9.
10. Russia, Turkey. Austria.

XXIX. WHAT RIVERS FLOW INTO THE BLACK SEA?

City School

1. Did not answer.
2. Did not answer.

3. Danube
4. Did not answer.
5. Dnieper Dniester
6. Don
7. Did not answer.
8. Dnieper and Dniester
9. Dnieper Dniester
10. Danube, Dneiper

Dudley School

1. Danube Dnieper Dniester, Bog.
2. Don Danube Dniester Bog Dnieper
3. Danube. Don, Volga, Ural.
4. Danube, Dniester, Dnieper.
5. Danube Bog Dnieper
6. Volga, Don, Dneiper, Danube, Dneister, Bog,
7. Danube, Dneiper, Bog, Dniester,
8. Don. Dneiper. Dneister. Danube
9. Dniester Dnieper Bog Danube
10. Danube, Don, etc.

XXX. NAME THE PRINCIPAL PORT OF RUSSIA ON THE BLACK SEA, ON THE WHITE SEA, AND ON THE GULF OF FINLAND.

City School

1. Did not answer.
2. Did not answer.
3. Did not answer.
4. Did not answer.
5. Sp Petersburg on the gulf of Finland
6. Did not answer.
7. Did not answer.
8. Did not answer.
9. Odessa, Moscow, St. Petersburgh
10. St. Petersburgh on the gulf of Finland

Dudley School

1. On the gulf of Finland is St. Petersburg. I do not know the others.
2. Did not answer.
3. Odessa on the Black sea, Archangel on the White, Riga on the Gulf of Finland.
4. Petersburge on the Gulf of Finland.
5. St. Petersburg
6. Odessa, Archangel, Riga,
7. Cronstadt
8. Oedssa Cronstadt
9. St. Petersburg on the Gulf of Finland
10. Petersburg on the Gulf of Finland,

XXXI. DRAW AN OUTLINE MAP OF ITALY.

City School

1.
2.
3.
4.
5.
6.   } Did not attempt it.
7.
8.
9.
10.

Dudley School

1. Succeeded.
2. Attempted and failed.
3. Attempted and failed.
4. Attempted and failed.
5. Succeeded.
6. Attempted and failed.
7. Succeeded.
8. Attempted and failed.
9. Succeeded.
10. Succeeded.

APPENDIX SIX

TABULATIONS OF 1845 RESULTS

EXPLANATION OF THE TABLES

These tables have been prepared with very great labor and care. It was necessary, however, to have them printed in haste, and a work which should have occupied several months has been done in a few weeks. It may be, therefore, that there are some errors in them; but it is believed that they will generally be found in favor of the schools. For instance, in looking for errors in definitions, the rule has been that when the scholar expressed himself obscurely, but seemed to have an idea of the meaning of the word, he should be considered as having answered correctly. So in geography, history, philosophy, etc., though the answers were ungrammatical, and contained errors in spelling and punctuation, still they have been recorded in the column of correct answers, if the scholar seemed to have a correct idea of the subject.

As to the columns containing the errors in spelling, grammar, and punctuation, they probably fall short of the real number, because while none would be found that were not in the scholars' answers, hundreds may have been overlooked in such a mass of papers. The number of errors in punctuation seems so enormous, that the Committee may be suspected of hypercriticism; it may be said that punctuation is a mere matter of taste, and that any man may point out hundreds of errors in the works of the best authors. But in looking over the answers written by our scholars, care has been taken to record only the most palpable errors in punctuation. The list has been swelled mainly by the omissions of commas and periods where the sense absolutely required them.

Sometimes errors will be found set down in the columns of errors in punctuation and spelling, against a question which is recorded as not having been answered; and this is the explanation: a boy writes against the question, "I don't know never studeid the subject" Here the question would be recorded as unanswered, and yet one error in spelling and two errors in punctuation would be recorded against him.

Lest the form of the tables should not be understood, we here observe that the first column on the left hand refers to the number of the question, to prevent repetition in printing, though at the time of writing every scholar had the questions plainly printed, before his eyes, and wrote his answers under them. The second column contains the number of answers correct as to sense; the third contains those incorrect as to sense; the third, fourth, fifth,

327

and sixth contain, respectively, the number of errors in grammar, spelling, and punctuation; the seventh contains the number of questions not answered; and the eighth the percentage of correct answers relatively to the whole number of answers that should have been given, supposing all the questions to have been answered.[1]

The column representing the percentage of correct answers in each school, in each study, is obtained by taking the number of scholars examined, and multiplying it by the whole number of questions; this shows the number of answers which they should have given; then taking the number of correct answers which they did give, and ascertaining the proportion between them.

The relative rank of each school in each study is obtained by multiplying the percentage of correct answers by the percentage of the scholars examined.

The mode of examination by written questions has been used with great success in many schools and colleges; but we are not aware of any tabularization like this having been attempted.

N. B. When the per cent of correct answers, or the proportion of the school examined, is one half per cent, it is counted in the scholars' favor; when less than one half it is omitted.

---

[1] The order of columns has been changed slightly in reprinting.

TABLE I

SHOWING THE RELATIVE RANK OF EACH SCHOOL IN THE "ALLOWED STUDIES"

PHILOSOPHY		ASTRONOMY	
Bowdoin	.0324	Johnson	.0216
Wells	.0315	Hawes	.0200
Mayhew	.0155	Franklin	.0135
Hawes	.0140	Mather	.0132
Brimmer	.0133		
Mather	.0116		
Otis	.0114		
Franklin	.0099		
Johnson	.0096		
Boylston	.0093		
Hancock	.0092		

TABLE II

SHOWING THE COMPARATIVE AGES OF THE CLASSES EXAMINED IN EACH SCHOOL

Phillips	12 yrs.	8	mos.	Hancock	13 yrs.	9	mos.		
Eliot	12 "	8	"	Hawes	13 "	9	"		
Adams	12 "	11	"	Boylston	14 "				
Brimmer	13 "			Franklin	14 "	6	"		
Endicott	13 "			Mather	14 "	6	"		
Otis	13 "	2	"	Winthrop	14 "	6½	"		
Wells	13 "	3	"	Bowdoin	14 "	8	"		
Mayhew	13 "	6	"						
Johnson	13 "	6½	"	Dudley	14 "	6	"		

Natural Philosophy had been studied in eleven Schools, and Astronomy in four out of the eleven. An allowance, therefore, should be made in their favor, but it is difficult to make it in this table, for some schools which did not offer classes for examination in Astronomy because they had not studied it, might still have given a considerable number of correct answers if they had been examined. The reader, bearing this in mind, and also the comparative ages of the scholars, will draw his own inference as to the real comparative rank of the schools and consider the following and final table, as he must the others, elements for the calculation.

TABLE III

RELATIVE RANK OF ALL THE SCHOOLS, IN EACH OF THE REQUIRED STUDIES, AS SHOWN BY THEIR ANSWERS TO THE PRINTED QUESTIONS

HISTORY		GEOGRAPHY		DEFINITIONS		GRAMMAR		TOTAL AMOUNT	
Bowdoin	.0384	Wells	.0387	Bowdoin	.0368	Bowdoin	.0440	Bowdoin	.1536
Adams	.0295	Bowdoin	.0344	Wells	.0342	Johnson	.0414	Wells	.1386
Wells	.0261	Adams	.0342	Boylston	.0280	Wells	.0396	Johnson	.0954
Boylston	.0190	Hancock	.0333	Eliot	.0275	Adams	.0305	Winthrop	.0954
Brimmer	.0182	Winthrop	.0276	Adams	.0272	Hancock	.0288	Boylston	.0920
Winthrop	.0174	Johnson	.0252	Winthrop	.0222	Phillips	.0288	Hancock	.0900
Eliot	.0170	Brimmer	.0248	Brimmer	.0165	Winthrop	.0282	Eliot	.0764
Johnson	.0162	Boylston	.0234	Johnson	.0126	Franklin	.0235	Brimmer	.0731
Mayhew	.0156	Eliot	.0215	Hancock	.0126	Boylston	.0216	Franklin	.0630
Hancock	.0153	Endicott	.0174	Franklin	.0110	Hawes	.0212	Mather	.0568
Franklin	.0130	Mayhew	.0168	Mather	.0108	Endicott	.0192	Mayhew	.0565
Mather	.0120	Phillips	.0165	Mayhew	.0085	Mather	.0184	Phillips	.0557
Hawes	.0096	Mather	.0156	Hawes	.0080	Mayhew	.0156	Hawes	.0520
Endicott	.0084	Franklin	.0155	Endicott	.0070	Brimmer	.0136	Endicott	.0520
Otis	.0054	Hawes	.0132	Phillips	.0064	Eliot	.0104	Phillips	.0520
Phillips	.0040	Otis	.0108	Otis	.0055	Otis	.0060	Otis	.0277
Smith	.0000	Smith	.0055	Smith	.0000	Smith	.0015	Smith	.0070
Dudley	.0336	Dudley	.0440	Dudley	.0360	Dudley	.0408	Dudley	.1544

TABLE IV

ILLUSTRATION OF REPORT OF TABULATIONS FOR EACH SCHOOL AND SUBJECT

ADAMS SCHOOL. *Examination in Worcester's History*

Total number of scholars, 418; number examined, 20; average age of those examined, 12 yrs. 11 mos.

NO. OF THE QUESTION	CORRECT ANSWERS	INCORRECT ANSWERS	ERRORS IN SPELLING	ERRORS IN PUNCTUA- TION	ERRORS IN GRAMMAR	NOT ANSWERED
1*	18	0	2	15	0	2
2	15	2	2	19	0	3
3	13	1	0	29	0	6
4	12	2	0	27	0	6
5	13	0	0	14	0	7
6	5	0	0	15	0	15
7	2	5	0	20	0	13
8	7	0	0	20	0	13
9	11	2	2	23	0	7
10	20	0	1	15	0	0
11	10	5	1	13	0	5
12	14	0	0	51	0	6
13	4	14	4	31	0	2
14	19	0	4	18	0	1
15	7	12	0	42	1	1
16	11	8	2	17	1	1
17	16	2	11	49	1	2
18	12	1	1	13	0	7
19	16	3	0	22	0	1
20*	11	9	1	24	0	0
21	16	4	6	28	0	2
22*	17	3	0	24	0	0
23	11	8	0	32	0	1
24*	15	3	0	14	0	2
25	16	1	8	29	1	3
26*	1	10	1	12	0	9
27	13	0	0	17	0	7
28	15	0	3	13	0	5
29	9	2	0	12	0	9
30	7	0	0	7	0	13
	354	97	49	665	4	149

Per cent of correct answers, .59.

Proportion of the school examined, .05; relative rank, .0295.

* Used in the 1919 test.

TABLE V. HISTORY

CONSOLIDATION OF SCORES IN 1845 TEST, ALL SCHOOLS
TOTAL NUMBER OF PUPILS IN "FIRST" CLASS, 1251
NUMBER TAKING TEST, 438 OR 35%

No. of Questions	Correct Answers	% of Correct Answers	In-correct Answers	Errors in Spelling	Errors in Punc-tuation	Errors in Grammar	Not Answered
1*	358	82	9	48	87	4	71
2	121	28	107	24	185	12	210
3	154	35	29	27	199	6	237
4	215	49	90	23	264	12	132
5	167	38	30	22	164	19	250
6	64	14	25	7	130	16	349
7	28	5	74	9	122	0	336
8	84	19	9	10	115	0	345
9	62	14	66	11	139	2	310
10	239	50	17	32	139	15	182
11	58	13	42	11	123	1	338
12	65	15	39	19	185	1	334
13	18	4	58	13	134	1	362
14	133	31	21	21	134	6	284
15	49	10	123	26	191	4	266
16	100	26	154	15	180	2	184
17	109	27	81	49	240	11	248
18	93	21	42	17	136	4	303
19	63	14	80	8	163	0	295
20*	256	59	128	59	288	20	54
21	117	27	157	48	257	15	164
22*	157	36	192	6	237	0	89
23	139	32	190	4	266	5	109
24*	166	38	93	3	161	0	179
25	119	27	161	46	239	12	158
26*	125	28	99	20	156	10	214
27	56	13	111	1	75	2	271
28	119	27	53	26	111	11	266
29	89	20	55	16	152	4	294
30	53	12	31	11	103	6	354
Total	3576	26%					

* Used in the 1919 tests.

TABLE VI

CONSOLIDATED RESULTS. HISTORY

Name of School	Total No. of Scholars in the School	No. Examined	Proportion of the School Examined	Average Age of Those Examined (Yrs. Mos.)	No. of Correct Answers Given to the Whole No. of Questions Given to the Whole No. of Scholars Examined	No. of Correct Answers There Would Have Been Had All the Scholars Answered Correctly	Percentage of Correct Answers	No. of Incorrect Answers Given	No. of Errors Committed in Giving, Spelling, in the Answers	No. of Errors Committed in Punctuation	No. of Errors Committed in Grammar	No. of Questions Not Answered	Relative Rank of the School
Adams	418	20	.05	12 11	354	600	.59	97	49	665	4	149	.0295
Boylston	534	25	.05	14 8	287	750	.38	161	69	445	51	302	.0190
Bowdoin	508	42	.08	14 8	607	1260	.48	335	39	757	14	318	.0384
Brimmer	513	36	.07	13	279	1080	.26	250	40	270	33	551	.0182
Eliot	456	21	.04	12 6	214	630	.34	112	62	326	12	304	.0170
Endicott	478	18	.05	13 9	114	540	.21	64	24	186	5	362	.0084
Franklin	418	19	.04	14 9	148	570	.26	90	12	119	4	332	.0130
Hawes	408	17	.04	13 6½	124	510	.24	114	32	167	1	272	.0096
Hancock	509	45	.09	13 6	234	1350	.17	124	42	270	8	992	.0153
Johnson	547	50	.09	13 6	264	1500	.18	185	16	229	30	1051	.0162
Mather	485	18	.04	14 2	161	540	.30	118	34	190	1	261	.0120
Mayhew	368	21	.06	13 8	163	630	.26	139	31	158	4	328	.0156
Otis	467	26	.06	12 3	68	780	.09	79	9	78	12	633	.0054
Phillips	440	23	.05	13 6½	52	690	.08	119	55	268	9	519	.0040
Wells	307	29	.09	14	254	870	.29	168	83	523	9	448	.0261
Winthrop	507	28	.06	13	244	840	.29	211	82	573	14	385	.0174
Dudley, Roxbury	350	29	.08	14 6	368	870	.42	148	13	449	7	354*	.0336

APPENDIX SIX

TABLE VII. GEOGRAPHY

CONSOLIDATION OF SCORES IN 1845 TEST, ALL SCHOOLS
TOTAL NUMBER OF PUPILS IN "FIRST" CLASS, 1251
NUMBER TAKING TEST, 487 OR 39%

No. of Questions	Correct Answers	% of Correct Answers	In-correct Answers	Errors in Spelling	Errors in Punctuation	Errors in Grammar	Not Answered
1	411	84	76	132	947	0	0
2*	329	65	154	290	1269	3	4
3	254	52	220	67	560	0	13
4	109	23	355	91	505	0	23
5	242	49	203	398	1539	0	42
6*	287	59	130	3	287	6	70
7	337	69	61	5	269	0	89
8	113	23	207	72	588	0	167
9	157	32	156	38	228	5	174
10	374	77	75	0	294	0	38
11	166	33	253	0	309	0	68
12	128	26	51	41	208	11	308
13*	405	83	14	0	295	0	68
14	179	37	187	30	522	0	121
15	166	34	189	138	1016	2	132
16	29	6	167	14	230	3	291
17*	182	38	176	0	230	0	129
18	25	5	160	17	205	6	302
19	91	19	154	7	203	12	242
20	132	27	199	1	225	3	156
21	35	7	118	108	584	9	334
22	244	50	104	1	248	0	139
23	38	8	187	17	411	0	262
24	126	26	177	35	498	1	184
25	71	14	103	6	135	1	313
26*	180	38	37	1	159	1	270
27	59	12	253	36	661	0	175
28	172	35	90	12	304	0	225
29	59	12	185	90	320	0	243
30	79	16	113	28	274	0	261
31	17	3	114	0	0	0	356
Total	5196	34%					

* Used in the 1919 tests

TABLE VIII

CONSOLIDATED RESULTS. GEOGRAPHY

NAME OF SCHOOL	TOTAL No. OF SCHOLARS IN THE SCHOOL	No. EXAMINED	PROPORTION OF THE SCHOOL EXAMINED	AVERAGE AGE OF THOSE EXAMINED (Yrs. Mos.)		No. OF CORRECT ANSWERS GIVEN TO THE WHOLE No. OF QUESTIONS BY THE WHOLE No. OF SCHOLARS EXAMINED	No. OF CORRECT ANSWERS THERE WOULD HAVE BEEN HAD ALL THE SCHOLARS ANSWERED CORRECTLY	No. OF INCORRECT ANSWERS GIVEN	PERCENTAGE OF CORRECT ANSWERS	No. OF ERRORS COMMITTED IN SPELLING, IN GIVING THE ANSWERS	No. OF ERRORS COMMITTED IN PUNCTUATION	No. OF ERRORS COMMITTED IN GRAMMAR	No. OF QUESTIONS NOT ANSWERED	RELATIVE RANK OF THE SCHOOL
Adams	418	36	.09	12	11	421	1116	447	.38	179	1451	5	248	.0342
Boylston	534	33	.06	14		397	1023	317	.39	98	1398	0	309	.0234
Bowdoin	508	42	.08	14	8	563	1302	493	.43	172	987	1	246	.0344
Brimmer	513	40	.08	13		379	1240	463	.31	231	1189	20	398	.0248
Eliot	456	22	.05	12	8	292	682	187	.43	57	829	6	203	.0215
Endicott	478	28	.06	13		252	868	318	.29	160	1088	3	298	.0174
Franklin	418	20	.04	14	6	192	620	216	.31	50	498	2	212	.0155
Hawes	408	17	.09	13	9	174	527	199	.33	35	261	3	154	.0132
Hancock	509	45	.09	13	9	515	1395	325	.37	94	617	1	555	.0333
Johnson	547	49	.04	13	6½	430	1519	457	.28	126	1012	2	632	.0252
Mather	485	17	.07	14	6	208	527	195	.39	83	774	4	124	.0156
Mayhew	368	24	.06	13	6	180	744	150	.24	133	609	3	414	.0168
Otis	467	27	.05	13		154	837	117	.18	46	309	2	566	.0108
Phillips	440	22	.05	12	8	225	682	222	.33	104	371	5	235	.0165
Smith	163	8	.09	13	3	27	248	38	.11	19	219	5	183	.0055
Wells	307	29	.06	14	6½	384	899	254	.43	72	805	1	261	.0387
Winthrop	507	28	.08	14	6	400	868	273	.46	100	1608	0	195	.0276
Dudley, Roxbury	350	29	.08	14	6	493	899	324	.55	51	1111	0	82	.0440

TABLE IX. ARITHMETIC

SCHOOLS	No. BELONGING TO SCHOOLS	No. IN FIRST CLASS	No. OF PUPILS EXAMINED	THE RESULT OF THE EXAMINATION. THE FIGURES 1, 2, 3, ETC., INDICATING THE No. OF THE QUESTION, BELOW WHICH IS STATED THE NUMBER OF CORRECT ANSWERS										AVERAGE AGE OF THE PUPILS IN EACH SCHOOL
				1*	2*	3*	4	5	6	7*	8	9*	10	
Eliot	470	80	24	24	24	13	0	0	0	5	0	13	0	13 6-12
Adams	420	72	17	17	17	9	2	0	0	10	0	4	0	13 2-12
Franklin	411	40	12	12	12	6	0	0	0	11	0	7	0	14 10-12
Mayhew	373	54	17	15	15	4	0	0	0	4	0	4	0	13 10-12
Hawes	424	52	20	20	20	5	0	0	0	5	0	11	1	14 4-12
Boylston	547	101	26	26	26	26	0	0	0	19	0	16	0	15 1-12
Bowdoin	511	143	19	19	19	18	0	0	0	11	0	11	0	15 4-12
Hancock	549	100	23	21	21	1	0	0	0	6	0	22	0	14 7-12
Wells	445	77	20	20	20	19	1	0	0	13	0	20	0	15
Johnson	504	113	16	15	13	9	6	0	0	5	0	5	0	15
Winthrop	553	81	20	20	19	13	0	0	0	16	0	14	0	13 10-12
Lyman	380	41	10	10	10	10	0	0	0	7	0	9	0	14
Endicott	518	81	22	22	17	11	0	0	0	13	0	11	0	18 6-12
Mather	485	59	11	11	11	4	0	0	0	11	0	10	0	15
Brimmer	532	40	15	11	10	5	0	0	0	1	0	5	0	14 6-12
Phillips	450	59	13	11	12	8	0	0	0	3	0	6	0	13 2-12
Otis	472	37	19	10	12	6	0	0	0	7	0	6	0	14
Smith	163													
New South	136	21	4	4	4	3	0	0	0	0	0	0	0	13 3-12

* Used in the 1919 tests.

TABLE X. GRAMMAR

Consolidation of Scores in 1845 Test, All Schools
Total Number of Pupils in "First" Class, 1251
Number Taking Test, 456 or 36%

No. of Ques- tions	Correct Answers	% of Correct Answers	In- correct Answers	No. of Errors	Errors in Spelling	Errors in Punctu- ation	Not Answered
1	117	25	258	484	313	3358	81
2*	142	31	277	386	323	2849	37
3*	356	78	41	39	8	183	59
4*	191	42	96	110	10	197	169
5	71	15	100	172	2	92	285
6	299	65	76	85	73	265	81
7	355	78	23	23	66	42	78
8	134	29	88	89	30	193	234
9*	143	31	65	66	61	133	248
10*	138	30	187	360	72	574	131
11	128	28	128	128	1	150	200
12	56	12	198	198	8	154	202
13	168	36	90	95	0	227	198
14	217	47	39	39	6	185	200
Total	2515	39					

* Used in the 1919 tests.

TABLE XI

CONSOLIDATED RESULTS. GRAMMAR

Name of School	Total No. of Scholars in the School	No. Examined	Proportion of the School Examined	Average Age of Those Examined (Yrs.)	(Mos.)	No. of Correct Answers Given to the Whole No. of Questions by the Whole No. of Scholars Examined	No. of Correct Answers There Would Have Been Had All Scholars Answered Correctly	Percentage of Correct Answers	No. of Incorrect Answers Given	No. of Errors Committed in Grammar	No. of Errors Committed in Spelling, in Giving the Answers	No. of Errors Committed in Punctuation	No. of Questions Not Answered	Relative Rank of the School
Adams	418	20	.05	12	11	171	280	.61	76	98	97	603	33	.0905
Boylston	534	34	.06	14		169	476	.36	136	199	91	882	171	.0216
Bowdoin	508	43	.08	14	8	333	602	.55	198	257	77	1014	71	.0440
Brimmer	513	20	.04	13		94	280	.34	114	149	67	389	72	.0136
Eliot	456	19	.04	12	8	70	266	.26	70	83	35	318	126	.0104
Endicott	478	30	.06	13		136	420	.32	102	140	87	821	182	.0192
Franklin	418	19	.05	14	6	125	266	.47	76	99	56	478	65	.0235
Hawes	408	17	.04	13	9	127	238	.53	73	92	26	310	38	.0212
Hancock	509	45	.09	13	9	203	630	.32	112	136	46	372	315	.0288
Johnson	547	49	.09	13	6½	315	680	.46	194	183	43	696	297	.0414
Mather	485	18	.04	14	6	116	252	.46	82	109	32	403	54	.0184
Mayhew	368	21	.06	13	6	75	294	.26	94	128	29	357	125	.0156
Otis	467	21	.04	13	2	43	294	.15	44	62	49	213	207	.0060
Phillips	440	35	.08	12	8	174	520	.36	133	219	100	446	183	.0288
Smith	163	8	.05	13		3	112	.03	5	8	9	75	104	.0015
Wells	307	29	.09	13	8	180	406	.44	100	108	56	765	126	.0396
Winthrop	507	28	.06	14	6½	183	592	.47	117	177	62	838	92	.0282
Dudley, Roxbury	350	29	.08	14	6	207	406	.51	99	121	14	663	100	.0408

TABLE XII. WORDS TO BE DEFINED

CONSOLIDATION OF SCORES IN 1845 TEST, ALL SCHOOLS
TOTAL NUMBER OF PUPILS IN "FIRST" CLASS, 1251
NUMBER TAKING TEST, 516 OR 41%

No. of Questions	Correct Answers	% of Correct Answers	Incorrect Answers	Errors in Spelling	Errors in Punctuation	Errors in Grammar	Not Answered
1*	218	42	144	2	239	3	154
2	173	34	83	6	178	2	260
3	25	5	197	2	176	2	294
4	87	17	65	2	154	1	364
5	101	20	179	11	200	1	236
6	21	4	237	11	185	1	258
7	120	23	136	3	178	1	260
8	105	20	120	11	174	1	291
9	62	12	100	0	146	2	354
10	116	22	131	13	183	2	269
11*	62	12	168	4	192	0	286
12	337	65	36	8	245	0	143
13*	114	22	129	6	170	6	273
14*	209	40	116	1	210	2	191
15	266	50	70	4	219	3	180
16	122	24	151	12	198	9	243
17	306	60	32	3	222	2	178
18	202	59	90	6	201	2	224
19	25	5	166	5	163	3	325
20	24	5	75	2	137	1	417
21	244	47	19	5	188	0	253
22*	160	31	158	9	225	2	198
23	13	3	160	3	167	0	343
24	137	26	21	4	129	3	358
25	126	24	21	1	12	0	369
26	9	1	95	3	107	0	412
27	7	1	94	4	85	0	415
28	118	22	43	1	129	0	355
Total	3509	27					

* Used in the 1919 tests.

TABLE XIII

CONSOLIDATED RESULTS. WORDS TO BE DEFINED

Name of School	Total No. of Scholars in the School	No. Examined	Proportion of the School Examined	Average Age of Those Examined (Yrs.)	(Mos.)	No. of Correct Answers Given to the Whole No. of Questions by the Whole No. of Scholars Examined	No. of Correct Answers There Would Have Been Had All the Scholars Answered Correctly	Percentage of Correct Answers	No. of Incorrect Answers Given	No. of Errors Committed in Spelling in Giving the Answers	No. of Errors Committed in Punctuation	No. of Errors Committed in Grammar	No. of Questions Not Answered	Relative Rank of the School
Adams	418	35	.08	12	11	333	980	.34	317	26	577	12	330	.0272
Boylston	534	36	.07	14	8	402	1008	.40	426	20	585	9	180	.0280
Bowdoin	508	43	.08	14	8	556	1204	.46	365	3	591	8	283	.0368
Brimmer	513	56	.11	13	6	235	1568	.15	310	18	369	1	1023	.0165
Eliot	456	21	.05	12	9	322	588	.55	127	9	363	4	139	.0275
Endicott	478	34	.07	13	9	93	952	.10	42	4	92	1	817	.0070
Franklin	418	19	.05	14	6½	117	532	.22	175	8	109	0	240	.0110
Hawes	408	17	.04	13	6	96	476	.20	160	10	110	1	220	.0080
Hancock	509	45	.09	13	6	179	1266	.14	84	6	110	2	997	.0126
Johnson	547	50	.09	13	6½	197	1400	.14	210	1	245	0	993	.0126
Mather	485	18	.04	14	6	134	504	.27	110	0	185	0	260	.0108
Mayhew	368	20	.05	13	2	95	560	.17	95	3	136	1	370	.0085
Otis	467	24	.05	12	8	76	672	.11	33	3	69	3	563	.0055
Phillips	440	35	.08			78	980	.08	99	10	294	1	803	.0064
Smith	163	6	.04	13	3	0	168	.00	16	1	16	0	152	.0000
Wells	307	29	.09	14	6½	309	812	.38	234	4	486	2	269	.0342
Winthrop	507	28	.06	14		289	784	.37	222	16	482	4	273	.0222
Dudley, Roxbury	350	29	.08	14	6	367	812	.45	183	5	384	1	312	.0360

TABLE XIV. NATURAL PHILOSOPHY

CONSOLIDATION OF SCORES IN 1845 TEST, ALL SCHOOLS
TOTAL NUMBER OF PUPILS IN "FIRST" CLASS, 1251
NUMBER TAKING TEST 279 OR 22%

No. of Questions	Correct Answers	% of Correct Answers	In-correct Answers	Errors in Spelling	Errors in Punctu-ation	Errors in Grammar	Not Answered
1	106	38	126	40	270	11	47
2	65	23	40	2	127	5	174
3	4	1	204	24	148	21	71
4	195	70	39	16	122	17	45
5	133	48	72	10	97	16	74
6*	60	22	75	5	75	10	144
7	81	29	74	4	130	5	124
8	19	7	115	2	85	2	145
9*	80	29	49	15	95	13	150
10	31	11	75	7	71	6	173
11*	76	27	153	1	112	9	50
12	24	9	28	5	62	2	227
13	150	54	16	13	71	23	113
14	68	24	22	0	53	0	189
15	9	3	17	0	27	2	253
16*	97	35	56	9	99	7	126
17	63	22	83	20	91	8	133
18	76	27	72	12	84	8	131
19*	44	15	111	17	103	20	124
20	73	26	151	1	108	4	55
Total	1450	24					

*Used in the 1919 tests.

TABLE XV

CONSOLIDATED RESULTS. NATURAL PHILOSOPHY

NAME OF SCHOOL	Total No. of Scholars in the School	No. Examined	Proportion of the School Examined	Average Age of Those Examined (Yrs.)	(Mos.)	No. of Correct Answers Given to the Whole No. of Questions by the Whole No. of Scholars Examined	No. of Correct Answers There Would Have Been Had All the Scholars Answered Correctly	Percentage of Correct Answers	No. of Incorrect Answers Given	No. of Errors Committed in Spelling in Giving the Answers	No. of Errors Committed in Punctuation	No. of Errors Committed in Grammar	No. of Questions Not Answered	Relative Rank of the School
Boylston	534	14	.03	14	8	86	280	.31	101	4	144	3	93	.0093
Bowdoin	508	45	.09	14		321	900	.36	268	22	361	110	311	.0324
Brimmer	513	35	.07	13	6	130	700	.19	217	54	206	13	353	.0133
Franklin	418	14	.03	14	9	91	280	.33	86	4	94	11	103	.0099
Hawes	408	17	.04	13	9	120	340	.35	139	36	153	3	81	.0140
Hancock	509	20	.04	13	6½	90	400	.23	75	4	52	6	235	.0092
Johnson	547	44	.08	13	6	103	880	.12	224	13	243	4	553	.0096
Mather	485	17	.04	14	6	97	340	.29	131	31	230	9	112	.0116
Mayhew	368	19	.05	13	2	119	380	.31	113	12	189	13	148	.0155
Otis	467	27	.06	13	3	104	540	.19	94	12	185	12	342	.0114
Wells	307	27	.09	13		190	540	.35	133	11	173	5	217	.0315
Dudley, Roxbury	850	29	.08	14	6	208	580	.36	140	12	290	0	232	.0288

TABLE XVI. ASTRONOMY

Consolidation of Scores in 1845 Test, All Schools
Total Number of Pupils in "First" Class, 1251
Number Taking Test, 104 or 8%

No. of Questions	Correct Answers	% of Correct Answers	In-correct Answers	Errors in Spelling	Errors in Punctu-ation	Errors in Grammar	Not Answered
1	56	40	12	14	24	1	36
2	13	9	40	1	34	4	51
3	95	68	6	0	26	0	3
4	19	14	79	0	59	1	6
5	17	12	7	2	31	0	80
6	32	23	13	4	32	2	59
7	3	2	9	1	11	0	92
8	3	2	17	1	15	0	84
9	0	0	7	0	9	0	97
10	0	0	3	0	2	1	101
11	24	17	54	1	39	0	26
12	59	42	19	0	48	0	26
13	10	7	4	0	10	0	90
14	35	25	13	0	25	4	56
15	32	23	20	0	26	1	52
16	10	7	19	0	11	0	75
17	32	23	6	0	28	3	66
18	23	16	22	7	47	3	59
19	6	4	31	0	15	1	67
20	20	14	20	0	21	0	64
21	8	5	22	3	23	1	74
22	52	37	37	2	75	12	15
23	62	44	19	1	49	6	23
24	45	32	45	0	9	0	14
25	77	55	8	0	14	0	19
26	52	37	8	0	11	0	44
27	89	64	3	0	12	0	12
28	44	31	44	0	56	0	16
29	30	21	16	3	41	2	58
30	16	11	14	3	25	2	74
31	13	9	17	2	18	2	74
Total	977	30					

TABLE XVII

CONSOLIDATED RESULTS. ASTRONOMY

Name of School	Total No. of Scholars in the School	No. Examined	Proportion of the School Examined	Average Age of Those Examined		No. of Correct Answers Given to the Whole No. of Questions by the Whole No. of Scholars Examined	No. of Correct Answers There Would Have Been Had All the Scholars Answered Correctly	Percentage of Correct Answers	No. of Incorrect Answers Given	No. of Errors Committed in Spelling, in Giving the Answers	No. of Errors Committed in Punctuation	No. of Errors Committed in Grammar	No. of Questions Not Answered	Relative Rank of the School
				Yrs.	Mos.									
Franklin	418	19	.05	14	6	158	589	.27	112	6	154	6	319	.0135
Hawes	408	17	.04	13	9	265	527	.50	141	20	192	25	121	.0200
Johnson	547	50	.09	13	6½	368	1550	.24	229	4	282	7	953	.0216
Mather	485	18	.04	14	6	186	558	.33	152	8	241	9	220	.0132

APPENDIX SEVEN

THE 1919 TESTS, RECORD SHEETS, AND DIRECTIONS FOR THEIR USE

INSTRUCTIONS FOR EXAMINERS

The tests should be given by a total stranger if possible, or by the principal of the school, a strange teacher, etc., but *not* by the room teacher. There should be absolutely no previous preparation, or warning, and no help should be given during the course of the tests. No books, maps, or other sources of information, should be available on the walls or desks, and there should be no work done except on the test papers.

Give the tests to the entire eighth grade, (both upper and lower divisions if the classes are so divided). Distribute the papers and direct the children to read and follow the explanations and instructions on the test sheets. Do not give other directions, answer no questions, and make no further explanations. Allow 100 minutes of working time. If pupils finish before the end of the time allowed, take their papers as they finish. Collect all the remaining papers at the end of 100 minutes whether the pupils have finished or not. Find and record the total attendance of the school on the day the tests are given. Instructions for scoring will be found with the tabulation sheets.

EXPLANATIONS

In 1845, there were 7,526 children in the Grammar Schools of Boston. In those days there were no grades. The schools were divided roughly into "classes." The tests were given to selected pupils from the "first" class. In the words of the report, "The whole number offered for examination — a number comprising the flower of the Boston Public Schools, was 530." The ages of the pupils selected varied from eleven to sixteen, the average being thirteen years and six months. A study of the results by schools, however, reveals the fact that there were great variations in the average age from school to school. In general the schools having the older pupils made the better records. Accordingly, tabulations of the 1845 results have been made in different ways: For the older and for the younger classes, and for the city as a whole. This will enable a fair comparison to be made with the scores of eighth grade classes of the present day.

Issued by Otis W. Caldwell and S. A. Courtis, 1807 East Grand Boulevard, Detroit, Michigan.

In 1845, the tests were given in June and July. The instructions for scoring are only fairly detailed, but fortunately, the actual answers written by one "medal" scholar [1] from each school, as well as other illustrative records, are published in full. The 1845 results are given question by question and school by school.

From the above it will be seen that no complete comparison between 1845 and the present day is possible owing to the many changes in the conditions. If the instructions above are followed exactly, however, it will be possible to learn many things of interest, and to determine what percentage of present day children attain the levels of achievement of the "best scholars" of 1845; also, whether or not this percentage is a larger proportion of the whole school than in 1845.

In particular it should be noted that many present day eighth grade children have received no school instruction in "Natural Philosophy." They should be given the test questions, nevertheless, as the occasion affords an opportunity to determine the relative attainments on the particular points covered.

[1] The honor scholars were awarded medals and were known as "medal" scholars.

	RESEARCH TESTS	Boston
1919	INSTRUCTIONS FOR SCORING	Survey

GENERAL SUGGESTIONS AND RECOMMENDATIONS

It is not wise to burden any one person with the scoring of a large number of papers. While uniformity may sometimes seem to be secured, fatigue and the delay in knowing the results may prove a more serious defect than lack of exact uniformity.

It is recommended that each eighth grade room teacher score one class (preferably not her own), when two or more eighth grade classes are examined, and if possible, that the different scorers read the instructions and work together in order that doubtful cases may be settled after discussion. Judgment enters largely into scoring like that demanded by this test. The scorers should make sure (1) that the instructions are thoroughly studied, and (2) that the situation is correctly observed. They should then make the best judgment of which they are capable, without spending a large amount of time on any one point. Steady, straight-forward, honest observance of the rules below, and the exercise of common sense judgment in doubtful cases, is all that can be hoped for in any general investigation of this character.

DIRECTIONS FOR SCORING

GENERAL RULE OF THE 1845 EXAMINERS
(To be followed also in 1919)

"We have put the most lenient construction upon the answers, and whenever it appeared that a scholar had any tolerable idea of the subject, we have recorded his answers as correct.

"For instance, in looking for errors in definitions, the rule has been, that when a scholar expressed himself obscurely, but seemed to have an idea of the meaning of the word, he should be considered as having answered correctly. So in geography, history, etc., though the answers were ungrammatical, and contained errors in spelling and punctuation, still they have been recorded in the column of correct answers, if the scholars seemed to have a correct idea of the subject. If we had put down as correct only those answers which were perfect in regard to sense, to grammatical construction, to spelling, and to punctuation, the record would have been very short indeed."

RULES

I. Look through the papers, compare each answer with the correct answer for that question as printed on the back of the corresponding record sheet, and mark on the test paper in the column headed A, either C (for correct), X (for wrong), O (for omitted), or a special record as provided for in the directions which follow. (See illustration, page 355.)

II. Read the answers through a second time, and draw a line around each error in punctuation, either of omission or commission.   The statement in the 1845 report is:

"The number of errors in punctuation may seem so enormous that the Committee may be suspected of hypercriticism; it may be said that punctuation is a mere matter of taste, and that any man may point to hundreds of errors in the works of the best authors.   But in looking over the answers written by our scholars, care has been taken to record only the most palpable errors in punctuation.   The list has been swelled mainly by the omission of commas and periods where the sense absolutely required them.   Sometimes errors will be found set down in the column of errors in punctuation and spelling, against a question which is recorded as not having been answered; and this is the explanation: a boy writes against a question, 'I don't know never studed the subject' Here the question would be recorded as unanswered, and yet one error in spelling and two errors in punctuation would be recorded against him."

To aid in standardizing the marking of the 1919 papers, look for the following "palpable" errors in capitalization and punctuation.

1. Omission of a period at the end of each sentence, or answer.

2. Omission of punctuation between the members of a series.

(As in enumerating the rivers of a country.)

3. The omission of a period after an abbreviation.

4. The use of a period in a situation in which it should not be used.

5. The omission of a comma where "the sense absolutely requires it."

6. Failure to begin an answer with a capital.

(If a period has been omitted at the end of one sentence and a small letter is used at the beginning of the next sentence, count the mistake as one error only.)

7. Failure to capitalize proper names.

8. The unquestionably wrong use of capitals.

9. A few gross errors not covered by the above rules may need to be scored.

Count the number of errors in punctuation in each answer and write the number on the test paper in the column headed P.

NOTE. — In the arithmetic test errors in punctuation are not scored.

III. Read the answers through a third time and underscore each word misspelled. Count a word as misspelled if :

1. It is illegible.

(But do not count failure to dot "i's" or cross "t's" unless it makes the word illegible.)

2. It has too many letters.

3. It has too few letters.

4. It has the right letters in the wrong order.

5. It is a homonym of the word called for by the sense.

(As "there" for "their")

6. If it is a mere slip.

(As dropping "d" from "and")

Count the number of errors in spelling in each question and write the number in the column headed S.

NOTE. — In the arithmetic test, the errors in spelling are not to be scored.

IV. In 1845 the answers were also scored for "errors in grammar," but as, in the main, the number of such errors was small, and as no hint is given in regard to what types of errors were counted, no tabulation of errors in grammar will be called for. The Boston results for grammatical errors will be given with the rest, however.

Check each point correctly given in the answers and count the number of checks. See illustration on the next page.

OUTLINE FOR SCORING QUESTION 16

     (1)   (2)   (1)   (2)   (3)

The: Definite article (or limiting adjective) modifies wages.

      (4)   (5)   (6)   (7)   (8)

Wages: Common noun, third person, singular number, neuter

            (9)   (10)

gender, nominative case, subject of verb is.

     (11)   (12)

Of: Preposition, shows relation between sin and wages, forms

         (13)   (14)   (15)

with sin an adjective phrase, modifying wages.

    (16)   (17)   (18)   (19)   (20)

Sin: Common noun, third person, singular number, neuter gender

    (21)   (22)

objective (or genitive) case, object of preposition of.

    (23)   (24)   (25)   (26)   (27)

Is: Copulative verb, third person, singular number, present tense,

    (28)   (29)

indicative mood, agrees with wages, shows the relation of the

    (30)

predicate noun death to the subject wages.

    (31)   (32)   (33)   (34)   (35)

Death: Common noun, third person, singular number, neuter

      (36)   (37)   (38)

gender, predicate nominative after is.

Allow 1 point additional for conjugation of verb, 1 point for each rule quoted, and 1 point for statement that the sentence is of the simple declarative type.

ILLUSTRATION OF SCORING

(Question 16)

The following answer is taken from the 1845 report. It should be given a credit of 18 points. The points allowed are indicated by check marks, and are listed below.

          √   √   √   √ √   √

"Wages is a noun 3rd Person Sin Nom to is of Preposition shows

  √   √   √

the relation between Sin and Wages Sin is a noun 3rd Person Ob-

  √   √   √ √   √   √
jective case govern by in is is a verb Indc mood Pres tense 3rd person
 √   √   √
Sin no Nom C after is

POINTS

1. Noun.	8. Noun.	15. Third person.
2. Third person.	9. Third person.	16. Sin no (singular num-
3. Sin (singular).	10. Objective case.	ber).
4. Nom (nominative).	11. Govern(ed) by in (of).	17. Nom C (nominative
5. To is (subject of is).	12. Verb.	case).
6. Preposition.	13. Indc (indicative).	18. After is.
7. Shows relation.	14. Pres (present).	

In the columns of errors, the answer above would be charged with 38 errors in punctuation and 1 in spelling as follows :

Errors in punctuation : the capitalization of 14 common nouns and the omission of proper punctuation marks after noun, Sin (2), Nom, is, of, Preposition, Wages, noun, Person, case, in, verb, Indc,
(2)
mood, Pres, tense, person, Sin, no, Nom, C, is.

Errors in spelling : govern for governed.

OUTLINE FOR SCORING QUESTION 19

Your brother was there (1) and he said to my sister and i (2) (3) (4) i am tired (6) and must go and lay (7) down to rest me (8) (9) (10) and when he was laying (11) down (12) we tried to lie (13) a vail (14) over his face.

POSSIBLE CORRECTIONS

1. Insert comma.	6. Insert comma.	11. Change laying to lying.
2. Change i to me.	7. Change lay to lie.	12. Insert comma.
3. Insert comma.	8. Omit me.	13. Change lie to lay.
4. Insert quotation	9. Insert period.	14. Change vail to veil.
mark.	10. Omit and and begin	
5. Change i to cap.	when with cap.	

ILLUSTRATION OF SCORING
(Question 19)

The following answer is taken from the 1845 report. It should be given a score of 6 points. The points allowed are indicated by check marks.

              √ √
Your Brother was there and he said to my Sister and me I must
        √   √
go and must go and lay down to rest myself and when he was lying
     √ √
down we tried to lay a veil over his face.

POINTS

1. Changed i to me.
2. Capitalized I.
3. Changed me to myself.
4. Changed laying to lying.
5. Changed lie to lay.
6. Changed vail to veil.

In the columns of errors, this answer would be charged with six errors in punction, as follows:

1, 2. Capitalization of brother and sister.
3. Omission of comma after me.
4. Omission of quotation marks.
5. Omission of comma after down.
6. Omission of period at end of sentence.

INSTRUCTIONS FOR RECORDS AND COMPUTATIONS

I. — HISTORY

1. When all the papers have been scored, fill out the blanks at the top of a history class record sheet, both original and duplicate.

2. Enter the names or initials of the pupils (or the papers may be simply numbered and entered by number). For each question enter the score in the proper column: C, X, or O under Ans., the number of punctuation errors under P, and the number of spelling errors under Sp.

3. When all the papers have been entered, find, and record at the bottom of the column, the total number of each type of answer. Find also the total number of errors in punctuation and spelling.

4. Transfer the totals to the summary on the back of the record sheet. Find the grand total of errors in punctuation and spelling. Then divide these totals by five times the number of children's records. The results are to be recorded as the average errors in punctuation and spelling.

5. For each question, divide the number of each type of answer by the number of children's records, and record the results in the column headed %. Find also the grand total of each type of answer, divide these grand totals by five times the number of children's records, and record the results as the average per cent. for the test.

The computations of per cent are best made by means of the tables. It saves time to learn to use these tables.

On the following page there is given a sample record for a class of five pupils.

No.	Names of Pupils	Question 1			Question 2			Question 3			Question 4			Question 5		
		Ans.	P	Sp.	Ans.	P	Sp.	Ans.	P	Sp.	Ans.	P	Sp.	Ans.	P	Sp.
1	J. McGAR	C	0	0	C	0	0	C	1	1	O	-	-	X	0	0
2	I. ROTH	C	0	0	C	0	0	C	0	0	O	-	-	X	0	0
3	D. COHEN	C	0	0	C	1	1	C	3	0	X	-	0	X	0	0
4	E. HINE	C	1	0	½C	1	0	C	1	0	X	-	0	X	0	0
5	A. ENGLE	C	1	0	C	0	1	½C	1	1	O	-	-	X	-	0
Totals	C	5	2	0	4.5	2	3	4.5	6	2	0	2	0	0	1	0
	X	0			.5			.5			2			5		
	O	0			0			0			3			0		

Summary of Results from the Front of this Sheet

Total Errors in	Spelling	Punctuation	Type of Answer					
			C		X		O	
			No.	%	No.	%	No.	%
Question 1	0	2	5	100	0	0	0	0
Question 2	3	2	4.5	90	.5	10	0	0
Question 3	2	6	4.5	90	.5	10	0	0
Question 4	0	2	0	0	2.	40	3	60
Question 5	0	1	0	0	5.	100	0	0
Grand Total	5	13	14.0	56	8.0	32	3	12
Average	.2	.52						

II. — GEOGRAPHY

The geography tabulations are made in precisely the same way except for question 6. For this question enter under Ans. the number of rivers given on each paper. For the total of the C answers, count the number of answers which are three or larger. For the X answers, count the number of 2's and 1's. For the O answers, count the number of zero's. The rest of the work is precisely like that for History.

ARITHMETIC

On this record sheet, copy not only the names but the ages of the pupils, and for each question record its C, X, or O score. Keep no record of the spelling and punctuation errors in this test.

Under "Important Data," write in the total adult population of your city, and the average daily attendance of your school system, grades, second to eighth inclusive. Make the computations indicated.

It is worth while getting the best record you can for these items as the data, compared with similar figures from 1845, will indicate how much larger a proportion of the children than formerly now attend public schools.

In similar fashion find and record the total attendance in your school building on the day of the test from grades 2 to 8 and the other data asked for. Make the indicated computations.

(If your school does not include all grades from 2 to 8, note that fact under "Remarks.") These data will measure the holding power of our schools as compared with that of 1845.

Divide the total of the ages by the number of children's records and record the result as the average age of the class.

The remaining computations are the same as for History.

GRAMMAR

For questions 16 and 19, enter on the record sheet the number of points made by each pupil. It will be noted that it was necessary to break up the answers to these questions into a relatively large number of points in order to provide for the wide range of replies which different schools give. But in estimating whether an answer is satisfactory or not:

For question 16, regard all answers of 6 or more points, C; answers of from 1 to 5 points, X; and no correct response, O.

For question 19, regard all answers of 3 or more points, C; answers of 1 or 2 points, X; no correct response, O.

The rest of the tabulations and computations are similar to those for History.

WORDS TO BE DEFINED, AND NATURAL PHILOSOPHY

The tabulations and computations are similar to those for History.

COMPARISONS WITH 1845 RESULTS

When you have sent in a copy of your results and have received in reply the sheet of 1845 scores, copy thereon the significant results from the summaries on the different class record sheets; then graph the results, following the instructions on the graph sheet which will be sent at the same time.

Special request: Return copies of your results before July 1st, 1919.

1919	**RESEARCH TESTS** Test Questions Given in **1845** to Pupils in the First Classes of the Boston Public Schools.	Boston Survey

Explanation to Eighth Grade Boys and Girls

This test is given to see whether or not the boys and girls of today have learned certain things as well as did their great grandfathers and grandmothers when they were pupils nearly seventy-five years ago.

The questions are taken from examinations given in Boston in 1845. Some of them are easy because they are the same as the questions you are asked in school today. Some are thought questions which you can answer easily if you have learned to think correctly. Others may prove difficult because you may never have studied anything about the subjects. However, **try them all.** Put down the best answers you can. Work calmly, but steadily. Do not hurry, but do not waste any time. Omit questions for which you cannot think of an answer. What you do will not affect your mark for this semester's work. Enjoy the tests as you would a game.

When you are sure you understand the above, fill out the blanks below, then open your paper and begin to work. Write your answers in the space provided. Do not work on any other paper. When you have finished, take your paper to the examiner.

Boy or
My name is.................................Girl?.....

I am.....years and.....months old.   I am in the......grade.

I live in....................(City)...............(State)

My school is...

The maximum time allowance for this test is 100 minutes.

Issued by Otis W. Caldwell and S. A. Courtis,
1807 East Grand Boulevard, Detroit, Mich.

[1] Tests as originally printed were on a page approximately 5 × 8 inches.

History

A	P	S

1. What is History? ....

....

....

....

2. About what year did the first colonists come to New England and what were the supposed motives for their leaving the mother country? ....

....

....

....

....

3. When did the war of the American Revolution commence, and who were the allies of the Americans? ..

....

....

4. About what year was the embargo laid by President Jefferson, and when was non-intercourse substituted for it? ....

....

5. What do you understand by an embargo? ....

....

....

....

....

Geography

A | P | S

6. Name the principal rivers in North America......

....

....

....

....

....

....

7. Do the waters of Lake Erie run into Lake Ontario, or the waters of Ontario into Erie?.................

....

8. Which is most accessible, in its interior parts, to ships and to commerce, Europe or Africa?...........

....

9. What is the nearest route from England to India, — by the Cape of Good Hope, or by the Red Sea?.....

....

....

10. If a merchant in Moscow dines at 3 o'clock, P. M., and a merchant in Boston at 2 o'clock, P. M., which dines first?...

....

....

Arithmetic

11. How much is $\frac{1}{2}$ of $\frac{1}{3}$ of 9 hours and 18 minutes?

(Do all your work in this space.) Answer...............

12. What part of 100 acres is 63 acres, 2 roods, and 7 sq. rods?

(Do all your work in this space.) A rood is a measure of land no longer in use. There were 40 sq. rods in a rood, and 4 roods in an acre. Answer...............

13. What is the quotient of one ten thousandth, divided by ten thousand? Express answer in decimal and common fractions.

(Do all your work in this space.) Answer...............

14. A sold goods for $1500, to be paid for one-half in 6 months, and one-half in 9 months. What is the present worth of the goods, interest being at 7 per cent?

(Do all your work in this space.) Answer...............

15. What is the square root of $\frac{5}{9}$ of $\frac{4}{5}$ of $\frac{4}{7}$ of $\frac{7}{9}$?

(Do all your work in this space.) Answer...............

(If you need more space, use the outside of last page.)

Grammar

A | P | S

16. Parse the following sentence, and write a full account of each word: *The wages of sin is death.*

. . . .
. . . .
. . . .
. . . .
. . . .
. . . .
. . . .

17. Write a short sentence, containing an active transitive verb, and an objective case.

. . . .
. . . .

18. Write a short sentence, containing an intransitive verb, a relative pronoun, and an adjective in the comparative degree.

. . . .
. . . .

19. Punctuate the following sentence: correct all the errors you may find in it; and write it out grammatically if you think it to be ungrammatical.

Your brother was there and he said to my sister and i i am tired and must go and lay down to rest me and when he was laying down we tried to lie a vail over his face.

. . . .
. . . .
. . . .
. . . .
. . . .
. . . .

Grammar (Continued)

A | P | S

20. What is an allegory?.........................

....
....
....

Words to be Defined

21. Monotony...............................

....
....

22. Dormant...............................

....
....

23. Infatuated...............................

....
....

24. Misnomer...............................

....
....

25. Connoisseur...............................

....
....

Natural Philosophy

A | P | S

26. What is the reason that when a car in motion is suddenly stopped, the passengers are thrown forward?.
....
....
....

27. What is the reason that you can cut a piece of pasteboard or hard substance, more easily by holding it close up to the rivet of a pair of scissors, than by holding it near the ends of the blades?.....................
....
....
....
....

28. Which could you stop most easily, a railroad car weighing a ton, going at the rate of ten miles an hour, or a car weighing 100 tons, creeping along at the rate of $\frac{1}{4}$ of a mile an hour?................................
....

29. In building a cistern should it be made stronger at the top or at the bottom? Why?................
....
....

30. In a small boat which is in danger of being upset, should the passengers stand up, or lie down in the bottom? Why?....................................
....
....
....
....
....

HISTORY

CORRECT ANSWERS AND SPECIAL INSTRUCTIONS

1. **History is a narrative of past events.**
   (Or story, record, account or any equivalent statement.)

2. **1620**, 1607, any year from 1600 to 1635, early part of the seventeenth century.

   Reasons: **To escape religious persecution,** to enjoy civil or religious liberty, to get liberty, or equivalent statements.
   Both a date and a reason should be given. If either is missing, and the other correct, call the answer $\frac{1}{2}$C.

3. **1775 or 1776.   The French.**
   Both a date and an ally should be given. Allow $\frac{1}{2}$C for one correct answer.

4. **1807, 1809,** any year from 1804 to 1812.
   Although there are two questions here, allow full credit for either answer or both.

5. **An embargo is a restriction of trade.**
   (A stopping of trade; prohibition to sail; etc.)

GEOGRAPHY

CORRECT ANSWERS AND SPECIAL INSTRUCTIONS

6. The list below contains most of the principal rivers that will be named. The names of other rivers will appear, however, and they should be counted, if they are names of American rivers and if, in the opinion of the teacher, they are of importance, either locally or because they have been taught. Such additional rivers should be recorded on this sheet.

1. Arkansas	10. Kennebec	19. Potomac	27. Saskatchewan
2. Alleghany	11. Kentucky	20. LaPlatte	28. Sacramento
3. Alabama	12. Mackenzie	21. Red	29. Susquehanna
4. Columbia	13. Merrimac	22. Red River of	30. Tennessee
5. Colorado	14. Mississippi	the North	31. Yellowstone
6. Connecticut	15. Missouri	23. Rio Grande	32. Yukon
7. Cumberland	16. Nelson	24. St. Lawrence	
8. Delaware	17. Ohio	25. Savannah	
9. Hudson	18. Penobscot	26. San Joaquin	

In the answers on the test papers, count the number of rivers which are found in the list above, and record this number in column A in place of the C and X answers. Write O for no correct response.

7. The waters of Lake Erie run into Lake Ontario.
(Or any equivalent statement, as "Into Ontario.")

8. Europe.   **9. By The Red Sea.**   **10. Moscow.**

NOTE. Strictly speaking, No. 10 is an ambiguous, unfair question, to which either Boston or Moscow is the right answer, depending upon the point of view. However the intent is plain, and it is *as* fair in 1919 as in 1845.

Record here names of North American rivers which are counted but not listed above.

ARITHMETIC

CORRECT ANSWERS AND SPECIAL INSTRUCTIONS

Only correct answers are to be counted. In case of decimal answers the number of places beyond the significant figures is unimportant; thus, the answer to 12 is to be considered correct if written .6; .64; .63; .635; etc., provided the decimal was derived from the proper common fraction.

11. One hour and 33 minutes; 93 minutes; 1.55 hours; and $1\frac{11}{20}$ hours.

12. .6354, or $\dfrac{10167}{16000}$.
(Full credit for either form.)

13. .000,000,01; $\dfrac{1}{100,000,000}$; one hundred-millionth.
(Two out of the three answers must be given. Half credit for one.)

14. **$1437.23.**

The answers on the papers may differ from this and still be right. Variations of one or two cents should not be counted wrong. If the example is worked correctly in principle, and no mistakes in computation have been made, it should be accepted. Possible correct answers are

$1442.44 $1440.75 $1438.92 $1436.89 $1434.08 $1433.40
$1441.09 $1440.41 $1437.57 $1435.43 $1433.74

An answer is not to be counted wrong, if the dollar sign is omitted.

15. $\frac{4}{9}$ or **.44.**

Important Data for Comparison with 1845

Present Adult Population of City (Best Estimate Available) . . . ——
Present Average Daily Attendance, Second to 8th Grade, Inclusive . ——
Per Cent. Average Daily Attendance is of the Total Population . ——
Total Attendance in This School Building on Day of Test, Grades 2–8 ——
Total Number of Eighth Grade Graduates This Semester . . . . ——
Per Cent. Eighth Grade Children Are of Total . . . . ——
Remarks : ————————————————————————
Average Age of This Eighth Grade Group————Years————Months.

GRAMMAR

CORRECT ANSWERS AND SPECIAL INSTRUCTIONS

16. In the outline on page 5 of the folder of instructions to scorers there are 38 possible points. Count the number of these points which are correctly given in each answer on the papers, and record the number in the column headed A, in place of the usual C, X or O. That is, check each point correctly given and count the number of checks. See illustration on page 352 of folder.

17. **I wrote a letter.**

(Or equivalent sentence.)

18. **He who is wise, grows constantly wiser.**

(Or equivalent sentence.)

19. The possible errors in the original sentence are numbered in
the copy on page 343 of the folder.   Count and record the
number of mistakes that have been successfully corrected in
the answers on the papers.

(If new mistakes in punctuation and spelling are made, they are scored
in the usual manner.)

20. **Allegory.**
An imaginative story told to illustrate a truth.

DEFINITION

CORRECT ANSWERS AND SPECIAL INSTRUCTIONS

After each word is given the correct definition, and in parenthesis,
a number of children's answers that were accepted as correct.

21. **Monotony.**   Tiresome uniformity.
(Sameness, no variety, all in one tone.)

22. **Dormant.**   Being in a state resembling sleep : torpid.
(Sleeping, sleepy, stupid, inactive, sluggish.)

23. **Infatuated.**   To inspire with such ardent passion as to deprive
of ordinary judgment.
(Blinded, without reason, crazy, impressed with some bad notion.)

24. **Misnomer.**   A name wrongly applied.
(A wrong name, misnamed, error, mistake.)

25. **Connoisseur.**   A competent and critical judge.
(A critic, a judge, a person who understands some particular business
but does not practice it.

NATURAL PHILOSOPHY

CORRECT ANSWERS AND SPECIAL INSTRUCTIONS

This will undoubtedly prove the most difficult test to score.   Any
answer which expresses the essential ideas of the answers below
is to be accepted as correct.

26. When the car is stopped, the passengers keep on moving until
they, too, are stopped.
(Inertia, momentum.)

27. The blades have a greater purchase near the rivet.
     (Because they move through a smaller distance; exert greater power, have greater leverage, etc.)

28. A car weighing a ton.

29. At the bottom, because the pressure is greater there.
     (Weight, force, tendency to break, etc.)

30. The passengers should lie down in the bottom to make the boat less top-heavy.
     (The lower the center of gravity, the less easily the boat is upset.)

Comparative Record and Graph Sheet
1845–1919

GENERAL DIRECTIONS

Copy from the various record sheets the "C" scores for each question, recording them in the column marked "City Scores." Subtract each "Boston Score" from the corresponding "City Score," or vice versa, depending upon which score is larger, and write the result in the column marked "Differences." If the Boston Score is the larger, give the difference a minus sign. Divide each difference by the corresponding Boston Score and write the result expressed as a rate per cent, (with its sign) in the column headed "Per Cent of Difference."

On each scale make a dot to indicate the per cent of difference for that test. If the per cent of difference exceeds 50%, make the dot just beyond the end of the line and write the result just after it: thus .87%. Join each point with the next by a straight line. A comparison of this line with the printed line marked "Boston Results" will give a picture of the changes which have taken place since 1845.

EXPLANATION

Any test yields only a score which shows what the children did with the particular material under the given conditions and should not be interpreted as having too extensive significance. Scores to be of value must be carefully interpreted, and accuracy of interpretation depends upon a knowledge of the conditions.

In considering the meaning of the 1919 results, we know at the outset that many conditions have changed from 1845 to 1919. For instance, in 1845 the words to be defined were taken from the children's readers, while in 1919, such words usually are not found in material judged suitable for eighth grade children. Therefore, in 1845, the Definition Test measured how well the children had profited by the explanations which were (or should have been) made in the reading classes; in 1919 it measures whether or not the words have found a place in the children's vocabulary chiefly through the incidental training afforded by general experiences. If the 1919 children make much lower scores in this test, the results might be interpreted as a sign of progress, since the 1845 reading material may thus prove to be poorly adjusted to the children's needs. In similar fashion, lower scores in some of the arithmetic and grammar questions are probably favorable signs. Following each question on the chart there has been placed an "M" (memory or mechanics) or a "T" (thought,) except for the questions on Definition and Natural Philosophy, both of which measure totally different facts than in 1845. It will probably be a favorable sign if the 1919 children do relatively better work with the thought questions than those involving merely memory or mechanical processes.

We should therefore not accept the results at their face value but try to interpret them in the light of the conditions. Judgment as to changes in efficiency of instruction may possibly be based best on the history and geography tests. Other tests bring out forcibly certain desirable changes which have taken place since 1845. For instance, in 1845 two and a half hours a day from the ages of 7 to 14 were set apart for arithmetic, and the inference from the test questions is that the emphasis was placed on the mechanics of the subject. As a whole, the results should be considered merely as indications of the direction in which the educational currents are at present tending. They should not be taken as an absolute comparison of the work of the present day schools with those of 1845. The changes in conditions are numerous and the defects in the statistical methods many. Nevertheless, the results, while not an exact measure of the changes, are significant of the character of the changes and should prove suggestive and valuable when rightly interpreted.

For convenience in graphing, all differences have been reduced to the percentage basis. Note that two items "Per Cent in School" and "Per Cent of Graduates" are taken from the arithmetic record

sheet, lines 3 and 8.   The first shows whether or not a larger proportion of the children now go to school than in 1845 and the second
whether or not a larger proportion stay through the eighth grade.
Note also that the scores for Punctuation and Spelling are the average of the scores for the five tests.   That is, add the average score
in Punctuation for the History, Geography, Grammar, Definition
and Natural Philosophy tests and divide the same by 5, recording
the results on line "D" of the record and graph sheet.   Statisti-
cally, this procedure is questionable, but probably not more so
than the scoring of the number of errors per question without regard to the number of words in the answers.   Here again the final
results should be taken as an indication of the general tendency
and not as an exact measure of fact.   Scores marked with a (*) are
unreliable in that there is no means of telling just how the answers
were scored in 1845.   On the other hand the following information
will render important comparisons possible.

Question 6.   The number of rivers in ten representative answers
as given in 1845 report varies from 4 to 14, median 6.   Ten answers
similarly chosen from one of the best girls' schools varied from 6 to
30, median $12\frac{1}{2}$.   All 1919 children giving 6 or more rivers in answer
to this question probably do as well or better than the average
child in Boston in 1845.

Question 16.   The median of five representative answers was
23 points.

Question 19.   The median of five representative answers was 2
points.

1845 RESULTS

1. GENERAL CONDITIONS

	Number	
Population of Boston in 1845, approximately	120,000	
Children in school, ages 7 to 14 (7 to 16 for girls)	7,930	6.6%
Children tested (corresponding to 8th grade graduates for year)	539	6.8%
Average age of children tested:		
Group A, Boys' Schools only*	91	12 yrs. 9 mo.
Group B, Boys', Girls' and mixed schools*	275	13 yrs. 5 mo.
Group C, Girls' and mixed schools*	144	14 yrs. 6 mo.
City as a whole, including one school in Roxbury*	539	13 yrs. 6 mo.

2. Errors in Punctuation, Spelling and Grammar. Average error per child per question:

Group	Spelling				Punctuation				Grammar			
	A	B	C	City	A	B	C	City	A	B	C	City
History	.68	.38	.54	.48	.09	.05	.05	.05	.01	.02	.02	.02
Geography	.93	.79	1.08	.93	.14	.11	.12	.12	.01	.00	.00	.00
Grammar	1.78	1.55	2.14	1.76	.28	.15	.23	.20	.53	.38	.46	.43
Definition	.55	.28	.54	.40	.03	.01	.08	.01	.01	.00	.07	.01
Natural Philosophy	..	.30	.42	.35	..	.03	.04	.03	..	.02	.09	.04
Average	.99	.66	.94	.78	.14	.07	.10	.08	.14	.07	.14	.10

* The grouping of the schools, the number of children in each group, and the average age of the group change slightly from test to test. For instance, in arithmetic and natural philosophy but 308 children were tested.

3. Per cent of each type of answers for each subject, question and group:

HISTORY*

Question	1				2				3				4				5				Average			
Group	A	B	C	City	A	B	C	City	A	B	C	City	A	B	C	City	A	B	C	City	A	B	C	City
Correct	61	79	96	83	46	53	74	59	53	37	26	36	46	29	50	35	18	23	43	28	45	44	58	48
Wrong	3	2	1	2	39	31	22	29	39	39	55	43	25	20	21	21	36	21	19	22	28	23	24	23
Omitted	36	19	3	15	15	16	4	12	8	24	19	21	29	51	29	44	46	56	38	50	27	33	18	29

GEOGRAPHY

Question	6				7				8				9				10				Average			
Group	A	B	C	City	A	B	C	City	A	B	C	City	A	B	C	City	A	B	C	City	A	B	C	City
Correct	82	63	66	68	54	58	66	61	87	80	92	84	55	36	33	40	41	35	40	39	64	54	59	58
Wrong	18	36	33	31	40	27	19	26	6	2	3	4	28	29	56	36	5	5	13	7	19	20	25	21
Omitted	0	1	1	1	6	15	15	13	7	18	5	12	17	35	11	24	54	60	47	54	17	26	16	21

ARITHMETIC

Question	11				12				13				14				15				Average			
Group	A	B	C	City	A	B	C	City	A	B	C	City	A	B	C	City	A	B	C	City	A	B	C	City
Correct Answers	98	89	99	94	92	86	97	92	52	33	83	55	43	36	64	48	44	62	67	56	66	61	82	70

* The History table is to be read as follows: Of all the children taking the test, in Group A 61% gave correct answers to Question 1, 3% gave wrong answers, and 36% failed to write any answer; in Group B, 79% gave correct answers to Question 1, and so on. For the city as a whole the average record based on the five history questions was 48% of correct answers.

GRAMMAR

Question	16				17				18				19				20				Average			
Group	A	B	C	City	A	B	C	City	A	B	C	City	A	B	C	City	A	B	C	City	A	B	C	City
Correct	38	26	37	32	81	77	83	80	38	39	51	45	21	28	40	32	21	32	36	31	40	41	49	44
Wrong	54	64	61	61	16	6	10	9	27	18	24	21	58	35	46	41	6	12	24	15	32	27	33	30
Omitted	8	10	2	7	3	17	7	11	35	43	25	34	21	37	14	27	73	56	40	54	28	32	18	26

DEFINITIONS

Question	21				22				23				24				25				Average			
Group	A	B	C	City	A	B	C	City	A	B	C	City	A	B	C	City	A	B	C	City	A	B	C	City
Correct	39	34	62	46	31	31	67	44	15	8	18	14	40	32	25	30	21	12	42	23	29	24	43	31
Wrong	27	25	32	26	26	22	21	22	29	21	58	33	18	26	49	30	30	17	38	24	27	22	40	27
Omitted	34	41	6	28	43	47	12	34	56	71	24	53	42	42	26	40	49	71	20	53	44	54	17	42

NATURAL PHILOSOPHY

Question	26				27				28				29				30				Average			
Group	A	B	C	City	A	B	C	City	A	B	C	City	A	B	C	City	A	B	C	City	A	B	C	City
Correct	..	21	23	26	..	28	30	29	..	25	31	27	..	26	51	34	..	9	31	17	..	22	33	27
Wrong	..	22	37	26	..	14	25	18	..	52	61	53	..	22	16	20	..	39	40	39	..	30	36	31
Omitted	..	57	40	48	..	58	45	53	..	23	8	20	..	52	33	46	..	52	29	44	..	48	31	42

APPENDIX EIGHT

SAMPLE PAGES FROM THE 1845 TEXTBOOKS

The textbooks in use in 1845 in the Boston schools bear little resemblance to those of 1923. They were small in size, averaging about 3 by $4\frac{1}{2}$ inches of reading, printed in small type, almost devoid of pictorial illustrations, and in content, mature, academic, uninteresting. The reader is asked to appraise for himself the content in the following pages from the viewpoint of modern educational ideals; namely, that subject matter should be of maximum intrinsic immediate worth both to the child and to society; that it should be selected in terms of the interests and development of the pupils by whom it is to be used; and that it should be presented in a natural (functional) order rather than in a logical (artificial) arrangement.

THE

NORTH AMERICAN READER;

CONTAINING

A GREAT-VARIETY OF PIECES IN PROSE AND POETRY,

FROM VERY HIGHLY ESTEEMED

AMERICAN AND ENGLISH WRITERS;

ALSO,

OBSERVATIONS ON GOOD READING ; THE DECLARATION OF INDEPENDENCE ;
THE CONSTITUTION OF THE UNITED STATES ; POLITICAL DEFINITIONS;
VARIABLE ORTHOGRAPHY ; CONCISE PRINCIPLES OF PRONUNCIA-
TION ; RULES FOR THE DIVISION OF WORDS ; AND THE RULES
FOR SPELLING THE PLURALS OF NOUNS, PARTICIPLES,
PRESENT TENSE, AND PRETERIT OF VERBS, AND
THE COMPARATIVE AND SUPERLATIVE
DEGREES OF ADJECTIVES.

DESIGNED FOR THE USE OF THE HIGHEST CLASSES IN SCHOOLS AND ACADEMIES.

BY LYMAN COBB, A.M.

Author of the First Book, Spelling-book, Expositor, School Dictionary, Miniature Lexicon, Primary Mon-
torial Lessons, Juvenile Reader, Nos. 1, 2, & 3, Sequel to the Juvenile Readers, Arithmetical Ru. tr
and Tables, Explanatory Arithmetick, Nos. 1 & 2, and Ciphering-book, Nos. 1 & 2.

FOURTH EDITION.

NEW YORK:

B. & S. COLLINS,

230 PEARL-STREET.

1 8 3 6.

Title page of the reader to which reference is made in the text and from
which the words for the definitions test were taken. Note the style.

CONTENTS.

[The names of American Authors are printed in small capitals.]

First page of the table of contents of the same reader. Note the subjects judged suitable for twelve-, thirteen-, and fourteen-year-old children. Note also the number of selections chosen for their supposed influence on the moral development of the pupils. This type of subject has disappeared from modern texts as completely as it has from the everyday conversations of adults.

LESSON XVI.

The Grave a place of rest.—MACKENZIE.

1. THE grave is a place where the weary are at rest. How soothing is this sentiment, "The weary are at rest!" There is something in the expression which affects the heart with uncommon sensations, and produces a species of delight, where tranquillity is the principal ingredient. The sentiment itself is extensive, and implies many particulars: it implies, not only that we are delivered from the troubling of the wicked, as in the former clause, but from every trouble and every pain, to which life is subjected.

2. Those, only, who have themselves been tried in affliction, can feel the full force of this expression. Others may be pleased with the sentiment, and affected by sympathy. The distressed are, at once, pleased and comforted. To be delivered from trouble; to be relieved from power; to see oppression humbled; to be freed from care and pain, from sickness and distress; to lie down as in a bed of security, in a long oblivion of our woes; to sleep, in peace, without the fear of interruption. How pleasing is the prospect! how full of consolation!

3. The ocean may roll its waves, the warring winds may join their forces, the thunders may shake the skies, and the lightnings pass, swiftly, from cloud to cloud: but not the forces of the elements, combined, not the sounds of thunders, nor of many seas, though they were united into one peal, and directed to one point, can shake the security of the tomb.

4. The dead hear nothing of the tumult; they sleep soundly; they rest from their calamities upon beds of peace. Conducted to silent mansions, they cannot be troubled by the rudest assaults, nor awakened by the loudest clamour. The unfortunate, the oppressed, the broken-hearted, with those that have languished on beds of sickness, rest here together; they have forgot their distresses; every sorrow is hushed, and every pang extinguished.

The selections on this and the opposite page are given that the reader may judge for himself both the appropriateness of the content and the style of the 1845 selections.

LESSON LXIII.

On the relative Value of Good Sense and Beauty in the Female Sex.—LITERARY GAZETTE.

1. Notwithstanding the lessons of moralists, and the declamations of philosophers, it cannot be denied that all mankind have a natural love, and even respect, for external beauty. In vain do they represent it as a thing of no value in itself, as a frail and perishable flower; in vain do they exhaust all the depths of argument, all the stores of fancy, to prove the worthlessness of this amiable gift of Nature.

2. However persuasive their reasonings may appear, and however we may for a time fancy ourselves convinced by them, we have in our breasts a certain instinct, which never fails to tell us that all is not satisfactory; and, though we may not be able to prove that they are wrong, we feel a conviction that it is impossible they should be right.

3. They are certainly right in blaming those who are rendered vain by the possession of beauty, since vanity is at all times a fault; but there is a great difference between being vain of a thing, and being happy that we have it; and that beauty, however little merit a woman can claim to herself for it, is really a quality which she may reasonably rejoice to possess, demands, I think, no very laboured proof.

4. Every one naturally wishes to please. To this end we know how important it is, that the first impression we produce should be favourable. Now this first impression is commonly produced through the medium of the eye; and this is frequently so powerful as to resist, for a long time, the opposing evidence of subsequent observation.

5. Let a man of even the soundest judgement be presented to two women, equally strangers to him, but the one extremely handsome, the other without any remarkable advantages of person, and he will, without deliberation, attach himself first to the former. All men seem in this to be actuated by the same principle as Socrates, who used to say, that when he

followed, in November, 1807, the *British Orders in Council*
by which all neutral vessels, trading with France, were compelled to stop at a British port and pay a duty. In consequence
of this measure, Bonaparte issued, in December, 1807, the
Milan Decree, by which every vessel, which should submit to
British search, or consent to any pecuniary exactions whatever,
was confiscated.

5. In the same month (December, 1807), on the recommendation of Mr. Jefferson, congress laid an *embargo* on all
the shipping of the United States. This measure was designed
to retaliate on both England and France, and also to put the
United States in a better state of defence, by retaining their
vessels and seamen at home; but, inasmuch as it annihilated
all foreign commerce, it operated with great severity on the
interests of the people, and became unpopular; and in March,
1809, the embargo was removed, and *non-intercourse* with
France and Great Britain was substituted.

6. While matters continued in this state, new causes of prov-
ocation continually occurred. The trade of the United States
was harassed by both of the belligerents; and the government
was accused in Britain of partiality to France, and in France
of pusillanimously submitting to the insults of Britain.

7. But one species of injury, which was keenly felt and
loudly complained of in this country, the United States suffered
exclusively from Britain. This was the impressment of her
seamen, on board the American vessels, by British men-of-
war. The similarity of language renders it difficult to distinguish American from British seamen; but there is reason to
believe, that, on some occasions, the British officers were not
anxious to make the distinction, being determined, at all haz-
ards, to procure men; and American seamen were compelled
to serve in the British navy, and fight the battles of Britain.

8. The British, on the other hand, complained that their
seamen escaped on board American vessels, to which they
were encouraged, and where they were carefully concealed;
and they contended for the right of searching American merchant vessels for their own runaway seamen. This custom
had been long practised; was a fruitful source of irritation;
and was submitted to, with extreme reluctance, on the part of
the Americans, who maintained that, under British naval officers, it was often conducted in the most arbitrary manner,
with little regard to the feelings of those against whom it was
enforced; and that, under the color of this search, native seamen were frequently dragged on board British vessels.

9. The custom of searching for British seamen had hitherto
been confined to private vessels; but, in 1807, it was ascer-

This illustration is the page of the history in use from which one of the
history questions is taken.

ARITHMETIC.

ARTICLE I.

DEFINITIONS OF QUANTITY, NUMBERS, AND ARITHMETIC.

QUANTITY is that property of any thing which may be increased or diminished—it is *magnitude* or *multitude*. It is magnitude when presented in a mass or continuity; as, a quantity of water, a quantity of cloth. It is multitude when presented in the assemblage of several things; as, a quantity of pens, a quantity of hats. The idea of quantity is not, however, confined to visible objects; it has reference to every thing that is susceptible of being more or less.

NUMBERS are the expressions of quantity. Their names are, One, Two, Three, Four, Five, Six, Seven, Eight, Nine, Ten, &c. In quantities of multitude, *One* expresses a UNIT; that is, an entire, single thing; as one pen, one hat. Then each succeeding number expresses one unit more than the next preceding. In quantities of magnitude, a certain known quantity is first assumed as a measure, and considered the unit; as one gallon, one yard. Then each succeeding number expresses a quantity equal to as many times the unit, as the number indicates. Hence, the value of any number depends upon the value of its unity.

When the unit is applied to any particular thing, it is called a *concrete* unit; and numbers consisting of concrete

3*

This illustration from Emerson's *Arithmetic*, published in 1835, is given to show the formal and academic character of the approach to arithmetic. It should be remembered that the report proves that the general custom was to learn such definitions by heart.

IX.   COMPOUND NUMBERS.   27

WINE MEASURE.

The denominations of Wine Measure are, the ton, $T.$, the pipe, $p.$, the puncheon, $pun.$, the hogshead, $hhd.$, the tierce, $tier.$, the barrel, $bl.$, the gallon, $gal.$, the quart, $qt.$ the pint. $pt.$ and the gill, $gi.$

4 gills . . . . = 1 pt.	1 gi. .. =	$\frac{1}{4}$ of 1 pt.
2 pints . . . . . . = 1 qt.	1 pt. .. =	$\frac{1}{2}$ of 1 qt.
4 quarts . . . . . = 1 gal.	1 qt. .. =	$\frac{1}{4}$ of 1 gal.
31$\frac{1}{2}$ gallons . . . . = 1 bl.	1 gal. .. =	$\frac{2}{63}$ of 1 bl.
42 gallons . . . . . = 1 tier.	1 gal. .. =	$\frac{1}{42}$ of 1 tier.
63 gallons . . . . . = 1 hhd.	1 gal. .. =	$\frac{1}{63}$ of 1 hhd.
84 gallons . . . . . = 1 pun.	1 gal. .. =	$\frac{1}{84}$ of 1 pun.
126 gallons . . . . . = 1 p.	1 gal. .. =	$\frac{1}{126}$ of 1 p.
2 pipes . . . . . . = 1 T.	1 p. .. =	$\frac{1}{2}$ of 1 T.

BEER MEASURE.

The denominations of Beer Measure are, the butt, $bt.$, the hogshead, $hhd.$, the barrel, $bl.$, the kilderkin, $kil.$, the firkin, $fir.$, the gallon, $gal.$, the quart, $qt.$, and the pint, $pt.$

2 pints . . . . = 1 qt.	1 pt. ... =	$\frac{1}{2}$ of 1 qt.
4 quarts . . . . . . = 1 gal.	1 qt. ... =	$\frac{1}{4}$ of 1 gal.
9 gallons . . . . . . = 1 fir.	1 gal. ... =	$\frac{1}{6}$ of 1 fir.
2 firkins . . . . . . = 1 kil.	1 fir. ... =	$\frac{1}{2}$ of 1 kil.
2 kilderkins . . . . = 1 bl.	1 kil. ... =	$\frac{1}{2}$ of 1 bl.
3 kilderkins . . . . = 1 hhd.	1 kil. ... =	$\frac{1}{3}$ of 1 hhd.
2 hogsheads . . . . . = 1 bt.	1 hhd. .. =	$\frac{1}{2}$ of 1 bt.

NOTE. In the United States, the Dry gallon contains 268$\frac{4}{5}$ cubic inches, the Wine gallon 231 cubic inches, and the Beer gallon 282 cubic inches. By an Act of the British government, however, the distinction between the Dry, Wine, and Beer gallon was abolished in Great Britain, in 1826, and an *Imperial Gallon* was established, as well for liquids as for dry substances. The Imperial gallon must contain " 10 pounds, Avoirdupois weight, of distilled water, weighed in air, at the temperature of 62° of Fahrenheit's thermometer, the barometer standing at 30 inches." This quantity of water will be found to measure 277$\frac{274}{1000}$ cubic inches. The same Act establishes the *pound Troy* at 5760 grains, and the *pound Avoirdupois* at 7000 grains.

In the old arithmetics are found many measures and processes which have since become obsolete. Note "puncheon," "tierce," "kilderkin," "Beer gallon," and "duodecimals" in the reproductions on this and the opposite page.

XXVII.

DUODECIMALS.

Duodecimals are compound numbers, the value of whose denominations diminish in a uniform ratio of 12. They are applied to square and cubic measure.

The denominations of duodecimals are the foot, (*f.*), the prime or inch, (′), the second, (″), the third, (‴), the fourth, (⁗), the fifth, (‴′′), and so on. Accordingly, the expression 3 1′ 7″ 9‴ 6⁗ denotes 3 feet 1 prime 7 seconds 9 thirds 6 fourths.

The accents, used to distinguish the denominations below feet, are called *indices*.

The foot being viewed as the unit, duodecimals present the following relations.

$1' = \frac{1}{12}$ of 1 foot.

$1'' = \frac{1}{12}$ of $\frac{1}{12}$ of 1 foot. . . . $= \frac{1}{144}$ of 1 foot.

$1''' = \frac{1}{12}$ of $\frac{1}{12}$ of $\frac{1}{12}$ of 1 foot. . . $= \frac{1}{1728}$ of 1 foot.

$1'''' = \frac{1}{12}$ of $\frac{1}{12}$ of $\frac{1}{12}$ of $\frac{1}{12}$ of 1 foot. $= \frac{1}{20736}$ of 1 foot.
&c.

Addition and subtraction of duodecimals are performed as addition and subtraction of other compound numbers; 12 of a lower denomination making 1 of a higher. Multiplication, however, when both the factors are duodecimals, is peculiar, and will now be considered.

When feet are multiplied by feet, the product is in feet. For instance, if required to ascertain the superficial feet in a board 6 feet long and 2 feet wide, we multiply the length by the breadth, and thus find its superficial, or square feet to be 12. But when feet are multiplied by any number of inches [primes], the effect is the same as that of multiplying by so many twelfths of a foot, and therefore the product is in twelfths of a foot, or inches: thus a board 6 feet long and 6 inches wide contains 36 inches, because the length being multiplied by the breadth, that is, 6 feet by $\frac{6}{12}$ of a foot, the product is $\frac{36}{12}$ of a foot,

120. If 240 men, in 5 days, of 11 hours each, can dig a trench 230 yards long, 3 yards wide, and 2 yards deep, in how many days, of 9 hours each, will 24 men dig a trench 420 yards long, 5 yards wide, and 3 yards deep?

Since 248 men, in 5 days, of 11 hours each, can dig a trench 230 yards long, 3 yards wide, and 2 yards deep, 24 men, working in days of the same length, would dig a trench of the same dimensions in $\frac{248}{24}$ of 5 days, which is $51\frac{16}{24} = 51\frac{2}{3}$ days; and, working in days of 9, instead of 11 hours each, the trench would occupy them $\frac{11}{9}$ of $51\frac{2}{3}$ days, which is $63\frac{4}{27}$ days. Again, since the trench to be dug by 24 men is 420, instead of 230 yards long, this length, (the width and depth remaining unchanged) would occupy them $\frac{420}{230} = \frac{42}{23}$ of $63\frac{4}{27}$ days, which is $115\frac{65}{207}$ days. Again, since the trench to be dug by 24 men is 5, instead of 3 yards wide, this width (the depth remaining unchanged) would occupy them $\frac{5}{3}$ of $115\frac{65}{207}$ days, which is $192\frac{118}{621}$ days. Lastly, since the trench to be dug by 24 men is 3, instead of 2 yards deep, it will occupy them $\frac{3}{2}$ of $192\frac{118}{621}$ days, which is $288\frac{177}{621} = 288\frac{59}{207}$ days, the answer.

121. If 12 men can build a brick wall 25 feet long, 7 feet high, and 4 feet thick, in 18 days, in how many days will 20 men build a brick wall 150 feet long, 8 feet high, and 6 feet thick?

122. If 15 men can dig a trench 75 feet long, 8 ft. wide, and 6 ft. deep, in 12 days, how many men must be employed to dig a trench 300 ft. long, 12 ft. wide, and 9 ft. deep, in 10 days?

123. If the carriage of 44 barrels of flour, 108 miles be worth $215, what is the carriage of 36 barrels, 162 miles worth?

124. If 175 bushels of corn, when corn is worth 60 cents a bushel, be given for the carriage of 100 barrels of flour, 58 miles, how many bushels of corn, when corn is worth 75 cents a bushel, must be given for the carriage of 90 barrels of flour, 200 miles?

125. If 12 ounces of wool make $2\frac{1}{2}$ yards of cloth, that is 6 quarters wide, how many pounds of wool would make 150 yards of cloth, 4 quarters wide?

In appraising the examples and problems in the Arithmetic pages shown on this and the opposite page, it should be kept in mind that children worked sums like these for seven years, two hours or two and one-half hours a day. Note particularly the clearness (?) of the explanation of the type problem at the top of the pages.

We will now extract the cube root of 178263.433152, in the abridged form, as in the preceding example; but without reference to the parts of the rule.

$$178263.433152(56.28 \quad \textit{Ans.}$$
$$125$$

75	53263
90	
36	
8436	50616
9408	2647433
336	
4	
944164	1888328
947532	759105152
13488	
64	
94888144	759105152
	. . . . . .

1. Extract the cube root of 614125.
2. What is the cube root of 191102976?
3. What is the cube root of 18399.744?
4. Find the cube root of 253395799552.
5. What is the cube root of 1740992427?
6. Extract the cube root of 35655654571.
7. Find the cube root of 27243729729.
8. What is the cube root of 912673000000?
9. What is the cube root of 67518581248?
10. Find the cube root of 729170113230343.
11. Extract the cube root of 643.853447875.
12. Find the cube root of .000000148877.
13. What is the cube root of 123?
14. Extract the cube root of 517.
15. Extract the cube root of 900.
16. Extract the cube root of $\frac{4}{15}$.
17. What is the cube root of $\frac{5}{9}$?
18. What is the cube root of $\frac{8}{27}$?
19. What is the cube root of $\frac{12167}{148877}$?
20. Extract the cube root of 26.

18   SUBTRACTION.

SUBTRACTION.

Note to Teachers. Here explain to the learners, that the cypher (0) represents nothing of itself being used only to occupy a place. Also lead them to observe the correspondence between addition and subtraction.

LESSON FIRST. I.

There was 1 pitcher on the table, but a careless boy knocked it off. What is left upon the table?

1 taken from where there was 1, leaves what?

2 trees stood near by, but the wind has blown 1 of them down. What number is left standing?

1 taken from 2, leaves what number?

3 chairs were standing in a row, but a child has thrown 1 of them down. How many are upright?

1 from 3 leaves how many?

7 sugar-loaves are on a shelf; one of them has the top broken off. How many of them are whole?

1 from 7 leaves how many?

Recite the table beginning, *One from one leaves nothing.*

1 from 1 leaves 0	1 from 6 leaves 5
1 from 2 leaves 1	1 from 7 leaves 6
1 from 3 leaves 2	1 from 8 leaves 7
1 from 4 leaves 3	1 from 9 leaves 8
1 from 5 leaves 4	1 from 10 leaves 9

In fairness to the authors of 1845 it must be stated that some attempt can be discerned to adjust the work to the abilities of children and to apply the formal principles of reckoning to life problems. See opposite page also.

XVII.

BANKING

A BANK is an institution which trafficks in money. It is owned in shares, by a company of individuals, called *stockholders;* and its operations are conducted by a President and board of Directors. It has a deposite of specie, and issues *notes* or *bills,* which are used for a circulating medium, as money. These bills are mostly obtained from the bank in loans, on which interest is paid; and the amount of bills issued being greater than the amount of specie kept in deposite, a profit accrues to the bank.

The interest on money hired from a bank, is paid at the time when the money is taken out—the hirer receiving as much less than the sum he promises to pay, as would be equal to the interest of what he promises to pay, from the time of hiring the money until the time it is to be paid. From this circumstance, the interest on money hired from a bank is called *discount,* and the promissory note received at the bank is said to be *discounted.*

A note, to be discounted at a bank, is usually made payable to some person, who endorses it, and who thereby binds himself to pay the debt, in case the signer of the note should fail to do so. Any person, therefore, who holds the note of another, payable at a future time, may endorse it, and obtain the money for it at a bank, by paying the bank discount; provided the credit of the parties is undoubted.

It is customary in banks, to compute the discount on every note for 3 days more than the time stated in the note; and the debtor is not required to make payment until 3 days after the stated term of time has elapsed. These 3 days are called *days of grace.*

1. What is the bank discount on 775 dollars for 30 days, and grace, when interest is 6 per cent. a year?

2. What is the bank discount on 900 dollars for 90 days, and grace, at the rate of 6 per cent. a year?

66

1	2	3	4	1	2	1	2

blade, man, hall, tar,—me, bed,—time, bid,—

cir cum am bi ent   bac cha na li an   sub ter ra ne an
prin ci pal i ty   cor nu co pi æ   tes ti mo ni al
tac i tur ni ty   dic ta to ri al   am mo ni a cal
                        im ma te ri al   dem o ni a cal
e lec tric i ty   in con ve ni ent   am bi gu i ty
ec cen tric i ty   im me mo ri al   con ti gu i ty
ar is toc ra cy   in con so la ble   con ti nu i ty
in ac ces si ble   in e bri e ty   op por tu ni ty
in ca pac i tate   con tra ri e ty   per pe tu i ty
in ca pac i ty   mat ri mo ni al   in ge nu i ty (140)
in sig nif i cance   or a to ri o   lon gi tu di nal
ir re sis ti ble   per i cra ni um   a man u en sis
rep re sent a tive   per i he li um   su per in cum bent
ris i bil i ty   sen a to ri al   su per in tend ant

TABLE X.

Con cil i a tor y   (132)   ad mi ra bil i ty
e jac u la tor y   (39)   ar is to crat i cal
re ver ber a tor y   cor ro si bil i ty
in tol er a ble ness   com pres si bil i ty
cir cum loc u tor y   (132)   dis sim i lar i ty
in de fat i ga ble   ef fu ma bil i ty
in de ter mi na ble   cor rup ti bil i ty
in de lib er a ted   im pla ca bil i ty
in ter rog a tor y   in com pre hen si ble
ir re cov er a ble   in con tro vert i ble
ir re plev i a ble   in cred i bil i ty
                                  in fal li bil i ty
ir re me di a ble   in fe ri or i ty
su per nu mer ar y   in stru men tal i ty

In appraising the matter shown above and on the opposite page, the reader should ask himself how many times he has had occasion to use the words in his personal correspondence. The same children who studied and spelled these words for their teachers made 3,733 errors in spelling in writing the answers to the examination questions, misspelling many simple words of their own choosing, such as "their," "which," etc.

67

1	2	3	4	1	2	3	1	2

tone, not, nor, move,—tube, sun, full,—rhyme, system.

pe cu li ar i ty
prac ti ca bil i ty
pu sil lan im i ty
su pe ri or i ty
sus cep ti bil i ty (132)

ad min is tra tor ship
me di a to ri al
pre des ti na ri an
en cy clo pe di a (132)
ir rec on ci la ble

el i gi bil i ty
ge ne a log i cal
me te o rol o gy
re fran gi bil i ty

im pen e tra bil i ty
in com pat i bil i ty
ir ref ra ga bil i ty (140)
me te o ro log i cal

—⚬⚬⚬—

TABLE III.

Words from the following reading lessons, defined.

A-corn, the seed of the oak.

Fame, renown, celebrity.

Fai-lings, imperfections.

Raise, (157) to lift, to elevate.

Aim, an intention; a design.

Praise, (157) renown, commendation.

Praise-wor-thy, deserving praise.

Grate-ful, having a due sense of benefits.

Ra-cer, runner, one that contends in speed.

Crea-tures, (167) beings created.

Rea-son, (157) the power by which man deduces consequences from premises.

Fee-lings, sensibility.

Ce-dar, a tree.

Ea-gle, a bird of prey.

Ear, the organ of hearing.

Pru-dence, wisdom applied to practice.

Ri-seth, groweth up.

Spite, defiance.

Course, race, career.

Glo-ries, splendour, brightness.

Oak, a well known tree.

Rose, (157) a flower.

Soar-eth, mounteth, riseth high.

Soul, the immortal spirit of man.

Mu-tu-al, (168) reciprocal, each acting in return.

Ac-tions, (167) deeds.

Branch, (134) the shoot of a tree.

Cher-ish, to support.

Char-i-ty, good will, benevolence.

CONTENTS.

INTRODUCTION.

PART I.

OF THE ADDRESS TO THE UNDERSTANDING, WITH A VIEW TO PRODUCE CONVICTION (INCLUDING INSTRUCTION.)

These two pages present the contents of a subject which in its old form has largely disappeared from our schools.

deed at first sight appear superfluous even to mention
so obvious a rule; but experience shows that it is by
no means uncommon for a young or ill-instructed writer to content himself with such a vague and indistinct
view of the point he is to aim at, that the whole train
of his reasoning is in consequence affected with a corresponding perplexity, obscurity, and looseness. It may
be worth while therefore to give some hints for the conduct of this preliminary process—the choice of propositions. Not, of course, that I am supposing the author
to be in doubt what opinion he shall adopt; the process of Investigation* (which does not fall within the·
province of Rhetoric) being supposed to be concluded;
but still there will often be room for deliberation as to
the form in which an opinion shall be stated, and, when
several propositions are to be maintained, in what order
they shall be placed.

Conviction
and In
struction.
On this head therefore I shall proceed to
propose some rules; after having premised
(in order to anticipate some objections or
doubts which might arise) one remark relative to the object to be effected. This is, of course, what may be
called in the widest sense of the word, Conviction; but
under that term are comprehended, first, what is strictly
called *Instruction;* and, secondly, *Conviction* in the
narrower sense; *i. e.* the Conviction of those who are
either of a *contrary opinion* to the one maintained, or
who are *in doubt* whether to admit or deny it. By Instruction, on the other hand, is commonly meant the
conviction of those who have neither formed an opinion on the subject, nor are deliberating whether to adopt
or reject the proposition in question, but are merely desirous of ascertaining *what* is the truth in respect of the
case before them. The former are supposed to have
before their minds the *terms* of the proposition maintained, and are called upon to consider *whether that particular proposition* be true or false; the latter are not

Logic, book iv. chap. 3.§ 2.

An illustration of the type of instruction provided for eighth-grade
children.

INDEX

Administration:
  Boston schools, 11, 12, 13.
  Detroit schools, 106, 107, 130–133.
  Schools of tomorrow, 158–160.
Adult education. *See* Continuation
  schools.
Age. *See* School age.
Algebra, 220.
Analysis of tests (1845), 29, 30.
Answers:
  Examinations (1845), 48, 49, 51,
    52, 54–61, 171–179.
  (1919), 365–369.
Appropriations. *See* School cost.
Architectural department, 106.
Arithmetic:
  Examinations (1845):
    Answers, 227, 228.
    Questions, 28, 30, 227, 276.
    Results, 265, 266.
    Tabulation of results, 336.
  Standard tests (1919):
    Answers, 68, 69, 70, 366, 367.
    Questions, 68, 69, 70, 361.
  Textbooks (1845), 381–387.
Assistant superintendent, 130, 131.
Astronomy:
  Examination (1845):
    Answers, 54, 177, 178.
    Questions, 52, 280, 281.
    Tabulation of results, 343, 344.
Attendance, 233, 234. *See also*
  Membership of schools.
Auditorium, 122–123, 136, 142.
Authors of tests, 125.

Board of Education. *See* Detroit
  Board of Education.
Books, 197–221.
Boston School Committee:
  Duties, 2, 3, 22, 23, 195, 197.
  See also Survey Committee.

Boston schools (1845):
  Comparative view of schools,
    181–186, 222–226.
  Corporal punishment, 20, 21, 206–
    213, 266–269.
  Curriculum, 16, 17, 232, 250, 251.
  Discipline, 19, 20, 201, 202, 207,
    213, 267, 268.
  Examinations, 27–43, 48–56, 168–
    181, 186, 187, 238–244, 283–
    323, 329–344, 372–374.
  Grading, 14.
  Instruction, 175, 177, 186–192, 230,
    231, 254–265.
  Membership, 103, 246.
  Number, 11.
  Organization, 11, 12, 13, 219.
  Rank, 228, 229, 329, 330.
  Salaries, 11, 103, 205, 229, 246, 247.
  School buildings, 11, 135–140, 231.
  School committee, 2, 22, 23, 100,
    101, 194, 196, 197.
  School cost, 4, 5, 11, 103, 105, 229,
    246, 247.
  Schoolmasters, 12, 21, 22, 188, 189,
    198–203, 206, 212, 230, 231,
    249–254.
  Sessions, 13.
  Supplies, 220, 221.
  Teachers, 11, 13, 19, 20, 60, 103,
    186, 205, 214–216, 229, 240,
    241, 246, 247, 252, 253, 254,
    269–271.
Boston school tests:
  Comparison of 1845 and 1919:
    Comparative results, 84–97.
    Conclusions, 85, 96.
    Graph, 86.
    Pupils participating, 84, 85.
    Scores, 88–91.
Boston Survey, 347–374. *See also*
  Standard tests (1919).

393

AMERICAN EDUCATION:
ITS MEN, IDEAS, AND INSTITUTIONS
An Arno Press/New York Times Collection

Series I

Culver, Raymond B. **Horace Mann and Religion in the Massachusetts Public Schools.** 1929.

Curoe, Philip R. V. **Educational Attitudes and Policies of Organized Labor in the United States.** 1926.

Dabney, Charles William. **Universal Education in the South.** 1936.

Dearborn, Ned Harland. **The Oswego Movement in American Education.** 1925.

De Lima, Agnes. **Our Enemy the Child.** 1926.

Dewey, John. **The Educational Situation.** 1902.

Dexter, Franklin B., editor. **Documentary History of Yale University.** 1916.

Eliot, Charles William. **Educational Reform: Essays and Addresses.** 1898.

Ensign, Forest Chester. **Compulsory School Attendance and Child Labor.** 1921.

Fitzpatrick, Edward Augustus. **The Educational Views and Influence of De Witt Clinton.** 1911.

Fleming, Sanford. **Children & Puritanism.** 1933.

Flexner, Abraham. **The American College: A Criticism.** 1908.

Foerster, Norman. **The Future of the Liberal College.** 1938.

Gilman, Daniel Coit. **University Problems in the United States.** 1898.

Hall, Samuel R. **Lectures on School-Keeping.** 1829.

Hall, Stanley G. **Adolescence: Its Psychology and Its Relations to Physiology, Anthropology, Sociology, Sex, Crime, Religion, and Education.** 1905. 2 vols.

Hansen, Allen Oscar. **Early Educational Leadership in the Ohio Valley.** 1923.

Harris, William T. **Psychologic Foundations of Education.** 1899.

Harris, William T. **Report of the Committee of Fifteen on the Elementary School.** 1895.

Harveson, Mae Elizabeth. **Catharine Esther Beecher: Pioneer Educator.** 1932.

Jackson, George Leroy. **The Development of School Support in Colonial Massachusetts.** 1909.

Kandel, I. L., editor. **Twenty-five Years of American Education.** 1924.

Kemp, William Webb. **The Support of Schools in Colonial New York by the Society for the Propagation of the Gospel in Foreign Parts.** 1913.

Kilpatrick, William Heard. **The Dutch Schools of New Netherland and Colonial New York.** 1912.

Kilpatrick, William Heard. **The Educational Frontier.** 1933.

Knight, Edgar Wallace. **The Influence of Reconstruction on Education in the South.** 1913.

Le Duc, Thomas. **Piety and Intellect at Amherst College, 1865-1912.** 1946.

Maclean, John. **History of the College of New Jersey from Its Origin in 1746 to the Commencement of 1854.** 1877.

Maddox, William Arthur. **The Free School Idea in Virginia before the Civil War.** 1918.

Mann, Horace. **Lectures on Education.** 1855.

McCadden, Joseph J. **Education in Pennsylvania, 1801-1835, and Its Debt to Roberts Vaux.** 1855.

McCallum, James Dow. **Eleazar Wheelock.** 1939.

McCuskey, Dorothy. **Bronson Alcott, Teacher.** 1940.

Meiklejohn, Alexander. **The Liberal College.** 1920.

Miller, Edward Alanson. **The History of Educational Legislation in Ohio from 1803 to 1850.** 1918.

Miller, George Frederick. **The Academy System of the State of New York.** 1922.

Monroe, Will S. **History of the Pestalozzian Movement in the United States.** 1907.

Mosely Education Commission. **Reports of the Mosely Education Commission to the United States of America October-December, 1903.** 1904.

Mowry, William A. **Recollections of a New England Educator.** 1908.

Mulhern, James. **A History of Secondary Education in Pennsylvania.** 1933.

National Herbart Society. **National Herbart Society Yearbooks 1-5, 1895-1899.** 1895-1899.

Nearing, Scott. **The New Education: A Review of Progressive Educational Movements of the Day.** 1915.

Neef, Joseph. **Sketches of a Plan and Method of Education.** 1808.

Nock, Albert Jay. **The Theory of Education in the United States.** 1932.

Norton, A. O., editor. **The First State Normal School in America: The Journals of Cyrus Pierce and Mary Swift.** 1926.

Oviatt, Edwin. **The Beginnings of Yale, 1701-1726.** 1916.

Packard, Frederic Adolphus. **The Daily Public School in the United States.** 1866.

Page, David P. **Theory and Practice of Teaching.** 1848.

Parker, Francis W. **Talks on Pedagogics: An Outline of the Theory of Concentration.** 1894.

Peabody, Elizabeth Palmer. **Record of a School.** 1835.

Porter, Noah. **The American Colleges and the American Public.** 1870.

Reigart, John Franklin. **The Lancasterian System of Instruction in the Schools of New York City.** 1916.

Reilly, Daniel F. **The School Controversy (1891-1893).** 1943.

Rice, Dr. J. M. **The Public-School System of the United States.** 1893.

Rice, Dr. J. M. **Scientific Management in Education.** 1912.

Ross, Early D. **Democracy's College: The Land-Grant Movement in the Formative Stage.** 1942.

Rugg, Harold, et al. **Curriculum-Making: Past and Present.** 1926.

Rugg, Harold, et al. **The Foundations of Curriculum-Making.** 1926.

Rugg, Harold and Shumaker, Ann. **The Child-Centered School.** 1928.

Seybolt, Robert Francis. **Apprenticeship and Apprenticeship Education in Colonial New England and New York.** 1917.

Seybolt, Robert Francis. **The Private Schools of Colonial Boston.** 1935.

Seybolt, Robert Francis. **The Public Schools of Colonial Boston.** 1935.

Sheldon, Henry D. **Student Life and Customs.** 1901.

Sherrill, Lewis Joseph. **Presbyterian Parochial Schools, 1846-1870.** 1932 .

Siljestrom, P. A. **Educational Institutions of the United States.** 1853.

Small, Walter Herbert. **Early New England Schools.** 1914.

Soltes, Mordecai. **The Yiddish Press: An Americanizing Agency.** 1925.

Stewart, George, Jr. **A History of Religious Education in Connecticut to the Middle of the Nineteenth Century.** 1924.

Storr, Richard J. **The Beginnings of Graduate Education in America.** 1953.

Stout, John Elbert. **The Development of High-School Curricula in the North Central States from 1860 to 1918.** 1921.

Suzzallo, Henry. **The Rise of Local School Supervision in Massachusetts.** 1906.

Swett, John. **Public Education in California.** 1911.

Tappan, Henry P. **University Education.** 1851.

Taylor, Howard Cromwell. **The Educational Significance of the Early Federal Land Ordinances.** 1921.

Taylor, J. Orville. **The District School.** 1834.

Tewksbury, Donald G. **The Founding of American Colleges and Universities before the Civil War.** 1932.

Thorndike, Edward L. **Educational Psychology.** 1913-1914.

True, Alfred Charles. **A History of Agricultural Education in the United States, 1785-1925.** 1929.

True, Alfred Charles. **A History of Agricultural Extension Work in the United States, 1785-1923.** 1928.

Updegraff, Harlan. **The Origin of the Moving School in Massachusetts.** 1908.

Wayland, Francis. **Thoughts on the Present Collegiate System in the United States.** 1842.

Weber, Samuel Edwin. **The Charity School Movement in Colonial Pennsylvania.** 1905.

Wells, Guy Fred. **Parish Education in Colonial Virginia.** 1923.

Wickersham, J. P. **The History of Education in Pennsylvania.** 1885.

Woodward, Calvin M. **The Manual Training School.** 1887.

Woody, Thomas. **Early Quaker Education in Pennsylvania.** 1920.

Woody, Thomas. **Quaker Education in the Colony and State of New Jersey.** 1923.

Wroth, Lawrence C. **An American Bookshelf, 1755.** 1934.

Series II

Adams, Evelyn C. **American Indian Education.** 1946.

Bailey, Joseph Cannon. **Seaman A. Knapp: Schoolmaster of American Agriculture.** 1945.

Beecher, Catharine and Harriet Beecher Stowe. **The American Woman's Home.** 1869.

Benezet, Louis T. **General Education in the Progressive College.** 1943.

Boas, Louise Schutz. **Woman's Education Begins.** 1935.

Bobbitt, Franklin. **The Curriculum.** 1918.

Bode, Boyd H. **Progressive Education at the Crossroads.** 1938.

Bourne, William Oland. **History of the Public School Society of the City of New York.** 1870.

Bronson, Walter C. **The History of Brown University, 1764-1914.** 1914.

Burstall, Sara A. **The Education of Girls in the United States.** 1894.

Butts, R. Freeman. **The College Charts Its Course.** 1939.

Caldwell, Otis W. and Stuart A. Courtis. **Then & Now in Education, 1845-1923.** 1923.

Calverton, V. F. & Samuel D. Schmalhausen, editors. **The New Generation: The Intimate Problems of Modern Parents and Children.** 1930.

Charters, W. W. **Curriculum Construction.** 1923.

Childs, John L. **Education and Morals.** 1950.

Childs, John L. **Education and the Philosophy of Experimentalism.** 1931.

Clapp, Elsie Ripley. **Community Schools in Action.** 1939.

Counts, George S. **The American Road to Culture: A Social Interpretation of Education in the United States.** 1930.

Counts, George S. **School and Society in Chicago.** 1928.

Finegan, Thomas E. **Free Schools.** 1921.

Fletcher, Robert Samuel. **A History of Oberlin College.** 1943.

Grattan, C. Hartley. **In Quest of Knowledge: A Historical Perspective on Adult Education.** 1955.

Hartman, Gertrude & Ann Shumaker, editors. **Creative Expression.** 1932.

Kandel, I. L. **The Cult of Uncertainty.** 1943.

Kandel, I. L. **Examinations and Their Substitutes in the United States.** 1936.

Kilpatrick, William Heard. **Education for a Changing Civilization.** 1926.

Kilpatrick, William Heard. **Foundations of Method.** 1925.

Kilpatrick, William Heard. **The Montessori System Examined.** 1914.

Lang, Ossian H., editor. **Educational Creeds of the Nineteenth Century.** 1898.

Learned, William S. **The Quality of the Educational Process in the United States and in Europe.** 1927.

Meiklejohn, Alexander. **The Experimental College.** 1932.

Middlekauff, Robert. **Ancients and Axioms: Secondary Education in Eighteenth-Century New England.** 1963.

Norwood, William Frederick. **Medical Education in the United States Before the Civil War.** 1944.

Parsons, Elsie W. Clews. **Educational Legislation and Administration of the Colonial Governments.** 1899.

Perry, Charles M. **Henry Philip Tappan: Philosopher and University President.** 1933.

Pierce, Bessie Louise. **Civic Attitudes in American School Textbooks.** 1930.

Rice, Edwin Wilbur. **The Sunday-School Movement (1780-1917) and the American Sunday-School Union (1817-1917).** 1917.

Robinson, James Harvey. **The Humanizing of Knowledge.** 1924.

Ryan, W. Carson. **Studies in Early Graduate Education.** 1939.

Seybolt, Robert Francis. **The Evening School in Colonial America.** 1925.

Seybolt, Robert Francis. **Source Studies in American Colonial Education.** 1925.

Todd, Lewis Paul. **Wartime Relations of the Federal Government and the Public Schools, 1917-1918.** 1945.

Vandewalker, Nina C. **The Kindergarten in American Education.** 1908.

Ward, Florence Elizabeth. **The Montessori Method and the American School.** 1913.

West, Andrew Fleming. **Short Papers on American Liberal Education.** 1907.

Wright, Marion M. Thompson. **The Education of Negroes in New Jersey.** 1941.

Supplement

The Social Frontier (Frontiers of Democracy). Vols. 1-10, 1934-1943.